The Law of War

The Law of War

Edited by

Richard I. Miller
Harbridge House, Inc.

Lexington Books
D.C. Heath and Company
Lexington, Massachusetts
Toronto   London

Grateful acknowledgment is made for permission to use excerpts from *Dominican Diary* by Tad Szulc, copyright © 1965 by the New York Times. Reprinted with permission of Delacorte Press and the New York Times.

Library of Congress Cataloging in Publication Data

Main entry under title:

The Law of War.

   Includes index.
   1. War (International law) I. Miller, Richard I.
JX4511.L38   341.6   74-16936
ISBN 0-669-95877-8

Published simultaneously in Canada.

Printed in the United States of America.

International Standard Book Number: 0-669-95877-8

Library of Congress Catalog Card Number: 74-16936

Contents

List of Abbreviations

AID	Agency for International Development (U.S. Department of State)
ARVN	Army of the Republic of Viet Nam
CARDC	Committee for Assisting the Return of Displaced Civilians (Korean Conflict)
CEP	Captured Enemy Personnel
CIE	Civil Information and Education Section
CPV	Chinese People's Volunteers (Korean Conflict)
CRP	Communist Rebel Prisoner (a South Vietnamese)
DRV	Democratic Republic of Vietnam (North Vietnam)
FAO	Food and Agriculture Organization (U.N.)
GC	Geneva Convention Relative to the Protection of Civilian Persons in Time of War
GPW	Geneva Convention Relative to the Treatment of Prisoners of War
GVN	Government of (South) Vietnam
GWS	Geneva Convention for the Amelioration of the Condition of the Wounded and Sick in Armed Forces in the Fields
GWS-Sea	Geneva Convention for the Amelioration of the Condition of the Wounded, Sick, and Shipwrecked Members of the Armed Forces at Sea
HR	Hague Regulations
ICRC	International Committee of the Red Cross
ILO	International Labour Organization
IPF	Inter-American Peace Force (Dominican Republic Conflict)
IRO	International Refugee Organization
ITU	International Telecommunication Union
MVD	Ministry of Internal Affairs of the USSR
NATO	North Atlantic Treaty Organization
NKVD	People's Commissariat of Internal Affairs (USSR)
NLF	National Liberation Front (organized South Vietnamese guerrilla army; also known as Viet Cong)
NNRC	Neutral Nations Repatriation Commission (Korean Conflict)
OAS	Organization of American States
ONUC	Organisacion Nation Unis de Congo
PG, PW or POW	Prisoners of War: The Geneva Conventions authorize the use of the marking, PW or PG (prisonnier de guerre). In the United States the article "Of" is also capitalized.
PRC	People's Republic of China
RSFSR	Russian Statutory Laws of the Federation of Soviet Republics

RVN   Republic of Vietnam (South Vietnam)
SEATO   Southeast Asia Treaty Organization
SEP   Surrendered Enemy Personnel (Malayan-Indonesian Conflict)
UCMJ   The Uniform Code of Military Justice
UNC   United Nations Command
UNCURK   United Nations Commission for the Unification and Rehabilitation of Korea
UNEF   United Nations Emergency Forces
UNESCO   United Nations Educational Scientific and Cultural Organization
UNFICYP   United Nations Forces in Cyprus
UNICEF   United Nations International Children's Emergency Fund
VC   Viet Cong (NLF)
WHO   World Health Organization

Preface

In 1968 the Department of the Army retained the firm of Harbridge House to conduct an 18-month study of the application of the international law of war to contemporary warfare. At the time the United States had half a million servicemen in Viet Nam; under domestic law the Army has jurisdiction over prisoners of war captured by all U.S. forces. The "prisoner of war" study was classified "secret" until November, 1974. The contents of this book are taken largely from the study report. Its declassification did not constitute an authorization or an approval of the publication by the Department of the Army or any other agency of the U.S. government.

Although substantially revised, edited and updated, the book follows the general development of the Army study; that is: (i) a restatement of the international law, with particular reference to the four Geneva Conventions of 1949; (ii) the application of the law to contemporary conflict and, (iii) an analysis of the law.

In addition to Richard I. Miller, who was the director of the study project staff and its major contributor, general authors of the work were Michael Bergner, Robert D. Crangle, Nicholas P. Flynn, and Seth M. Kalberg. The staff was especially grateful to Professor R.R. Baxter of Harvard Law School for having guided its research, contributing much of his own thoughts and material, and reading large portions of the manuscript. Professor Baxter must receive much of the credit for any scholarly merit this work possesses; the project staff is obliged to accept the opprobrium for the scholarly deficiencies which invariably arise when one tries to abstract a readable volume from a government tome.

Along with Professor Baxter, the staff owes a special debt of gratitude to Jerome Alan Cohen, of Harvard Law School and author of Chapter 8, and other academicians. Professor Cohen's contribution on the People's Republic of China and the assistance of others on various aspects of comparative law and sociology were somewhat constrained by the peculiar format of the original project. Part III, which deals with application of the law overseas, was responsive to a hypothetical mode which eminent scholars, unlike management consultants, will adopt only with the greatest reluctance.

Finally, the authors would like to express their appreciation to Suzanne Endemann and Tami L. Miller, whose technical editing was largely responsible for the distillation of five rough manuscript volumes into a single book.

The authors and editors dedicate this book to the military, diplomatic, and humanitarian personnel who continue to labor to reduce the ravages of war, even as all men of good will work toward the day when nations shall war no more.

The Law of War

Part I:
Statement of the Law

1 The Legal Setting

The book deals with both the treaty (or conventional) law of war and the customary law of war relating to the treatment of prisoners of war, the wounded and the sick, and detained civilian persons. Historically, the customary law antedates the conventional. The modern law is very largely the law of the treaties codified over the past 100 years. This chapter presents an overview of the development of both the conventional and customary law and describes the persons and the types of conflicts covered by these laws. A more detailed treatment of the persons to whom the law applies and of the complementation of the law in selected conflicts is found in subsequent chapters.

Conventional Law

The United States and other nations and political entities are parties to the four Geneva Conventions for the Protection of War Victims, signed at Geneva on August 12, 1949. These are:

1. Geneva Convention for the Amelioration of the Condition of the Wounded and Sick in Armed Forces in the Fields (GWS-1949).
2. Geneva Convention for the Amelioration of the Condition of Wounded, Sick, and Shipwrecked Members of Armed Forces at Sea (GWS Sea-1949).
3. Geneva Convention Relative to the Protection of Civilian Persons in Time of War (GC-1949).
4. Geneva Convention Relative to the Treatment of Prisoners of War (GPW-1949).

The number of parties to the conventions is somewhat inflated by the fact that the Swiss government, which acts as depositary of the treaties, has been willing to accept ratifications or accessions from both governments of a number of divided states on the sound principle that it is wise to have as many governments as possible bound by the conventions. Thus, both governments of the partitioned states of Germany, China, Korea, and Vietnam have ratified or acceded to the conventions. A list of parties to the Conventions of 1949 is set forth in Table 1-1.

Each one of the Geneva Conventions of 1949 is the product of an earlier treaty or of several antecedent treaties, some of which are still in force. Figure 1-1 is a graphic representation of the development of and relationship among these treaties. The wounded and the sick were the first persons to receive treaty protection.

3

Table 1-1
States that are Parties to All Four Geneva Conventions of 1949

Without Reservation

Afghanistan	Indonesia
Algeria	Iran
Austria	Iraq
Bangladesh[a]	Ireland
Barbados	Ivory Coast
Belgium	Jamaica
Botswana	Japan
Burundi	Jordan
Cambodia	Kenya
Cameroon	Laos
Canada	Lebanon
Central African Republic	Lesotho
Ceylon	Liberia
Chile	Libya
Colombia	Liechtenstein
Congo (Brazaville)	Luxembourg
Congo (Kinshasa)	Madagascar
Cuba	Malaysia
Cyprus	Mali
Dahomey	Malta
Denmark	Mauritania
Dominican Republic	Mauritius[a]
Ecuador	Malawi
El Salvador	Mexico
Fiji[a]	Monaco
Finland	Mongolian People's Republic
France	Morocco
Gabon	Nepal
Gambia	Nicaragua
Germany (Germany, Fed. Rep.)	Niger
Ghana	Nigeria
Greece	Norway
Guatemala	Panama
Guyana	Paraguay
Haiti	Peru
Holy See	Philippines
Honduras	Rwanda
Iceland	San Merino
India	Saudi Arabia

Table 1-1 (cont.)

Without Reservation

Senegal	Togo
Sierra Leone	Trinidad & Tobago
Singapore	Tunisia
Somali Republic	Turkey
South Africa	Uganda
Sudan	United Arab Emirates[a]
Sweden	United Arab Republic
Switzerland	Upper Volta
Syrian Arab Republic	Venezuela
Tanzania: Tanganyika & Zanzibar	Viet Nam
Thailand	Zambia

With Reservation

Albania	Kuwait
Argentina	Netherlands
Australia	New Zealand
Brazil	Pakistan
Bulgaria	Poland
Byelorussian S.S.R.	Portugal
China, Peoples Republic	Romania
Czechoslovakia	Spain
Germany, Dem. Rep.	Ukrainian S.S.R.
Hungary	United States
Israel	United Kingdom
Italy	U.S.S.R.
Korea	Vietnam, Dem. Rep.
Korean Dem. Rep.	Yugoslavia

[a]Countries established since 1968 with possible reservations.

Wounded and Sick Conventions

The first convention on the subject of the wounded and the sick, the Convention for the Amelioration of the Wounded in Armies in the Field, was drawn up at Geneva in 1864. The 1864 convention was superseded in 1906 by a new convention, which was itself replaced in 1929. The convention presently in force, the Geneva Convention for the Amelioration of the Condition of the Wounded and Sick in Armed Forces in the Field, was signed at the conclusion of the Diplomatic Conference for the Establishment of International Conventions for the Protection of War Victims on August 12, 1949. According to article 59,

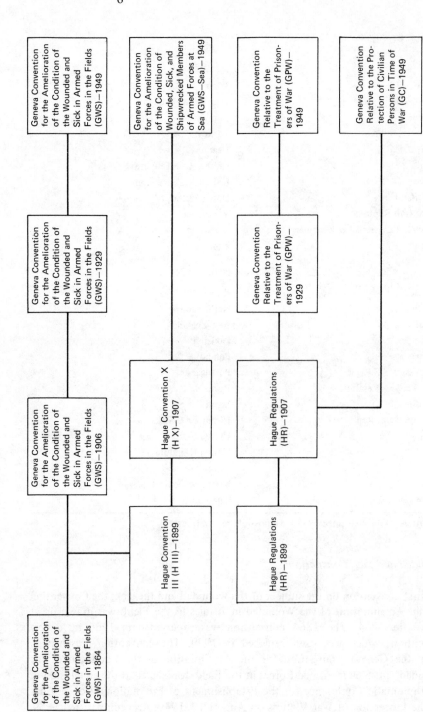

Figure 1-1. Schematic Representation of the Development of the Conventions

"the present Convention replaces the Conventions of 1864, 1906, and 1929 in relations between the High Contracting Parties." In addition to the conventions drawn up at Geneva, the international law of war has also been shaped by conventions drawn up at the Hague, first in 1899 and again in 1907. At the Hague Conference of 1899 it was decided to supplement the existing Wounded and Sick Convention with a new treaty relating to the position of wounded and sick persons in maritime warfare. The Maritime Convention drawn up in 1899 was revised in 1907, and a new Convention for the Amelioration of the Condition of the Wounded, Sick, and Shipwrecked Members of Armed Forces at Sea was drawn up at the Geneva Conference of 1949. The United States is a party to both the 1907 and 1949 conventions.

Prisoner of War Conventions

There was no codification of the law relating to prisoners of war until 1899, when Convention II respecting the Laws and Customs of War on Land was drawn up at The Hague. The regulations annexed to this convention contained twenty articles dealing with prisoners of war. These regulations were somewhat revised at the Hague Conference of 1907 and the Convention to which they were annexed was renumbered "Convention IV." This convention with its annexed regulations is still in force, and the United States is among the parties to it.

At the same conference in 1929 that provided a new wounded and sick convention, the participating states drew up the first multilateral treaty dealing exclusively with the protection of prisoners of war. The new Geneva Convention Relative to the Treatment of Prisoners of War (GPW) defined its relation to the Hague Regulations in the following way:

In the relations between Powers bound by the Hague Convention respecting the Laws and Customs of War on Land, whether it is a question of that of July 29, 1899, or that of October 18, 1907, and who participate in the present Convention, the latter shall complete Chapter II [relating to prisoners of war] of the Regulations annexed to the said Hague Conventions. (art. 89)

The use of the term "complete" was probably suggested by the much greater detail and amplitude of the 1929 convention, as contrasted with the corresponding provisions of the Hague Regulations. In all likelihood, it means that if there should be a conflict between the Hague Regulations and the convention, the latter would apply without prejudice to the continuing force of the Hague Regulations. At the Geneva Conference of 1949 the participating states drew up a new Convention Relative to the Treatment of Prisoners of War. This convention contained a provision almost identical to that quoted above, defining its relation to the Hague Regulations of 1899 and 1907.

Civilians Conventions

There was no separate convention concerning civilians until the Geneva Convention Relative to the Protection of Civilian Persons in Time of War was concluded in 1949. However, parts of the Hague Regulations of 1899 and 1907, notably Sections II and III dealing with "Hostilities" and "Military Authority over the Territory of the Hostile State," do contain some provisions bearing on the protection of civilians. The Convention of 1949 was declared to be "supplementary" to Sections II and III of the Hague Regulations in relations between states bound by the Conventions of 1899 and 1907.

Applicability and Reservations

The above conventions are applicable between each pair of opposing belligerents only insofar as both are parties to the particular convention. For example, if State A is a party to GPW-1949 and GPW-1929 and State B is a party only to GPW-1929, GPW-1929 will be applicable to the hostilities between them. The obligations of the parties to these instruments may be limited by reservations they have entered to particular articles. If a state enters a reservation to a provision of a multilateral convention, it is open to each of the other parties to determine whether it will accept or reject the reservation. The standard that the individual state is expected to use is whether or not the reservation is "compatible" with the purposes of the treaty, but that determination is usually a wholly subjective one for each state to make. If the reservation is accepted, the convention enters into force between the reserving and accepting state subject to the reservation. If the reservation is rejected, no treaty relations exist between the reserving and objecting states. It is possible, of course, for a reserving and an objecting state to work out a compromise whereby, for example, the convention enters into force minus the article as to which there has been a reservation and an objection. In effect, the parties agree to disagree about the article that has been the source of controversy.

A number of reservations have been entered to various articles of the four Geneva Conventions of 1949 by the United States, the members of the Soviet bloc, and other nations. The United States reserved as to article 68, paragraph 2 of GC, concerning the death penalty for offenses committed by inhabitants of occupied areas, and as to article 53 of GWS, relating to the use of the Red Cross emblem. The Soviet Union reserved as to seven articles of the conventions, and the same reservations were made by the other Communist states at the time that they ratified or acceded to the treaties. These reservations relate to article 10 of GPW and the corresponding articles of the other conventions, concerning a neutral state's or a humanitarian organization's undertaking the function of a protecting power for prisoners of war and civilians transferred to the custody of another power; and article 85 of GPW, concerning the extensions of the application of GPW to persons convicted of war crimes and crimes against humanity.

Subsequent to the ratification of the conventions by the United States, the Department of State further complicated the reservations by a highly ambiguous statement:

Rejecting the reservations which States have made with respect to the Geneva convention relative to the treatment of prisoners of war, the United States accepts treaty relations with all parties to that convention, except as to the changes proposed by such reservations.[1]

The meaning and legal significance of this statement have never been made clear. The statement seems to do two wholly inconsistent things. It rejects the reservations, in which case the conventions would not be in force between the United States and any state entering a reservation; but at the same time the statement accepts treaty relations with the reserving states, which could happen only if the United States were willing to accede to the reservations that had been made. The language "except as to the changes proposed by such reservations" strongly suggests that the United States government did not wish to be bound by the conventions as they would be changed by the reservations. The possibility is opened up for a reserving state to maintain that—as its reservations had been rejected and had not been withdrawn—no treaty relations existed. This has never been asserted by the Soviet Union or any other reserving state, but it nevertheless remains a disquieting possibility. One may hazard that in a conflict between the United States and a reserving state, the United States would simply demand strict compliance with all of the articles to which the other party had entered reservations, while the other party would maintain that its obligations to the United States should be measured by the reserved articles of the conventions.

Customary Law

Source of the Law

Although the conventional law is detailed, precise, and broad in scope, it has not preempted the field, and customary law continues to exist side by side with the treaty law, even among those states that have accepted the largest measure of treaty obligations without reservation. The classic statement of the role of customary law is found in the preamble of Hague Convention IV of 1907 (H IV-1907):

Until a more complete code of the laws of war has been issued, the High Contracting Parties deem it expedient to declare that, in cases not included in the Regulations adopted by them, the inhabitants and the belligerents remain under the protection and the rule of the principles of the law of nations, as they result from the usages established among civilized peoples, from the laws of humanity, and the dictates of the public conscience.

The source of the customary law of war is, in the language of the Statute of the International Court of Justice (art. 38, para. 1G), "in international custom, as evidence of a general practice accepted as law." The language "accepted as law" is important because it is not sufficient that nations act in a particular way; they must also act in a way that reflects a sense of obligation or of acting in a legal context (*opinio juris*).

The Statute of the International Court also mentions as a source of international law "the general principles of law recognized by civilized nations," that is to say, principles of law that have attained widespread recognition in municipal legal systems. In the law of war, principles derived from municipal law have most often been applied to the regulation of war crimes proceedings. In the *Hostage* case, the tribunal said:

In determining whether . . . a fundamental rule of justice is entitled to be declared a principle of international law, an examination of the municipal laws of states in the family of nations will reveal the answer. If it is found to have been accepted generally as a fundamental rule of justice by most nations in their municipal law, its declaration as a rule of international law would seem to be fully justified.[2]

What customary usage can create, custom can also undo. As the matter was put by the Nuremberg Tribunal:

The law of war is to be found not only in treaties, but in the customs and practices of states which gradually obtained universal recognition, and from the general principles of justice applied by jurists and practiced by military courts. This law is not static but by continual adaptation follows the needs of a changing world.[3]

The same theme was taken up in the *I.G. Farben* case, in which the tribunal responded to a defense plea concerning the obsolescence of the law of war under conditions of total war by stating:

As custom is a source of international law, customs and practices may change and find such general acceptance in the community of civilized nations as to alter the substantive content of certain of its principles. But we are unable to find that there has been a change in the basic concept of respect for property rights during belligerent occupation of a character to give any legal protection to the widespread acts of plunder and spoilation committed by Nazi Germany during the course of World War II.[4]

Thus, customary international law is neither changed nor destroyed on any of the following bases:

- That the law is alleged to be vague or uncertain.
- That military necessity makes it impossible to comply with the law. There are points in the treaties when a state is relieved of what would otherwise be its obligation by reason of special circumstances, but these circumstances must be specially identified in the relevant provision. Military necessity offers no general excuse for failure to comply with international law.
- That the opposing state is guilty of the same or other violations of the law. The international law of war is not based on reciprocity, and it is not bilateral. It is universal in character, and no state may relieve itself of its obligations by pointing to violations by the other party.
- That the law—and this applies more particularly to treaty law—has been so widely violated that it is no longer binding. As in municipal law, the law does not become any less obligatory because others violate it, so long as those in a position to enforce that law continue to regard the departures from the law as violations of it.

Evidence of the Law

For *evidence* of what this customary international law of war is, one turns to a variety of sources. Examination of the records in law and history books concerning "general practice accepted as law" is the basic way of determining the usages of states that have become accepted as law. This practice has often been recorded and synthesized in those writings forming "the teachings of the most highly qualified publicists" (art. 38, para. 1, of the Statute of the International Court). Such writings are characterized in the statute as "subsidiary means for the determination of rules of law."

Other evidence may be found in national military regulations and military manuals, which reflect the attitudes of various states toward international law and the standards that they expect of their own forces. However, some cloud has been thrown over such manuals as evidence of the law; the tribunal in the *Hostage* case found acceptable the position on superior orders taken in the British and American military manuals (They were later revised to deny that superior orders are a defense to a charge of having committed a war crime.). The tribunal said:

We point out that army regulations are not a competent source of international law. They are neither legislative nor judicial pronouncements. They are not competent for any purpose in determining whether a fundamental principle of justice has been accepted by civilized nations generally. It is possible, however, that such regulations, as they bear upon a question of custom and practice in the conduct of war, might have evidentiary value, particularly if the applicable portions had been put into general practice.[5]

Although ascertainment of what is a general practice accepted as law is attended with some difficulty and uncertainty, the law is to a certain extent nailed down when it is enunciated in the decision of a tribunal. Because the International Military Tribunal for the Trial of Major War Criminals of the European Axis and the International Military Tribunal for the Far East were international tribunals—international in their authority and in their composition—and included judges from a variety of legal systems, they spoke with particular forcefulness. That authority was underscored by the fact that the General Assembly of the United Nations "affirmed the principles of international law recognized by the Charter of the Nuremberg Tribunal and the Judgment of the Tribunal." On the other hand, the number of separate and dissenting opinions in the *Tokyo* trial undercuts confidence in that decision.

There are also a certain number of decisions of other international tribunals—ad hoc arbitral tribunals, commissions charged with the duty of determining responsibility for violations of international law, investigatory bodies established to decide disputes under peace treaties, and kindred postwar agreements—that provide a limited amount of evidence of the state of the law. Since the law that they apply is often the law of the treaties under which they are established, they do not in their totality shed much light on customary international law.

A great abundance of case law has been laid down by national civil and military tribunals, not all of which is accessible. For the most part, these decisions were rendered in prosecutions for war crimes, but there are a number that resulted from prosecutions for other offenses (such as collaboration with the enemy by nationals for unlawful hostilities in arms) or from civil proceedings (such as actions to recover property unlawfully seized from individuals by belligerent occupant). National and ideological biases are sometimes to be discerned in these cases, and the intermingling of domestic and international issues may obscure the contribution of the cases to international law. Nevertheless, these judicial decisions should not be overlooked, since such resources are not available in many other areas of international law.

In recent years the United Nations General Assembly has sometimes expressed itself on questions of the law of war in the form of resolutions. For example, in considering the repatriation of prisoners in the Korea conflict, the General Assembly adopted a resolution in 1952 that seemed to speak both to the interpretation of article 118 of GPW and to the state of customary international law. Resolutions of this character carry weight in proportion to the number of states voting for them.

Finally, the determination of what precisely is the state of customary international law has been very substantially facilitated by the declaration of the International Military Tribunal at Nuremberg that the Hague Regulations had become declaratory of customary international law. In the words of the tribunal:

The rules of land warfare expressed in the convention undoubtedly represented an advance over existing international law at the time of their adoption. But the convention expressly stated that it was an attempt "to revise the general laws and customs of war," which it thus recognized to be then existing, but by 1939 these rules laid down in the convention were recognized by all civilized nations, and were regarded as being declaratory of the laws and customs of war which are referred to in Article 6 (b) of the Charter.[6]

The International Military Tribunal for the Far East receded somewhat from this bold position. Speaking generally of the conventions adopted at The Hague in 1907, that tribunal said that "the Convention remains as good evidence of the customary law of nations, to be considered by the Tribunal along with all other available evidence in determining the customary law to be applied in any given situation."[7]

In the *High Command* case, the Nuremberg Tribunal (constituted under Control Council Law No. 10 and in actuality an American tribunal acting under international authority) effected a selective incorporation of certain provisions of GPW-1929 into customary international law, provisions that were in large measure those that provided basic safeguards to prisoners of war and did not deal in detail with their treatment. There are other isolated instances in which particular articles of the two foregoing conventions were held to be declaratory of customary international law.

None of the provisions of the Wounded and Sick Conventions has been singled out by a tribunal as being a codification of customary international law, although it is quite clear that many of the provisions of GWS-1929 and GWS-1949 do reflect customary international law. GWS-1906 is probably sufficient evidence of customary international law on the treatment of the wounded and the sick.

The Nature of Customary Law

Before turning to the actual state of international law on the treatment of prisoners of war and detained persons, something must be said about what we conceive to be the nature of the established law set forth in this section. We deal here with those rules and principles of law about which there is no dissent or no substantial amount of dissent. These include the following:

- Rules incorporated in a treaty, binding *qua* treaty or as a restatement of customary international law.
- Rules that can be firmly established from the drafting history of a treaty provision, as reflected in the working papers (*travaux preparatoires*).

It is, of course, always possible to manufacture controversy where none should exist and to call black white, and there can be no guarantee that any or all of the law set forth in this section would be assented to or applied by a particular belligerent. On the other hand, there is no requirement that a rule of customary international law be the subject of universal, unanimous express consent before it can be regarded as binding.

In areas of the law that have been heavily codified over the past century, such as the protection of prisoners of war, there are difficulties today in determining what is the present state of customary international law. When almost all of the states of the world are bound by treaties on the subject, there is no room for the development or reaffirmation of customary international law. The most recent evidence of the customary law may date from the nineteenth century and may have doubtful relevance to the relations of belligerents in the second half of the twentieth century.

The Role of Neutral Nations

Neutral nations, private international organizations (such as the International Committee of the Red Cross and other humanitarian organizations), and public international organizations (such as the United Nations) play an important part in securing to prisoners of war and other war victims the protection to which they are entitled under customary and conventional international law.

In principle, the most important role that can be performed by a neutral state is to serve as a protecting power, charged with the responsibility of looking after the interests of persons from the designating state in the hands of the enemy. Naturally, the protecting power must be a state acceptable to both the nation it serves and the nation with which it deals. It provides a wide range of services as set forth in the Geneva Conventions of 1949, such as communication and liaison by transmitting lists of prisoners of war and wounded and sick persons, and by acting as a channel of communication for certain other types of information, notices, and funds. Its representatives visit places of internment for prisoners of war and civilians and receive their complaints. The protecting power may also offer its good offices for the settlement of disputes but has no authority to reach decisions binding on the belligerents.

If the protecting power is unable to continue its services, the two states concerned may designate a successor. If the country on which the prisoners of war or other war victims depend ceases to exist, then the detaining power is to designate a substitute for the original protecting power or accept or request the services of a humanitarian organization such as the International Committee of the Red Cross (ICRC), to assume the "humanitarian functions" of the protecting power.

Aside from their functions as protecting powers, neutral nations may also transmit complaints of violation of the law of war, offer their good offices for the settlement of disputes, and serve as a general channel of communication between belligerents. Under GPW-1949 they may also undertake to accommodate seriously sick and wounded prisoners of war, prisoners who have been long in captivity, and even the ordinary run of prisoners of war by agreement with the belligerents. Finally, neutral states often serve as members of international commissions dealing with the repatriation of prisoners of war and with the supervision of the execution of armistices.

Side by side with neutral nations, the International Committee of the Red Cross looks after the interests of war victims. The organization has historically had the function of initiating, drafting, and revising the various conventions for the protection of war victims, the most recent of which are the Geneva Conventions of 1949. Under these treaties the ICRC can, under certain circumstances, perform the humanitarian functions of a protecting power. It operates central agencies for the recording and exchange of information about prisoners of war and other war victims. Its delegates have the right to visit places where prisoners of war and civilians are interned and to interview them privately. The International Committee carries on extensive relief activities, lends its good offices to secure agreement of hospital and safety zones, and assists in the dissemination of information about the Geneva Conventions. Besides these functions expressly recognized by the conventions, the ICRC also assists in the conduct of pacific relations between belligerents by acting as a go-between and by bringing the belligerents to agreement. As the guardian of the Geneva Conventions, it often issues appeals to belligerents to comply with the conventions or to bring them into operation. The Geneva Conventions also make provisions for the activities of other humanitarian organizations, including relief societies and National Red Cross Societies.

The United Nations concerns itself to some degree with the law relating to war victims. The General Assembly has called upon nations to comply with the law and has from time to time expressed its judgment on the correct interpretation of the treaties. It has drafted instruments dealing with war crimes but has otherwise not attempted to enter the particular domain of the ICRC. Persons acting on behalf of the United Nations often times perform functions resembling those of representatives of the ICRC and of other humanitarian organizations.

Sanctions

Violations respecting the protection of war victims are encouraged to be dealt with through the imposition of a number of sanctions, criminal or civil in nature, or through measures of self-help.

Individuals who violate the law of war or are responsible for violations of the law of war are to be held criminally responsible. Any violation of the law of war is a war crime for which the actor may be punished. The Geneva Conventions of 1949 have created a new category of the most serious war crimes that the treaties characterize as "grave breaches." Grave breaches and other violations of the conventions constitute war crimes if singly or on a small scale but are alluded to as "crimes against humanity" when committed on a large scale.

In the past, war criminals have been tried by international tribunals such as the International Military Tribunal at Nuremberg, and by national courts either of the enemy or of the country to which the war criminal belongs. The actual law under which the criminal is tried may be either international law or provisions of municipal law that serve to implement and spell out the international law of war.

It must be emphasized that jurisdiction over war crimes and the particular form of war crimes called grave breaches is universal; any nation, including a neutral state, may prosecute a violator of the law of war. In addition, the Geneva Conventions require that any party to the treaties holding a person charged with a war crime must either try him or turn him over to a state that can make out a *prima facie* case against the prisoner and is prepared to try him.

As the result of new requirements of national treatment imposed by the Geneva Conventions of 1949, it appears unlikely that any state will be permitted to turn over persons charged with war crimes to an international tribunal for trial. A prisoner of war must now be tried by the same courts and according to the same procedure as members of the armed forces of the detaining power. This means that the Nuremberg trials are a chapter in history that may never be repeated.

The legality of measures taken by a belligerent may also be collaterally challenged in the courts of third states or in the courts of one of the belligerents before or after the termination of hostilities. The basis for the legal challenge in each instance would be the incompatibility of the measures taken by a belligerent with international law.

A belligerent state that violates the law of war is itself under an obligation to pay compensation to the injured state. This compensation has normally taken the form in the past of "reparations" paid by one state to another under the terms of the peace settlement. The facts that only a victor is in a position to exact reparations and that these payments are often in these days exacted for economic and political reasons (that is to bring about the economic disarmament of a defeated enemy) have eliminated much of the legal significance that reparations may once have had. The General Assembly may act in a quasi-judicial capacity in determining responsibility for an alleged violation of the law of war.

Under customary and conventional international law prior to the coming into force of the Geneva Conventions of 1949, the two modes of self-help that belligerents could lawfully employ under the law of war were reprisals and the taking of hostages. *Reprisals* are the taking of measures otherwise unlawful in response to unlawful acts of the opposing belligerent. *Hostages* are enemy persons taken into custody by a belligerent in order to induce compliance with the law of war or with orders of a belligerent. Now, under the Geneva Conventions of 1949, reprisals against protected persons, the taking of hostages, and collective punishments are absolutely forbidden. The only legal scope left for reprisals is that they may be directed against military personnel who are not yet in the hands of the opposing belligerent and against civilians outside of occupied territories.

Types of Conflict to Which the Law of War Applies

Before establishing the types of conflict to which the law of land warfare applies, we must consider the different types of cross-boundary and within-boundary conflict with which international law is concerned. For legal and other purposes, the various types of conflict often differ only in degree, but the distinctions must nevertheless be made if the law is to perform its task.

The distinction between one type of conflict and another usually turns on the scale of the violence and the intention or fault of the state or the authorities initiating the violence or allowing it to be used. The type of weaponry employed—whether conventional weapons or tactical or strategic nuclear weapons—does not of itself carry legal significance, although it may shed some light on the purpose or intention of the aggressor.

The basic type of conflict to which the law of war applies is *international* armed conflict. This may take a variety of legally significant forms:

- Unauthorized incursion by soldiers.
- Authorized small-scale incursion or border incident.
- Permitting hostile activity by private persons or persons acting on behalf of a third state.
- Hostile short-term expedition for a limited purpose.
- Full-scale violence between states.
- Occcupation of territory of another state without combat but through the threat or use of force.

The Hague Regulations apply only if the hostilities are of sufficient scale to constitute "war," which must be taken to mean the use of force by one state against another, with or without declaration of war, with the object of imposing the will of one state on the other. The Geneva Conventions of 1949 have wider application to "all cases of declared war or of any other armed conflict" between parties to the conventions.

So far as *internal* conflicts are concerned, customary international law imposes no requirements with respect to the treatment of persons involved in the conflict. The institutions of recognition of belligerency and recognition of insurgency were nineteenth-century attempts to provide a basis for bringing into operation the law governing international armed conflicts when civil strife had escalated to a scale resembling international war. The Geneva Conventions of 1949 dealt with the problems by laying down a few general principles of humanity binding on both parties to an "armed conflict not of an international character."

Modern conflicts are often of a mixed civil and international character, in that a civil war leads to or is accompanied by assistance and participation by outside states. The existing law provides no clear guide as to whether the law ordinarily regulating international conflicts is to govern conflicts of this mixed character and, if so, to what degree. Moreover the applicability of the law governing international war may be obscured by uncertainty about whether the conflict is civil or international. For example, was the war between North and South Vietnam a civil war or an international conflict for the purposes of the Geneva Conventions?

The establishment of the United Nations has led to the new phenomenon of operations conducted by forces of international composition engaged in maintaining or reestablishing peace. United Nations activity in the form of observation, truce supervision, and mediation gives rise to few problems under the law of war, since these operations are usually conducted without gunfire. United Nations combat forces, however, were constituted in the Korean conflict, and forces were established by the secretary general of the United Nations at the behest of the General Assembly or Security Council in the Middle East (UNEF), the Congo (ONUC), and Cyprus (UNFICYP). In all of these conflicts the United Nations forces were directed to comply with the humanitarian principles of the conventions in their entirety. No United Nations forces have been constituted in the manner contemplated by articles 43 and 48 of the charter, which looked to the provision by the Security Council of national military contingents. International forces have also been established by regional organizations. The most important instance is the Inter-American Armed Force established in the Dominican Republic in 1965.

Finally, the type of conflict to which the law applies has a temporal dimension, since one must determine under what circumstances the law ceases to be applicable as well as under what circumstances the law begins to be applicable; while the terminal dates must be dealt with expressly, the latter question is answered by implication when one ascertains to what type of conflict the law applies.

Under the law as it existed prior to the Geneva Conventions of 1949, the application of the law of war ceased when peace had been restored, normally under the terms of a peace treaty. Difficulties about the application of the existing treaties to the occupation of Germany after World War II led the Geneva Conference to incorporate in the conventions a variety of terminal dates for the operation of various provisions of the treaties.

Types of International or Cross-boundary Conflicts

The following levels of conflicts are arranged in ascending order of intensity of violence, breadth of purpose, and international delinquency:

A state may be internationally responsible for its failure to control the troops that it supports if, without orders or in violation of orders, they cross a frontier and do violence to the persons or property on the other side.

A state may, for a variety of reasons (to test another state's response, as a warning, or to assert a claim to territory), send a small body of troops across a frontier. If fighting breaks out, it may prove extremely difficult to determine who initiated the combat and whether the shooting started with a deliberate purpose or because of a mistake. What is significant is that the fighting is localized and that no attempt is made to deploy the full force of one state against another state, or to impose the will of one state on another through violence. Although such fighting may not be war for the purposes of international law, it may nevertheless constitute a "threat or use of force against the territorial integrity or political independence of any state" according to the United Nations Charter. As a consequence, it may be a dispute or a situation involving a threat to the peace, breach of the peace, or act of aggression that will call for action by the General Assembly or the Security Council.

If a state gives support to hostile activities against another state or harbors persons, whether its own inhabitants or persons acting on behalf of a third state, who are engaged in hostile action against another state, the state allowing or supporting the use of force may be internationally delinquent. If such a state is regarded as an aggressor or even as having mounted an armed attack, the state against which that attack is directed may avail itself of the privilege of individual or collective self-defense under article 51 of the charter. The term "indirect aggression" has often been applied to such conduct.

If a hostile, short-term expedition is initiated for a limited purpose, force of some magnitude may be deployed, falling short of an attempt on the part of the state employing force to impose its will upon another state and to deny it its political independence. It may be by way of retaliation against prior border violations by another state, or it may be a modern exercise of the alleged right of "humanitarian intervention" for the purpose of protecting nationals of the state concerned against public or private violence when no other remedy is available (for example, the Congo rescue operation or the United States action in the Dominican Republic at the inception of the military operation). It is characteristic of actions of this sort that the infringement of the independence of the state subjected to violence is temporally and geographically limited and that no acquisition of territory or sovereignty is intended or effected.

Full-scale violence between states is war in its conventional sense, involving an attempt by one state to impose its will upon another by the use of force and looking to the acquisition of territory or the denial of the political independence of the victim of the use of force. Even in this context, the declaration of war is in these days only of marginal importance. A state, whether in fact the aggressor or the victim of aggression, will seek to justify its resort to force as an act of self-defense. If war has been thrust upon one state by another, there is no need to declare war. If, on the other hand, a state is fatally bent on mischief, it will probably not pause to declare the war that it has legally inflicted on another. A more powerful state may occupy the territory of another state without combat but through the threat or use of force.

A state commanding such overwhelming military superiority over another may be able to send its troops into the territory of the victim without resistance on the part of the invaded state. The state employing the force does not thereby absolve itself of its responsibilities under the law of war. The classic case was the invasion of Denmark by Germany, largely without resistance on the part of the former. The Nuremberg Tribunal nevertheless held that Germany had engaged in "aggressive war" against Denmark as well as Norway.[8]

To which of the above categories of conflict does the law relating to prisoners of war and detained persons apply? By its literal terms, HR (Hague Regulations) *qua* treaty applies between contracting powers "and then only if all the belligerents are parties to the Convention" (H IV, art. 2). This is the *si omnes* provision meaning that if a single participant in a conflict was not a party to H IV-1907, the convention and the annexed regulations would be inapplicable as between all of the states that were actually parties to the convention. But as a restatement of the customary law of war, the regulations apply to the relations of all states. Although neither H IV nor HR define expressly the circumstances under which they will be operative, the frequent use of the word "war" in the text suggests that it is to war in its orthodox sense—primarily declared war and excluding lesser levels of use of force—to which the regulations apply. However, members of armed forces captured in lower levels of conflict, extending even to unauthorized operations, have been treated as prisoners of war when retained. The alternative, if the captured troops were not promptly repatriated, would be to hold them as criminals, and that would hardly be admissible as a rule of the game. However, it would always be open to a state to adopt a strict and literal interpretation of the word "war" as used in HR and to deny prisoner of war treatment to captured soldiers. This is a matter about which there can be no certainty.

The draftsmen of the Geneva Conventions of 1949 were anxious to rectify the imprecision of the existing conventional and customary law. Each convention by its own terms is to apply to "all cases of declared war or of any other armed conflict which may arise between two or more of the High Contracting Parties, even if the state of war is not recognized by one of them." "Any other armed conflict" should be accorded the broad scope that was intended for it. In the language of the Pictet Red Cross commentary, "any difference arising between two states and leading to the intervention of members of the armed forces is an armed conflict within the meaning of Article 2" (GC-1949, art. 2). All that is required in the case of prisoners of war is that the armed forces of one party shall have captured members of the armed forces of the other. An ambiguity lurks, however, in the clause "even if the state of war is not recognized by one of them." Literally the proviso suggests that the conventions may not be for application if the state of war is not recognized by *both* parties, but if war victims are to be protected, their protection should not turn on the attitudes of the antagonists.

Types of Internal Conflicts

Just as there are varying degrees of intensity in international conflicts there is also a whole spectrum of internal conflict, ranging from a single political assassination to a full-scale civil conflict. When the activity is localized and limited in scope, it may even be difficult to tell whether the action is for private or public ends—whether it is banditry or guerrilla action against the government.

Customary international law imposed no requirements with respect to the treatment of the participants in a civil conflict, of whatever degree of intensity. International law was envisaged in its orthodox role as the law governing the relations of states. An internal conflict remained within the domestic jurisdiction of the state concerned, except when the actions of the contending factions (including the lawful and recognized government) impinged upon other states. Such action as the closure or blockade of ports, the seizure of neutral property, and dealings with the rebel government were matters of international concern because they affected state-to-state relationships.

In the past, international law attempted to deal with the international aspects of civil strife through two institutions—recognition of insurgency and recognition of belligerency. Recognition of insurgency was the characterization placed upon what the third state was willing to concede to the rebels in the particular instance.

However, once there is a general armed conflict within a state and the rebels, constituting themselves as a government, are in control of a substantial portion of the territory of the state and wage war through armed forces that act in accordance with the law of war, third states may recognize (or are under a duty to recognize, according to another view) the belligerency of the insurgents. This means that the outsiders that have accorded this recognition will thereafter, treat the conflict as if it were an international one and will assume a position of neutrality.

All of what has been said up to this point applies to the relation of third parties with the rebels and the lawful government and does not affect the relationship of the lawful government to the rebels. Recognition of insurgency by third states may influence the lawful government to treat the members of the rebel forces according to the law applicable to international conflicts. However, the lawful government of a state may, as a matter of its strict legal right, treat the rebels as traitors and criminals for the duration of the conflict, whatever may be the position of third states. The established government will treat the rebels as prisoners of war only when the conflict has reached such a scale that there are actually two competing governments, each controlling armies and territory. However, observance of the laws of war involves no recognition of the rebellious government. Thus, the nineteenth century body of law about the recognition of insurgency and of belligerency has, for the most part, quietly expired.

At the Geneva Conference of 1949 an attempt was made to work out some firm basis on which both of the opposing belligerents in a civil conflict might, under appropriate circumstances, be required to apply the international law of war. This attempt was unsuccessful, and the weak provisions of common article 3 provide merely a basic bill of rights for persons taking no active part in hostilities, including those who have laid down their arms, in "the case of armed conflict not of an international character occurring in the territory of one" of the parties. The law is apparently applicable to all forms of armed conflict, although it is reasonable to suppose that the opposing faction in the conflict must act with a political or public purpose and not for private gain. The obligation is imposed on "each Party to the conflict," which means that the rebels are, under the literal language of the conventions, as much bound as the lawful government. Although there may be practical difficulties in securing performance of this obligation by members of the rebellious faction, in strict law their duty arises from the fact that they are nationals of the state that has assumed the obligations of a treaty binding upon individuals as well as states. The parties to the conflict are encouraged to bring into force by special agreements all or part of the conventions, and the ICRC may òffer its services to the parties.

Conflicts of a Mixed Civil and
International Character

As the whole pattern of post-World War II relationships has taught us, civil conflicts have a dangerous way of escalating into international conflicts if not damped down by conventional or parliamentary diplomacy. For international law the significance of this phenomenon is that conflicts may be of a mixed civil and international character. A third state may come to the assistance of the government of a state, at the government's invitation, when it is faced with disorder, insurrection, or revolt.

This kind of situation can become extremely complicated, for that government may either be the universally recognized government of the state, or its claim to legitimacy may be challenged by one or more states. The position of the third state may be called into question if it aids what is, in the view of other states, not the lawful government but a usurper. In this case, the state may find itself accused of aggression by the rebellious faction and by those other states that recognize the rebellious faction as the government. On the other hand, aid to rebels or premature recognition of insurgents are both international delin-quencies, and as we have seen above, the aid to the rebels may be considered a form of indirect aggression against a lawful government. Further, several different states may go to the aid of opposing factions in the state, each state claiming that it is aiding the legitimate government at its request. An example of this is the war in Vietnam, even though the aid to the government of North Vietnam by the USSR and Communist China did not reach the level of supplying troops.

A number of authorities on international law have proposed a variety of rules in an attempt to deal with the dangers posed by an outsider or outsiders becoming involved in a family quarrel that could turn into a neighborhood brawl. Some have asserted that any participation by an outside state in a civil conflict, even at the invitation of the government, is unlawful intervention; others, that aid to the government to "overcome an insurgent movement of large proportions" is unlawful; and yet others, that a duty to abstain from assistance to government as well as to the rebels arises upon general recognition of belligerency. As the recent controversy about the legality of United States aid to the government of South Vietnam bears witness, there is no agreement on the applicable law.

Customary international law does not regulate the conduct of internal conflicts, and the law with respect to aid by an outside state to the government of a state faced with insurrection is itself unclear. Thus, there has been no room for the development of a distinctive body of law applicable to military and civilian personnel in a mixed civil-international conflict. The distinction drawn by common articles 2 and 3 of the Geneva Conventions does not resolve the application of the treaty law, and the existing law provides no clear answers.

International Operations

The United Nations may assume activity in the form of observation, truce supervision, and mediation. The Security Council has often requested or authorized the secretary general to send observers or supervisors to various troubled spots in the world. Among these groups have been the United Nations Truce Supervision Organization in Palestine, first established in 1948; the United Nations Military Observer Group in India and Pakistan, established in 1948; the United Nations Observor Group in Lebanon, established in 1958, and the United Nations Observation Mission in Yemen. The personnel to staff these organizations have been secluded from national military forces, have been individually recruited, and have not had the status of members of the Secretariat of the United Nations. These operations have had as their various purposes the gathering of information for the Security Council, the supervision of truces, and the establishment of a United Nations presence on the ground with a view to cooling down the situation and providing a medium of communication between the contending forces. There is no thought that the individuals making up these bodies should engage in hostilities, and there would, therefore, be no question of their taking prisoners or detaining civilians. If members of these bodies were to be taken into custody or otherwise interfered with while they were in the proper performance of their official duties, the secretary general and the Security Council would look upon such action as unlawful and would, in appropriate cases, demand satisfaction. For example, when Count Bernadotte, the United Nations mediator in Palestine, was killed, it was ruled that the organization could bring an international claim reparation against the responsible government.

Sometimes United Nations forces are constituted that are authorized to engage in combat. These forces in the strict sense have been constituted under the authority of both the Security Council and the General Assembly to deal with various threats to the peace or breaches of the peace. Some of these forces have engaged in combat. The principal forms of United Nations activity of this character have been as follows, in ascending order of control by and responsibility of the General Assembly and the Security Council:

The United Nations Command in Korea. When North Korean forces attacked the Republic of Korea in 1950, the Security Council first recommended that the members furnish assistance to the victim of aggression and then recommended "that all Members providing military forces and other assistance pursuant to the ... Security Council resolutions make such forces and other assistance available to a unified command under the United States." The United States was requested to designate the commander of the force and to provide the Security Council with periodic reports, and the "unified command" was authorized to use the United Nations flag. This was the extent of United Nations participation. Neither the Security Council nor the General Assembly exercised any substantial control over the unified command, either directly or through the secretary general.

There are differing views about whether the United Nations Command acting under the unified command of the United States actually could be regarded as United Nations forces in the sense of the United Nations bearing responsibility for them. The following two positions by various authorities on the subject reflect how controversial the question is:

These relations, it is submitted, are not sufficient to establish the United Nations as bearer of the rights and duties in respect of the Force, either alone, or concurrently with the United States or other Governments.[9]

There can be no doubt that, in practice, the overwhelming majority of States involved in the Korean action were fully prepared to regard it as a United Nations action involving United Nations forces.[10]

Even states of similar political persuasion were not in agreement. Communist China was prepared and, at the time, even delighted to concede that it was dealing with United Nations forces, while the Soviet Union denied that this was a United Nations action.

At the time the conflict broke out the United States and other nations allied with it, as well as North Korea and Communist China, were not parties to the Geneva Conventions of 1949, and the principal participants indicated in differing terms their willingness to comply with all or part of the conventions. The United States, speaking on behalf of the United Nations Command, stated at different times, with doubtful consistency, that it was applying the humanitarian principles of the conventions, particularly article 3 (relating to civil conflicts) and the detailed provisions of GPW and that forces had been directed to observe at all times the four Geneva Conventions of 1949 as well as H IV. North Korea declared that it was complying with the "principles" of GPW, and Communist China "recognized" the four Conventions in 1952, relatively late in the conflict.

Forces Constituted by the Secretary General of the United Nations at the Direction of the Security Council or of the General Assembly. There have been three forces of this character constituted since the establishment of the United Nations: the United Nations Emergency Force in the Middle East (UNEF), the United Nations Force in the Congo (ONUC), and the United Nations Force in Cyprus (UNFICYP).

UNEF was constituted by the General Assembly in 1956 in order "to secure and supervise the cessation of hostilities" in the Middle East following the conflict between Israel, France, and Great Britain, on the one hand, and the United Arab Republic and other Arab states, on the other. As the secretary general put it, UNEF should not be regarded as a military force temporarily controlling the territory in which it was stationed, but it had to be considered more than an observer's corps. The establishment of UNEF by the General Assembly was consistent with the Uniting for Peace Resolution of the General Assembly, which looked to the General Assembly to take measures for the maintenance of international peace and security, when the Security Council had, as the result of a veto, taken no action to deal with a situation.

ONUC came into existence in 1960 under the authority of resolutions of the Security Council and was charged with providing military assistance to the Republic of the Congo, which had been torn asunder by civil conflict, and securing the withdrawal of foreign military personnel. These measures were necessary in order to avoid having the country become the scene of a confrontation authorized by the Security Council to take "requisite measures of force" against foreign military personnel.

UNFICYP was likewise constituted on the basis of a resolution of the Security Council. Its function was the maintenance of peace and the restoration of normal conditions in Cyprus. That country was then in the midst of a civil war between the Greek and Turkish factions in the island, and there was a grave danger that foreign intervention, which had already assumed substantial proportions, would bring on a full-scale international conflict. The force, as in the case of UNEF, did not engage in combat. By the time the Turks invaded Cyprus in 1974 the force had been withdrawn.

All three of these forces had certain common characteristics. They were all made up of national contingents, with the exception of the post of commander and the higher staff positions. All three were subordinated to the secretary general, to whom the Security Council and General Assembly had gladly turned over the task of establishing the force and supervising its activity. And in all three cases, the force was stationed on the territory of the state concerned, with the consent of that state, and even the composition of the force was subject to veto by the state on whose territory the force served. The consensual basis of the stationing was emphasized by the existence of agreements with the host states that resembled status of forces agreements and, to a lesser degree, the civil affairs agreements concluded during World War II between the United States and countries which were to be liberated.

Only in the activity of UNEF was the conflict purely international. In the other two—the Congo and Cyprus—a conflict that was in its inception normally an internal one threatened to turn into an international conflict—and, in the case of Cyprus, in fact did so. In all three instances the situation was sufficiently dangerous to threaten the maintenance of international peace and security and thus fell within the competence of the General Assembly, the United Nations Charter, and the Security Council.

In all three of these operations the regulations prescribed for the forces by the secretary general provided that the Force observe and respect the principle and spirit of the general international Conventions applicable to the conduct of military personnel. The view taken by the ICRC was that since the United Nations was not a party to the conventions, when supplying a contingent to the United Nations, each State was personally responsible for the application of these Conventions. In the case of the one conflict in which the United Nations forces engaged in combat, the Republic of the Congo (Zaire) was bound by the conventions, while the Katangese forces agreed to respect the humanitarian principles generally recognized.

True United Nations Forces Constituted Under Articles 43 to 48 of the Charter. It was contemplated by the draftsmen of the charter that the enforcement measures by "air, sea, or land forces" envisaged by article 42 would be carried out by armed forces made available to the Security Council by member nations. Since such measures would be taken against a state that had been guilty of a threat to the peace, breach of the peace, or act of aggression, the acquienscence of that state would naturally not be required, and the consensual basis for the placing of United Nations forces on the territory of a member state, characteristic of the forces referred to in the preceding paragraph, would be irrelevant.

The forces would be made available under agreements to be concluded between the furnishing states and the Security Council. The troops would be deployed under the strategic direction of a Military Staff Committee subordinated to the Security Council. It has not been possible to conclude the requisite agreements, and forces have therefore never been constituted under these provisions of the charter.

The Soviet Union and other Communist countries maintain that the establishment, financing, and employment of forces by the United Nations must be under the control of the Security Council, where the veto may be employed. The Soviet challenge to the legality of the financing of UNEF and ONUC was decided by the International Court adversely to the USSR. The ensuing refusal of the USSR and other countries to pay their contributions led to a great financial crisis in the U.N., which was resolved only when the United States yielded to the Soviet position. The position of the Communist states must be borne in mind in assessing the degree of cooperation or obstruction to which United Nations forces of the future may be subject. Since no supranational forces independent of national forces have ever been constituted, there is no precedent concerning the extent to which the activities of such forces would be subject to the conventional or customary law of war.

Forces Established by a Regional Organization Constituted Under Article 53 of the United Nations Charter. International forces may be constituted not only by the United Nations but also by the regional organizations recognized by article 53 of the charter of the United Nations. From the point of view of the United States, the most important instance of the use of such forces was the Inter-American Armed Force established by the Tenth Meeting of Consultation of Ministers of Foreign Affairs of the Organization of American States to deal with the situation in the Dominican Republic in 1965. The United States forces, which had initially been sent to the Dominican Republic for the protection of United States citizens and other foreigners, were made a part of this force.

End of Application of the Law of War

The orthodox way of ending a war—in theory, if not in the practice of nations—is through subjugation or the conclusion of a treaty of peace, which is preceded by a general armistice or capitulation bringing the active hostilities to a halt. For the duration of the armistice the state of hostilities is suspended but not terminated. A state of peace is reestablished only when the peace treaty comes into force.

Under customary international law the repatriation of prisoners is to take place as quickly as possible "after the conclusion of peace." The word "peace" is to be taken literally, as meaning the coming into force of the peace treaty. Nothing, of course, stands in the way of their earlier repatriation if the detaining power so desires. Reflecting a practice of earlier repatriation of prisoners under the terms of the armistice, GPW-1929 enjoins the belligerents to make provision for the repatriation of prisoners in the armistice itself.

When Germany unconditionally surrendered, its government was assumed by the occupying powers. The anticipated delay in the conclusion of any treaty of peace created obstacles after the defeat of Germany to the application of the provisions of HR relating to belligerent occupation. The position taken by the occupying powers to the capitulation of Germany and the succession of the occupying powers to the government of that country made HR inapplicable. In their view the provisions of HR relating to belligerent occupation referred to a state of affairs in which the outcome of the war was still uncertain and the occupation therefore precarious. Those circumstances no longer existed. But as a matter of policy it was decided that such of the provisions as were consistent with the position and policy of the occupants would be applied. Thus, the rules that the United States followed in the seizure and requisitioning of property were those of HR. The most telling argument made against the failure of the Allied powers to apply HR was that this policy deprived the inhabitants of Germany of the protection of the law of war at the very time when they were most in need of it, in the sense that they were at the mercy of the occupants and had no government of their own.

This history had its impact on the Geneva Conventions of 1949, which provide for various terminal dates for certain purposes. Under GWS, protected persons who have fallen into the hands of the enemy continue to benefit from the convention "until their final repatriation." Under GPW, protection of prisoners continues until their "final release and repatriation" (art. 5). Prisoners are to be repatriated "without delay after the cessation of active hostilities" (art. 118). As a response to the problem of Germany after World War II, GC took a new line, with different dates provided for the cessation of application of various provisions of the convention with respect to civilians (art. 6):

- In the territory of parties to the conflict the application of the convention ends at the "general close of military operations."
- In occupied territories the application of the convention ends one year after the general close of military operations, except that:
  a) The application of certain identified provisions, dealing with the most basic protection of human life and welfare, continues "for the duration of the occupation, to the extent that such Power exercises the functions of government in such territory."
  b) Protected persons who are released, repatriated, or reestablished at a date

later than those above continue to be protected by the convention in the meanwhile.

Persons to Whom the Law of War Applies

There are basically three categories of war victims under the protection of international law—prisoners of war including certain civilians accompanying armed forces; medical personnel, chaplains, and related persons ministering to the armed forces; and civilians who are not involved in the conflict. Both under customary law and GPW-1949, members of the land, sea, and air armed forces and of militias and volunteer corps forming part of the armed forces are entitled to treatment as prisoners of war. Because of somewhat different wording in HR and GPW-1929 on the one hand and GPW-1949 on the other, how the individual came into the hands of the detaining power can be a question of some importance. Under the customary law, as reflected in articles 1 and 3 of HR, the member of the armed forces must have been "captured" to claim such treatment. The scope of GPW-1949 was deliberately broadened through the use of the expression "who have fallen into the power of the enemy." The purpose of this language was to cover the case of "soldiers who had surrendered without resistance or who had been in enemy territory at the outbreak of hostilities. This clause applies to all the categories of persons who are entitled to prisoner of war treatment under GPW, article 4, paragraph A.

Under the somewhat elliptical language of HR, militias and volunteer corps are counted as members of the armed forces if such bodies constitute or form part of the army. If they do not constitute or form part of the army, they must fulfill the following four conditions. First, they must be commanded by a person responsible for his subordinates. This requirement can be met through command of the resistance movement by an officer of the armed forces or some other person in authority, whether he is appointed by the government of a party to the conflict or elected or appointed within the resistance movement. Since military operations can hardly be carried on effectively by forces lacking a leader, this requirement should be easily satisfied in almost all instances.

Second, a distinctive emblem must be recognizable at a distance. The distinctive sign must be "fixed," which means that it must be worn regularly and not taken off to permit concealment of the character of the individual. (It may be observed that the proposal made in 1947 to require that the sign be displayed "habitually and consistently" was not adopted.) A distinctive uniform is best, but a distinctive type of headgear or helmet would do, and a brassard or badge would also help to fix the identity of the individual.

Third, the member of the resistance movement must not conceal his arms at times when he is not using them or when he wishes to pass himself off as a peaceful civilian. He must be a full-time soldier. There are obviously problems in the application of this standard. The farmer who drops his regular occupation in order to join a partisan band for a week will probably qualify, but a farmer who works nights as a soldier and hides his weapon by day will not.

Fourth, operations must be conducted in accordance with the law and customs of war. It is physically impossible for members of a resistance movement, especially in an occupied area, to comply with the four Geneva Conventions and HR in all of their detail, and what must be looked for is substantial compliance, especially as regards such matters as prohibitions on the "employment of treachery, denial of quarter, maltreatment of prisoners of war, wounded, and dead, improper conduct toward flags or truce, pillage, and unnecessary violence and destruction."[11] The fact that an individual has committed a war crime cannot be the cause for denying him prisoner of war status, if his unit or organization generally complies with the law, but there can come a time when the level of compliance is so low that all members of the organization or unit will be denied prisoner of war treatment and those individually guilty of violations of the law will be subject to trial for their war crimes.

The last three of the four requirements probably would not be satisfied by most guerrilla forces and resistance movements, which depend heavily on stealth and dissimulation. Thus, there are relatively few persons other than those specifically identified in the other parts of GPW, article 4, who can expect to meet all four of these conditions and so qualify for treatment as prisoners of war.

Another category to which the law applies is to the members of a levy en masse. These are persons "who on the approach of the enemy spontaneously take up arms to resist the invading forces, without having had time to form themselves into regular armed forces" (GPW, art. 4). The two requirements they must meet are that they must carry arms openly and respect the laws and customs of war. There is no such thing as a levy en masse in occupied territory, although it is not always easy to distinguish areas that are occupied from those that are merely invaded. The levy must be en masse, and isolated civilians who take up arms for what Professor James Molony Spaight has called "some amateur hedgerow fighting in his spare moments" and franctierurs do not qualify. The crucial line between individual and mass resistance is not easily drawn. But if the opposing forces are faced by nonformed and unorganized masses of civilians in arms, they may presume that all persons capable of bearing arms are enemies and take all men of military age as prisoners of war, even if these men have laid down their arms and have returned to their normal pursuits. The concept of the levy en masse is of little current utility, since modern war simply does not permit operations of this sort. However, there is a certain sentimental attachment to the idea of popular resistance, and Communist states that place emphasis on this notion and on wars of national liberation may be expected to favor this concept.

The regulations say nothing about resistance in occupied areas by militias and volunteer corps meeting the avoce specifications. Before, during, and after the two Hague Conferences in 1899 and 1907, there was a conflict of views between countries that had been occupied—and therefore had advocated a right of resistance in occupied areas—and the great military powers who had been occupants. Indeed, there was enough controversy about the matter that members of a resistance movement in occupied territory could not count on being treated as prisoners of war upon capture even though they might comply with the four conditions.

The unwillingness of the German forces to grant prisoner of war status to members of resistance movements in World War II led to demands for a new formulation in the Geneva Conference of 1949. GPW-1949 recognizes no general right of resistance in occupied areas and limits prisoner of war standing to "members of other militias and members of other volunteer corps, including those of organized resistance movements, belonging to a Party to the conflict and operating in or outside their own territory, even if this territory is occupied," provided they comply with the four requirements of HR quoted above. Quite aside from the first requirement—command by a person responsible for his subordinates—the deliberate use of the language "organized resistance movements" suggests activity by groups operating within an overall organization of some size, rather than individual acts of resistance. Moreover, the movement must "belong to a Party to the conflict," which means that a resistance movement, even if organized and fulfilling all of the other requirements, cannot claim prisoner of war treatment for its members if it stands in opposition to both or all of the parties to the conflict. A secessionist movement in a war fought between two states—each claiming the territory in question to be its own—would thus not qualify, except if those in arms supporting it could establish that they were "members of regular armed forces who profess allegiance to a government or an authority not recognized by the detaining power" (GC, art. 4, para. A (3)).

Members of *regular* armed forces who profess allegiance to a government or an authority not recognized by the detaining power are also covered by the law. This government or authority must purport to act on behalf of a party to the conventions, for otherwise the treaties would not be operative at all. This provision was intended to secure treatment as prisoners of war for forces like the Free French Forces of General de Gaulle and the Italian troops that fought against Germany after 1943, as well as forces acting on behalf of a government in exile. The position of such forces was not clear under customary international law. The situation of General de Gaulle's forces was complicated by the fact that the French Armistice of 1940 had stated that persons who continued to fight would not be treated as prisoners of war. The International Committee of the Red Cross was successful in pursuading Germany to renounce this provision and to treat these troops as prisoners of war.

Under customary law the position of civilians accompanying the armed forces states that individuals "who follow an army without directly belonging to it" and come into the hands of the enemy are entitled to prisoner of war treatment, so long as they possess identification provided by the army they accompany. However, the loss of identity documents, which might be facilitated by the detaining power, would mean that the individual would forfeit prisoner of war treatment. GPW-1949 made only one substantive change in the article, providing that the person must have received authorization from the armed forces that he accompanies, and that the armed forces are to provide him with an identity card. However, the possession of the card is not a condition of being treated as a prisoner of war, and the status of the individual may be established by other means.

The categories of persons specifically mentioned in GPW—civilian members of military aircraft crews, war correspondents, supply contractors, members of labor units or of services responsible for the welfare of the armed forces—are only exemplary. There is no significance to the fact that HR contains a shorter list and mentions sutlers, whereas GPW does not. However, civilian laborers accompanying guerrilla forces and other irregular combatants would not qualify.

Members of crews of the merchant marine and crews of civil aircraft or parties to the conflict are treated as prisoners of war under GPW-1949 if they "do not benefit by more favorable treatment under any other provisions of international law" meaning Hague Convention XI relative to the Right of Capture in Naval War. In these days enemy civilians in the hands of a belligerent are often interned, and it is not clear that Hague Convention XI would exempt captains, officers, and crews from being placed in such custody. If they were interned, they would benefit from GC. It will be observed that neutral nationals forming part of the crew (including masters, pilots, and apprentices) are not accorded a privileged position under GPW, unless they can bring themselves within Hague Convention XI.

One totally new category of people accorded prisoner of war status by the Geneva Conventions of 1949 were present or former members of the armed forces of an occupied country who are interned. This innovation was introduced as a consequence of the facts that such persons had been interned by occupants, notably Germany, during World War II and the intervention of the ICRC had been necessary in order to secure treatment as prisoners of war for such persons. Thus, article 4, paragraph B (1) of GPW-1949 provides that if the occupant considers it necessary to intern "persons belonging, or having belonged, to the armed forces of occupied country," they benefit from prisoner of war treatment even if they had been liberated while hostilities were going on outside the occupied territory. Two categories of such persons are specifically mentioned: (1) persons who have made an unsuccessful attempt to rejoin their own armed forces, and (2) persons who have failed to respond to a summons to internment. This is because during World War II, such persons had often been treated more severely than escaping prisoners.

The international law of war also covers persons interned in neutral territory. Under customary international law, belligerent forces that were allowed to enter the territory of a neutral state had to be interned, but they were not characterized as prisoners of war. In the case of individual soldiers, the neutral was required to take measures to keep them from rejoining their own forces. Escaping prisoners of war and prisoners carried in by the troops granted asylum could not be interned and would be allowed to rejoin their own forces.

Under conventional law, on the other hand, persons who are received by a neutral state and are required to be interned by that state are treated as prisoners of war. These persons include the following:

1. Troops belonging to the belligerent armies.
2. Individual soldiers (excluding escaped prisoners of war or prisoners of war brought in by troops granted asylum).
3. Wounded, sick, and other prisoners interned in a neutral state by agreement between that state and a detaining power.
4. Officers and crew of a ship that has been interned because of failure to leave a neutral port in which it is not entitled to remain.
5. Wounded, sick, and shipwrecked personnel and other persons in naval warfare who are required to be interned under H IV-1907.

However, GPW also provides that certain articles inappropriate to the relationship of a neutral state with persons interned on its territory do not apply. If the neutral state and the parties to the conflict maintain diplomatic relationships, the articles relating to the protecting power may not apply, but the neutral state will be permitted to exercise the functions of a protecting power under the convention.

Another innovation of the Geneva Conventions of 1949 was that they accorded prisoner of war protection to persons in doubtful status. Article 5, of GPW provides that "should any doubt arise as to whether persons, having committed a belligerent act and having fallen into the hands of the enemy, belong to any of the categories . . . [discussed above], such persons shall enjoy the protection of the present convention until such time as their status has been determined by a competent tribunal." New law is laid down in this paragraph, and there is no corresponding duty imposed by customary international law other than that a person who *is* actually a prisoner of war be treated as one. The past evil that this paragraph was intended to guard against is clear. During World War II persons such as escaping prisoners in civilian clothes, deserters, and civilians who had lost their identity cards were frequently asserted not to be prisoners of war and were taken out and shot, often at the command of an enlisted man. Article 5 provides that in doubtful cases the individual will enjoy prisoner of war treatment and that he may be deprived of that standing only as the result of the proceedings of a competent tribunal.

If assistance is furnished by staff of aid societies of neutral countries, their personnel who have fallen into the hands of the opposing party cannot be detained and must be returned to their own country or to the territory of the party to the conflict where they were serving as soon as practicable. In the meanwhile, they are to continue their work, preferably in the care of the wounded and sick of the party in whose service they were. Certain basic safeguards are afforded to such persons under GWS, article 32.

Finally, it is necessary to mention prisoners of war charged with or convicted of war crimes. Analytically these prisoners do not form a category separate from prisoners of war in general. However, reservations to article 85 of GPW would deprive certain of such persons of their standing as prisoners of war. This group as well as medical and related personnel, and civilians will be discussed in chapters 2 and 3, respectively.

Notes

1. Vol. 6, U.S. Treaties, p. 3514. (Treaties in International Agreements Series 3364, p. 200).

2. United States v. List et al. (11 Trials of War Criminals before the Nuremberg Military Tribunals under Control Council Law No. 10) 1230, 1235 (1948).

3. Nazi Conspiracy and Aggression: Opinion and Judgment [The Nuremberg Judgment] 51 (1947).

4. United States v. Krauch et al. (8 Trials of War Criminals before the Nuremberg Military Tribunals under Control Council Law No. 10) 1081, 1138 (1948).

5. United States v. List et al. (11 Trials of War Criminals before the Nuremberg Military Tribunals under Control Council Law No. 10) 1230, 1237 (1948).

6. Nazi Conspiracy and Aggression: Opinion and Judgment 83 (1947).

7. In re Hirota and Others, 15 Ann. Dig. 356, 366 (1948).

8. Nazi Conspiracy and Aggression: Opinion and Judgment 38 (1947).

9. Baxter, Constitutional Forms and Some Legal Problems of International Military Command, 29 Brit. Y.B. Int'l L. 325, 336 (1952).

10. Bowett, United Nations Forces 47 (1964).

11. Field Manual 27-10, Law of Land Warfare, para. 64d (1956).

2 The Combatants

Captivity and Internment

General Protection of Prisoners

Preceding the specific rules of GPW-1949 (Geneva Convention Relative to the Treatment of Prisoners of War—1949) governing the treatment of prisoners of war is a statement of general principles that condition the entire relationship between the detaining power and the prisoner of war. The first and most important of these is the principle of humane treatment, which is fundamental to both GPW and customary international law. Under GPW-1949, prisoners of war are entitled to humane treatment "at all times" (art. 13), even during battle, provided they no longer resist their captors or take part in combat. This standard underlies all aspects of their captivity and extends even to instances where disciplinary action is taken because of an infraction of rules. The convention prohibits unlawful acts causing death or illness, physical mutilation and medical or scientific experiments. Prisoners are also protected against violence, intimidation, insults, and public curiosity. Reprisals are expressly forbidden, both because of their inhumanity to prisoners, who are in no way responsible for the acts committed, and because of their corrosive effect on the observance of the other rules of the convention.

Article 14 of GPW-1949 elaborates the concept of humane treatment and provides that prisoners are entitled to respect for their persons and honor. With regard to the physical well-being of prisoners, the convention requires not only protection against direct injury, but also care as to living conditions provided, as well as protection against the effects of military operations. It also applies to the psychological well-being of prisoners and to religious, intellectual, and social activities, which are provided for in later articles of the convention. Respect for personal integrity is also addressed by other articles of GPW-1949 that cover such matters as permission to wear badges of rank and nationality; treatment of officers with the respect due their rank and age; prohibition against humiliating types of labor; dishonorable forms of punishment; and honorable burial in the event of death. Women are covered expressly in article 14 and are guaranteed treatment as favorable as that provided men.

With respect to their legal rights as private persons (as distinguished from prisoners of war), article 14 provides that prisoners retain the "full civil capacity that they enjoyed at the time of their capture," since their detention is not

35

penal. The detaining power may not restrict the prisoners' exercise of their rights except as required by their captivity. In fact, there is an affirmative duty to allow prisoners to consult legal counsel and to facilitate the preparation and transmission of legal documents on the prisoners' behalf.

Article 16 requires equality of treatment of prisoners subject to any special provisions of the convention itself. Differences in treatment may be based on rank, sex, aptitude for work, age, and state of health, but no adverse distinction may be based on "race, nationality, religious belief or political opinions, or any other distinction founded on similar criteria."

The detaining power is responsible for treatment of prisoners from the time of their capture. In order to make this clear, article 12 expressly provides that prisoners "are in the hands of the enemy Power, but not of the individuals or military units who have captured them." Even though agents of the detaining power may be individually responsible for their conduct toward prisoners, the detaining power remains primarily (but not exclusively) responsible for the treatment provided them. Reflecting that obligation, article 15 requires the detaining power to provide free maintenance and medical care to the prisoners. In this respect the convention departs from customary law, under which the costs of maintenance could ultimately be passed on to the power on which the prisoner depended.

Civilian Assistance

In addition to the responsibilities of the detaining power, the law also sets forth the standards of behavior for civilians regarding their relation to enemy wounded and sick. Perhaps the most vulnerable period for an individual who has fallen into enemy hands is the time between his incapacitation, surrender, or capture and his incarceration in a prison camp. During this time he is at the mercy of persons close to or involved in combat whose feelings of violence and retaliation may be running high. To protect the wounded and the sick from violence or neglect on the part of the civilian population, the law prohibits civilians from doing harm to combatants and encourages them to offer assistance to the wounded and sick.

Although there are few references to civilian assistance in customary law, it appears that the universal principle that accords a fallen combatant respect and protection is extended to civilians. Article 18 of GWS (Geneva Convention for the Amelioration of the Condition of the Wounded and Sick in Armed Forces in the Fields) enjoins civilians from doing violence to any wounded or sick combatant. It may even be argued that the law places a positive obligation upon anyone who finds a fallen combatant to assist him and give him help. In order to encourage the civilian population to assist the fallen, the Geneva Convention of 1864 granted neutral status to civilians who quartered the wounded and sick.

Such quarters were exempted from being further requisitioned by an occupying power. The concept invited abuse and was not continued in 1906 or any other subsequent conventions. Three principles of civilian assistance to the sick and the wounded have been continuously elaborated upon by the 1906, 1929, and 1949 conventions. They are that:

1. The protection and medical facilities accorded to the inhabitants by one party to the conflict must also be available to other parties to the conflict.
2. The inhabitants must be encouraged to offer spontaneous care to the wounded.
3. Having cared for enemy wounded is never a reprehensible act.

Article 18 authorizes the military authorities to appeal to the charity of the inhabitants by assuring that similar immunities would be granted if the adverse party should recapture the territory, and that no person would be molested or convicted for having tended the wounded or sick. The civilian who assists the incapacitated combatant is, in effect, offered the immunity of medical personnel who are placed above the conflict under the law. However, an occupying power is not relieved of its obligation with respect to the wounded and sick because of any assistance that may be rendered by the inhabitants or by relief societies.

Transfer Between Countries

GPW-1929 was silent on the subject of transfer of prisoners of war between powers, although belligerents had, as a matter of practice, been transferred from one ally to another. This was generally accepted as allowable under customary international law, although it was not clear what responsibility the captor state retained for prisoners' maintenance and treatment after they had been transferred. The question was further complicated by the fact that GPW-1929 prescribed treatment similar to that given their own nationals, in a number of instances, but these standards varied greatly. During World War II the International Committee of the Red Cross (ICRC) took the view that the captor retained a responsibility with respect to the treatment of prisoners whom it had transferred to an ally, and the United States adhered to this view. For example, on being apprised by the ICRC that prisoners transferred to France lacked adequate subsistence because of the general shortage of foodstuffs in France, the United States furnished clothing and equipment to the prisoners in French hands and took back a number of prisoners. Definite rules are set forth in GWP-1949 that permit the transfer of prisoners to another party to the convention under prescribed safeguards. Before the transfer the detaining power must assure itself of the willingness and ability of the transferee to apply the convention. However, the types of assurances that must be obtained or investigations that should be conducted to satisfy these general standards are not indicated.

After the transfer the transferee is responsible for applying the convention while the prisoners are in its custody. The transferee power has all the responsibilities of a detaining power with respect to the transferred prisoners. It is the national standards of the transferee that now apply where the transferor's standards had before. However, if the transferee fails to carry out the convention "in any important respect" the transferor is bound (upon notification by the protecting power) to take effective steps to correct the situation or to request the return of the prisoners and that the transferee comply. The respective responsibilities of the transferor and transferee were a practical solution to the conflicting views of the delegations to the 1949 conference. The compromise finally arrived at avoids joint responsibility but imposes on the transferor a secondary obligation to act when important deficiencies are revealed.

The Communist states, however, did not accept the compromise and deposited reservations to the article. The Soviet Union declared that it refused to consider a power released from responsibility for applying the convention merely because it had transferred prisoners to another power. The reservations of the other Communist states are similar. Hungary, for example, declared that the transferor and transferee must be held jointly responsible.

Article III of GPW-1949 expresses for the first time in conventional law the permissive rule that the detaining power, the power on which the prisoners depend, and a neutral may agree upon the transfer of prisoners to the neutral for internment on its territory. The article recommends that the parties endeavor to reach such an agreement, but it may not adversely affect the prisoners' rights. Transfers of this sort present no problem in customary international law because the opposing belligerents may naturally enter into mutually acceptable agreements.

Beginning of Captivity

The beginning of captivity is a critical period for the prisoner of war. Capture normally places him in the hands of forces who are in the midst of battle. Because of the high degree of danger to the prisoner during these early stages of his captivity, the convention deals explicitly with three important matters arising at that time—interrogation, confiscation of property, and evacuation from the combat zone.

Interrogation

In recognition of the prisoner's obligation not to disclose military information to the detaining power, article 17 requires only that he give his name, rank, date of birth, and serial number (or equivalent information) on demand in order to establish his identity with the detaining power. The detaining power must know this in order to determine the treatment the prisoner is entitled to by law and to provide the necessary notification of capture to the state on which the prisoner depends through the Central Prisoners of War Information Agency. The detaining power is to supply identity documents to prisoners who have none. Prisoners may not be subjected to any form of coercion to secure information of any kind. However, if they do not provide the information required by article 17, they may have their privileges restricted. Curtailment is limited to special privileges allowed commissioned and noncommissioned officers and does not extend to the basic guarantees of the convention. Prisoners who are unable to state their identity because of their physical or mental condition are to be handed over to the medical service.

Confiscation and Impounding of Property

GPW-1949 confirms the generally recognized principle of international law that a belligerent's right of booty applies only to property of the enemy state and not to the private property of a person of enemy nationality. This principle prohibits confiscation of all effects and articles of personal use to the prisoner of war, except arms, horses, military equipment, and military documents, which may be seized even if personally owned by the prisoner. However, articles used for personal protection, such as metal helmets, gas masks, and the like, and articles used for clothing and feeding of the prisoner, even though these are the property of his government, may not be confiscated.

A distinction is also drawn in GPW-1949 between those personal articles that may be impounded (and returned to the prisoner later) and those that may not. Impounding is permitted in recognition of the security interests of the detaining power. Cash and items of monetary value may be impounded, primarily so that the prisoner cannot use them to facilitate an escape. This action may be taken only after the items have been recorded in a special register and only if a receipt is provided to the prisoner. Articles having a personal or sentimental value may not be impounded, nor may be the prisoner be deprived of indications of rank and nationality or his decorations.

Evacuation of Prisoners

Once captured, the primary concern under GPW-1949 is the safety of the prisoners of war. The timing and manner of evacuation from the point of capture to the internment camp frequently mark the difference between life and death. Article 19 requires that prisoners be evacuated as soon as possible after capture to camps removed from the danger of the combat zone. The only basis for temporarily detaining a prisoner in the combat area is if detention would result in less risk, because of his wounds or sickness, than would evacuation from the battle area. In response to cases of flagrant maltreatment of prisoners during evacuation from battle in World War II, GPW-1949 strengthened the provisions of GPW-1929. Article 20 not only requires humane treatment, but also applies a national standard to the conditions under which evacuation must take place, which should be similar to those under which the detaining power must supply prisoners with "sufficient food and potable water" and "necessary clothing and medical attention," and must take "all suitable precautions" for prisoners' safety during the evacuation. These precautions have been interpreted to prohibit evacuation across the fighting lines where prisoners might come under fire, and to include protection against aerial bombardment and attacks by the civilian population. To help establish accountability for prisoners early in their capture, the detaining power is required to establish "as soon as possible" a list of the prisoners who are evacuated.

Internment of Prisoners of War

Nature, Circumstances, and Conditions of Internment. Under customary international law, as reflected in HR (Hague Regulations), prisoners of war are "in the power of the hostile government" but "must be humanely treated." The same principle is affirmed and amplified in GPW-1949. The confinement of a prisoner of war is conceptually limited by "detention" at one extreme and by "parole" or repatriation at the other. Whereas internment usually refers to keeping a prisoner within the limits of a camp or other prescribed geographical area, "detention" refers to close confinement in a cell or a room, or as the result of disciplinary or judicial proceedings. The text of the convention is to be posted in the camps so that both prisoners and guards may be clearly informed of camp regulations and of prisoners' rights under international law.

Parole is the promise of a prisoner of war to conform his conduct to specified standards in consideration of limited or complete freedom from captivity. Historically, parole was granted only to officers and, more often than not, regulated by agreements between the parties to the conflict. During the Seven Years War (1750), for example, England and France agreed that prisoners who broke parole could be returned to their captors or even imprisoned by their own country. The practice of granting parole for humanitarian reasons, as well as to reduce the economic burden of the detaining power in maintaining its prisoners, was recognized in customary international law, but a person who broke parole would lose the protection of the convention if recaptured, GPW-1949 acknowledges the traditional right of the detaining power to offer partial or full release on parole, subject, however, to the municipal law of the prisoner's own country on the matter. In shifting the emphasis of the customary law from sanction to purpose, it encourages release on parole in cases where it may contribute to the improvement of a prisoner's state of health.

The principal limitation on the offer of parole by the detaining power is the law of the prisoner's own country. Upon the outbreak of hostilities, the parties to the conflict are to exchange laws and regulations allowing or prohibiting nationals to accept liberty on parole. Even though the prisoner may be unaware of the laws of his own country in this regard, the detaining power may offer parole only to the extent permitted by the power on which the prisoner depends. The offer of parole ordinarily involves a conflict of interests; in exchange for physical freedom, the prisoner of war must acknowledge the legitimacy of his captivity and foreswear attempts to escape. In order to avoid this conflict many nations have, from time to time, refused to allow their nationals to accept parole. The United States authorizes an American prisoner to accept a limited parole only for the specific purpose of performing certain acts contributing to his welfare or that of his fellow prisoners. However, article III of the Code of Conduct, prescribed by Dwight D. Eisenhower in 1955 and since revised several times, flatly states that American personnel "will accept neither parole, nor favors from the enemy." These two statements have been reconciled by the judge advocate general of the army as meaning that a military commander in the field may permit his captured personnel to accept parole if authorization to this effect has been given by the power on which he depends.

The penalty for breach of parole differs according to whether customary or conventional international law is being applied. Under customary law prisoners liberated on parole and recaptured bearing arms against their former detainors or one of its allies lose their right to be treated as prisoners of war and can be punished for their conduct under municipal law. Under conventional law, GPW-1949 provides that prisoners of war prosecuted for acts committed prior to capture retain the benefits of the convention and may not be punished.

Places and Conditions of Internment. There would seem to be no evidence of customary law relating to the place of internment, in spite of negotiation and protest among combatants regarding the geographical location of internment camps. HR, article 5, merely provides that prisoners may be "interned" in "a town, fortress, camp, or other place" but does not state that there is any place where they may not be interned. GPW-1929, article 9, exhorts the detaining power to remove prisoners originating in temperate climates as soon as possible from an unhealthy locality in which they may have been captured. This legal ethnocentricity was not perpetuated in GPW-1949, which prohibits internment of a prisoner in any area where the climate or prevailing conditions may be injurious to health. Thus, although military exigencies may call for the removal of prisoners from the place of capture to a location far from the prisoner's place of origin, it would not be legal to transport natives of a tropical climate to an internment camp in the Arctic. Furthermore, after their arrival in camp, prisoners of war should not be transferred to locations that would increase the difficulty of repatriation. They may be interned only on land as internment at sea is unlawful. Thus, prisoners taken by the navy must be turned over to the ground forces for internment. Under the 1929 convention, internment camps were to be segregated by race and nationality as far as possible. The 1949 convention provides that prisoners of war are to be assembled in compounds by nationality, language, and customs with no adverse distinctions based upon race. Finally, unless they consent, they may not be interned separately from the armed forces with which they were serving when captured.

Neither the location of the camps nor the prisoners themselves may be used as shields to protect the forces or installations of the captor. The illegality of exposing prisoners to fire in combat zones was conceded by the major participants in World War I and such exposure was expressly proscribed by GPW-1929. The principle is elaborated in the 1949 convention, which requires that the camps be located far enough from the combat zone to be out of danger and that they be marked with the "PW" (prisoners of war) or "PG" (prisonniers de guerre), which must be clearly visible from the air. The belligerents are enjoined to exchange information regarding the location of camps. Prisoners are also entitled to use of bomb shelters and any other protective measures available to the general population (whether in permanent or temporary camps).

Food, Clothing, and Shelter. The 1949 convention considerably expanded the scope of GPW-1929 and radically altered the alimentary standard with regard to the quantity and quality of food to be provided prisoners. Earlier, the detaining power was merely required to provide rations commensurate with those of its own troops. GPW-1949, however, changed the requirement so that the detaining power must supply a sufficient quantity, quality, and variety of food to prevent weight loss or "the development of nutritional deficiencies" (art. 26). By explicitly requiring that account be taken of the habitual diet of prisoners, the convention repudiates the theory that what is good enough for natives is good enough for the prisoners. The monthly medical inspections, which are required by article 31, must include periodic checks of weight and nutrition.

The promise or denial of food as an incentive to increase work output is prohibited, as is any use of food rations as a collective disciplinary measure that would detrimentally affect the health of the prisoners. Although a prisoner may not be put on bread and water he may be punished by a reduction of his rations to the minimum required to maintain health. The detaining power is enjoined to facilitate the supervision of mess by prisoners—officers and enlisted men alike—and prisoners of war are associated with the preparation of their own food whenever possible.

GPW-1949 also sets forth standards for clothing prisoners of war. Prisoners must be supplied by their captors with clothes, underwear, and shoes suited to the climate in which they are interned. The issue may be supplemented by captured uniforms from home, and relief shipments that the prisoners are authorized to distribute.

The convention allows the use of any type of clothing as long as it is of "sufficient quantity" (art. 27). However, the provision of uniforms with national markings used by the detaining power's troops violates the principles expressed in GPW-1949 article 14. The detaining power must alter these garments, stripping off all insignia, prior to their issuance to prisoners of war. However, the tradition of clothing with an emblem or uniform pattern designating the wearer as a prisoner of war is perfectly acceptable. Clothing must be regularly repaired and replaced by the detaining power. Appropriate work clothing must be supplied to protect the health and safety of the prisoner, and it must be commensurate with that provided similarly employed nationals of the detaining power.

In addition to food and clothing standards, international law also provides standards of shelter for prisoners of war. By the end of the nineteenth century, it was understood that the detaining power was obliged to furnish proper accommodation for prisoners. The law laid down by HR is that, in the absence of agreement between the belligerents, prisoners are to be provided with lodging of the same character as that furnished to the troops of the detaining power. The 1929 convention employed both relative and absolute criteria. The amount of space and bedding provided were to be equivalent to those of the custodial troops of the detaining power. Adequate lighting and heat, protection from dampness, hygienic safe-guards, and precautions against fire were also required, whether or not they were utilized by the captor's own armed forces.

Basically the same standard of quartering is laid down by the current treaty. Conditions must be at least as favorable as those for "the forces of the detaining power who are billeted in the same area" (GPW-1949, art. 25), although prisoners may be required to build their own barracks. To the requirements of the 1949 convention has been added specific obligation to maintain heat and light "in particular between dusk and lights out." Segregation between the sexes extends only to dormitories and need not be applied to mess halls, recreation rooms, and similar common areas. Quarters set aside for disciplinary punishment must meet the same sanitary requirements as other accommodations. However, the law significantly omits any reference to the other minimal amenities such as bedding, lighting, and heat. Thus, the only governing standard would be the medical well-being of the prisoner as determined by the monthly inspections under article 31.

Labor. GPW-1949 and the earlier law attempt to reconcile a number of conflicting considerations concerning employment: the need of the detaining power for labor, the humane view that prisoners of war should not be required to take part in operations of war against their own country and that they should not be unnecessarily exposed to danger, and the fact that idleness is bad for the morale of prisoners and may at the same time lead to mischief against the detaining power.

Customary law gave no legal guidelines concerning employment prior to the Hague and Geneva Conventions. HR-1907 treats employment in one brief article (art. 6). The detaining power may employ prisoners of war (except officers) "according to their rank and aptitude." The work must have no connection with the operations of the war and must not be excessive. Although prisoners of war may be required to work for the public service or private persons (as well as on their own account), work conditions must always be arranged with military authorities, who remain responsible for the prisoners during their employment.

To avoid the difficulty encountered in World War I caused by the blurring of lines between civilian and war-related activities, article 31 of GPW-1929 prohibits compulsory work that has a *direct* connection with the operations of the war and employment in manufacturing or transporting arms or munitions of any kind, or for transporting material intended for combatant units. Prisoners are authorized to use the grievance procedures of the convention if the provisions of article 31 are violated.

GPW-1949 goes much farther than either the earlier conventions or the customary law in defining how prisoners of war may be employed. The standards of the earlier conventions as to who may be required to work are adopted with regard to commissioned and noncommissioned officers. That is, noncommissioned officers can be required to perform only supervisory work, although they may request nonsupervisory work if they wish. Commissioned officers may request "suitable" employment even though they may not be compelled to work. Four categories of personnel are given special treatment. First, medically trained personnel not assigned to medical duties in their own armed forces may be required to provide medical services to prisoners of their own country. Second, ministers of religion not acting in that capacity when captured are to be left free to minister to prisoners. Third, orderlies in the camps of officers prisoners are exempt from other work. Fourth, prisoners' representatives are also exempt if accomplishment of their duties as representatives is made more difficult by the added work.

GPW-1949 merely authorizes classes of work and abandons the "connection with the war" test, which proved virtually impossible to apply in World War II. Besides camp administration, installation, or maintenance, article 50 of the GPW-1949 provides that prisoners of war may be required to work in or at:

1. Agriculture.
2. Industries connected with the production or the extraction of raw materials, and manufacturing industries, with the exception of metallurgical, machinery and chemical industries; public works and building operations that have no military character or purpose.
3. Transport and handling of stores that are not military in character or purpose.

4. Commercial business, and arts and crafts.
5. Domestic service.
6. Public utility services having no military character or purpose.

It is a condition of employment in the above work that the assigned tasks not be unhealthy or dangerous in nature and not be looked upon as humiliating; that is, if it would be deemed humiliating if performed by a member of the detaining power's own forces. To eliminate a practice often employed in World War II, article 52 specifically classifies removal of mines or similar devices as dangerous work, which prisoners of war may not be compelled to perform. Compensation for work done for the detaining power itself is provided for at rates in force for similar work by soldiers of the detaining power or, if none exists, "at a rate according to the work executed." The wages must be applied toward improving the lot of the prisoners of war. The cost of their maintenance may be deducted from their wages, but the balance must be paid to the prisoners of war when they are released.

Health and Medical Personnel. Customary law requires that the belligerents take measures to promote general health and to prevent epidemics among prisoners of war. The conventions, however, set forth specific standards for the maintenance of public health and require the detaining power to insure provision of medical attention if required. The detaining power must provide clean latrines, accessible day and night (separate ones for women), and necessary hygienic facilities, such as soap, water, baths, and showers.

An adequate infirmary, with any necessary isolation wards, must be established, and prisoners must have free access to medical personnel. The language of GPW-1949 respecting camp infirmaries, like that of GPW-1929, suggests that these facilities are intended to be equipped only for less serious injuries or illnesses. Critical cases requiring special hospital or surgical care should be transferred to military or civilian hospitals. Upon request, certificates are to be furnished by the detaining power, indicating the nature and extent of any illness or injury. These certificates may be used by prisoners in securing accident and disability compensation from their own governments. Each prisoner must receive a monthly medical inspection that includes, in addition to weight checks, diagnostic tests for contagious diseases. Daily medical checkups must be given upon request to prisoners in disciplinary confinement, as well as any other medical care that may be required. A prisoner is entitled to medical inspection and attention even if his reputation is contemplated shortly.

In order to meet its obligations, the detaining power may require prisoners of war who are medically trained, although not attached to the medical service, to perform services in the interest of fellow prisoners. Such personnel are entitled to the same treatment as corresponding medical corps personnel, except that the former are still "prisoners of war" whereas the latter are "retained personnel."

Regular medical personnel and chaplains have traditionally been considered noncombatants, entitled to immediate repatriation upon capture. However, they may be retained subject to the regulations of the medical service of the detaining power when their presence is indispensable to the welfare of the prisoners, preferably those of their own armed forces. If sufficient retained personnel and other medically trained prisoners are not available, the detaining power should recruit the requisite persons from among its own nationals.

The senior medical officer in each camp is responsible for all activities of medical personnel and has direct access to the camp authorities in all questions arising out of his duties. Like the prisoner representative, he must be allowed facilities for unlimited correspondence. Medical personnel may not be compelled to do any work other than the practice of medicine. They are to be given transportation to labor detachments and hospitals. The convention enjoins belligerents to negotiate agreements concerning the possible relief of retained personnel. The personnel protected under GWS-1949 (Geneva Convention for the Amelioration of the Condition of the Wounded and Sick in Armed Forces in the Fields—1949) and the conditions governing their protection are:

1. Permanent medical personnel of the armed forces, including those exclusively engaged in searching, collecting, transporting, and healing the wounded and sick, or in administering medical units and establishments, and chaplains (art. 24).
2. Auxiliary personnel of the armed forces, that is, military personnel employed part time as stretcher bearers or as hospital orderlies and nurses (art. 25).
3. Personnel of recognized relief societies such as the Red Cross who are employed in the performance of the same duties as permanent or auxiliary personnel (art. 26).
4. Personnel of recognized relief societies of neutral countries (art. 27).
5. Civilians rendering spontaneous assistance (art. 18).

Religion and Leisure-time Activities. Subject to the disciplinary routine of the camp, prisoners should be granted every opportunity to participate in religious, intellectual, and physical activity while in confinement. Prior to GPW-1949, the recreational activities of internees were not singled out for particular consideration. Now the detaining power is obliged to provide prisoners with sporting equipment to pursue a recreational program. HR (Hague Regulations), article 18, provided that the prisoners should enjoy freedom of religion, including attendance at church services. The law currently requires the detaining power to permit attendance at religious services of the prisoner's faith. There may be no practice of religious rites of such a nature as to conflict with usual camp organizations and administration. However, the detaining power should attempt, whenever possible, to accommodate the prisoner's right to worship. GPW-1949 includes an obligation to provide for holding religious services.

When no chaplain of the armed forces of the prisoners is available, an ordained prisoner of war who is not serving as a chaplain, or a civilian from the local population, may be called upon to perform these duties, with the concurrence of the detaining power. A minister of a different faith from the prisoners, or a layman, may serve at the request of the prisoners themselves. The person so designated is subject to the approval of the detaining power and must comply with its regulations.

The law relating to the physical and intellectual well-being of prisoners of war is somewhat less rigorous than the provisions concerning spiritual well-being. The 1929 convention encouraged belligerents to organize "intellectual diversions" and sports among the prisoners. Articles 38 and 72 of the 1949 convention elaborate the earlier requirements by calling for adequate equipment and space and assuring that prisoners may receive parcels that include books, musical instruments, sporting outfits, and the like. The convention neither encourages nor expressly prohibits the use of recreational activity by the detaining power for propaganda or psychological warfare purposes.

Camp Order and Discipline. Order is maintained within prisoner of war camps through the establishment of a legal regime that, among other things, puts the camp under the command of a responsible officer, makes the prisoners subject to the same law as members of the armed forces of the detaining power, and requires prisoners of war to show external marks of respect to officers of the detaining power. Traditionally, prisoners of war have been subject to the laws and regulations in force in the captor's army only for military offenses. HR-1907 additionally stipulates that acts of insubordination warrant the use of measures of such severity as may be deemed necessary. Because prisoners of war owe no loyalty to the detaining power, applying a rule of strict assimilation led to serious disciplinary abuses in World War I. In GPW-1949 the detaining power is free to reduce the penalty to below the minimum ordinarily provided by law as the accused has no duty of allegiance to the power. In making the choice between disciplinary and judicial proceedings, the detaining power should adopt the "greatest leniency" and should try to use, if at all possible, disciplinary instead of judicial proceedings (art. 83).

The authority to deal with offenses against discipline is vested in the camp commander, who must be commissioned officer of the regular armed forces of the detaining power. He may be replaced by a responsible officer or delegated authority but not by a noncommissioned officer or a prisoner of war. The prisoner of war owes the camp commander and his officers the external marks of respect (such as saluting) to the extent provided in the regulations of the armed forces to which the prisoner belongs, rather than in the regulations of the detaining power. The camp commander's responsibility for proper application of the provisions of the convention is owed not only to his own government, but, apparently, to all of the countries that are parties to the convention. The convention requires that, at the outbreak of hostilities, the belligerents exchange information about the titles and ranks they employ. Both commissioned and noncommissioned officers retain the privileges of their rank in captivity and must be permitted to wear their own insignia and decorations. Promotions in rank during imprisonment must be recognized if the detaining power has been notified by the prisoner's government. This is a new rule that is contrary to the past practice of the United States and of other countries of refusing to recognize promotions of prisoners during captivity.

The convention, camp regulations, and camp orders are required to be posted so that prisoners can read and understand them. Copies must be also provided, upon request, to any prisoner who, because of sickness, detention, or other circumstances, does not have access to the place of posting. The text of the convention or any other document that is posted must be in the language of the prisoner. Unlike the test of the convention itself, special agreements arrived at by the belligerents may be posted in abbreviated form as long as they include the essential provisions of the agreement.

Neither HR-1907 nor GPW-1929 included provisions regarding the use of weapons against escaping prisoners. However, GPW-1949 expressly provides that the use of weapons against a prisoner, even if he is trying to escape, is regarded as an extreme measure that must always be preceded by appropriate warnings. Warning may be given by a whistle, siren, or other instrument or by a warning shot. The requirements in this respect are a reaction against the establishment of death-lines around camps, which, when crossed, automatically leads to firing upon the prisoner without further warning. Other measures designed to deter potential escapers are also subject to limitation on the use of weapons.

Relations of Prisoners of War with the Detaining Power. History records that prisoners of war have, on various occasions, addressed petitions and complaints to the civil and military authorities of the detaining power, to protecting powers and other neutral nations, and to the ICRC. Complaints that were screened by welfare committees and camp military authorities rarely reached their destination. The custom of appointing a "trustee" as spokesman for the prisoners arose during World War I. Both the 1929 and 1949 Geneva conventions formalized the relations of prisoners with the detaining power by requiring the appointment of prisoners' representatives. They also preserved the right of direct appeal to the military authorities and the protecting power.

Representatives must be of the same language, nationality, and custom as the prisoners they represent. Medical personnel and chaplains, technically not prisoners of war, are not eligible to serve as representatives. In camps where officer prisoners are detained, the senior officer automatically becomes the representative. In camps where no officers are captive, the representative is elected by the prisoners themselves, by secret ballot, for a six-month term. Prisoner's representatives may appoint assistants as required. In camps where there are both officers and enlisted men, the assistants must be enlisted men.

The elected representative is subject to the approval of the detaining power. If the detaining power fails to approve him or withdraws its approval—which it may do any time, as long as it reports its reasons to the protecting power—the prisoners may hold new elections. If a representative is transferred he must be given a reasonable time to brief his successor on current affairs. Although the detaining power may dismiss a representative, under article 80 it may not hold him responsible for offenses committed by other prisoners. The convention does not provide a procedure for the recall of a representative by the prisoners prior to the expiration of his term of office.

The prisoners' representative is concerned with relief activities, relations between prisoners of war and authorities, and verification of various matters under the convention. He may not be required to do any work if it interferes with the performance of his duties. Article 81 authorizes a certain freedom of movement to the representative in order to permit him to visit prisoners' premises, work camps, and the like, and to facilitate prisoners' freedom of access to him. The representatives must also be given the facilities to communicate with the detaining authorities, the ICRC, the protecting power, and the organizations that assist prisoners of war. Periodic reports on camp conditions may be sent to representatives of the protecting power. The representative's duties include acting as the spokesman for any sanctioned mutual assistance group organized by the prisoners. His position in this respect may be rather delicate, because effective performance of the office requires cooperation with the detaining power, which may come close to collaboration with the enemy.

The convention also preserves the historical right of prisoners to address requests or complaints directly to representatives of the detaining power, either verbally or in writing, or to submit them through the prisoner's representative. Requests and complaints are not included in the correspondence quota allotted prisoners, and complaints may not give rise to punishment even if unfounded.

Relations of Prisoners with the Exterior. Prisoners of war are entitled to minimal contacts with their own country through the notice of capture, correspondence, and relief shipments. These contacts with the world outside are so vital that both GPW-1929 and GPW-1949, require that, upon capture, the detaining power inform the prisoners of the regulations controlling them. Belligerents have normally followed the practice of allowing prisoners of war to send and receive mail in limited quantities, subject to censorship, but there was no hard-and-fast rule of customary international law on the amount of correspondence that a prisoner might send or receive or the circumstances under which correspondence could be interrupted. Under the present treaty law, a prisoner is allowed, within one week after his arrival in a camp (whether permanent or transit), to send a "capture card" to his family and to the Central Prisoners of War Information Agency. Thereafter, each prisoner is allowed to send at least two letters and four cards monthly. Further limitations on outgoing mail may be imposed only if the protecting power is satisfied that the detaining power cannot find sufficient linguists to carry out the necessary censorship. Limitations on the amount of incoming mail may be ordered only by the state on which the prisoners of war depend. To simplify censorship, prisoners may be compelled to correspond only in their native language. Mail may be censored only once, as quickly as possible and the difficulties of censorship may not be used as a pretext to delay the mail. Mail may not be delayed or withheld for disciplinary reasons. In general, prisoner of war mail must be sent by the most rapid method at the disposal of the protecting power. Prisoners of war must be allowed to receive relief parcels containing food, clothing, medical supplies, books and materials to meet their religious, intellectual, and recreational needs. The only limits that may be imposed on these shipments is to be proposed by the protecting power, the ICRC, or other assisting organizations, only on account of exceptional strain on transport or communications. Mail, relief shipments, and money orders to and from prisoners of war are exempt from postage. The examination of packages by the detaining power must be carried out in the presence of the addressee or a designated fellow prisoner.

In the case of collective relief shipments, possession will ordinarily be taken by the prisoners' representatives for disposition to the prisoners. Regulations for the receipt and distribution of collective relief shipments are provided in GPW-1949. These apply in the absence of special agreements between the powers. The regulations reflect the experience gained during World War II when a large volume of such shipments was sent to prisoners. If special agreements between the powers do apply, they may not restrict the right of the prisoners' representative to take possession of the shipments and use them for the benefit of the prisoners. Nor may they restrict the right of the protecting power, the ICRC, or any donor organization responsible for forwarding collective shipments to supervise the distribution of such shipments to the prisoners.

In spite of the sweeping language of GPW-1949, both correspondence and relief shipments may be suspended. The parties to the conflict may temporarily suspend the correspondence of prisoners of war, but for as short a time as possible. Although relief shipments may place a very substantial strain on the warehouse and transport facilities of the detaining power, only the protecting power or the charitable organization furnishing the supplies can order their limitation. Presumably, these agencies would respond favorably to a request from the detaining power to suspend shipments temporarily.

Prisoners' Financial Resources and Account. GPW-1949 contains a complete and detailed system for management of the prisoner's financial resources. This system is quite different from the simple provisions of HR-1907, which stipulate that wages of prisoners shall go toward improving their lot and that the balance shall be paid to them at the time of their release, after deducting the cost of maintenance. Officers shall be paid in full by the detaining power (at the same rates as the detaining power's forces), subject to ultimate reimbursement by the power on which the prisoners depend. The same basic principles were carried over, with some expansion, into GPW-1929. Under GPW-1949, all prisoners are to receive monthly advances of pay from the detaining power, which will normally be only a fraction of their regular pay, as well as remittances of money addressed to them individually or collectively by, for example, their next of kin or a relief society. When their captivity is terminated, the detaining power, instead of paying the prisoners the balance in their accounts (as was previously done under GPW-1929), is supposed to credit statements that must be honored by the power on which the prisoners depend.

The detaining power must establish an account for each prisoner, including in it funds impounded from the prisoner at the beginning of captivity, the prisoner's regular advances of pay, his working pay, and any supplementary payments made by his government, his family, or relief organization. However, the maximum amount or ready money that prisoners may possess at any time "in cash or similar form" (for example, coupons or vouchers for camp purchases) may be set by the detaining power, subject to the agreement of the protecting power (art. 58). A particular reason for limiting funds in this manner is to prevent escapes through bribery. No express standards are provided for determining the amount of ready money, but it is expected to be reasonable and to take into account the prisoner's well-being and his everyday needs.

The prisoner may use the ready money for purchases from the canteen. If the detaining power permits, he may also make purchases outside the camp. In addition, a system has been introduced to enable a prisoner of war to make payments in his home country (especially to his family). The prisoner's account is debited by the detaining power and credited by his own country through a notification transmitted by the protecting power, without any material transfer of funds. There will probably be less need for these transfers than in the past, since under GPW-1929, an officer's entire pay came from the detaining power, whereas now his own country remains liable for his pay, subject to the advances made by the detaining power.

GPW-1949, articles 59 through 63, are concerned with the various sources from which prisoners may put themselves in funds. Currency of the detaining power taken from the prisoner is credited to his financial account. Currency of nations other than the detaining power is not converted to the currency of the detaining power except at the prisoner's request. This is to protect the prisoner from fluctuations in exchange rates that might operate to his disadvantage.

As noted above, regular advances of pay are made monthly, sometimes in the form of credit entries on which the prisoner may draw for ready money. The pay is called an advance to show that the amount is only a part of the pay given the prisoners in their own army. The amounts are very small; they correspond to about $1.84 per month for prisoners of war below sergeants, $2.76 per month for sergeants, $11.50 for those above sergeant but below major, $13.80 per month for majors, lieutenant colonels, and colonels, and $17.25 per month for generals (based on a conversion rate of one Swiss franc to $0.23 United States). They are said to have been set at approximately one-tenth of the pay received in most forces in 1949. The belligerents may modify these amounts by agreement. If the advances are unduly high as compared with the pay of members of the detaining power's own armed forces, the detaining power, while continuing to credit the prisoners' accounts with the full amounts due, may temporarily limit the amounts made available for the prisoners' own use to sums that are reasonable. In the case of the prisoners ranking below sergeant, this amount may not be less than the pay given by detaining power to its own forces. The unilateral action of the detaining power, in reducing the amount of advances of pay, should then yield to arrangements made with the power on which the prisoners depend concerning advances of pay. This prevents embarrassment to countries with weak currencies and low standards of living.

The amount of pay must be established impartially, and the nature of the services rendered must be taken into account. However, it is not expected that prisoners of war, who are being fed and housed at the cost of the detaining power, will also be remunerated for their work at a rate corresponding to that paid a civilian worker responsible for maintaining himself and his family out of his wages.

In the management of the prisoner's individual financial account GPW-1949 adopts a system of close control and gives both prisoners and the protecting power the possibility of checking the accounts regularly. Each entry is to be countersigned by the prisoner or the prisoner's representative, and the prisoner may consult the account and obtain copies of it. Accounts are transferred along with a prisoner and, if he is transferred from one detaining power to another, he is entitled to a certificate of the money in his account. Other money not in the currency of the detaining power is to follow him.

The winding up of a prisoner's account is accomplished when the detaining power issues a certificate of the credit balance. The power on which the prisoner depends must pay the entire credit balance, regardless of its source, including amounts that are attributable to working pay or supplementary payments. There are limited provisions for settling prisoners' accounts between the opposing belligerents at the close of hostilities. These provide for a joint settlement concerning advances of pay made to the prisoners and prior remittances to the prisoners' countries of origin (which may have been made out of credit balances attributable to sums impounded at the time of capture, for which the power on which the prisoners depend should be reimbursed). It appears that settlement may also be made between the parties as to prior transfers attributable to working pay.

In addition, GPW-1949 provides rules covering prisoners' claims arising out of the failure of the detaining power to return articles and effects that were impounded at the beginning of captivity, and claims for other losses alleged to be attributed to the fault of the detaining power or any of its servants. The prisoner of war presents these claims to his own government. There are also rules for claims for compensation for injuries or disabilities arising out of their work. While the detaining power's laws on compensation for injuries in employment apply to prisoners, the power on which the prisoners depend is to pay the amounts due, based on certificate issued by the detaining power. This payment will generally be made after the prisoner's captivity has ended. The payments are to be taken into account in the final settlement between the opposing belligerents to the extent that such payments are made by the power on which the prisoner depends. Thus, the detaining power may be ultimately responsible. The purposes here, as generally, are to protect the prisoner's rights first and after that, to leave the question of financial responsibility for settlement between the parties.

Transfers of Prisoners Between Camps. The memories of the horrors of the Death March of Bataan and other fearful tragedies were fresh in the minds of the representatives at the 1949 conference, and there was a determination to outlaw any such barbarities in the future. Previously, the only customary law having any bearing on transfers was simply the general rule that prisoners be treated humanely. GPW-1929 specifically prohibits the transfer of sick and wounded if their recovery might be prejudiced by the journey, unless the course of military operations demands it. While military necessity is the dominant consideration in determining whether a prisoner should be transferred, GPW-1929 requires that prisoners be evacuated from dangerous areas as quickly as possible except when military operations would be facilitated by delaying evacuation. The only other exception is one in favor of those prisoners who are wounded or sick and whose condition would be worsened if they were to be evacuated.

The 1949 conference eliminated these inconsistencies by accepting the suggestion that the same general principle be applied to transfers as to initial evacuations. These principles apply, for the first time in conventional law, to prisoners in good health. Transfers are prohibited if the combat zone approaches the camp unless the transfer can be carried out in adequate safety or if the prisoner "would be exposed to greater risks by remaining on the spot than being transferred" (art. 47). This new rule was motivated by experiences in Germany at the end of World War II, in which prisoners were compelled to embark on inhuman marches until finally the authorities had to agree to let them fall into the hands of the enemy.

In deciding upon transfer, the detaining power is to take into account the interests of the prisoners themselves, "especially so as not to increase the difficulty of their repatriation" (art. 46). This may be more a moral or practical injunction than a legal one, considering that the immediate interests of the detaining power and of the prisoner are of more importance than the distance that a prisoner will have to cover when final repatriation occurs. The detaining power is generally expected to have the time and to take the effort to make the necessary previous arrangements for conveying the prisoners under suitable conditions. The conditions are to measure up to the standards applied by the detaining power in transferring members of its own armed forces. Climatic conditions also must be taken into account. In no case may the transfer be prejudicial to prisoners' health, and the detaining power must provide them with sufficient food and water and the necessary clothing, shelter, and medical attention. Specific attention is called to the need to take safety precautions in connection with a transfer by sea or air, primarily to prevent avoidable exposure to bombing and attacks.

Administrative conditions of transfer require that:

1. Lists be drawn up of prisoners being transferred (art. 46).
2. Prisoners be notified in advance in time to make preparations (art. 48).
3. Prisoners be allowed to take with them their personal effects, subject to weight limitation of 25 kilograms (55.12 lbs.) (art. 48).
4. Mail and parcels as well as luggage left behind be forwarded to them at the new camp without delay (art. 48).

Judicial and Disciplinary Sanctions
Against Prisoners

Basic Standards

It has long been a principle of the laws of war that prisoners of war are subject to the laws, regulations, and orders of the army detaining them. This, however, does not prevent the power on which the prisoner depends from taking later disciplinary or judicial action against its soldiers for acts committed in captivity. The maintenance of control over prisoners by butt and bullet and the shooting of prisoners as punishment for attempted escape are violations of customary law. The *High Command* case[1] cited as customary law the following rules of the HR and GPW-1929:

- Prisoners must be humanely treated (HR, art. 4).
- A prisoner may only be disciplined if he has escaped from custody and may not be punished at all after rejoining his own army (HR, art. 8, para. 2; GPW-1929, art. 50).
- Corporal punishment, confinement in quarters not lighted by daylight, and any form of cruelty are prohibited (GPW-1929, art. 48).
- Prisoners of war may not be transferred to penitentiary establishments to undergo disciplinary punishment (GPW-1929, art. 56).

Customary law requires that a prisoner of war be given a trial before being severely punished, although the minimum requirements in this regard are not clear. The requirement of a trial was indicated as early as the Hague Peace Conference of 1899. The right to a trial may reflect merely an elementary principle of humane treatment—that a prisoner may not be executed or otherwise seriously punished without an impartial hearing before an authority vested with the appropriate powers. A possible alternative expression of the customary law is that a prisoner is entitled to a trial of the same type as that provided by the detaining power to its own nationals or members of its armed forces. This view of customary international law makes municipal law applicable to prisoners but obviously does not impose adequate standards where municipal law is lacking.

The right of prisoners of war and civilians to a trial in occupied territory was a dominant theme in many of the lesser war crimes cases after World War II. The major tribunals had little occasion to consider the elements of a fair trial except in terms of the rights they considered themselves bound to provide to defendants (itself of some relevance), and in connection with the wholesale perversion of justice shown in the *Justice* case, in which the tribunal appeared to allow the execution of spies and guerrillas, as unprivileged belligerents, caught in the act. A trial was required, however, before civilian hostages and reprisal prisoners could be executed.[2] A number of the lesser war crimes proceedings held that judges, magistrates, and members of military tribunals who direct the killing of prisoners or civilians in occupied territories without providing the fundamentals of an impartial hearing are guilty of war crimes. While it is not possible to define with particularity the requisites of a fair trial, these cases would require a court to consider: (1) Whether the prisoner was informed of the charges against him in a language he understood. (2) The extent to which the prisoner was allowed to defend himself. (3) Whether outside directives existed that limited the impartiality of the judge. (4) The time spent in convicting the accused, weighed in light of the difficulties of the legal and factual issues involved. There appears to be no requirement of customary law that trial be before any particular type of tribunal or that it be conducted under the same law and procedure prevailing in trials of members of the armed forces of the detaining power.

Customary law also limits the severity of the punishment that a prisoner may receive for relatively minor offenses. Judicial or disciplinary punishment for a minor offense should not be such that it outrages the sentiments of humanity. Even if capital punishment is allowed, corporal punishment or torture before execution is unlawful.

GPW-1949 now provides some standards applicable to both judicial and disciplinary proceedings, criteria for choosing between judicial and disciplinary punishment, and separate requirements for each, including specific rules about discipline for attempted escape. The choice of judicial or disciplinary sanctions is to be made according to the principles toward which the detaining power is bound to show the greatest leniency, and to use disciplinary rather than judicial measures whenever possible to punish the violation of any laws, regulations, or rules that apply exclusively to prisoners of war and not to the detaining power's own personnel. Combined national and international standards are provided in GPW-1949 to assure that prisoners receive a fair trial. The national standards invoked are the detaining power's judicial procedures for trying its own military personnel. The international standards constitute a bill of rights incorporating the fundamentals of a fair trial.

According to the national standards, a prisoner is to be tried by a military or civil court if the detaining power would try its military personnel thereby for the particular offense. In either case the detaining power's municipal procedures, such as its rules of evidence, are to be followed except as international standards otherwise require. The fundamental principle is that a prisoner must be tried in a court that "offers the essential guarantees of independence and impartiality as generally recognized" (art. 84, para. 2). Specific rules prohibit coerced confessions, collective punishments, *ex postital facto* laws, and give the prisoner rights to a speedy trial, to be informed of the details of the charge against him, to present his defense, and to have the assistance of a qualified counsel. Some degree of international supervision is provided through the jurisdictional requirement that the protecting power receive three weeks' notice of a pending trial of a prisoner and may usually send a representative to be present at the trial.

The following rules control the punishment and sentencing of prisoners in both judicial and disciplinary proceedings:

1. A prisoner may not be punished more than once for the same act or on the same charge (double jeopardy) (art. 86).
2. Collective punishment may not be imposed for individual acts (art. 87, para. 3).
3. Corporal punishment, imprisonment in premises without daylight, and any form of torture or cruelty are forbidden (art. 87, para. 3).
4. In assessing penalties, the detaining power is to take into consideration that the prisoner owes it no allegiance and is not a prisoner by choice. For these reasons, the greatest leniency in setting penalties is enjoined (art. 87, para. 2).
5. The courts and authorities may set a penalty that is less than the minimum penalty which may be given the detaining power's military personnel for the same offense (art. 87, para. 2).
6. In no case may a prisoner receive a harsher penalty than the detaining power gives to its own military personnel for the same acts, except in respect to those disciplinary offenses that are only offenses if committed by a prisoner (art. 87, para. 1).
7. A prisoner undergoing judicial or disciplinary punishment may receive no harsher treatment than would be imposed on the detaining power's military personnel of equivalent rank (art. 88, para. 1).
8. Women prisoners may receive no greater punishment, or be treated more harshly during punishment, than women members of the armed forces of the

detaining power who have committed the same or similar offense (art. 88, para. 2), and they may never be punished more severely or receive harsher treatment than male members of the armed forces of the detaining power (art. 88, para. 3).

9. A prisoner may not be treated differently from other prisoners at the end of his judicial or disciplinary punishment (art. 88, para. 4).

All of the convention's rules with regard to judicial proceedings against prisoners apply to prisoners prosecuted for acts committed prior to capture as well as to offenses they commit while in captivity. Thus, war crimes proceedings, including those for "grave breaches" (under art. 129), must comply with all the requirements of articles 82 through 87 and 99 through 108, if brought against prisoners of war. Moreover, willfully depriving a prisoner of war of the "rights of fair and regular trial" prescribed by the convention itself is a "grave breach" (art. 129).

This application of GPW-1949 to precapture offenses is a major development and reversal of the interpretation given GPW-1929 by the United States and other powers. Under the current rules, which oblige the detaining power to hold judicial proceedings in the same type of courts that try members of its own armed forces, it is no longer possible to establish international tribunals or other special courts outside the framework of the regular judicial process to try war criminals who are prisoners of war. As noted above, the trial of war prisoners by courts like the International Military Tribunals of Nuremberg and Tokyo is no longer possible unless (as appears unlikely) the detaining power turns members of its own armed forces over to such a tribunal. The numerous other rules applicable to offenses committed in captivity apply with equal force to prosecutions for "grave breaches" and other war crimes. The Communist countries as mentioned earlier reserve the rights to treat prisoners sentenced to confinement according to their regular prison procedures. At the end of a sentence, however, the prisoner of war once more comes under the protection of GPW.

Disciplinary Punishment

Imposition of Disciplinary Punishment. The authority to impose disciplinary punishment is vested in the camp commander and may be delegated to a responsible officer of the detaining power. The courts and superior military authorities may also discipline prisoners. Prisoners themselves may not be used to impose discipline as this would put them in a compromising position, which would be considered close to collaboration. Disciplinary offenses are to be investigated immediately, and the accused must be provided precise information about the offenses with which he is charged and must have an opportunity to defend himself and explain his conduct. He may call witnesses and have the services of a qualified interpreter. The decision is to be announced to him and to his representative.

The maximum disciplinary punishment for all acts with which a prisoner is charged in one proceeding may not exceed thirty days, and only the following types of punishment are permitted (arts. 89 and 90):

1. A fine not in excess of one-half of the prisoner's monthly regular and working pay.
2. Discontinuance of privileges over and above the treatment provided for by the convention.
3. Fatigue duties not in excess of two hours daily, but this punishment may not be imposed on officers.
4. Confinement.

A prisoner may not be kept in confinement pending a hearing for a disciplinary offense unless the detaining power's military personnel would be confined if accused of a similar offense or unless confinement is essential to maintain camp order and discipline. Such confinement is to be kept to a minimum and may not exceed fourteen days. The period of confinement must be deducted from the punishment awarded. The punishment may not include curtailment of an adequate diet.

Treatment of Prisoners Undergoing Disciplinary Punishment. A prisoner is entitled to all the privileges of the convention while undergoing disciplinary punishment, except those necessarily made inapplicable by his confinement or other punishment. Even if confined, prisoners undergoing discipline may exercise and stay in the open air at least two hours daily, they may read and write and send and receive letters, and they may attend daily medical inspections and receive proper medical attention, including being removed to the infirmary or hospital if their condition requires. On the other hand, parcels and remittances of money may be withheld from them until the completion of punishment.

A prisoner's right to present grievances and complaints may not be curtailed while he is being disciplined. Other prisoners, representatives of the protecting power, and delegates of the ICRC may visit and interview him. The prerogatives of his rank may not be denied. An officer may not be confined with enlisted prisoners, and women prisoners must be confined separately under the direct supervision of women. Confinement must be in appropriate buildings that meet the general health standards.

Escape

The rules of the convention about escape attempt to reconcile the prisoner of war's natural desire and duty to attempt escape, and the detaining power's interest in retaining him in its custody and discouraging just such attempts. Consequently, only disciplinary punishment may be imposed on a prisoner who is caught while trying to escape, even if the offense is repeated. There is the same limitation upon the punishment of a prisoner for assisting a fellow prisoner's escape. A recaptured prisoner must be turned over to the military authorities without delay to prevent the prisoner from being handed over to a special organization, such as the secret police, for arbitrary punishment or execution, and to get the prisoner quickly back into the hands of the authorities most directly concerned with compliance with the convention.

The detaining power's legitimate interests are also recognized. Its right to take necessary measures to prevent escapes is recognized by both customary and conventional law. However, GPW-1949 is the first convention to make this rule explicit; it adds the restriction that the use of weapons to prevent escape is an extreme measure that must always be preceded by appropriate warnings. This subject was previously omitted from the treaties because of hesitance to lay down rules that might sanction the killing of escaping prisoners, but experiences during World War II with quick-shooting guards and the facile use of the classic police excuse "shot while attempting to escape" showed that explicit restrictions were necessary. The appropriate actions that a detaining power may take to prevent escape also include special surveillance of prisoners who have been punished for an unsuccessful escape attempt. This surveillance may not affect the prisoner's health, must be undergone in a prisoner of war camp, and may not cause the denial of any of the safeguards granted prisoners by the convention.

The duty of a prisoner to escape is further recognized in limitations on punishment for criminal acts committed in the course of an attempt to escape. While serious offenses of a prisoner in the course of an escape, such as assault or killing, are punishable, lesser types of escape-connected offenses, that is, all acts of the prisoner that are solely intended to facilitate his escape and that do not entail any violence against life or limb, may lead to disciplinary punishment alone. Examples are offenses against public property, theft without intention of self-enrichment, drawing up and using false papers, and wearing of civilian clothes. All other types of escape-connected offenses may be punished judicially, but escape, or an attempt to escape, may not be considered an aggravating circumstance in any such trial. A prisoner successfully completes an escape by doing any of the following (art. 91):

- Joining the armed forces of his own power or an allied power.
- Leaving the territory controlled by the detaining power or any ally of that power.
- Joining, in the territorial waters of the detaining power, a ship flying the flag of his own power or one of its allies if the ship is not under the control of the detaining power.

It follows that the prisoner would also successfully complete an escape by joining a ship of his own power or one of its allies in international waters. Merely reaching international waters, as on a raft, would not constitute a completed escape.

Judicial Proceedings

Assurance of Fair Trial. The principle of *nullem crimen sine lege* (no crime without a law) is reflected in the provision of the convention that trial and sentence may occur only if an act is forbidden by "the law of the Detaining Power or by international law" in effect at the time the act is committed. "International law" in this context—according to a report at the Diplomatic Conference of 1949—means the generally recognized provisions, including customary law, if they have not been covered or superseded by the convention or by any other treaty. The prisoner's rights to be tried by the same courts and under the same procedures that the detaining power applies to its own military personnel include the right of appeal or petition from any sentence, with a view to quashing or revising the sentence or reopening the trial. He must be fully informed of his rights. The protecting power is responsible for finding counsel for the prisoner if he does not choose one himself, and the detaining power must appoint competent counsel if one is not secured by the prisoner or through the endeavors of the protecting power. Counsel for the accused is to have the time (at least two weeks before the commencement of the trial), the facilities, and the client relationship permitting him to prepare the case. Throughout, and until the term of appeal or petition has expired, he may freely visit and interview the accused in private (if the detaining power allows this for its nationals) and may confer with defense witnesses, including prisoners of war. The convention is silent on the assumption of the costs of the defense, although drafts of it contained rules on the subject.

Communications to Protecting Powers and Other Conditions of Trial. The detaining power is required to communicate specified information about judicial proceedings to the protecting power. In a number of instances the information provided to the protecting power must also be furnished to the prisoner's representative and to the prisoner. The rules regarding these notifications—some of which are extremely important jurisdictional requirements—are as follows:

1. Prisoners and the protecting powers have to be informed as soon as possible of offenses subject to the death penalty under the laws of the detaining power. Other offenses may not be made punishable by the death penalty without the concurrence of the power on which the prisoners of war depend (art. 100).
2. The detaining power has to notify the protecting power of the decision to institute any judicial proceedings against a prisoner. This notification is to be

made as early as possible, and not later than three weeks before the trial commences (art. 104). The notification must contain the following information:

a) Name of the prisoner and his rank; army; regimental, personal, or serial number; his date of birth; and his profession and trade, if any
b) Place of internment or confinement
c) Specification of the charges on which the prisoner is to be arraigned and the applicable legal provisions
d) The court that will try the case and the date and place fixed for opening of the trial.

Unless evidence is obtained at the opening of the trial that both the protecting power and the prisoner's representative received notification at least three weeks before the opening of the trial, the trial cannot take place and must be adjourned. Any judgment and sentence imposed on a prisoner must be reported immediately to the protecting power by a summary communication, which shall also indicate whether the prisoner has a right to appeal the sentence or to reopen the trial. If the death sentence is pronounced, it may not be carried out before a period of six months has expired after the protecting power has received proper notice.

Termination of Captivity

During Hostilities

Repatriation and Exchange of Prisoners of War in General. During hostilities the parties to the conflict may reach any agreement they desire for the exchange of prisoners of war. Under both customary and conventional law a belligerent may unilaterally repatriate prisoners who desire to return to their own country. There is a duty, however, to repatriate seriously sick and wounded prisoners who likewise desire to return to their own country. The conferees at the Hague in 1899 did not include terms about repatriation during hostilities for they felt that the parties to a conflict might do as they pleased by way of agreement. A duty to repatriate the seriously sick and wounded was first established in GPW-1929 and has been carried over and developed in GPW-1949. GPW-1949 does, however, encourage, for the first time in conventional law, the repatriation of able-bodied prisoners who have been long in captivity. The parties may agree on the direct repatriation or internment in a neutral country of such prisoners.

Any exchange of prisoners satisfactory to the parties is possible, and highly varied arrangements have been made, such as exchanging rank-for-rank or man-for-man. The motives for reaching agreement on an exchange vary widely in different circumstances. They may range from the humanitarian desire of the power on which the prisoners depend to have its soldiers returned to the desire of the detaining power to relieve itself of financial and administration responsibilities for prisoners. An exchange of prisoners will rarely be carried out during hostilities except by agreement between the governments concerned, although governments may, if they desire, delegate the authority to agree to exchange under field conditions to commanders of forces. Exchange negotiations can be complex, and, as a result, in recent conflicts general exchanges have been extremely rare. In the past, exchanges have generally been man-for-man and rank-for-rank with adjustments to establish equivalency.

Agreements for exchange during hostilities may often contain a condition that the exchanged men should not again participate as soldiers in the war. In the absence of this type of stipulation, there is a question of whether subsequent active military service is prohibited. Although GPW-1949 does not specifically mention exchanges of able-bodied prisoners, other than those in long captivity, it states that "no repatriated person may be employed on active military service" (art. 117). This rule, taken on its face, would appear to apply to general exchanges, especially if any prisoners in "long captivity" are exchanged.

Repatriation of Medical Personnel. Medical personnel whose retention is not vital are to be returned to the party to the conflict to whom they belong, as soon as transportation for their return and military requirements permit. On their departure they must be allowed to take with them their effects, personal belongings, valuables, and instruments.

In selecting personnel for return to their own side, article 31 prohibits any discrimination founded on race, religion, or political opinions. In the absence of a bilateral agreement to the contrary, medical personnel are to be repatriated, preferably according to their date of capture and state of health; those who have been held the longest and those whose health has deteriorated are to have priority. Article 31 also permits the belligerents, from the outbreak of hostilities, to determine by special agreement the percentage of personnel to be retained, in proportion to the number of prisoners and the distribution of medical personnel in the camps.

Article 32 prohibits the retention of neutral medical personnel against their will. If possible, they are to be returned to their country as soon as possible. Otherwise they must be returned to the country that they served. Pending their return, they may continue their work under the direction of the party who controls them. Unlike medical personnel of the belligerents, they must be given the same treatment as the medical personnel of the detaining power with respect to food, lodging, allowances, and pay. Upon their departure, they may bring with them, in addition to their effects, personal articles, valuables, and instruments, their arms, and, if possible, their means of transport.

Repatriation of the Seriously Sick and Wounded. It is an imperative duty of each belligerent to repatriate seriously sick and wounded prisoners of war to their own countries when they are fit to travel, but no prisoner in this category may be repatriated against his will. This was explained at the 1949 conference as being designed principally to prevent the German practice during World War II of listing able-bodied prisoners as sick and wounded and of repatriating them to occupied territories, where they were compelled to collaborate. The needs of the prisoners—the degree of their incapacity, rather than any consideration of man-for-man exchange or rank—are the bases for carrying out this obligation. This was also the rule of GPW-1929, but practical difficulties were experienced in enforcing it in World War II. As a result, GPW-1949 contains more detailed and forceful procedures, which are intended to minimize the extent of agreement needed between the belligerents to effect the repatriation. This repatriation normally, it seems, will be effected on the basis of an understanding between the parties, most probably under the aegis of the ICRC or neutrals; otherwise, fundamental matters relating to timing and transport could not be worked out.

General standards have been established for determining who is to be classified as seriously sick and wounded in order to reduce the area of negotiation. A prisoner is seriously sick or wounded if his mental and physical fitness seems to have been gravely diminished and is incurable, is not likely to recover within one year and requires treatment, or has recovered but his mental or physical fitness seems to have been gravely and permanently diminished. Self-inflicted injuries do not entitle a prisoner to repatriation, although injuries that are the result of accidents do. Injuries and diseases that existed before the war and have not become worse, and war injuries that have not prevented subsequent military service shall not entitle a prisoner to direct repatriation.

Mixed Medical Commissions. Those seriously sick and wounded prisoners who are to be repatriated are selected by Mixed Medical Commissions, each composed of two persons who belong to a neutral power and of a representative of the detaining power. These are to be established at the beginning of hostilities, and thereafter as necessary. Prisoners whom the medical authorities of the detaining power consider clearly to be seriously injured or sick may be repatriated without examination by such a commission. Following are the legal requirements for the Mixed Medical Commissions:

1. That the two neutral members (who generally are to be a physician and a surgeon) be appointed by the ICRC at the request of the detaining power with the consent of the protecting power (art. 3); or, if the ICRC is unable to act, by the protecting power of the prisoners (art. 5).
2. That one of the neutral members be chairman (art. 1).
3. That the neutral members shall be entirely independent of the parties to the conflict (art. 7).
4. That the commission's decisions proposing repatriation, rejection, or later examination be made by majority vote (art. 10).

5. That the detaining power "shall be required" to carry out a decision of the Mixed Medical Commission within three months after being notified of the decision (art. 12).
6. That the commission function permanently and visit each prisoner of war camp at least every six months (art. 14).

The following prisoners have first priority for examination by Mixed Medical Commissions (art. 113): (1) Prisoners designated by the medical authorities of the detaining power. (2) Wounded and sick proposed by a doctor of the prisoner's nationality, or of the nationality of an ally of the prisoner's power, who acts as a doctor in the camp. (3) Wounded and sick proposed by the prisoner's representative. (4) Those proposed by the power on which the prisoner depends or an organization acting for it. Any other prisoner may present himself for examination by a Mixed Medical Commission. He is to be examined, by a doctor of the same nationality, only after examination of the priority category prisoners. The purpose of this priority system is to permit the most deserving prisoners to be considered first, since it was found during World War II, in the absence of any priorities in GPW-1929, that the functioning of the Mixed Medical Commissions became congested and disorganized when all prisoners had the right to present themselves for examination without further controls.

Transfer of Prisoners to Neutrals. Prisoners may be transferred to a neutral country by agreement between the detaining power, the power on which the prisoners depend, and the neutral. The convention recommends that the parties "endeavor" to reach such agreement. One reason for encouraging transfers of this type that appears in the proceedings of the Diplomatic Conference of 1949 is to ensure a reasonable standard of living for prisoners if the detaining power is unable to comply with the minimum standards for their treatment. But difficulties of this type are not preconditions to transfers by agreement, which are encouraged under all conditions. Furthermore, as long as prisoner's rights are not adversely affected, nothing restricts the parties from agreeing on a system of internment in a neutral country that provides greater freedom to the prisoners than that normally contemplated by the convention. Since these transfers are by agreement between the opposing belligerents, they can be made to a nonparty to the convention.

The convention also recommends that the parties to the conflict endeavor during hostilities to make arrangements, with the cooperation of neutral powers, to accommodate sick and wounded prisoners who are not seriously sick and wounded, in neutral countries. The type of accommodation contemplated is a hospital or other similar institution. The following prisoners may be so accommodated:

- Wounded and sick whose recovery may be expected within one year of the date of the wound or the beginning of the illness, if treatment in a neutral country might increase the prospects of a more certain and speedy recovery.
- Prisoners whose mental or physical health is seriously threatened by continued captivity, but whose accommodation in a neutral country might remove the threat.

If the health of any such prisoners in a neutral country deteriorates to the extent that they become seriously sick and wounded, or if their mental or physical powers remain considerably impaired after treatment, they "should be" repatriated home (art. 110, para. 3).

Additional Restrictions. No sick and wounded prisoner otherwise eligible for repatriation or accommodation in a neutral country may be kept back because he is undergoing disciplinary punishment, awaiting judicial proceedings, or undergoing judicial punishment. There is the further condition, noted above, that "no repatriated person may be employed on active military service" (art. 117), although the meaning of the words "active military service" is not defined in the convention. The convention establishes rules that the parties are to follow in apportioning the costs of repatriation and of transporting prisoners for accommodations in neutral countries. These costs are to be borne from the frontiers of the detaining power on which the prisoners depend.

The End of a Conflict

Duty to Repatriate. Considering the fundamental premises of the laws of war— that wars are conflicts between states rather than individuals and that the status of prisoners is one of the protective custody—there is no basis in customary law (other than in the specific limited instances considered below) for a state to hold a prisoner, who is an innocent person according to these concepts, after peace has been concluded. This principle was expressed in HR-1899 and HR-1907 as the duty to carry out repatriation as quickly as possible "after the conclusion of peace," which normally came about through the coming into force of a treaty of peace.

The fourteen months delay after World War I between the Armistice of November 1918 and the Treaty of Versailles, which was not concluded until January 1920, as well as the extended delay of Germany in repatriating Russian prisoners, showed the inadequacy of the rule of customary law. The Geneva Conference of 1929 responded by providing that the parties "must, in principle" agree on repatriation in the armistice or, if this has not been practicable, must conclude a special agreement on the subject as soon as possible. GPW-1929 requires, in any event, that repatriation be effected "with the least possible delay" after the conclusion of peace.

After World War II there was no treaty of peace between the United Nations and Germany. The Western allies continued to use German prisoners for labor after the unconditional surrender of the German forces, releasing them over approximately a two-year period. Russia held many German prisoners after the war and never made a full accounting. The defeat of Germany had left it without a government with which the agreements could be concluded. This situation provided the impetus of GPW-1949, for completely discarding the rule that arrangements for repatriation should be made in the treaty of peace, replacing it with a unilateral obligation to repatriate.

Whether or not repatriation is by agreement, GPW-1949 requires that it take place "without delay after the cessation of active hostilities." The words "without delay" reflect an intent to impose a definite objective obligation that precludes a state from claiming impossibility of repatriation for its own reasons or as a matter of policy under the circumstances. For example, the desire to use the prisoners for labor would not be valid excuse for the failure to repatriate, nor would a claim that it would be improvident to repatriate prisoners to a war-ravaged country where food and other basic necessities are in short supply.

While the obligation to repatriate rests squarely on the detaining power (even in the absence of agreement), repatriation will usually be effected by agreement in the armistice, capitulation, or other agreement terminating active hostilities or may be incorporated in a separate agreement. If there is no provision in an agreement between the parties to repatriate at the cessation of hostilities, each belligerent must establish and execute a plan of repatriation that must be brought to the knowledge of the prisoners. Failure to agree on the equitable apportionment of the costs of repatriation does not justify any delay in this repatriation.

GPW-1949 also sets forth standards for apportioning the costs of final repatriation between the parties. Conventional and customary law previously had left this matter entirely to agreement. These costs are to be equitably apportioned between the detaining power and the state on which the prisoners depend (art. 118, para. 4). When the detaining power and the power on which the prisoners depend are contiguous the latter must bear the "costs of repatriation from the frontiers of the detaining power." The converse also appears to be true, although the convention does not specifically say so. In the event that the powers are contiguous and the most direct or suitable route for repatriation is by sea or over the territory of a third power, literal reading of the convention would also require the prisoner's power to bear the costs of repatriation from the frontiers of the detaining power. The requirements in this instance are not clear and the principles of equitable apportionment might override the literal language.

GPW-1949 does not impose responsibilities for the transport and care of prisoners during their repatriation although the responsibilities for paying these costs may tend in practice to run parallel. None of the terms of the convention appears to limit the rights of the prisoner's power and the detaining power to assign between themselves the responsibility for obtaining transportation and providing care for the prisoners during repatriation. However, if the parties fail to agree, the detaining power has to establish and execute a plan of repatriation to an appropriate receiving point in the home territory of the prisoners. There are, however, minimum standards about the conditions of repatriation. Article 119 itself specifies certain requirements and additionally provides that repatriation is to be effected under conditions similar to those for transfer of prisoners between camps having regard to the specific requirements applicable to final repatriation.

Exceptions to Repatriation. Nothing is said in GPW-1949 or earlier prisoner of war conventions about a right of asylum for prisoners of war at the end of hostilities. It was this issue—whether prisoners must be repatriated against their will—that was the subject of the long, drawn-out negotiations that brought an end to the Korean conflict of 1950 to 1953. These negotiations concerned more than 22,000 prisoners of war in the custody of the United Nations Command and several hundred in the hands of the Korean People's Army and Chinese People's Volunteers who did not want to be repatriated. The resolution of this dispute, which must be taken to establish the present state of the law, was brought about through a resolution of the United Nations General Assembly and the subsequent armistice, adopting the position of the United Nations Command against forcible repatriation. The resolution of the General Assembly (which the Soviet bloc voted against) affirmed that the Korean conflict, "The release and repatriation of prisoners of war shall be effected in accordance with the Geneva Convention relative to the Treatment of Prisoners of War, dated 12 August 1949, the well-established principles and practice of international law and the relevant provisions of the draft armistice agreement," and that, "Force shall not be used against the prisoners of war to prevent or effect their return to their homelands."

While there is a well-recognized principle of asylum in peacetime that entitles a state *at its discretion* to provide sanctuary to political refugees, it does not necessarily follow that states have the same rights with regard to prisoners of war without procedures that guarantee that the prisoners have been granted a free choice. The conditions of captivity and the opportunity that the detaining power has to influence the decisions of prisoners readily offer possibilities of abuse. As stated in a resolution of the General Assembly dealing with the German prisoners that the USSR continued to detain long after World War II, prisoners must be given "an unrestricted opportunity of repatriation." The Korean Armistice of 1953 met this problem by establishing a Neutral Nations Repatriation Commission (NNRC), which took custody of the prisoners who refused to be repatriated. The armistice provided detailed procedures, under the supervision of the NNRC, to assure a free expression of choice, which included permitting the power on which the prisoners depended to offer "explanations" to the obdurate prisoners of why they should return. As an alternative to granting asylum to prisoners of war, treaties have contained provisions for amnesty that guaranteed that there would be no retaliation against repatriated prisoners. The Korean repatriation dispute and the principle of nonforcible repatriation, as accepted there, should not obscure the fact that granting asylum is left entirely to the discretion of the detaining power. There is no such thing as a legal duty to grant asylum.

Death of Prisoners. In customary and conventional law the belligerents have a right to expect that dead soldiers shall not be disgracefully treated or mutilated. Military courts following World War II, for example, found the following to be war crimes: decapitation and preservation of a dead soldier's head; bayoneting and mutilating the dead body of a United States prisoner of war; and precluding an honorable burial by the cannibalism of the bodies of prisoners of war. All possible measures are to be to search for the wounded, sick, and dead—particularly after an engagement—and to prevent the despoilation of the dead. The dead on the battlefield and in captivity must be honorably buried, and their graves must be respected, maintained, and marked.

Death certificates are required for deceased prisoners, whether found in camps or on the battlefield, to be forwarded to the Prisoner of War Information Bureau. Burial or cremation is to be preceded by examination (a medical examination under GPW-1949, and under GWS (Geneva Convention for the Amelioration of the Condition of the Wounded and Sick in Armed Forces in the Fields) whenever possible). Cremation is permitted only for imperative reasons of hygiene, because of the deceased's religion, or in accordance with his expressed wish; and burial is to be in individual graves grouped in the burying grounds by country if possible, unless unavoidable circumstances require otherwise. Each party is to establish a Graves Registration Service to record burials, graves, and ashes, and to transmit lists of them to the power on which the prisoners depend.

Any death or serious injury of a prisoner caused by a person, or by a cause which is unknown, is to be made the subject of an inquiry by the detaining power, and must be immediately reported to the protecting power, followed by a report, to include statements of witnesses. If the inquiry indicates the guilt of one or more persons, the detaining power is to take the necessary measures to prosecute them. A main purpose of this requirement, new in GPW-1949, is to deter and punish inexcusable killings passed off under the false characterization, "killed while attempting to escape." Wills of prisoners are also treated in the provisions on death of article 120 and separately in article 77. Taken together, these articles oblige the detaining power to help (and to permit a lawyer to help) the prisoner prepare his will. They require that the country of origin furnish the necessary legal information and that wills be forwarded to the protecting power at the prisoner's request or, in any event, on his death.

Information Bureaus

During the second half of the nineteenth century belligerents had in several instances unilaterally established national bureaus to receive and transmit information about prisoners of war. HR, article 14, turned practice into law, and states are thus under a customary as well as conventional obligation to establish Information Bureaus to receive and furnish to the government on which the prisoners depend, information concerning internments, transfers, releases, escapes, admissions to hospital, and deaths, as well as to serve as a channel for the restoration to prisoners of property from which they may have become separated.

Under GPW-1949, belligerents and neutrals receiving prisoners of war are required to set up official Information Bureaus to receive the categories of information about prisoners of war set forth in article 14 of HR. This information is then in turn to be communicated by the bureau to the state from which the prisoners come (through the protecting power) and also to the Central Prisoners of War Information Agency. The functions of the bureaus also included answering all inquiries about prisoners of war and collecting and forwarding personal valuables of prisoners who have been repatriated or released or have escaped or died.

Medical Property

Medical Facilities and Equipment

Under customary and conventional law, both mobile medical units and fixed medical establishments are entitled to protection at all times. GWS-1949 also protects hospital ships entitled to protection under GWS-Sea-1949 from land attack and capture. Protective rights cease if medical units and establishments are used to commit acts harmful to the enemy, such as espionage and concealment of arms and ammunitions. The following conditions do not justify the loss of rights: (1) The armed defense of the unit, and its wounded and sick. (2) The use of pickets, guards, or escorts, in the absence of armed orderlies. (3) The presence of small arms taken from the wounded and sick, and not yet given to the proper authorities. Appropriate warning must be given by the adverse party of acts alleged to forfeit immunity; only after such warning goes unheeded are protective rights lost.

Under customary law the mobile medical unit and its material would be released at the same time as the medical personnel. The materials and stores of medical establishments become the property of the captor. GWS-1949 changes this customary law and provides that medical material, when taken, is to remain in the hands of the captor for the continued care of all of the wounded and sick. Conventional law also prohibits intentional destruction of these materials and stores either by the enemy or by those who would want to prevent the property from falling into enemy hands. Permanent medical installations may not be used for purposes other than medical, except in cases of military necessity, and then only if suitable arrangements are previously made for the wounded and sick. The real and personal property of recognized aid societies is regarded as private property. Thus, it is subject to requisition by belligerents, but only in case of urgent necessity and after the welfare of the wounded and sick has been ensured.

Hospital Zones and Localities

In time of peace and after the outbreak of hostilities, the parties may establish "hospital zones and localities," specially organized to protect wounded and sick personnel connected therewith from the effects of war. These areas may be established in the territory of the party concerned or, if need be, in occupied areas. Agreements between the parties may be concluded for the mutual recognition of the zones and localities created. The protecting power and ICRC are also united to assist in the institution and recognition of these areas.

Medical Transports

Transports of wounded and sick and medical equipment are entitled to the same respect and protection as mobile medical units. If they fall into enemy hands, they become the property of the captor provided he ensures the care of the wounded and sick. If such care cannot be provided, he must allow the convoy to continue on to its own lines. These provisions do not affect medical vehicles belonging to National Red Cross societies or other recognized aid societies, as these vehicles are considered private property and exempt from capture, although they may be requisitioned.

Article 35 also provides that civilian personnel and all transport obtained by requisition are subject to the rules of international law, which reflects customary law. If not requisitioned by the occupying power, civilian inhabitants of occupied territory may not be retained as prisoners of war if captured while engaged in the evacuation of the wounded and sick, neither may their vehicles be taken. However, if requisitioned by the belligerent in its own territory, they would be entitled to the benefits of GC-1949 (Geneva Convention Relative to the Protection of Civilian Persons in Time of War—1949). The requisitioned means of transportation may be seized, but later it must be restored and compensation must be paid.

Aircraft

Aircraft, including helicopters, flying alone or in convoys, exclusively employed for the removal of wounded and sick and for transportation of medical personnel and equipment, must be respected when flying at heights, times, and on routes specifically agreed upon between the belligerents. Unless otherwise agreed, flights over enemy or enemy-occupied territory are also prohibited. Lacking such agreement, belligerents may use medical aircraft only at their own risk. Aerial medical convoys must be clearly marked with the distinctive emblem described in article 38. They must obey every summons to land. After landing and examination they may continue their flight. In the event of involuntary landing in enemy-occupied territory, the wounded and sick, as well as the aircraft crew, are to be treated as prisoners of war; medical personnel are to be treated appropriately as discussed earlier.

Aircraft may fly over territory of neutral powers, land there if necessary, or use it as a port of call. However, they are immune from attack only on the conditions and restrictions of passage specifically agreed upon between the parties to the conflict and the neutral power concerned. Unless the neutral power and the parties to the conflict agree otherwise, the wounded and sick disembarked on neutral territory by medical aircraft shall be detained by the neutral power so that they cannot take part in operations of war again. The cost of their accommodation and internment is to be borne by the power on which they depend.

Distinctive Markings

Under both customary and conventional law, the sign of a red cross on a white ground, first sanctioned by the Geneva Convention of 1864, is the emblem and distinctive protective sign of the medical service of the armed forces. GWS-1949 has also approved the emblems of the red crescent, or the red lion and sun on a white ground for countries that use them. The use of the official emblem is permitted to signify that personnel or material are connected with the Red Cross, without invoking the protection of the convention. Protection is only extended to medical (and religious) personnel and medical equipment displaying the distinctive emblem. In addition to an identity disc described in article 16, permanent medical personnel, and those of recognized relief societies, must wear a water-resistant armlet on their left sleeve and carry an identity card, each bearing the distinctive emblem. In no circumstances may they be deprived of such identification. Under customary law, personnel not in uniform attached to the medical service of armies are given certificates of identity. Medical personnel also carry regular military identification tokens so that in case of death their bodies can be identified.

Notes

1. Nazi Conspiracy and Aggression, Opinion and Judgement 59, 61-62, 117, 165 (1947); U.S. v. Von Leeb et al. (11 Trials of War Criminals before the Nuremberg Military Tribunals under Control Council Law No. 10) at 536-58.

2. U.S. v. Altstoetter et al. (3 Trials of War Criminals before the Nuremberg Military Tribunals under Control Council Law No. 10) 954 (1947). In U.S. v. List et al. [the *Hostage* case] , 12 id. 1230 at 1244-46, 1250, 1253, 1290 (1948).

3 Civilians

Introduction

Notwithstanding the actual fate of civilian populations from the conquests of Rome through two twentieth-century world wars, it has long been a fundamental principle of the law of war that military operations should be limited to the armed forces and that the civilian population should enjoy immunity from violence. Although scholars may find a few specific applications of this humanitarian principle scattered through the pages of history, the customary international law is scanty and lacking in detail. HR (Hague Regulations) contains some provisions applicable to the inhabitants of territory occupied by an enemy army. But until the unprecedented slaughter and brutal treatment of civilians during World War II inspired the Civilians Convention of 1949, there was no conventional declaration that explicitly set forth the fundamental rights and safeguards of noncombatants in time of war.

The organization of the convention is rather complicated: Part I states general provisions, including articles common to all four Geneva Conventions of 1949. Part II, comprising articles 13-26, relates to the protection of entire populations of the belligerent states, including areas invaded but not yet occupied. The provisions, which are largely humanitarian in nature, are broadly drafted and do not apply to individual protected persons. Part III defines the status and dictates the treatment of protected persons. It amplifies and extends the customary law applicable to inhabitants of occupied territory. In other sections it creates new rights for enemy aliens in the territory of a party to the conflict and any protected persons who may be interned.

Under GC (Geneva Convention Relative to the Protection of Civilian Persons in Time of War) "protected persons" (as defined in article 4) who are in "occupied territory" come under the specific protection of Part II (General Protection of Populations against Certain Consequences of War), Part III, Section 1 (Provisions Common to the Territories of the Parties to the Conflict and to Occupied Territories), and Part III, Section 3 (Occupied Territories), as well as the sections governing the treatment of internees and information bureaus and the central agency.

Part II of GC covers the whole of the populations in the territories of the parties to the conflict. Its provisions, which relate to the medical care and protection of the wounded and sick and to family welfare, are "intended to alleviate the sufferings caused by war" (art. 13). This part covers the whole of the territories of the belligerents; the area of hostilities, including territories invaded but not yet occupied; and the whole of the populations of the belligerent states, whether nationals or aliens. It should be particularly noted that the convention thus includes the relationship of a party to its own resident population. These provisions, which are principally concerned with humanitarian relief such as removal of the wounded and the sick, hospital convoys, and the like are discussed below. The basic rights of protected persons to humane treatment and to respect for their persons, honor, family rights, and religious convictions, under article 27, do not extend to the members of populations protected by articles 13-26. Thus, the general protection of entire populations is broader in jurisdiction and narrower in substance than the rights of either enemy aliens in the territory of a belligerent or the inhabitants of occupied territories. Customary international law, as it will hereafter appear, is not equally broad in scope. Moreover, neutral nationals and persons protected by other bodies of law are not within the protection of the customary international law of war.

The effect of GC, Part III, Section 1 (Provisions Common to the Territories of the Parties to the Conflict and to Occupied Territory), is to amplify certain provisions of HR applicable to occupied territories and then to extend these broadened and more detailed rules to the territories of the belligerents, as well as to occupied areas. In a number of respects, these articles do no more than give greater particularity to what would be the customary international law even in the absence of HR.

Categories of Protected Persons

Protected and Unprotected Civilians

Under article 4 of GC, protected persons consist of those who, for any reason, "find themselves, in case of a conflict or occupation, in the hands of a Party to the conflict or Occupying Power of which they are not nationals," with the following exceptions: (1) Nationals of a party not bound by the convention. (2) Nationals of a neutral state in the territory of a belligerent, so long as the state of which they are nationals has normal diplomatic representation with the state that they are in. (3) Nationals of a co-belligerent, so long as the state of which they are nationals has diplomatic representation with the state that they are in. (4) Persons protected under any one of the other three conventions, that is, the prisoners of war, and the wounded, the sick, and the shipwrecked members of the armed forces.

Nationals of Neutral Nations

Some, but not all, neutral nationals in occupied territory are "protected persons" within the meaning of GC, whether or not entitled to the full scope of protection of GC. Neutral nationals in occupied territory will inevitably find themselves subjected to many of the same restraints as enemy nationals (notably in respect to legislation promulgated by the occupant), and their property will likewise be subject to seizure or requisition. However, a neutral state would be justified in claiming that a neutral national should be given no worse treatment than an enemy national, which would mean that HR would constitute a ceiling on what the belligerent occupant could do. HR would thus retain some of its force when brought to bear on neutral nationals, even though the principle is that the regulations are not applicable to neutral nationals, either as treaty law or as evidence of customary law.

Enemy Aliens in the Territory of a Party to the Conflict

Enemy aliens in the territory of a party to the conflict are among the persons whose protection is defined by the convention as a function of the political status of the territory in which they are located. Civilians of enemy nations living in the territory of a belligerent were treated as slaves under Roman law. Their position gradually improved under customary law and by the time of Grotius in the 16th century they were entitled to at least the protection of prisoners of war. Nevertheless, prior to GC they were, at best, refugees with uncertain rights of resettlement and repatriation. The customary right of a state to expel all enemy aliens has not been abrogated by the convention. Enemy aliens who are neither expelled nor interned must be permitted to leave the territory. Aliens who are expelled on short notice have less protection than those who elect voluntary departure. Those who choose to remain and are not otherwise interned are regulated by the provisions concerning aliens in time of peace.

Enemy Nationals in Occupied Territory

Enemy nationals who inhabit occupied territory are a second group of persons whose protection is defined as a function of the political status of the territory in which they are located. Under HR, article 42, "territory is considered occupied when it is actually placed under the authority of the hostile army." The article goes on to provide that the occupation extends only to areas where the authority of the occupant has actually been established and can be exercised. The concept envisages a certain stability of control, in the sense that the particular territory is not being actually fought over at the moment. To precisely what area the authority of the occupant extends is highly uncertain in modern warfare; in a war of movement, towns and cities may be bypassed by fast-moving tank or motorized columns. Nevertheless, one normally thinks of populated centers or military bases as being the core of occupied areas even though control may not be established over every meter of the surrounding countryside. However, exactly when a sufficient stability of control has been achieved and the authority of the occupant actually extends to particular area is a subjective judgment. Consistent with the humanitarian objectives of the Convention of 1949, such provisions as would operate to the maximum benefit of the local inhabitants should be given as early and as wide an application as possible.

Interned Persons

A separate subcategory of protected persons in occupied areas and in the territory of a party to the conflict consists of those persons who are interned or imprisoned, either for "imperative reasons of security" (GC, art. 78) or for the commission of an offense. Customary international law provides no specific protection for persons so deprived of their liberty. Under GC they may, at the most, be subject to assigned residence or internment with a right of appeal. However, one who is regarded as a "spy or saboteur, or a person under definite suspicion of activity hostile to the security of the Occupying Power" (GC, art. 5) belongs to a special class of persons who may be denied rights of communication. He is to be restored the full rights and privileges of a protected person as soon as the security of the occupant permits.

Chiefs of State

Under customary international law, enemy chiefs of state and high civilian officials, such as cabinet ministers, were liable to detention as prisoners of war upon capture. The present position seems to be, however, that such individuals fall under the comprehensive protection of GC and may be interned if the measure is required in the interests of the security of the detaining power. Nevertheless, a high civilian official accompanying the armed forces, or a chief of state who was also the commander-in-chief of the armed forces of that state, could continue to be held as a prisoner of war under GPW (Geneva Convention Relative to the Treatment of Prisoners of War), article 4. The occupying power may accept the characterization of the civilian official under his own municipal law. Thus the president of the United States, who is constitutionally the commander-in-chief, would be entitled to protection as a prisoner of war. The president of the USSR, who is constitutionally a civilian, would be entitled to protection under GC.

Medical Personnel

Under article 20 of GC, medical personnel of civilian hospitals and other persons engaged in the care of the wounded and the sick, the infirm, and maternity cases are to be respected and protected. The provision runs parallel to the articles of GWS (Geneva Convention for the Amelioration of the Condition of the Wounded and Sick in Armed Forces in the Field) and GWS-Sea (Geneva Convention for the Amelioration of the Condition of Wounded, Sick, and Shipwrecked Members of Armed Forces at Sea) relating to medical personnel, but the clause is so brief that it would not be proper to regard it as establishing a whole separate category of persons for legal purposes. However, there is no counterpart in the customary law.

Protection of Populations in Civil Conflicts

Except with respect to humanitarian relief of populations, the relationship of a state with its own nationals is outside the scope of customary international law. However, article 3, common to the four Geneva Conventions of 1949, grants certain basic rights even to "persons taking no active part in the hostilities, including members of armed forces who have laid down their arms and those placed *hors de combat* by sickness, wounds, detention, or any other cause." These rules apply to each party to the conflict in its relations with personnel of the other party; thus they bind insurgents as well as the lawful government.

The parties to such an armed conflict not of an international character are encouraged to bring into force all or part of the conventions. If they do, the participants in a civil war are put on the same footing as if the war were an international one of the character described in article 2 common to the four conventions. Civilians taking no active part in the hostilities are to be treated humanely and without discrimination. The following acts are specifically prohibited:

- Violence to life and person, particularly murder, mutilation, cruel treatment, and torture.
- The taking of hostages.
- Offenses against personal dignity, "in particular humiliating and degrading treatment."
- The imposition of criminal penalties except after judgment by a competent tribunal, acting according to international standards of justice.

The wounded and the sick must be provided for.

Although the parties to the conflict are encouraged to enter into an agreement bringing GC into force in whole or in part, the application of article 3 or the bringing into force of GC as a whole do not affect the legal status of the parties to the conflict. This means that treating civilian victims of a civil war humanely or in full conformity with GC is without legal significance as a matter of law. For example, it does not constitute an implied recognition of the rebels as a government, as insurgents, or as belligerents for any other purposes. Forbearing from such acts as murder, torture, and the taking of hostages does not constitute an implied recognition of insurgents, affect the legal status of either party to the conflict, or inhibit the application of municipal law. It does not deter the government's dealing with civilian rebels as violators of the municipal law of the state. Civilians may continue to be tried for crimes that they have committed, even if these be of a political character. Indeed, this privilege of the government of the state is implicitly recognized in the provisions of article 3 regarding fair trials. Although article 3 is explicitly without political significance, it appears to have an implicit political significance that has handicapped its application in civil insurrections. Thus, the French in Algeria were loath to apply the article for political reasons during Algeria's war for independence.

Limited Protection of Populations in International Conflicts

The protection international law accords to particular categories of civilians depends upon their physical location, the activities in which they are engaged, the nature of the conflict, and the legal position of the state that is a party in the conflict (that is, whether it is a party to the conventions). Part II of GC-1949 provides limited protection for the entire populations of countries engaged in an international conflict, as well as populations of an occupied territory, without any adverse distinction based on race, nationality, religion, or political opinion. The language of the convention has led to the view that there are two separate spheres in the protection of civilians: One relates to the general humanitarian concern for population, taken as a whole; the other is directed to the right of the protected person in his relation with the belligerent. The limited protection for entire populations, insofar as it deals with occupied areas, supplements the Hague Conventions of 1899 and 1907 for those states that are bound by them. The rights given to this broad sweep of "protected persons," as defined by article 13 of GC-1949, are without precedent in customary or conventional law.

Hospital and Safety Zones

The idea of establishing hospital and safety zones dates back to the Franco-Prussian War of 1870. It was discussed at various international conferences prior to 1949, and there were attempts to set up such zones, with differing degrees of success, in the Spanish Civil War, World War II, and the 1948 conflict in Palestine. It remained for the Geneva Conference of 1949 to draft provisions on this subject. The zones dealt with in GC-1949 are of two types. In peacetime or after the outbreak of hostilities, the belligerents may establish "hospital and safety zones and localities" in their own territory or in occupied areas to shelter the wounded and the sick, the aged, children, pregnant women, and mothers of infants. These zones correspond to the hospital zones and localities referred to in GWS-1949, article 23. The same zone may harbor both military and civilian wounded and sick. Establishment of the zones is not enough to give them a protected position; the belligerents must agree on recognition of these zones and localities. The International Red Cross and protecting powers are to use their influence to secure the establishment of such zones.

Civilian Hospitals

Civilian hospitals may not be attacked and must be respected and protected. When authorized by the government of the state in which they are located, civilian hospitals are to be marked with the Red Cross or other authorized emblem. The convention recommends that such hospitals be situated as far as possible from military objectives. It also provides that if hospitals are used to commit acts harmful to the enemy, which are confirmed after due warning, they shall lose the protection of the law. Caring for sick and wounded members of the armed forces is not considered to be an act harmful to the enemy.

The full-time hospital staffs, like the institutions themselves, must be respected and protected. They are to be identified in occupied territory and in zones of military operations by means of identity cards and armlets issued by the state. Part-time personnel are entitled to wear armlets while actually performing hospital duties. It should be observed that the use of the authorized emblem (Red Cross, Red Lion, and so forth) is strictly controlled by international and domestic laws.

GC also provides for the first time for the marketing and control of aircraft used exclusively for the removal of wounded and sick civilians, the infirm, and maternity cases, and for the transport of medical personnel and equipment. The conditions under which such aircraft are used must be agreed upon by the belligerents. The aircraft must obey every summons to land. Wounded and sick members of the armed forces aboard such aircraft, or for that matter in civilian hospitals, are subject to capture.

These principles mark some departures from the customary law. HR, article 27, had merely required commanders to spare hospitals (as well as museums, monuments, and the like) and had placed a duty upon the besieged to indicate the presence of such places by visible signs. GC precludes hospitals and medical convoys from being made the objects of attack under any circumstances, unless protection has been forfeited by an improper use of facilities or personnel. Thus the bombardment of a hospital in Hanoi by the U.S. Air Force, which might have been condoned under HR, was strictly prohibited by GC.

Noncombatants on the Battlefield

A general obligation to protect and to refrain from attacking the wounded and the sick, the infirm, and expectant mothers applies to all parties to the conflict and to all military and civilian personnel. To the extent that military considerations allow, the belligerents, are also obliged to search for and to protect the wounded, the dead, and other noncombatants exposed to grave danger. Personnel and materiel engaged in the removal of these victims of war are entitled to respect and protection. Military necessity must be the paramount consideration in the decision of a commander whether to permit evacuation of the wounded, infirm, children, and maternity cases from besieged or encircled areas. Although belligerents are encouraged to remove these noncombatants from besieged places, no rule of international law compels evacuation. The matter is left to agreement by the parties. An example would be the relief of the Egyptian city of Suez and the encircled Third Army by Israeli Forces in the 1973 conflict.

Relief Supplies

After World War I the ICRC (International Committee of the Red Cross) had tried unsuccessfully to persuade the international community to accept the principle of mercy shipments through blockades. During World War II the combatants were willing to permit such shipments to the populations of occupied territories, but not to a party to the conflict. Under the Geneva Conventions of 1949, however, a belligerent must permit the free passage of medical supplies, religious objects, and essential food and clothing for children through a land or sea blockade. The obligation of a commander to allow free passage of the consignments is subject to his being satisfied as to the following points:

- That the material will not be diverted from its destination.
- That the control will be effective.
- That the enemy will not realize a distinct economic or military advantage by the substitution of relief supplies for material that would otherwise be produced by its own economy.

Family Welfare

All parties to a conflict must insure the support and education of children under fifteen who are orphaned or separated from their parents as a result of warfare. They must also facilitate inquiries made by members of families dispersed by war and encourage the work of organizations engaged in this task if they conform to security regulations. Personal communications may be exchanged by persons in occupied territory or in the territory of parties to the conflict who desire to communicate with their families. The mechanics of transmitting the mail are not stipulated by the treaty except to recommend application to a neutral intermediary such as the Central Information Agency, if necessary.

Provisions Common to Territories of the Belligerent and to Occupied Territory

GC, article 27, requires humane treatment of and respect for the protected person at all times, protecting him against acts and threats of violence and disrespect to his person, honor, family rights, religious beliefs and practices, manners and customs. It also prohibits any adverse distinction in the treatment of protected persons on account of sex, race, religion, and political beliefs. HR, article 46, provides many of these protections, but GC goes further in specifically citing as prohibited the following acts of violence and disrespect:

- Insults and exposure to public curiosity (art. 27).
- Rape, enforced prostitution, and indecent assault on women (art. 27).
- Using the physical presence of a person to make a place immune from military operations (art. 28).
- Physical or moral coercion, particularly to obtain information from the person or from third parties (arts. 31 and 33); forcing inhabitants to provide military information is also prohibited by article 44 of HR.
- Actions causing physical suffering, intimidation, or extermination, including murder, torture, corporal punishment, mutilation, brutality, and medical or scientific experimentation (art. 32).
- Pillage (art. 33); pillaging (not simply in occupied areas but anywhere at all) is prohibited by articles 28 and 47 of HR.
- Punishment of a person for an offense he did not commit (art. 33).
- Collective penalties (art. 33).
- Reprisals against the person or his property (art. 33).
- Taking of hostages (art. 34).

Reflecting the normal rule of responsibility, a party to the conflict is also responsible for the treatment afforded to protected persons by its agents, irrespective of any individual responsibility (that is, for a war crime) that may be incurred. However, the parties to the conflict may take such control and security measures with respect to protected persons as are necessary because of the war.

Protected persons must be allowed to communicate with the protecting power, the International Red Cross, the local national Red Cross Society, and other organizations that might assist them. Detaining or occupying powers are also required to facilitate the work of such organizations, including visits designed to provide protected persons with spiritual or medical relief.

The prohibitions on collective punishment, reprisals, and the taking of hostages in articles 33 and 34 of GC represent a fundamental change from the customary law. The ancient theory of collective responsibility, which is recognized to a limited extent by HR, article 50, is clearly abolished, and the principle of strict personal responsibility is substituted in its place. This fundamental change of international law was a specific reaction to the destruction of Lidice, Czechoslovakia, by Nazi Germany during World War II. Reprisals, which custom recognized as a legitimate sanction for enforcing compliance with the rules of civilized warfare, may no longer be taken against protected persons and their property. Similarly, customary law condones the taking of hostages, subject to their being treated as prisoners of war. But under GC, the taking of protected persons as hostages is absolutely prohibited. While it would be sanguine to believe that outrages of warfare against protected populations will be eliminated by the convention, it is somewhat consoling that such atrocities are now indefensible by law.

Scope of Protection

Basic Human Rights

Food, Clothing, and Shelter. Insofar as customary law concerned itself at all with this subject, it looked primarily to the maintenance of the occupation forces. HR, article 52, restricts requisitions to the needs of the army of occupation, and the requisitions must be in proportion to the resources of the country. The Civilians Convention, on the other hand, chiefly concerns itself with the provisions of the necessities of life to protected persons left at liberty (in occupied territories and in the territory of parties to the conflict), in transit, and in internment camps. GC, articles 83-92, regulating the rights of internees with respect to food, clothing, and shelter, are closely modeled on articles 25-68 of GPW-1949. Whenever possible, the draftsmen used identical language in both conventions.

Alien enemies allowed to leave the territory of a belligerent under article 35 of GC-1949 are entitled to leave under "satisfactory conditions" as regards food (as well as hygiene, sanitation, and safety) (art. 36). When an occupying power evacuates a territory in the interest of military security, it must insure adequate food for the transferees. Article 55 reiterates the rule of HR that supplies may be requisitioned only for the use of the occupation forces. It mentions foodstuffs and medical supplies expressly where HR had not. Not only must the occupying power now refrain from requisitioning food until "the needs of the civilian population have been taken into account," but its responsibility also extends to insuring the provision of food and medicine to the population "to the fullest extent of the means available to it" (art. 55). The protecting power may verify the food supplies at any time, except when imperative military requirements prevent this.

The detaining power must provide a sufficient quantity, quality, and variety of food to internees to maintain good health and prevent nutritional deficiencies. The standard is like that applicable to prisoners of war under GPW-1949, article 26. As civilian internees may include women and children, GC requires that expectant and nursing mothers and children under 15 years of age be supplied with supplementary rations as required by their physiological needs. GC requires only that internees be given the facilities to prepare any supplementary rations in their possession, by contrast with the right of prisoners of war to participate in the daily preparation of meals, in accordance with the military practice. In other respects the standards relating to food are similar to those for prisoners of war.

There is no customary or conventional law regarding the clothing of civilians left at liberty. GC, article 90, however, requires merely that civilian internees be provided with the facilities to clothe themselves and to procure additional apparel as required. Any internee lacking the means to purchase garments suitable for the climate in which he is interned is to be clothed by the detaining power. Clothes that are supplied by the captors, and the markings that may be required by the camp authorities on the internee's own clothes, may not expose him to ridicule or opprobrium. This provision was specifically directed against such practices as the use of the Star of David in World War II to identify Jewish internees. Clothes may not be used in any way that would create adverse distinction based upon race, religion, or political opinion.

With respect to shelter, customary law required merely that an occupying force must pay for the use of privately owned quarters that are requisitioned. Even under GC-1949 an occupying power does not have any affirmative obligation to provide shelter to civilians not interned. Civilian internees must be accommodated in quarters separate from those of prisoners of war and persons legally detained for any other reason. The standards relating to light and heat, protection from dampness, and so forth, are identical to those applicable to prisoners under GPW, article 25. In many respects GC, article 85, resembles a housing code, detailing in a single article the location of quarters, minimum criteria of habitation, and public health standards. It differs from GPW only in particulars reflecting the housing requirements of military personnel, who are presumed to be largely adult males, and interned civilians, who are presumed to include families, women, and children. There are no provisions concerning intermediate transit camps. Sanitary facilities must be provided from the outset of internment. Bedding may differ depending upon the age and sex of the internee. Because women are generally part of a family unit, separate accommodations for women are regarded as "exceptional and temporary." Protective measures against air attack and fire available to the general population must also be extended to internees. Civilians interned in their own homes may either use available shelters in case of alarm or remain to protect their quarters. Camps should be marked with the letters "IC" clearly visible from the air.

Hygiene and Medical Attention. Protected persons leaving the territory of a belligerent at the outset of, or during, a conflict are to depart under "satisfactory conditions as regards . . . hygiene, [and] sanitation" (GC, art. 36). Those who remain are, in principle, entitled to such medical attention and hospital treatment as would have been available to them in time of peace, and specifically to the same care given to nationals of the country where they are located.

There is no customary law and no provision of the earlier treaties requiring the belligerent occupant to concern itself with health in the occupied area, other than the general obligation under HR, article 43, "to restore and ensure . . . public order and safety." Now under GC, article 56, the occupying power, working with the national authorities, has a duty to keep hospital and public health services going to the extent that it has the means of doing so. Civilian hospitals may be requisitioned only if there is urgent necessity and only if arrangements have been made to look after the patients and the civilian population that rely on the hospital. The occupant has an obligation to insure medical supplies for the population if the existing resources are not adequate. It may not interfere with any preferential medical care that may have been adopted for mothers and children prior to the occupation. When an occupying power is obliged to transfer or evacuate civilians, it must insure that removals take place under satisfactory hygienic conditions.

Internees are required to be provided with adequate infirmary facilities and medical attention corresponding to those provided in prisoner of war camps under GPW, article 30. They may not be prevented from seeking medical examination at the daily inspection that must be held under article 125, and each internee is to receive at least a monthly inspection that includes weight checks and diagnostic tests for contagious diseases. The seriously ill and maternity cases must be admitted to an institution that will offer care that is not inferior to that available to the general population. Whenever possible, the physician shall be the same nationality as the patient. Medical inspections and treatment are to be paid for by the detaining power, which must also provide clean latrines, accessible day and night; soap, bathing and washing facilities; and the time to utilize them.

Religion and Leisure. The right of an alien in a hostile country to practice his religion and to receive spiritual assistance from a minister of his faith is among the basic protections extended by GC, article 38. The law provides a measure of protection against special discrimination based upon religion and an end to any religious persecution preceding the war.

Customary law requires the occupying power to respect the religious convictions of inhabitants and to permit public worship. The clear, detailed, and unequivocal judicial affirmation of this principle by the International Military Tribunal at Nuremberg in the case of the persecution of the Jews in territory occupied by Nazi Germany appears to have preempted further conventional statement. GC, article 58, requires the occupying power to permit ministers of religion to give spiritual assistance to members of their religious communities. This includes the acceptance and distribution of Bibles, prayer books, and other articles and publications required for religious needs. In countries where clergy are paid by the state, their salaries must be continued if the occupant collects the taxes. The freedom of the clergy in occupied territory may not be used as a cover for agitation against the occupying power. Civilian internees enjoy precisely the same freedom in the exercise of their religion as prisoners of war. They must be provided with premises suitable for religious services; interned ministers of religion shall be allowed to minister to internees of the same religion and nationality, and if there is a shortage of interned ministers, local religious authorities may, with the approval of the detaining power, appoint qualified personnel as substitutes.

Although article 94 requires the detaining power to encourage "intellectual, educational, and recreational pursuits," the internees are free to participate or not as they wish. The difference in emphasis between the internee's right to "take part or not" and the respect to be accorded to the "individual preferences" of prisoners of war suggests a sensitivity in GC to the psychological warfare potential of educational and intellectual activities that is lacking in GPW. GC expresses a special concern for the continuation of education, not only for the children and young adults, whose schooling must be insured within or outside the compound, but also for any internee who so desires. Recreational areas must be provided for young people.

Relations with the Exterior. The customary law did not define or protect the communication rights of individuals in occupied territory. Nevertheless, the preservation of submarine cables to neutral countries by HR, article 54, provides some assurance that the occupied territory will not be totally cut off from the outside world. The Civilians Convention somewhat extends contact with the outside world by facilitating the passage of individual relief consignments to aliens in the territory of a belligerent and to inhabitants of occupied territories. The vital right of contact between individuals who have been deprived of their liberty by placement in assigned residence or an internment camp is protected by means analogous to those applicable to prisoners of war; notification to the protected person of the measures taken by the detaining power to assure communications is required, as is notice of internment to relatives and to the Central Information Agency.

Correspondence rights and censorship burdens of prisoners and internees are similar. An inexplicable difference is that prisoners of war in confinement under due process of law have a limited right to receive and dispatch correspondence, while GC grants civilians merely a right to receive parcels under similar conditions. A similar obscurity clouds the total omission of a postal exemption for internees, such as enjoyed by prisoners under GPW. The detailed mechanics of individual and collective relief shipments set forth in GC are merely extensions of the prisoner of war law applicable to civilian internees.

An important right granted to internees that has no counterpart in GPW is the allowance of family visitations and the right of internees to visit their homes, particularly in the case of illness or death in the family. Presumably, the right could be exercised only by those whose homes and families are in the country of internment itself.

Death. Death certificates, which must be certified by a doctor, are required for all deceased internees, and an official record of the death of an internee must be drawn up and registered in accordance with the laws in effect in the territory of the place of internment. A copy of this record is to be transmitted to the protecting power and to the Central Information Agency.

A deceased internee is to be honorably buried, if possible in accordance with his religious beliefs, and the burial must be in an individual grave unless unavoidable circumstances make it necessary to use collective graves. Cremation is permissible only for imperative reasons of hygiene, because of the deceased's religion, or in accordance with his expressed wish. The fact of cremation and the reasons therefor must be noted on the death certificate. Graves are to be respected, maintained, and marked in such a way that they can always be recognized. Lists of graves are to be transmitted to the powers on which the deceased internees depend as soon as circumstances permit and not later than the close of hostilities. Ashes shall be retained for safekeeping by the authorities and transferred as soon as possible to the next of kin on their request.

Any death or serious injury of an internee caused by a person, or the cause of which is unknown, is to be the subject of an injury by the detaining power. The occurrence of such a death or injury must be communicated immediately to the protecting power; a repeat of the inquiry is also to be reported to the protecting power including evidence presented by witnesses. If the inquiry indicates the guilt of one or more persons, the detaining power is to take necessary measures to prosecute them.

The detaining power is to facilitate the execution of wills and other legal documents by internees and allow the internees to consult a lawyer for these purposes. Wills will be received for safekeeping by the responsible authority and in the event of death shall be sent without delay to the person previously designated by the internee.

Transfer and Movement of Persons

Departures and Transfers of Aliens in the Territory of a Belligerent. Under Roman law, subjects of a belligerent on enemy territory at the outbreak of war could all be detained as prisoners of war. Under treaties of the eighteenth and nineteenth centuries, however, the practice developed of permitting alien enemies categorized as not active or as reserve combatants to depart within a reasonable time after the outbreak of war. Although this practice became "almost a rule of international law," there has been a trend in this century to broaden the categories of aliens who may be prevented from leaving. In codifying the practice, GC-1949 reflects this trend. It permits protected persons to depart unless their departure is contrary to "the national interests of the State" (art. 35, para. 1). These national interests, which are broader than security considerations, include economic interests.

Applications of protected persons to leave must be decided in accordance with regularly established procedures. Any denial is to be reconsidered, upon proper request, by an appropriate court or administrative board of the detaining power. The protecting power, if it requests, is entitled to know who has been denied permission to leave and the reasons, unless security considerations are to the contrary or the persons concerned object. The parties to the conflict may arrive at special agreement for mutual exchanges, provided the rights of protected persons are not violated. In any event, departures are to be carried out under satisfactory conditions as regards safety, hygiene, sanitation, and food. If the persons leaving do not finance their own trips, the costs from the point of exit in the detaining power are to be borne by the country of destination or, if there is to be accommodation in a neutral country, by the power whose nationals are benefited.

GC-1949 also provides safeguards with respect to transfers of protected persons in the territory of a belligerent to a third power. Transfers of this type have been made in the past without any clear definition of the legal responsibilities of the transferor and transferee powers. GC-1949 establishes rules that are the same as those for transfers under article 12 of GPW-1949. Transfer may be made only to a party to the convention; the transferor must satisfy itself of the willingness and ability of the transferee to comply. The transferee is responsible for the civilians in its custody, but the transferor has a contingent responsibility if the transferee fails to carry out the convention "in any important respect." The Communist nations, however, objected to these rules, as they did to article 12 of GPW, and deposited reservations that refuse to recognize the failure to provide for joint responsibility on the part of the transferor and transferee for protected civilians in the latter's custody.

The following movements are excepted from these rules about transfers between powers: repatriations, returns of protected persons at the close of hostilities to their countries of residence, and extradition under extradition treaties concluded before the outbreak of hostilities for ordinary criminal offenses. Expulsion or deportation of undesirables on an individual basis is apparently not intended to be precluded, but a protected person may not be transferred to a country where he has reason to fear persecution of political opinions or religious beliefs.

Departures and Transfers from Occupied Territory. Protected persons in an occupied territory who are not nationals of the occupied state have the same right to leave the territory as protected persons in the territory of a party to the conflict. They may leave unless their departure is contrary to the national interests of the occupying power. They are also entitled to have denials of their requests for permission to depart reconsidered by an appropriate board or court designated by the occupying power. It is not clear whether the right of neutrals to leave occupied territory was previously a rule of the customary law.

In World War II at least 5 million persons were deported from occupied territories to Germany as part of the Nazi program of slave labor, persecution, and death. Although HR-1907 does not prohibit deportation per se, its articles with respect to the safety and order of the inhabitants and requisitioning of supplies and services lead to the conclusion that forcible deportation is beyond the legitimate activities of an occupying power. The International Military Tribunal and Nuremberg and the Military Tribunals under Control Council Order No. 10, pursuant to their charters that defined "deportation to slave labor or for any other purpose" to be war crimes, held the Nazi deportations to be unlawful. The enormity of the offenses connected with this deportation of civilians in World War II made it generally unnecessary for the tribunals to dwell extensively on fine points as to whether deportation apart from compulsory labor and persecution was illegal. Nevertheless, forcible deportation alone was held in the Krupp Trial to be a violation of customary law,[1] as well as deportation for an illegal purpose (for example, forced labor in the territory of the occupying power) and deportation that disregards recognized standards of decency and humanity.

Accordingly, GC-1949 provides that "individual or mass forcible transfers" and deportations of protected persons from occupied territory to the territory of the occupying power, or any other country, are prohibited regardless of motive. The total or partial evacuation of a given area is permitted if the security of the population or imperative military reasons demand. This evacuation is a protective measure, designed to remove civilians from areas of bombing and hostilities and to avoid their interfering with military operations. The language of the article would also appear to permit the evacuation of inhabitants of a particular area who are suspected by the occupying power of supporting a band of guerrillas. No such evacuation, however, may displace protected persons outside of the bounds of the occupied territory except when it is impossible, for material reasons, to avoid their displacement. Finally, evacuations must be effected under satisfactory conditions of hygiene, health, safety, and nutrition. Members of the same family are not to be separated. In any case, evacuated persons are to be transferred back to their homes as soon as hostilities have ceased in the area.

Similarly, protected persons may not be detained in areas particularly exposed to the dangers of war unless the security of the population or imperative military reasons otherwise demand. The purpose of this rule is to avoid a repetition of the disastrous consequences of the mass flight of civilians in World War II on roads exposed to bombardment.

On the other hand, the occupying power must not deport or transfer its own civilian population into the territory it occupies. This restriction upon the movement of nationals of the occupying power is intended to prevent transfers for political or racial reasons or for the purpose of colonizing the occupied territory. It does not prevent the occupying administration from being properly staffed. The rule grew out of the Nazi policy in World War II of deporting civilians from occupied territories and resettling the same areas with Germans.

Transfers of Internees. The minimum physical conditions of a transfer of civilian internees from one place to another—hygiene, safety, sustenance, and so forth—correspond to those prescribed for transfers of prisoners of war. In addition, as a rule, transfer must be by train or other vehicle instead of by foot. Before there is any transfer by foot, it must be assured that the internee is in fit condition, and he must not be exposed to excessive fatigue. Humane treatment must be provided that at least meets the standards of the detaining power in transferring its own armed forces. The standards of GPW and GC in this regard were largely a reaction against the infamous "death march" from Bataan during World War II in which thousands of United States and Philippine troops perished.

Release, Repatriation, and Accommodation in Neutral Countries. When the reasons for interning a person no longer exist, he is to be promptly released. This would be the case, for example, if he was interned because of military age that he later exceeds. Other provisions of the convention require periodic six-month reviews of the cases of internees. Moreover, the parties to the conflict are to endeavor to agree upon release, repatriation, return to their places of residence, or accommodation in neutral countries, of certain classes of internees. Children, pregnant women, mothers with infants, wounded and sick, and internees who have been detained for a long time are especially to be considered. In World War II a number of exchanges of this type took place. There is flexibility here that recognizes varying circumstances, including the desires of the internees—whether to be interned, to be returned to their situation before internment, or to be repatriated to their countries of origin—and their ability to maintain themselves if released. Accommodation in a neutral country may be particularly suitable when hospital treatment is necessary.

Internment is to cease as "soon as possible" after the close of hostilities (art. 133, para. 1), with the exception that persons awaiting trial or undergoing judicial sentence may be retained. The parties to the conflict must endeavor, upon the close of hostilities or occupation, to return all internees to their last places of residence, or to facilitate their repatriation. However, this does not mean that in all cases internment must promptly cease. The ICRC states that "the disorganization caused by war may quite possibly involve some delay before the return to normal." What is intended to be avoided is the indefinite prolongation of internment and lack of good faith action. Initial drafts of the convention presented to the Geneva Conference would have required that persons be resettled if conditions have changed. These attempts to meet the problems of refugees were considered, however, to go beyond the proper scope of the convention.

The expense of moving the internees is borne as follows:

- The detaining power bears the expense of transport to the place of residence at the time of internment, or, if custody was taken when the person was in transit or on the high seas, the cost of completing the journey or of return to the point of departure.
- The detaining power bears the cost of repatriation if it refuses permission to reside in its territory to a detainee who previously had his permanent domicile there. This appears to be the only place in the convention in which forced repatriation of an individual is expressly referred to.
- However, if the internee on his own or in obedience to his own government elects to return to his own country, the detaining power pays only the expense of his journey to the point of departure from its territory. The detaining power need not pay the cost of repatriation of an internee interned at his own request.

Economic Rights in International Conflicts

Taking and Destruction of Property. Both the Hague Regulations and the Geneva Civilians Convention restate the prohibition of the customary law on destruction of the property of private persons—or for that matter of the state—except if such destruction of property is absolutely necessary for military purposes. Likewise, both customary and conventional international law contain outright prohibitions on pillage, that is, looting of public or private property by members of the occupying forces.

However, both the Hague Regulations and the Geneva Civilians Convention of 1949 permit the belligerent occupant to take public or private property under certain circumstances defined with some particularity in the conventions. The basic law in this respect is laid down in Section III of the Hague Regulations, the articles of which have been extensively considered and interpreted in a number of cases arising before international and municipal courts.

Since the principal concern of this book is the protection of persons, no detailed attention is given to the treatment of public property belonging to the occupied territory of a state. However, it should be noted that the property of municipalities and of religious, charitable, and educational institutions (even those belonging to the state) are to be treated as private property. The category of property that may be seized from private persons under the Hague Regulations is defined as "all appliances, whether on land, at sea or in the air, adapted for the transmission of news, or for the transport of persons or things, exclusive of cases governed by naval law, depots of arms, and, generally, all kinds of ammunition of war" (HR, art. 53). In essence, this provision means of communication and transport and generally all types of military supplies and equipment in the hands of private persons subject to seizure.

Particular difficulties have been occasioned by the definition of the term "ammunition of war" (in the original French, "munition de guerre"). The term in the abstract lends itself to two polar constructions—one being "munitions" in their strict sense, as that term is understood in the English language, and the other embracing all supplies and equipment that could in any way contribute toward the prosecution of the war. The correct interpretation of this term was squarely posed in the *Singapore Oil Stocks* case, decided by the Court of Appeal of Singapore in 1956.[2] In that case it was held that privately owned oil in the ground, characterized as movable property, did not constitute "ammunition of war" because further fabrication, by way of refining, was required before it could be put to military use. The expression must, in light of the law of this case, be taken as referring to those supplies and goods that are susceptible of being placed to military use in their present condition without any substantial amount of further processing or manufacture. While the Singapore Oil Stocks case has clarified the law somewhat, continuing difficulties in the interpretation may be foreseen.

The requirement of the Hague Regulations is that private property of a military character must be restored and compensation fixed when peace is made. The draftsmen were apparently thinking about the situation in which telegraph apparatus or a wagon might be taken for the needs of the occupying forces, entailing a duty on the part of the authorities to restore the objects to the owners with suitable compensation for the use of their property. Under conditions of prolonged conflict, it can be foreseen that a substantial proportion of the private movable property that is seized will either be consumed in use or destroyed by the termination of the war. In that event, compensation for the use of the property until the time of its consumption plus the value of the property at the time of its consumption or destruction would be an element of the war accounts to be settled in the postwar settlement of financial matters generally.

If the occupying power requires any other privately owned movable property, it must requisition that property under article 52 of HR and may use such property only for the needs of the army of occupation within the occupied area. (The law in this respect is to be contrasted with the law concerning the *seizure* of property under article 53 of HR: Seized property may be used for any purpose whatsoever by the belligerent occupant, and there is no territorial limitation on the places in which it may be employed.) GC, article 55, goes somewhat beyond the Hague Regulations in prohibiting the requisition of foodstuffs or medical supplies if the requirements of the civilian population have not been taken into account. As to these items, the needs of the occupant are subordinated to those of the local population. The same rule is applied with respect to the supplies of civilian hospitals. However, even though the occupant has the duty of insuring the food and medical supplies of the population "to the fullest extent of the means available to it," this does not mean that the occupant must requisition for the needs of the civilian population generally. If food supplies were available in the occupied territory and could be secured through requisition it would be incongruous to require the occupant to bring in scarce food supplies from its own country in order to satisfy the needs of the population of the occupied territory.

Goods that are requisitioned must be paid for in cash at their fair market value, or a receipt must be given and then taken up and the property paid for as soon as possible. The funds with which to pay for requisitioned property can be secured by the occupant through "contributions" levied on the local population. These contributions are actually taxes levied by the occupant (sometimes in recent practice referred to as "occupation costs," as the case of Germany). These contributions must likewise be levied only for the needs of the army or the administration of the occupied territory. The governing principle thus seems to be that the occupied territory may be called upon to support with funds and supplies the army of occupation but not the war in general. The effect of the provisions relating to requisitions and contributions is to spread evenly over the population of the occupied territory the cost of privately owned property that is taken, exclusive of property of a distinctively military character, dealt with in HR, article 53.

The seizure of works of art is specifically prohibited by HR, article 56. In order to give fuller protection to cultural property, a Convention of Protection of Cultural Property in Time of War was concluded in 1954. The United States has not become a party to this convention because certain of its provisions relating to historic monuments and areas would prohibit conventional aerial bombardments, let alone the use of nuclear weapons (the improvement of accuracy through the use of "smart bombs" may lead to a change in the position of the United States).

If the belligerent occupant wishes to secure privately owned immovable property, such as a factory or quarters for the housing of troops, it must requisition the property on the same terms that it requisitions privately owned movable property. There are various devices that have been used in recent conflicts in order to circumvent the rules of international law with respect to the seizure and requisitioning of privately owned property. Contracts will be negotiated by the occupant with inhabitants of the occupied territory under duress; goods will be paid for in valueless occupation currency; and the imposition of exchange controls will cut off any effective payment for goods that are taken out of the occupied country against payment in the currency of the occupant. It is fair to say that the provisions of the Hague Regulations are not effective to protect the economic life of the occupied territory. The governing rule that can be enunciated today is only the general principle that the belligerent occupant has an obligation to maintain the economic health of the occupied territory to the extent of the means available to it. Thus, although Israeli administration of occupied Arab territories after the Six Day War often violated HR, the economy of the occupied territory was preserved and even prospered.

Financial Matters. Financial activities of enemy persons in the territory of a party to the conflict are governed by "trading with the enemy" legislation. In addition, if a party to the conflict applies a method of control to a protected person that makes him unable to support himself, the state has an obligation to insure his and his dependents' support. This is to guarantee the basic living conditions of enemy civilians who remain at liberty if they lose their jobs because of their enemy nationality, or if the head of a family is interned or deported, leaving his next of kin without support. Protected persons in the territory of a party to the conflict may also receive allowances from their home country, the protecting power, or relief societies.

In occupied territories the rules regarding the seizure of private property that have been described above apply equally to cash, securities, and tangible property. The occupying power may levy contributions in excess of local taxes for the needs of the army or for the administration of the territory. The existing tax system continues to function during the occupation. "Cash, funds, and realizable securities which are strictly the property of the state" may be seized by the occupying power (HR, art. 53). Bearer bonds and other bearer instruments of the occupied state are, of course, "realizable securities." It would appear that HR adversely discriminates against Socialist countries, where property that is held by the state would be privately owned in capitalist countries. There has been conflicting opinion about whether or not other debts that are payable to the occupied state or to its order may be seized, but the proper rule would appear to allow their seizure. The occupying power will not usually pay the external debts of the occupied state. It will supervise the spending of money to prevent its hostile use.

Sums of money taken from an internee are to be paid into his account. Currency may not be converted unless conversion is required by legislation in force or is consented to by the internee. The detaining power must provide internees a regular allowance that is sufficient for small purchases of tobacco, toilet articles, and so forth. Internees with personal funds as well as those who lack them are entitled to these allowances. They may keep ready money on their persons in cash or in scrip issued by the detaining power.

The internees may also receive an allowance from the power to which they give allegiance, from organizations, or their families; they are entitled to the income on their own property in accordance with the law of the detaining power. Any allowances from the power to which internees own allegiance must be the same for all categories of internees, such as the infirm, sick, or pregnant. The internees may draw on their accounts within limits fixed by the detaining power and may make remittances to their families and dependents to the extent consistent with the detaining power's legislation.

Labor. The labor provisions of GC, like those of GPW with regard to prisoners of war, permit compulsory employment of civilians at prescribed tasks and under prescribed conditions. In the case of civilians, the rules naturally differ depending upon whether the protected person is an alien residing in the territory of a belligerent, an inhabitant of an occupied territory, or an internee.

Aliens who are at large in the territory of a belligerent and have lost their jobs as a result of the war must be granted an opportunity to find work equal to that of the nationals of the belligerent. Their right to seek work is subject, however, to security considerations and to the provisions of the convention regarding compulsory labor. With respect to the latter, GC, article 40, establishes different rules for aliens of enemy nationality and others. Aliens of enemy nationality may not be required to work at jobs "directly related to the conduct of military operations" and may only be compelled to perform tasks "normally necessary to ensure the feeding, sheltering, clothing, transporting and health of human beings" (art. 40). All other aliens are governed by a national standard that provides that they may be compelled to work only to the same extent as nationals of the belligerent. *All* aliens compelled to work, however, are entitled to the same working conditions and safeguards enjoyed by nationals of the territory in which they reside.

Further safeguards are provided in the event that these aliens are unable to support themselves because of measures taken by the belligerent to restrict their activities. Article 39 requires the belligerent to insure their support and that of their dependents in that case. If their rights with regard to employment are infringed, they may exercise their right of complaint under article 30 of the convention.

Under customary law, as reflected in HR, article 52, the occupying power may requisition the labor of inhabitants of an occupied territory needed to meet the needs of the army of occupation. The demands for labor must be in proportion to the resources of the country and must not require the inhabitants to take part in military operations against their own country. Reflecting the broader scope of the occupant's responsibilities under article 51 permits compulsory labor to meet the requirements of the occupying forces for public utility services, and for the "feeding, sheltering, clothing, transportation or health of the population of the occupied country." But inhabitants may not be compelled to work at tasks that would either require them to take part in military operations or to use force to protect installations where they are performing compulsory labor. The convention establishes eighteen years of age as the minimum age for compulsory labor and enjoins the occupying power not to require inhabitants to serve in its armed or auxiliary forces and even forbids pressuring or persuading them to accept "voluntary enlistment" (art. 51).

To guard against the practice of deporting labor from the occupied territory, as was done in World War II, GC requires that work be carried out only in the occupied territory, "where the persons whose services have been requisitioned are" (art. 51). Workers are to be paid a fair wage and are entitled to the benefits of legislation in force in the occupied country concerning working conditions and safeguards. Moreover, GC, article 52, prohibits steps to create unemployment in order to induce workers to work for the occupying power.

Internees, whether aliens or inhabitants of occupied territories, are governed in labor matters by GC, articles 95 and 96. Unlike protected civilians left at liberty, they may not be compelled to work. Degrading or humiliating work is prohibited, as is work that would be a violation of articles 40 or 51, discussed above. The detaining power may employ medical personnel on behalf of fellow internees. It may also employ internees at specified tasks in places of internment, including duties connected with protection of internees against war risks, provided such persons are not required to perform tasks for which they are physically unsuited. The detaining power has full responsibility for working conditions, medical care, wages, and compensation for occupational accidents and diseases of internees. Working conditions and pay must conform to national laws and regulations as well as existing practice and may not be inferior to those for similar work in the same district. Wages are to be equitably determined by special agreement among the internees, the detaining power, and others, if necessary.

Law and Order

The law of belligerent occupation is concerned primarily, although not exclusively, with criminal law. It is also involved with the maintenance of the law and the courts in occupied areas. The occupying power may remove public officials and judges from office, but while they are in power it may not alter their status or apply sanctions or coercion against them should they not fulfill their office for "reasons of conscience."

Aliens in the Territory of a Party to the Conflict. In the case of protected persons left at liberty within the territory of a party to the conflict, the only provision of customary or conventional law indisputably having any application to them is article 37 of GC guaranteeing humane treatment to those in pretrial custody or serving a sentence.

Protected Persons in Occupied Areas. As part of its responsibility to maintain public order and safety in occupied territories, the belligerent occupant under the Hague Regulations has the duty, "unless absolutely prevented," to respect the laws in force in the country (art. 43). Additionally, it is expressly forbidden to declare the rights and actions of the nationals of the hostile party abolished, suspended, or inadmissible in a court of law. These provisions reflect the underlying concept of belligerent occupation, which is that although the occupant has the military authority and control that entitles it to take all legitimate actions required by the necessities of war, it is not substituted in law for the existing state and government as sovereign. The rules are also grounded in the consideration that it is conducive to a stable occupation and the quiescence of the inhabitants if the existing laws, institutions, and customs are respected to the maximum extent.

GC-1949 supplements HR-1907 by more precise rules that provide that the penal laws of the occupied territory may not be repealed or suspended except where they constitute a threat to the security of the occupying power or an obstacle to the application of the civilians convention. The latter exception is designed to make it abundantly clear that the occupant does not have to honor discriminatory and unjust penal laws like those of Nazi Germany. Similarly, the occupant must permit the local courts to continue to function in enforcing those penal laws, except if doing so would be an obstacle to the application of GC. (This was the usual interpretation of HR-1907 but not the invariable one.) There is no exception, as there is with regard to the substantive penal law itself, which permits the occupying power to deprive such courts of jurisdiction on the ground that they are a threat to its security. It was considered by the 1949 conference that the functioning of the local courts would never threaten the security of the occupying power and that such an exception would lead to abuse. However, there is the qualification that the courts must be capable of the "effective administration of justice"; this takes into account the possibility of a breakdown of the judicial system of the occupied states, as in the case where the judges have fled. In that event the occupant would have to establish courts to enforce the local penal law.

While the courts of the occupied state continue to administer the pre-existing penal laws of the occupied state, as described above, the occupying power may, and invariably will, establish its own system of penal laws to support its authority as administrator of the territory. GC-1949 provides that these laws may be promulgated,

- "To enable the Occupying Power to fulfill its obligations under the . . . Convention."
- "To maintain the orderly government of the territory."
- "To ensure the security of the occupying power, of the members and property of the occupying forces or administration, and likewise of the establishments and laws of communications used by them."

The occupant is permitted to enforce a wise variety of regulations with penal sanctions. For example, it may suspend the political as well as the military activities of the inhabitants; prohibit looting and black marketing; enforce curfews; establish regulations governing espionage, sabotage, resistance, possession of weapons, travel, work, and forbidden areas; provide for economic and fiscal administration of the territory; and, under article 78, establish procedures for the internment of civilians. In view of the expanded obligations of the occupying power under the Civilian Convention (for example, in connection with its obligation to insure that the population is adequately fed) the occupant will necessarily have to legislate on a wider range of matters than was true when HR-1907 was drafted.

The penal laws enacted by the occupant may not come into force before they have been *published* and brought to the knowledge of the inhabitants in their own language. The original text of this article presented to the 1949 conference required only that the laws be brought to the knowledge of the inhabitants in their own language. Under that text it would have been legitimate for the occupying power to bring its laws to the knowledge of the inhabitants verbally, by radio or loudspeaker announcements, without actual publication. The convention does not prescribe any particular mode of publication.

The penal laws enacted by the occupant may not be retroactive. The courts may enforce only those provisions of law that were applicable prior to the offense, and protected persons may not be arrested, prosecuted, or convicted by the occupying power for acts committed or for opinions expressed before, or during a temporary interruption of, the occupation, other than war crimes. These provisions emphasize the importance of the occupant's prompt promulgation of its penal law at the very outset of occupation. It has been said, however, that if offenses are committed against the occupying forces before such announcements, the occupying power may punish them by having recourse to the military law of the occupied territory. It is doubtful that an occupant can avail himself of local law in this way. It is to be noted that the prohibition against retroactive application of penal laws, as stated in article 67, is expressed as being directly applicable to the courts, regardless of any action of the occupying power.

The occupying power's courts, which may prosecute breaches of the penal provisions promulgated by it, must be "properly constituted, nonpolitical military courts" and must sit in the occupied country. Courts of appeal of the occupying power should "preferably" sit in the occupied country. A reference to civil courts in the draft submitted to the 1949 conference was deleted in order to prevent an occupying power from extending its domestic civil court system to the occupied territory and because of a fear that civil courts set up in an occupied territory would be likely to be political in character. Whether the military courts may have civilian judges is not clear. The words "properly constituted" (substituted for "regular" in the draft) are equally troublesome.

The dual system of justice in an occupied country may take various forms. While the occupying power may require that all offenses against its legitimate laws and regulations be prosecuted in its courts, it does not have to; the courts of the occupied country may be given concurrent jurisdiction over the same offenses. In any event, the occupation law is binding on the indigenous courts; and insofar as the occupant assumes jurisdiction, the converse is also true—that the regular penal law of the country, except as modified by the occupant, is binding on the courts of the occupying power. The occupant may, for example, decide that trials of inhabitants for offenses against other inhabitants, although involving violations of occupation laws, will be before the existing local courts, whereas the occupation courts will have jurisdiction of other offenses that are a direct threat to the members and property of the occupying forces or administration.

The military courts of the occupying power may apply only those provisions of law that are "in accordance with general principles of law" (art. 67). They are specifically directed to apply the principle that the penalty be proportionate to the offense. They also must take into account that the accused is not a national of the occupying power.

These principles are humanitarian refinements of the customary law. The term "general principles of law" is imprecise, but it may be surmised that it excludes such violations of "due process" as enforcement of excessively vague penal laws and arbitrary misconstruction of the announced law. This rule also reaffirms principles set forth elsewhere in the convention, such as the prohibition in article 33 against punishing a person for an offense committed by someone else. The principle that the punishment be proportional to the offense moves away from the older customary law, which tended to authorize the death penalty for almost every offense during wartime. Similarly, the new rule of the convention that the courts take into account that the accused is not a national of the occupying power, with its implication that leniency should therefore be granted whenever possible, is a departure from the notion once entertained in the customary law that inhabitants of occupied territory had a duty of allegiance to the occupying power.

GC-1949 contains rules that implement in considerable detail the principle of proportionality in punishment. These rules attempt to reconcile the need of the occupying power to be free from hostile acts with the inhabitant's right not to suffer arbitrary or unwarranted punishment. A distinction is drawn between lesser offenses and serious offenses. The lesser offenses are those that do not constitute an attempt on the life or limb of members of the occupying forces or administration; or a grave collective danger; or serious damage to the property of the occupying forces, their administration, or the installations used by them. For these, the maximum punishment is "simple imprisonment," which presumably is imprisonment of a less severe kind, not including imprisonment with hard labor or solitary confinement.

The right to impose the death penalty on a protected person for violation of the occupant's penal laws may be given only for espionage, serious acts of sabotage against the military installations of the occupying power, and intentional offenses that have caused the death of one or more persons. In addition, the death sentence is permitted only if the offense was punishable by death under the law of the occupied territory in force before the occupation began. The death sentence may not be imposed on a protected person who was under eighteen when the offense was committed.

Substantial controversy developed over these requirements when they were proposed and discussed at the Diplomatic Conference of 1949. A number of nations, including the United States and the United Kingdom, questioned whether the right to impose the death sentence, even for murder, espionage, or sabotage, should depend on the laws of the occupied country in force just before the beginning of the occupation. This would permit a government, which foresaw that its territory might be occupied, to abolish the death penalty in its own law to preclude its use by the occupant. Accordingly, the United States signed the Civilians Convention with a reservation to article 68 that declared that the United States would be free to impose the death penalty for the offenses specified in article 68, without regard to whether such offenses were punishable by death under the law of the occupied territory at the beginning of the occupation. A similar reservation was made at the time of signing by the United Kingdom, Canada, the Netherlands, and New Zealand.

GC-1949 contains certain entirely new rules relating to judicial proceedings against refugees who are nationals of the occupying power but who obtained refuge in the occupied country before hostilities began. These new provisions were responsive to Nazi roundups of German refugees found in Nazi-occupied territories. The convention makes it unlawful for the occupying power to arrest, prosecute, or deport from the occupied territory any such refugees who left the territory of the occupying power before hostilities began, subject to two carefully drawn exceptions: The first exception applies to offenses committed after the outbreak of hostilities and permits the occupant to arrest, try, or remove its own nationals who have violated laws while in the occupied country after the outbreak of hostilities. This would include the traitor as well as the common-law criminal. The second exception permits arrest, deportation, and trial of refugee nationals who before hostilities committed "common-law" crimes that, under the law of the occupied state, would have been extraditable under the law of the occupied country in peacetime. This protects political refugees but not a person who commits a crime before hostilities and who flees the country in order to avoid the consequences.

The rules as to judicial proceedings in the courts of the occupying power are based on the same principles that apply in the Prisoners of War convention, but they are somewhat less detailed. The requirements for a regular trial include procedures to insure that the accused is informed of the charges against him, has the right to present his defense and to be assisted by competent counsel, as well as the right of appeal. However, courts of appeals need not be established if the occupant's law does not provide for them; the minimum requirement is that in the absence of a court of appeals a convicted person must be able to petition against the findings and sentence to a competent authority of the occupying power. The protecting power is to be notified of a pending trial if the charge may involve the death penalty or two or more years of imprisonment, and the trial may not proceed unless there is evidence that this notification has been given. The protecting power also may take part in providing the accused with counsel, may have its representatives attend the trial, and is to receive notice of any sentence of death or imprisonment of two years or more. The death sentence generally may not be carried out until six months after it is final and after notification to the protecting power. In any case, the duration of pretrial arrest is to be deducted from a sentence of imprisonment. Accused and convicted persons are entitled to proper food and hygiene, medical attention, spiritual assistance, visits by representatives of the protecting power and the ICRC, and relief parcels at least monthly. If possible, they are to be separated from common criminals. In accordance with the rule against deportation, they must serve their sentence in the occupied country. If the country is liberated, the accused or convicted persons must not be taken with the forces of the occupying power in retreat but are to be handed over to the authorities of the liberated territory.

Interned Persons. Under customary international law, as noted above, aliens in the territory of a party to the conflict are subject to internment at the discretion of the power in whose territory they are. Under customary law, belligerent occupants also had resort to the practice, of placing persons who might be a threat to their security in internment. Who was to be interned, the procedures by which this was to be accomplished, and the conditions of internment were left to municipal law. Internment was simply left unregulated by the customary law, although such persons were from time to time, at the option of the interning state, granted the same treatment as prisoners of war.

The freedom of detaining powers has now been circumscribed by GC. Aliens in the territory of a party to the conflict and civilians in occupied territory may be placed in assigned residence (that is, required to stay in a prescribed building or area) or interned if such action is absolutely required by the security of the detaining power. In the case of belligerent occupation, decisions regarding assigned residence and internment are to be made according to published regulations of the occupying power. In order to maintain his safety, a protected person may be interned at his own request if his situation requires it. Finally, a sentence to imprisonment of an inhabitant of occupied territory who has been found guilty of an offense may be converted to a term of internment at the discretion of an occupation court.

The final decision as to the necessity for interning a protected person may be made after he has been interned. Article 43 requires the detaining power to establish a court or board for reconsidering the cases of protected persons who have been involuntarily interned or placed in assigned residence. The procedure includes a right appeal, and such cases are to be automatically reviewed semiannually. Subject to the requirements of military security in the case of spies or saboteurs under article 5, the names of such persons are to be given to the protecting power as rapidly as possible. When the reasons for internment no longer exist, the protected person is to be released. An occupying power may take no more drastic steps in the interest of security than placing civilians in an assigned residence or an internment camp.

As far as possible, a detaining power must accommodate internees according to their nationality, language, and customs. GC, article 82, in this respect corresponds generally to GPW, article 22. GC is also necessarily concerned, however, with the preservation of family life, likewise protected under the customary law enunciated in HR, article 46, which enjoins an occupying power to respect "family honor and rights." Family units shall not be broken up except for reasons of employment, health, or disciplinary confinement. If the internment of adults has left their children without parental care, they may request that the children be interned with them. Protected persons who are interned retain whatever legal rights are compatible with their status, such as the capacity to draw wills and to enter into contracts. This is the counterpart of GPW, art. 14.

The maintenance of order within civilian internment camps poses legal and administrative problems similar to those encountered in prisoner of war camps. However, international law takes account of the sociological distinction between military prisoners, whose social structure is based on command and control, and civilians, who are likely to bring into the internment camp a society in which familial, religious, social, and political norms are the bases of public order. The only rules of customary law that would be applicable to the maintenance of order within the internment camp are the general requirement of humane standards and the specific prohibition against group punishment for the acts of individuals. The laws in force in the territory in which civilians are detained continue to apply to offenses committed by internees during internment. Acts that are made punishable by camp regulations rather than municipal law may incur disciplinary action only.

The responsibility for the application of the convention is vested in a camp commander who shall be either a regular military officer or a regular civil administrator of the detaining power. Even when the commander is a military officer, discipline should not be ordered by strict compliance with military rules, although his obligations with respect to the posting of the convention, language of communication, and so forth, are similar to those imposed on the commander of a prisoner of war camp under GPW, article 41.

Article 100 is a partial enumeration of prohibited disciplinary measures based largely upon illegal practices by the Nazis in World War II German concentration camps. Essentially, it reiterates that acts and threats of violence, disrespect for persons, and inhumane treatment of internees may not be employed by the detaining power in the interest of camp order and discipline. It proscribes reduction of food rations, marking an internee's body in any manner, and other regulations that would impose conditions of dangerous physical exertion or moral victimization.

Civilian internees shall elect an Internees' Committee to represent them before the detaining power, the protecting power, the Red Cross, and other organizations that may assist them. The convention is deliberately vague about the number, composition, and leadership of the committee. The committee holds office for six-month terms and has obligations and authority similar to those exercised by Prisoner's Representative described in Chapter 2. Internees, like prisoners, have the right to file petitions and complaints without incurring punishment, as well as analogous rights respecting mutual assistance and correspondence.

Internees continue to be subject to the laws in force in the territory in which they are detained. Consequently, internees in occupied territories have all the protection afforded by articles 64 to 78 of GC-1949, as discussed above. On the other hand, GC-1949 makes applicable to internees in the territory of a party to the conflict only a selected part of these rules. This part covers articles 71 to 76 relating to the right of fair trial, notices to the protecting power, delay in execution of the death sentence, and the conditions of confinement of an accused or convicted person. Other rules about judicial and disciplinary sanctions of GC-1949 specially applicable to internees follow the rules of GPW-1949 with respect to penal and disciplinary sanctions against prisoners of war without exception but with various omissions. Almost all of these rules pertain only to disciplinary actions.

Internees may not be singled out as a class for judicial punishment; any acts by them that are not punishable judicially when committed by others may entail only disciplinary action. Leniency is to be exercised in choosing between judicial and disciplinary punishment, and double jeopardy is prohibited. Disciplinary punishment is limited to fines, not to exceed fifty percent of monthly wages, discontinuance of special privileges, two hours a day of fatigue duties or confinement, which may not exceed thirty days. Only disciplinary punishment may be imposed for escape or an attempted escape. However, the Civilians Convention does not exculpate escaping prisoners from judicial liability for lesser offenses connected with escape, or define successful escape, as does GPW. The procedures for imposition of disciplinary punishment—limited preventive arrest, speedy investigation, opportunity to know the charges, and explain the conduct—follow the Prisoners of War Convention, as do those relating to conditions of confinement.

Information Bureaus

There is no customary international law for civilians at liberty or in custody that is applicable to information bureaus. The notorious "night and fog decree" under which the Nazis secretly transported civilians in occupied territory to Germany for trial and punishment were cited by the Nuremberg Tribunal as evidence of the ill treatment of the civilian population. Now articles 136 through 141 extend to civilians many of the rights to public accountability that had been secured for prisoners of war through the Hague Regulations and the GPW Conventions.

Each party to the conflict must establish an official information bureau and transmit to it, within the shortest possible time, information concerning any protected persons who have been kept in custody for more than two weeks, or have been interned or placed in assigned residence. In addition to detailed identification data the information shall include news of transfers, releases, repatriations, escapes, hospitalizations, births, and deaths. There may exist a single information bureau for prisoners and civilians. The Civilians Convention, however, does not include any of the administrative and staffing regulations that are explicit in GPW. Thus, while employment in the bureau is a permissible occupation for prisoners of war, the law is silent on such employment for civilian internees. There is no civilian requirement analogous to the GPW obligation for neutral powers to transmit information regarding protected persons within their territory.

At the request of the protected person, the information bureau may not transmit information to the adverse party if its release could be detrimental to the person concerned or to his relatives. Such information, when communicated to the Central Information Agency, shall be held in confidence. Indeed, unlike prisoners who are obligated to supply certain basic identification information, civilians may withhold all such information from the detaining power.

Notes

1. United States v. Krupp (9 Trials of War Criminals before the Nuremberg Military Tribunals under Control Council Law No. 10) at 1327, 1429-1433 (1948), adopting the concurring opinion of Judge Phillips in United States v. Milch, 2 id. 860, 864-865 (1947).

2. N.V. de Bataafsche Petroleum Maatschappij and Others v. War Damage Commission, Singapore, Court of Appeal, 23 I.L.R. 810 (1956).

**Part II:
Application of the Law:
The United States in
Modern Conflict**

4   Korea

Introduction

The Korean conflict was the first attempt by the United Nations to prevent aggression through collective military action. It had, in addition to United Nations involvement, both civil and traditional international aspects. These hostilities were also the first major test of GPW-1949 (Geneva Convention Relative to the Treatment of Prisoners of War—1949) in the post-World War II era. The conflict is discussed in this book because of the attitudes shown by North Korea and the People's Republic of China (Communist China) toward prisoners of war and their entitlement to humanitarian treatment as prescribed by the Geneva Conventions. Important, too, is the position of the United Nations on nonforcible repatriation of prisoners at the close of the war.

Full-scale hostilities began in Korea on June 25, 1950, with the invasion of South Korea by North Korean forces. Events leading to that outbreak started at the close of World War II. In establishing terms for the Japanese surrender, the USSR and the United States agreed that Soviet troops in Korea would accept the surrender of Japanese troops north of the 38th parallel, while the United States would accept their surrender south of that line. Occupation of Korea by the Allied Powers took place on that basis, and it soon became apparent that the USSR considered the 38th parallel a political boundary.

After two years of unsuccessful efforts to reach agreement with the Soviet Union on the independence of Korea, the United States referred the problem to the United Nations. In August 1948 the United Nations established the Republic of Korea (South Korea) in the American zone, and Syngman Rhee was chosen as its first president. In reaction, the Soviet Union recognized the Democratic People's Republic of Korea (North Korea), which controlled Korean territory north of the 38th parallel.

By 1949 the United States had withdrawn its troops from South Korea, leaving only 500 men to assist in organizing the South Korean Army. During 1949 and 1950 the North Korean government took all measures short of overt war to create trouble in South Korea. Then, on June 25, 1950, the North Korean Army invaded South Korea. The United Nations Security Council passed a resolution that day, calling for an immediate cease-fire and withdrawal of North Korean troops to the 38th parallel. On June 27 the Security Council, noting that the North Koreans had not complied with its resolution of June 25, passed a second resolution recommending that the United Nations assist the

Republic of Korea in repelling the armed attack and in restoring peace and security in the area. A third resolution on July 7, 1950 requested United Nations members to provide military forces and other assistance and asked the United States to designate the commander of United Nations forces, or the United Nations Command (UNC). The United States had sent the initial forces that aided South Korea, and fifteen other United Nations member states eventually contributed military units to the United Nations force. (These included Australia, Belgium, Columbia, Canada, Ethiopia, France, Greece, Luxembourg, the Philippines, the Netherlands, New Zealand, Thailand, Turkey, Union of South Africa, and the United Kingdom.)

As United States resistance to the North Koreans increased in the summer of 1950, the North Koreans began to fan out, and fighting escalated throughout South Korea. The United Nations mounted an offensive from Inchon Harbor on September 15, which shattered the North Korean Army, and on October 9 the United States Eighth Army followed South Korean troops into North Korea with the approval of the United Nations General Assembly.

On October 26 military forces of Communist China entered the war in ambushes on South Korean units in North Korea. On November 25 they struck the United Nations Army in a massive and unexpected attack. Further advance by the United Nations forces was forgotten as efforts were concentrated on saving them from being overrun. By the end of December United Nations forces had been withdrawn from North Korea.

On December 31, 1950 the Communists began their second invasion of South Korea. Meanwhile, Communist China denied any official participation in the Korean war. Unconvinced, the United Nations General Assembly voted on February 1, 1951 to brand Communist China an aggressor. By late February 1951 the Communist advance was halted and United Nations forces again moved northward. In April 1951 they crossed the 38th parallel. After a two-phase Communist offensive in April and May of that year, the United Nations forces counterattacked and continued north.

On June 23, 1951 the Soviet representative to the United Nations proposed that cease-fire negotiations be undertaken between the participants. Truce talks began on July 10 at Kaesong but broke down completely by August. Meanwhile, fighting continued. Negotiations resumed in Panmunjon in November 1951, and the United Nations forces ceased offensive operations. Small clashes continued while the Communists used the relative quiet to build up their combat strength. The effectiveness of their army was neutralized, however, by command of the air by United Nations forces.

The prisoner of war repatriation issue occupied the armistice negotiations from December 1951 to July 1953. More than one half of the Korean prisoners and two thirds of the Chinese prisoners in United Nations hands did not wish to return to their Communist homelands. The United Nations proposed that no prisoners be forcibly repatriated. In an effort to change the attitudes of these prisoners, Communists planted organizers among prisoners captured at the front. Although an effective organization was achieved within the prison camps, it failed to change the attitudes of most anti-Communist prisoners.

As armistice terms were being negotiated, South Korea asserted it would not be party to any agreement that perpetuated the division of the country and demanded that the military offensive be resumed. On June 18, 1953 President Rhee ordered the release of 27,000 North Korean anti-Communist prisoners held under South Korean guard. But a new Communist attack convinced President Rhee that South Korea was dependent upon the United Nations for its existence, and he agreed to cooperate. On July 20, 1953 negotiations were resumed and on July 27 an armistice was signed.

Repatriation came soon after, and with it came knowledge of the extent of Communist mistreatment of prisoners. Nearly 60 percent had died from torture or neglect. On the United Nations side more than 23,000 anti-Communist prisoners held by the United Nations forces were screened by a Neutral Nations Repatriation Commission (NNRC) to determine their preferences concerning repatriation. In spite of threats from pro-Communist prisoners, only 700 agreed to go home. The remainder were later released, 15,000 Chinese going to Formosa and 8,000 North Koreans remaining in South Korea.

Type of Conflict

The Korean hostilities involved civil and international war as well as "enforcement" action by the United Nations. The governments of North and South Korea both claimed sovereignty in Korea, and their conflict was civil in character. The classification of United States involvement depends upon categorization of United Nations actions in Korea. Although United States forces were initially deployed in June 1950 in response to a direct appeal for aid from the Korean National Assembly (South Korea), aid was provided in accordance with the Security Council resolution of June 25, requesting member states to render every assistance to the United Nations in obtaining a cease-fire and withdrawal of North Korean forces to the 38th parallel. Therefore, the status of the conflict in relation to United States participation was the same as that of the United Nations, whose forces the United States was to command shortly thereafter.

The legal status of United Nations actions in Korea is a matter of debate. Many states hold the view that the United Nations' military actions were not "war." They argue that because the United Nations was limited to resisting aggression and restoring peace rather than completely subjugating the other side, its acts were enforcement or police action. The Soviet Union and Communist China, on the other hand, held that the United Nations was a belligerent in the conflict. The distinction is important because rules of the law of war turn on it.

However, the United Nations conducted itself in Korea as if all the laws of war applied, so the issue had little practical effect on its actions.

Communist China entered the conflict in October 1950 on the grounds of defending itself from United States aggression. It alleged that United States actions in Korea were a threat to Chinese national security. The United Nations General Assembly, however, named Communist China the aggressor in its acts against South Korean and United Nations forces. Regardless of the justification for it, Chinese involvement in Korea provided a traditional international aspect the war did not have until that time.

A wide variety of forces were deployed in the Korean War. The initial North Korean invasion force comprised 60,000 men of the North Korean Army, about 100 tanks, and 100 to 150 aircraft. South Korea had, in defense, elements of four infantry divisions along the border, one division in Seoul, and others in training farther south. The South Korean Air Force consisted of sixteen trainers.

The United Nations forces comprised national contingents of sixteen member states. Three army corps and one marine division were provided by the United States. The United Kingdom, the next largest contributor, provided two brigades. The United States also provided naval and air forces, as did the other contributors to a lesser degree. The ground forces provided by member states were incorporated as units into divisions of the United States Eighth Army. Naval and air units were handled similarly and were attached to the Seventh United States Fleet and the Far Eastern Air Force. These forces made up the United Nations Command. The forces of South Korea were also brought under United Nations command early in the conflict. The chain of command of United Nations forces extended from divisional commanders through the United Nations commander, the chief of staff of the United States Army, the United States Joint Chiefs of Staff, and the secretary of defense to the president of the United States. However, the senior military representative of each member state contributing forces was given direct access to the United Nations commander on "matters of major policy affecting the operations capabilities of the forces concerned."[1] The United States provided biweekly reports on the conflict to the Security Council and, after the Chinese intervention, held weekly conferences with the advisory "Committee of Sixteen"—a group of member states whose forces were serving under the United Nations Command.

Communist China initially committed two full field armies to the conflict. Estimates place their strength at a minimum of 200,000 men and possibly as high as 550,000 men. With North Korean units integrated into Chinese formations, as they came to be, the Chinese may have controlled as many as 700,000 troops. The Chinese Air Force was also committed to the battle.

Systems of Control

The Korean war erupted when the Geneva Conventions of 1949 were signed but had not yet been ratified by the parties to the conflict. The day after the invasion of South Korea, ICRC (International Committee of the Red Cross) cabled North and South Korea and proposed that the humanitarian principles of the conventions be applied. South Korea responded by signing article 3 of all four conventions (which contains minimum provisions applicable to "armed conflicts not of an international character"). North Korea stated it would apply the "principles" of GPW. The United Nations Command instructed its forces to observe all the provisions of GPW-1949. However, it did not undertake to apply the detailed provisions of the other conventions, because it did not believe it had the authority to accept them or the means to insure compliance with them, except by personnel under the control of the United Nations Command. With respect to acts of these personnel, it agreed to abide by the principles of all the conventions. The Chinese government did not recognize the conventions until July 1952 and did so then with reservations.

The United Nations Command attempted to designate a protecting power but was unsuccessful. On June 26, 1950 ICRC offered its services to both parties to the conflict. It expressed willingness to send a delegate to each of the governments to work out practical steps for implementing the conventions. This was not an offer to mediate the dispute, as some then interpreted it, but only an attempt to insure application of the humanitarian principles of the conventions. South Korea and the United Nations Command responded affirmatively to the ICRC suggestion, but North Korea did not respond at all.

On July 7, 1950 ICRC placed the services of the Central Prisoners of War Agency at the disposal of the belligerents. Also in July it was able to set up a delegation in South Korea. However, in spite of numerous attempts, it was unable to arrange for its delegates to enter North Korea during the conflict. Notwithstanding North Korea's failure to respond to ICRC appeals, the Central Prisoners of War Agency regularly transmitted data to it concerning prisoners in the hands of United Nations forces. By the end of 1951 these transmissions covered 192,495 PWs of whom 13,814 were deceased and 235 seriously ill. In return, ICRC received only two lists, covering 110 prisoners in North Korean hands. ICRC visited over 50 PW camps in South Korea and furnished regular reports to the detaining authorities and to the home powers of the prisoners. A few civilian prisons were also visited, and steps to improve the lot of prisoners were recommended to South Korea authorities.

The United Nations itself took steps to ameliorate the war's effects on South Korea. In late July 1950 the Security Council requested the United Nations Command to determine relief requirements of the civilian population in Korea, since an estimated one million people had been driven from their homes by the invasion and were concentrated in an area without sufficient food, shelter, clothes, or medical care.

In October the General Assembly established the United Nations Commission for the Unification and Rehabilitation of Korea (UNCURK); among its functions was the performance of relief duties as determined by the General Assembly. Aid and assistance were also volunteered by specialized agencies and subsidiary bodies of the United Nations—such as the International Labour Organization (ILO), the Food and Agriculture Organization (FAO), the United Nations Educational Scientific and Cultural Organization (UNESCO), the World Health Organization (WHO), the International Refugee Organization (IRO), the International Telecommunication Union (ITU), and the United Nations International Children's Emergency Fund (UNICEF). To bring these efforts together, a unified plan for Korean relief and rehabilitation was prepared by the United Nations Economic and Social Council and adopted by the General Assembly in November. The estimated cost of executing the plan from January 1951 to early 1952 was $250 million. Funds for this work were provided by voluntary contributions from member states.

The armistice agreement of July 27, 1953 established elaborate means for the repatriation or release of prisoners of war and the return of displaced civilians to their homes. Separate procedures were adopted for prisoners who insisted on repatriation and those who did not. These procedures are outlined below and their application is discussed under "Release and Repatriation."

With regard to the prisoners who wished repatriation, the Military Armistice Commission (established under the armistice agreement) was delegated, among other duties, overall responsibility for PW repatriation. It provided general supervision of the Committee for Repatriation of Prisoners of War (Repatriation Committee), which had operational responsibility for insuring accomplishment of the task. The Repatriation Committee, comprising three officers appointed by the commander-in-chief of the United Nations Command and three appointed jointly by North Korea and Communist China, was to coordinate the specific repatriation plans of both sides and supervise their execution.

The Repatriation Committee was to be assisted in its work by three joint Red Cross teams whose functions were also defined by the armistice agreement. The teams consisted of representatives of Red Cross societies of nations involved on both sides of the conflict: countries contributing forces to the United Nations Command, the Democratic People's Republic of Korea, and the People's Republic of China. One team assisted in the delivery and the receipt of prisoners at designated places. Its chairmanship alternated daily between representatives of the two sides, and its work was coordinated by the Repatriation Committee. A second team was to visit the PW camps of North Korea and Communist China and also to provide services to prisoners in transit to delivery and reception centers. Its chairman was to be a representative of the Red Cross Society of North Korea or Communist China. A third team, having duties similar to the second, was to visit PW camps under the administration of the United Nations Command. It was to be headed by a representative of a Red Cross Society of a nation contributing forces to the United Nations Command. The Red Cross teams and the Repatriation Committee were to be dissolved upon completion of the repatriation task.

Prisoners who did not insist on repatriation were to be placed in the custody of the Neutral Nations Repatriation Commission (NNRC) for disposition in accordance with the provisions of the annex to the armistice agreement. The NNRC consisted of members appointed, one each, by India, Sweden, Switzerland, Poland, and Czechoslovakia. The Indian representative was also the commission's chairman and executive agent, and India alone was authorized to provide the armed forces and operating personnel required to carry out NNRC's duties. It was also designated the umpire in accordance with article 132 of GPW-1949. The NNRC operated by majority vote and was the sole interpreter of the agreement that established its functions.

The armistice provided the following procedures for handling prisoners in NNRC's care. After receiving custody of prisoners, NNRC was to arrange for the nations from which the prisoners came to explain their rights to them; precautions were to be taken to prevent prisoners from being coerced to repatriate; interviews had to be conducted in the presence of a representative of each member nation of NNRC and of the detaining power; and prisoners were to be free to communicate with the NNRC concerning all matters affecting them. If they decided to repatriate, they were to make application to that effect to NNRC, which would vote on the validity of the application. Once their applications were validated, they were to be segregated immediately and delivered to the PW exchange point at Panmunjon for repatriation.

Those who did not exercise their right to repatriation within the time allotted for interviews were to be referred for disposition to the political conference recommended in the armistice agreement. If the conference did not settle the question within 30 days, the NNRC was authorized to declare the remaining prisoners relieved of PW status and, in conjunction with the Red Cross Society of India, to assist those who chose to go to neutral nations to do so. Upon dissolution of NNRC, responsibility for assisting those who later decided to return to their fatherlands was stated by the annex to reside in the authorities of the localities where the released prisoners lived.

A Committee for Assisting the Return of Displaced Civilians (CARDC) was established under the armistice to facilitate the return of displaced persons of North and South Korea to their homes. CARDC was to consist of four military officers, two appointed by the UNC commander and two appointed jointly by the commanders of the North Korean and Chinese forces. It operated under the general supervision of the Military Armistice Commission, and its duties were to coordinate the plans of both sides for assisting in the return of displaced civilians and to supervise the execution of the plans. CARDC was to make the necessary arrangements for movement of displaced civilians, select the points at which they would cross the Military Demarcation Line, arrange for security at the crossing points, and carry out other unspecified tasks that might be required to accomplish civilian return. Matters on which the committee were unable to reach agreement were to be referred to the Military Armistice Commission for decision. CARDC was to be dissolved once it had accomplished its mission.

Sanctions and Reprisals

Parties on both sides of the conflict claimed commission of atrocities by the other side and brought charges before the United Nations. As early as August 1950 the United Nations Command began to receive reports of atrocities involving military personnel and civilians on the part of forces of the North Korean Army. On August 19, 1950 General Douglas MacArthur publicly warned the premier of North Korea that he would hold the premier and his commanders "criminally accountable" for their acts "under the rules and precedents of war."

Even before the August reports, General MacArthur's headquarters had assigned responsibility to the staff judge advocate to investigate reports of atrocities and to prepare to conduct trials of enemy personnel who committed atrocities and other crimes in violation of the laws of war. The investigations were to meet two objectives; to obtain evidence that alone would permit trial of an alleged war criminal, and to collect additional evidence that, with evidence from other sources, would make possible the fixing of responsibility for criminal acts at levels above that of the immediate perpetrators.

The rapid advance by United Nations forces to the north in September 1950 revealed the truth of the reports of atrocities. Evidence from Korean civilians, captured North Korean and Chinese troops, and United Nations and South Korean troops repatriated in 1953 helped piece together the story. The atrocities fell into four main categories: (1) the killing of prisoners at or near the scene of battle; (2) the killing of Korean civilians for political reasons; (3) violent abuse, neglect, and killing of prisoners during long marches far behind the battle zone; and (4) abuse, neglect, and killing of prisoners in temporary or permanent prison camps. Cases of battle atrocities numbered in the hundreds, with the vast majority occurring in the first year of the war. These incidents, involving some 11,600 victims, happened either a few hours after capture or when the firing line approached the places of captivity. In the latter case, prisoners were killed, usually just before their captors retreated, in order to gain a military advantage.

The intentional killings of civilians occurred mainly during the early months of the war. Most involved imprisoned Koreans and were committed primarily by the North Korean Communist political security police. Business and professional people, government employees, landowners, and policemen—all considered to be political enemies of North Korea—accounted for most of the reported victims. An estimated 17,000 civilians lost their lives in this way.

Atrocities on the march behind the battle zone claimed the lives of an estimated 1,900 prisoners. Without food, suitable clothing, rest, or medical care, prisoners were marched from places of captivity to other PW collecting points or to temporary or permanent PW camps. Those too weak to keep up with the march were beaten to death and shot, and others were brutalized or killed on no pretext at all. According to available evidence, 81 such death marches took place, almost all between November 1950 and March 1951.

Deaths in the prison camps occurred from many causes—lack of food and clothing, disease, exposure to the elements, lethal injections, and shooting—and claimed the lives of an estimated 7,300 prisoners. North Koreans were in charge of 53 camps at which atrocities were reported; Chinese Communists, in charge of five; and both groups jointly supervised six. The Chinese Communists had charge of several large camps, including Camp Number 5 near Pyoktong, where the number of prisoners reported to have died is larger than at any other camp under enemy control. The evidence of atrocities was gathered with the expectation of identifying and trying perpetrators of war crimes after hostilities ceased. No trials were to be held during the war, however, because of the possibility of reprisals against prisoners held by North Koreans and Chinese.

As repatriation became the central issue of armistice negotiations in 1952 and charges of waging bacteriological warfare were brought against United Nation forces on the basis of "confessions" by prisoners in North Korean and Chinese hands, concern over the fate of Communist-held prisoners grew. The final repatriation agreement made no provision to retain prisoners suspected of war crimes, and no such trials were held. Instead, the United States placed the evidence of atrocities before the United Nations General Assembly and requested adoption of a resolution condemning such acts by any government against captured military personnel or civilians. The resolution was adopted by the General Assembly on December 3, 1953.

The USSR and North Korea alleged two types of war crimes on the part of United Nations forces—mass murder of prisoners and use of bacteriological weapons. The charge of mass murder on the island of Pongam in December, 1952 was brought before the United Nations General Assembly later the same month. The USSR alleged that the United States guards of the PW camp situated there killed 82 and wounded 120 Korean and Chinese prisoners who were demanding repatriation. The USSR requested adoption of a resolution condemning the United States for its acts and calling upon it to curtail such actions and to punish the offenders.

The United States explained to the General Assembly that guerrillas rather than prisoners of war from enemy armies were held at Pongam and that force was necessary there to prevent riot and pitched battles. Coded documents had been intercepted in several compounds disclosing plans for a mass break. Upon reports that internees of two compounds were massing, the camp commander dispatched 110 guards—20 armed with shotguns—into the first of the compounds where they were pelted with rocks by hundreds of rioters. It was alleged that the direction of the wind made use of tear gas impossible. When the rioters disobeyed an order to quiet down and disperse, volleys were fired to quell the riot. Following a full debate of the incident by the General Assembly, the proposed resolution of the USSR was defeated.

North Korea and China repeatedly accused the United States of using bacteriological weapons in Korea. The United States requested the United

Nations General Assembly to arrange for an impartial investigation of the charges to prove the falsity of the charge. General Assembly Resolution 706 (VII) established a five-nation commission to investigate the allegations, but North Korea and China refused to participate in the investigation. The United States presented proof that the confessions of its personnel to the use of bacteriological weapons were extorted during their captivity and were false. When the matter was discussed by the General Assembly, the USSR attempted to divert the discussion to a consideration of the Geneva Protocol for the prohibition of the use of bacteriological weapons, but the failure of North Korea and China to participate in the investigation was widely accepted as an admission that the charges were false.

Persons Entitled to PW Status

The question of persons entitled to PW status in the Korean conflict is clouded somewhat by the terms under which the belligerents were bound to the conventions. As noted in "Systems of Control," above, the North Koreans agreed to abide by the principles of GPW-1949, whereas South Korea signed the provisions of article 3 of all four conventions.

The United Nations forces presented a varied picture. States making up the United Nations contingents each replied separately to the ICRC request to apply the conventions. Some accepted article 3; others agreed to observe GPW-1929 and to comply with the principles of GPW-1949; and still others indicated they would apply GPW-1949 on a de facto basis. The United Kingdom stated that since North Korea had not acceded to them, the conventions were applicable only to the extent they represented accepted principles of international law. Later, some of the member states declared they would abide by any undertakings regarding PWs, entered into on behalf of the United Nations forces by the United Nations commander-in-chief, who instructed United Nations forces to observe all provisions of GPW-1949. The Chinese government, however, did not recognize the conventions until 1952, long after its entry into the war. Thus, all belligerents except China had some commitment to the conventions during the period that most prisoners were taken. What it meant in terms of practice was not clearly defined, but much can be inferred from their conduct during the war.

With the success of the Inchon invasion in September 1950, the number of internees in United Nations and South Korean hands increased from 6,000 in August to 90,000 one month later. The taking of prisoners was made difficult by the anonymity of significant numbers of enemy troops. A besieged Communist force, estimated by the Republic of Korea at 600,000, simply melted into the rural civilian population subsequent to the Inchon invasion. Civilians and North Korean infiltrators wore the same white garments and were virtually indistinguishable from one another, particularly to the Western troops of the United Nations Command. As a result, every Korean who was suspected of carrying a gun for the enemy was taken into custody by the South Koreans or United Nations Command, interrogated, and either interned as a prisoner of war or civilian internee or released.

The issue of the number of captives taken was second in importance only to the repatriation question itself at the Panmunjon truce negotiations. Of the approximately 173,200 internees held by United Nations Command at the time of repatriation, about 102,300 were North Korean soldiers, 49,300 were interned civilians, and 21,700 were Chinese. However, there was wide discrepancy between the public claims of prisoners taken and the more modest PW lists that were exchanged. The problem was compounded by escapes, disappearances, and clerical errors. In one instance, the United Nations Command had sent more than 2,000 prisoners through the screening cycle at least twice, and the refusal of many Communist prisoners to identify themselves made it difficult to correct errors. The return of 37,000 civilian internees to civilian life by the United Nations Command during the war was a factor in the negotiations on the exchange of former South Korean Army personnel impressed into the Communist armed forces.

Little is directly known of North Korean policy concerning prisoners of war because of its refusal to provide information on, or access to, internees during the war. Reports from prisoners indicate that in the early stages of the war the North Koreans tended to shoot captives rather than to take them prisoner. The period from capture until a permanent camp was reached was one of critical danger to detainees. Neglect, privation, and atrocities were frequent. Prisoners who survived capture were marched to collecting points 20 to 100 miles away. After a stay of two weeks to five months, they were marched again to more permanent camps. Incidents documented by the United States Army Korea War Crimes Division of the Judge Advocates Section, Korean Communications Zone, illustrate some of the dangers detainees faced.

For example, in July 1950 North Korean soldiers overran a group of eighteen to twenty wounded United States soldiers being attended by a regimental surgeon, wearing the Red Cross brassard, and an army chaplain, all unarmed. The North Koreans opened fire and executed the group.

On August 15, 1950 a mortar platoon was captured by North Korean soldiers and escorted to a nearby orchard where their boots and dog tags were removed and all their personal property taken. Their hands were tied behind them, and for two days they were hidden in ravines by day and marched at night. On August 17 their guards opened fire without warning and left them for dead. Only four of 38 United States soldiers survived the episode.

In August 1950 about 376 United States detainees were held in Seoul, awaiting movement north. About half were wounded but received virtually no medical care. They were beaten often, and their personal belongings were stolen.

In September they were marched to Pyongyang in a two-week ordeal. No medical care was provided, and food consisted of one or two rice balls per day. Detainees were left to find their own water, which they obtained from roadside ditches and rice paddies. The inevitable diarrhea and dysentery resulted. The sick and wounded who were unable to maintain the pace were summarily executed and left unburied along the roadside. Only 296 men survived the march.

On November 6, 1950 sixteen infantrymen were captured near Tagan-ni, stripped of their clothes and shoes, and marched five miles to a headquarters for interrogation. One of the officers was brutally beaten for telling the men of their rights as PWs. Soon after, they were led to the vicinity of Yieltong-ni, having been promised a warm meal, at which point their captors shot them.

Atrocities persisted even late in the war. On September 21, 1952 a United States forward observer team and a squad of South Koreans were overrun near Samchi-yong. The mutilated bodies of two United States and several South Korean soldiers were recovered the following day. One of the men had no head and his feet had been cut off above the ankles. Another had been bayonetted all over the body and his eyes gouged out. No means of identifying either body were found.

The United States Army Korea War Crimes Division of the Judge Advocates Section, Korean Communications Zone, concludes from its investigations that North Korean policy was to execute summarily any prisoner whose physical condition would burden their operations. This pattern was allayed somewhat in favor of taking prisoners as the invaders consolidated their grip on occupied South Korean territory. Before the United Nations Pusan-Inchon offensive of September and October 1950, North Korea held only 750 United Nations prisoners, all of whom were from the United States. However, murder became commonplace again as North Korean forces withdrew. The prisoners were moved northward, and approximately 200 died during the evacuation. Although it is difficult to estimate the proportion of persons detained to the number captured, it is known that by 1953 North Korea held 8,321 South Korean Army personnel, 3,746 United States personnel, and 1,377 personnel from other national contingents of the United Nations Command. Significantly, at this time South Korea and the United States counted, respectively, over 88,000 and 11,500 men missing in action. As noted above, the reconciliation of this disparity was a principal item of contention during the truce negotiations.

Standards of Internment

United Nations Command

All prisoners captured by South Korean and United Nations forces were detained by the United Nations Command. The principal internment camps of the United Nations were located near the city of Pusan and on the island of Koje-do. There were transit camps at Chungju, Taejon, and elsewhere, and a large temporary facility at Inchon established shortly after the United Nations offensive of 1950. At these, prisoners were housed in makeshift barracks and tents in the compound and in clusters throughout the city. The structures were primitive and unsanitary and were regarded as temporary by the detaining power. The number of compounds increased rapidly but never kept pace with the growing PW population. The quality of shelter, however, was gradually improved. The main camp at Koje-do when fully developed consisted of twenty-eight compounds distributed among four enclosures. Each compound was designed to hold 4,500 men, but many were overcrowded during much of the war. Compounds within the camps were clearly marked by the letters "PW" painted on corner tents, as well as by a Red Cross emblem that was illuminated at night. As the detaining power had military command of the skies at all times during the conflict, markings served principally to prevent inadvertent attack by its aircraft on its own facilities.

On September 1, 1950 Pusan Camp Number 1, constructed for 2,000 prisoners, contained 6,000 persons. On September 30, 1950 ICRC reported 6,284 prisoners taken at the Inchon landing. Only eight days later, on October 8, ICRC reported that the Inchon camp held 32,107 internees. A similar report of rapid build-up was filed on the transit camps at Chungju and Taejon, which during the same period held 222 and 452 prisoners, respectively. By December 10, 468 prisoners were taken in the vicinity of Pyongyang. However, the camp population had been redistributed by that time so that Camp Number 1 in Pusan housed only 2,252 prisoners. During the subsequent two to three weeks, the total PW population rose to 90,000. Ninety-five percent of the approximately 170,000 prisoners taken by the United Nations Command during the conflict were captured during the first year of the war.

The nutrition provided prisoners taken during the 1950 United Nations offensive was extremely poor. The ICRC delegate in Korea was at first of the opinion that the daily ration was insufficient to restore or to maintain health. However, "on being informed that it was about the same as that of the Republic of Korea army he declared himself satisfied."[2] Initially, the prisoners were fed Western-style rations. This food not only was disliked but appeared to aggravate the prevalent problem of dysentery. Even by January 1951, when the food had satisfactory caloric and nutritive value, it was flat and tasteless by Korean standards, lacking their normal strong condiments. Subsequently, the detaining power switched to regional fare. The official daily ration consisted of 5 hops (26 ounces) of rice, one half-hop of barley and wheat, Korean pepper sauce and seaweed leaf, and 230 wons in cash to purchase perishables from local merchants through a prison canteen.

Food was prepared by the prisoners. Serving of meals within the huge camps was complicated by a score of logistical problems. For example, the supply of bowls was insufficient, and portions were often measured out by hand. Moreover, as investigations into the reasons for disorder in the camps subsequently revealed, the hands that received the food usually belonged to the strongest prisoners. Nevertheless, monthly weight records indicated that prisoners gained an average of two to three pounds per month during internment.

The logistical obstacles that plagued the United Nations Command in supplying shelter and food did not extend to clothing. The prisoners' own clothing was supplemented with GI clothing and shoes. At the Inchon camp ICRC reported that all had "sufficient blankets, comforters and wraps" to protect them from the Korean winter. PW garments were not marked as such. However, a summer issue of red shirts and shorts in 1951 was a principal factor in some of the serious commotion preceding the breakdown of order in the Koje-do camp later that year. The detaining power was unaware of the odious connotation of red garments, which had overtones of Japanese imperialism and connotations of death to the Koreans. The red clothing was vigorously rejected by the prisoners. Upon repatriation, many North Korean and Chinese "People's Volunteers" discarded their serviceable United States clothing and footwear and chose to cross the Yalu river exchange point clad only in breechclouts fashioned from towels.

Each prisoner was deloused and vaccinated upon arrival at a camp. The principal public health problems in the large compounds were lack of potable water and sewage disposal. The waste-disposal system for a community of over 200,000 people on the island of Koje-do consisted of removal of waste by contractors in open containers that were dumped into the sea. Adequate hospital facilities, including X-ray and laboratory units, were available and were staffed completely by United States personnel. There were few Korean physicians among the detainees because professional positions prior to World War II had been largely filled by Japanese colonial administrators. The main field hospital at Pusan, which had 450 beds, was inspected and reported on favorably by ICRC on February 22, 1951. A clean bill of health was also given to the hospital at Koje-do, which, at that time, contained 3,000 of the total camp population of 91,662 men.

No religious activity or facilities were reported at any of the United Nations camps. Labor consisted exclusively of camp maintenance, which, like most other camp activities, was organized by the prisoners themselves. In many compounds, particularly those containing the 22,000 Chinese prisoners on Koje-do, there was a great deal of crafts and gardening activity. The ingenuity and proficiency of the prisoners was such that they actually manufactured wooden replicas of carbines and machine guns, which featured in the uprisings at Koje-do.

The voluntary recreational program of the detaining power included sporting events (principally volleyball), agricultural and literary activities, theatre, motion pictures and—at Koje-do—even a Boy Scout troop. Nevertheless, the recreational program was a mere gloss on camp life, which was tightly controlled by

Communist prisoners. The Civil Information and Education Program had a distinct political orientation and was viewed by Communist PW leaders as a threat to their leadership. Investigators identify it as a major focus on the riots of 1951.

The United Nations Command sporadically filed prisoner capture cards with ICRC, but full accountability was eventually achieved. The task was complicated by the high rate of capture after the Inchon offensive, the refusal of prisoners to cooperate with the detaining power, language barriers, and the sheer administrative magnitude of the task. At a time when Pusan Camp Number 1 contained 6,000 prisoners, the United Nations forwarded 1,535 cards to ICRC with the endorsement, "remainder in course of preparation." Full mail service, in accordance with GPW article 71, was available to prisoners at Koje-do by February 1951, after a board of United States officers mentioned it in a report on the causes of unrest and violence in the camps. However, ICRC reported that the Korean and Chinese prisoners made little use of the privilege. As a result of the same report, GPW-1949 was posted in all compounds in Korean and English. In general, the prisoners did not receive relief packages from their own countries, nor did they have any other personal communications with the outside during confinement. There was evidence, though, of substantial underground political communication with the Communist command during both the conflict and the Panmunjon negotiations.

North Korea and China

Any discussion of standards of internment maintained by North Korea and Communist China must consider the wide variations in conditions and treatment of prisoners from time to time and place to place during the conflict. Several periods comprising overall differences in PW treatment can be identified:

North Korean Offensive (June to September 15, 1950). Prisoners received generally adequate treatment during the offensive, with sufficient food and medical attention. However, there were isolated cases of mistreatment, sometimes related to interrogation or attempts to secure cooperation in propaganda activities. One thousand Americans captured during this period were transported by train from Seoul to Pyongyang and later to Mampojin.

North Korean Defeat (September 15 to Mid-November 1950). As the United Nations forces began their advance to the Yalu River in late September, conditions began to change. The Chinese moved in their troops and occupied former PW barracks, driving the prisoners outdoors into the cold, or into overcrowded mud huts. Food rations were drastically limited, and the number of brutalities increased substantially. During this time the first of the Death Marches occurred.

Large-scale Captures by the Chinese: Internment in Temporary Camps (November 1950 to March 1951). During the Chinese offensive large numbers of men were captured and held in temporary camps, and then moved—without transportation—over long (often circular) routes. Prisoners were often stripped of clothing. Those captured during the summer who had survived were held in severely overcrowded mud huts. Battle wounds were seldom treated, and malnutrition, dysentery, pneumonia, louse infestation, and frostbite were commonplace. Food, which was scarce, consisted of indigestible, boiled cracked corn.

The prisoners captured after the summer were held at transit points, which might be no more than holes in the open areas. PWs referred to them by names such as "The Caves" or "Death Valley." Less than half of the prisoners captured during this period survived. Both North Koreans and Chinese frequently committed atrocities. They demanded information and cooperation in propaganda efforts. Failure to comply meant a reduction in food and general care for everyone. Individuals were punished by confinement in vegetable pits or other cramped, solitary conditions. Physical punishment was common at this time.

The Chinese had an experimental indoctrination camp called "Peaceful Valley" by PWs. Here, under relatively good living conditions, about 500 Americans were subjected to intensive indoctrination, and a few were released at the front.

Establishment of the Permanent Camps (March to June 1951). Talk of an armistice led to the establishment of the first permanent camps along the Yalu. Conditions were better, although many prisoners died even before reaching them. At the first camp, Number 5, about one-fifth died before summer.

The North Koreans began organizing PW "peace fighters" in April and May. Prisoners in the transit camps where death rates were so high were offered an opportunity to move to Camp Number 12, "The Peace Fighter's Camp." Once there, they were threatened with return to the transit camps if they did not cooperate in indoctrination and propaganda efforts. The Chinese used subtler methods but the intent was the same.

Compulsory Indoctrination (July 1951 to May 1952). Treatment improved after the truce talks started. The Chinese then took custody of all PWs, although the North Koreans managed to hide General Dodd. Efforts to involve prisoners in the "peace campaign" were intensified, with compulsory attendance at lectures and discussions. Officers and noncommissioned officers were separated from private soldiers. In August a penal camp for uncooperative prisoners was established where conditions were harsh and punishment was severe.

In November 1951 Colonal James M. Hanley, judge advocate general of the United States 8th Army, released an unauthorized report on Communist war crimes. The Chinese were said to be responsible for 2,513 deaths among

American prisoners. The Chinese worked hard to refute the charges, and attempted to get favorable statements from American prisoners. The report aided PWs and prompted more efforts to prevent further deaths.

Controversy Regarding PW Repatriation (May 1952 to April 1953). In the United Nations camps a bitter conflict had arisen between the pro-Communist minority and the anti-Communist majority. At least half of the Chinese and North Korean PWs, who were anti-Communist, feared repatriation. Chinese Communists grew concerned that prisoners might be allowed to choose between communism and freedom, encouraging mass defection. As a result they changed their tactics with American PWs and compulsory indoctrination sessions were dropped. On March 28, 1953 they agreed to the principal of voluntary repatriation, and began a program to improve the appearance of PWs before they were exchanged.

Repatriation (April 20, 1953 to September 6, 1953). Armistice talks continued, but release of sick and wounded prisoners began on April 20 with the "Little Switch PW" exchange. Communists used the prospect of exchange as bait to make PWs cooperate further.

Intensive fighting occurred during the last weeks before the truce as each side sought a strong final position. Recent PWs were sent to Camp Number 9. Then the truce was signed on July 27 and the "Big Switch" exchange began, ending on September 6.

Throughout each period the Chinese Communists treated prisoners according to how well things were going in negotiations. Not all prisoners, however, were held among the major groups of PWs. Some, alone or in small groups, were paraded about in public; some were sent to interrogation centers; about 75 were pressured for confessions of bacteriological warfare; and a few ended up in North Korean hospitals.

Following the United Nations invasion at Inchon in September 1950, the North Koreans took their prisoners on the retreat to the Yalu River. Statements of the 120 survivors of the "long March" recount every kind of physical and mental privation. When the prisoners protested the location of a transit camp in a Chinese ammunition dump, specifically citing the Geneva Conventions, they were told that the exposure was a consequence of the indiscriminate bombing of peaceful Korean villages. Other transit shelters were not appreciably better; a major collecting station north of the Yalu, referred to as "Bean Camp," was set up in an old mining quarry. The camp held 700 prisoners, packed eight or ten to each eight-foot-square room.

The permanent North Korean camps were generally unmarked wooden compounds with corrugated metal roofs. Both the Chinese and the North Koreans refrained from marking the camps on the grounds that it would merely target the locations. Prisoners attempted to mark the camps themselves; in one case, by arranging cabbage leaves that were drying on the compound roof into the letters "POW"; in another case, by trampling "POW" in the snow. Both attempts were foiled by their captors. United States planes did, in fact, strafe unmarked PW compounds in the autumn of 1951, and the Chinese insisted that the location of the camps was known to the attackers.

The daily food ration in transit camps in 1950 was two 2-inch by 2 1/2-inch cakes of soybean, whole-kernel corn, millet, and sorghum. The evening meal included soybean soup and water. A special supplement for the sick and wounded was a mineral-rich turnip dish. An interned United States doctor estimates that this diet provided approximately 1,600 calories per day. The diet in permanent Camp V (administered by the Chinese) through the winter of 1951 also had a corn-millet base; the daily amount of food was variously estimated at 300 to 600 grams per prisoner, yielding as little as 1,200 calories per day. Because of the weakened condition of prisoners there, the food was inadequate to sustain health. Food was used as a psychological weapon, and men were fed when they attended lectures. However, the food was so little and so bad that prisoners were eating grass and bark off trees. The death rate in the camp that winter was 10 to 12 prisoners each day. A total of 1,500 of the 3,500 United States prisoners died in Camp V before repatriation. In most instances, diarrhea, beriberi, and pellagra among the dying were related to nutritional deficiencies.

The amount of quality of the food began to improve by early spring of 1952. Prisoners then cooked their own food on campfires. Mess groups were organized by nationality, and some prisoners, notably the Turks, supplemented camp rations with edible herbs and tubers.

The Chinese related food to propaganda. They took pains to explain to the prisoners that the prison fare they received was the equivalent of that given to class enemies (landlords, merchants, and property owners) in their own country. Prisoners who zealously studied and disseminated Communist propaganda were rewarded with better food. The Chinese did not distribute relief packages because the prisoners would then have enjoyed a higher standard of living than the captors. They argued that "prisoners of war must live like the poor peasants they were trying to enslave." The diet of North Korean and United States physicians (who worked together) included fish twice a week, a food that was denied the PWs. The nutritional standards of all prisoners improved as the negotiations at Panmunjon continued. Fresh vegetables began to enrich the diet in the spring of 1952. Rice and bread were substituted for cracked corn in the summer.

Prisoners were generally permitted to keep the clothes in which they were captured (although instances involving confiscation of clothes were reported); however, officers' insignia of rank were removed. At times, detainees were ordered to remove their garments in order to expose them to the elements as punishment. This appeared to have been particularly prevalent in early 1951, when other forms of torture were also common.

Recreational activities planned by the detaining power were largely confined to education propaganda. Toward the end of captivity, the Chinese began to provide books, tobacco, and other amenities. Prisoners were permitted to organize their own leisure activity. However, since the Chinese segregated officers, senior noncommissioned officers, junior noncommissioned officers, and enlisted men from each other and regularly transferred prisoners who appeared to be assuming leadership within their groups, organized activity by prisoners was negligible. Morale among the United States internees was extremely low throughout most of their captivity, a factor that investigators later related to poor nutrition, inadequate medical care, and, at least on the part of Chinese captors, the psychological effects of "brainwashing" activities.

Medical care of prisoners was inadequate due to a chronic shortage of medicine and medical personnel. When precious antibiotics were made available, the camp commanders often instructed the doctors to distribute them among such a large number of prisoners that few received any benefit from the inadequate dosage. Although camp infirmary facilities were usually inadequate, the principal Chinese hospital, which was housed in the Pyoktong Buddhist temple, was a competent facility. Prisoners receiving treatment at the hospital were requested to sign a statement that they had, in fact, received adequate food, medication, and medical attention. Medical care in the camps, like food and recreation, improved substantially during the truce negotiations, including monthly medical checks, for example, during which blood counts and urinalyses were performed.

The Chinese insisted that their "lenient policy" regarding contacts with the outside was superior to the Geneva Conventions and, in general, refused to respond to communications from ICRC. For example, announcements of the desire to deliver a ton of medical supplies went unacknowledged. Efforts to secure the names of prisoners through the Chinese Red Cross were equally unsuccessful. In December, 1951 the detaining power announced that it was holding 11,559 United Nations prisoners, of whom 3,198 were United States personnel; 571 were said to have died in the camps. The accuracy of these figures, particularly the deaths, was questioned by the United Nations Command.

Interrogation, Indoctrination, and Propaganda

The battle for the minds of prisoners of war is one of the stark chapters of the Korean War. A sharp distinction must be drawn between the conduct of North Korea and of China in this respect. North Korean efforts to interrogate and propagandize prisoners were limited, crude, and largely ineffective. To induce cooperation, they relied heavily on threats and beatings, and these measures often increased PW resistance to their demands. North Korean propaganda involving prisoners was aimed at influencing others, not the prisoners themselves.

Thus, prisoners were paraded through large towns for display to the local population, photographed, and the photographs disseminated widely throughout Communist countries. In addition, some prisoners who had not been mistreated were asked to make recordings—ostensibly for their families—that included a required word of kindness for their captors. These were then broadcast throughout the Communist world. While North Korean techniques were harsh and deceitful, the Chinese manipulated the total camp environment to sway men's minds.

The Chinese assumed control of several PW camps in 1951 and set about systematically to undermine the beliefs of their captives. Men captured by the Chinese, expecting North Korean brutality, were received instead with a friendly welcome. Notwithstanding the show of friendship, the first months of captivity were a struggle for survival because of marginal living conditions that the Chinese blamed on United Nations bombing of supply lines. The outward sympathy of the Chinese for the prisoners' plight kept the men from banding together against the Chinese. Morale was further adversely affected by Chinese offers of better food and medical care to those who were willing to cooperate with them.

The prisoners were marched north during the winter of 1950-51 and were moved into more permanent camps along the Yalu river in the spring. Although food, shelter, and medical care improved, psychological pressures were kept up to achieve the political and military objectives of their captors. The Chinese strategy was to destroy the formal and informal organization of prisoners and to force the men into psychological isolation. Emotional support from family and friends was severed by curtailment of contact with the outside world, and a variety of psychological techniques were employed that, through promotion of fear, distrust, and confusion, seriously weakened the will to resist. The Chinese program assumed the view that prisoners were military and political tools in the fight for communism. It involved total control of the camp environment for the purposes of indoctrinating prisoners with Communist ideology, interrogating them for military information and confessions with propaganda value, and developing a corps of collaborators within the prison camp.

The United Nations Command routinely interrogated prisoners in its custody for information having military value. It also prepared a voluntary indoctrination and educational program that it applied to prisoners in its hands.

The Chinese Program

In contrast with the crude interrogation methods of the North Koreans, the Chinese played subtly upon the fears and anxieties of prisoners to encourage their cooperation. Physical torture was rarely used, even when prisoners refused to cooperate. Chinese interrogation had three objectives: to obtain military information; to secure information that could later be used against prisoners;

and to break down social ties among PWs to pave the way for Communist indoctrination.

The responsibility for interrogation was assigned to the camp commander, who delegated it to his interrogation section. It was the job of one of his staff officers to collect intelligence information, while another, the education and training officer, analyzed and evaluated the data received. The interrogation section was staffed by trained personnel fluent in English and well informed about various aspects of life in the United States. These personnel were issued the following directive:

After the United Nations prisoners arrive at the camps that we have prepared for them, they will be organized and interviewed every day and night until they have told us all the information we need to help us teach them our policies. We are interested in all of the prisoners from the capitalistic countries, but we have a special interest and concern in the American prisoners. We have our best opportunity to win over these prisoners for use in the future. They are weak and don't understand what is behind the war in Korea. Be patient with them and don't beat them or shoot them. They are our prisoners for a long time.[3]

Interrogation sections were usually equipped with recorders, exposed and hidden microphones, two-way mirrors, and some form of a "lie detector." Open twenty-four hours a day, they were manned by interrogators with extensive backgrounds in United States customs who pretended to befriend captives to decrease their resistance and manipulated the captives' fear and anxiety to generate cooperation.

Interrogations were carried on at all stages of internment. Almost all prisoners of war were interrogated for information useful in the war effort. In addition, they were interrogated on their backgrounds and beliefs for data useful in the indoctrination program. Deception, harassment, repetition, implied threats, fear, accusation, surprise, biographical essays, walking conferences, cumulative files of interrogation data, and the "Mutt and Jeff" approach were among the interrogation techniques employed to achieve these ends.

Deception was used to create confusion, insecurity, anxiety, and mistrust to fellow detainees. The Chinese were quite successful in creating the impression that they could obtain any information from anyone. A variety of tactics were used to establish this idea. A prisoner would be drilled for hours, days, or weeks on a question. After his repeated refusals at great cost in time and energy, the interrogator would display a complete and often detailed answer, frequently written by a fellow prisoner. The same procedure would be used repeatedly with new topics until the prisoner could no longer guess what the Chinese did not know. In many cases, he began to believe that his compatriots had already provided the information, and would decide that his cooperation would not provide any further knowledge to the enemy.

The appearance of extensive collaboration was further promoted by presenting statements written and signed by prisoners. Frequently, signatures were obtained from detainees by requiring them to sign material copied from a manual or by requesting them to sign blank paper. They were encouraged to write on subjects like banking, industrial finance, and bridge building that on the surface appeared to have no military significance or propaganda value. To obtain cooperation, interrogators would display publications on the subjects, stating that all they were interested in was the prisoners' views. The information provided was then used in the indoctrination and propaganda program, for military purposes, and to blackmail the prisoners into further collaboration.

Prisoners were subjected to persistent harassment to destroy psychological resistance through mental and physical exhaustion. The detainee would be summoned at any hour of the day or night for lengthy interrogations. Often he would be awakened from his sleep or called during meals and told that if he would answer the simple questions requested of him he would be left alone. However, when he complied, he was subjected to more harassment, drilling, and blackmail—all to obtain additional information. Endless repetition of questions was used as a separate tactic to wear down stubborn subjects. This technique frequently revealed whether they possessed any useful information and often produced answers that were an attempt to escape the exhaustive questioning.

A complete file was compiled on each prisoner to convince him that the Chinese knew his entire background. The file held the results of all previous interrogations, information from numerous forms completed upon capture, data culled from letters he had received and written, and even blank paper bearing his signature. Faced with his file and claims of more data, some PWs succumbed and provided useful information.

The walking conference, an informal approach to interrogation, took advantage of the PW's hunger for social contacts and friendships. A walk outside the compounds provided a break from the monotonous routine. During the walk, the interrogator usually began by engaging the prisoner in personal and informal conversation frequently about United States sports figures, cities, or books. In this manner, the Chinese attempted to undermine his natural suspicions, lull him into a sense of false security, and make him susceptible to providing information.

A tactic referred to as the "Mutt and Jeff" approach was employed to woo the PW into a cooperative state of mind. His first interrogator would treat him harshly, hitting or kicking him when he refused to cooperate. After a time, he would be replaced by a second interrogator who would apologize to the frightened prisoner, assuring him that his assistant's behavior was crude and dishonorable and certainly unnecessary in view of the intelligence of the prisoner. This approach frequently fostered a sense of confidence in the second interrogator, which led the prisoner to cooperate.

Prisoners were required to write detailed autobiographical essays with particular emphasis on their social and cultural backgrounds. The purpose was apparently to determine which prisoners might be predisposed by background toward the Communist philosophy and thus make them apt subjects for special indoctrination. Once some information was provided, additional details were always requested. Clarification often led to inclusion of information about fellow prisoners and statements increasingly favorable to the Communist cause. Discrepancies were uncovered by requiring the prisoner to repeat the details of these autobiographies many times, making it impossible to remember all fictitious details. In this way material was provided for further questioning. Thousands of pages of personal and general information were generated in this manner for exploitation by the Chinese.

Implied and open threats were used to encourage prisoners to collaborate. The threat of disclosure of collaboration to fellow prisoners and the United States government induced many to cooperate or to continue to do so. The threat of nonrepatriation was very effective in inducing cooperation. The implied threat of physical violence for failure to cooperate, in light of known stories of North Korean torture and brutality, motivated many to cooperate to some degree.

Interrogations frequently lasted for hours, days, or weeks. In some instances the interrogator lived with his subject, attempting to create an atmosphere of friendship and trust in order to encourage discussion. Any weakness or inconsistency in the prisoner's beliefs was quickly exploited. The above techniques kept continuous psychological pressure on prisoners that, coupled with physical exhaustion, produced severe hardship.

The Chinese indoctrination program was based upon total control of the environment of the prison camp to achieve two major objectives: (1) to indoctrinate fully a small, select group of prisoners—through special training, counseling, and privileged treatment—in the theory and practice of communism; and (2) to undermine the faith of the prisoner in his country, its leaders, and its political system in order to foster sympathy toward the Communist cause. The Chinese organizational unit responsible for the indoctrination program was the training and education section, which was staffed with well-trained personnel, some of whom were educated in the United States. The staff prepared material for the indoctrination program, planned courses, developed class schedules, determined the scope of training, and selected the instructors. The training and education section operated through such subordinate organizations as:

- The Central Peace Committee, composed of prisoners and headed by two United States captives whose purpose was to help prepare literature for American consumption and prisoner indoctrination programs.
- The Camp Peace Committee, composed of prisoners who traveled to various camps to promote the Communist cause.
- The Company Peace Committee, ostensibly established by the prisoners for participation in the indoctrination program to give the impression that they rather than their captors were promoting it.

- The Squad Peace Committee, composed of prisoners in daily contact with the members of their squad who helped implement the lecture program.

Indoctrination began at the time of capture and permeated all daily activities in the internment camp. Steps were taken to control the social environment through destruction of ties among the prisoners. This was accomplished in the following way:

- Prisoners were segregated by race, nationality, and rank in order to apply special indoctrination pressures on members of minority groups and to undermine the internal structure of the group by removing its traditional leaders.
- Leaders were selected by the Chinese from among the lowest ranking soldiers to remind prisoners that their old rank system was no longer valid.
- Prisoners were prohibited from holding any type of group meeting not sanctioned by their captors.
- All forms of religious expression were prohibited.
- Informers and spies were systematically sought out and used within the camp, breeding mutual distrust and destroying personal contacts among prisoners.
- Loyalties to home and country were undermined by manipulating mail. Usually only mail containing bad news was delivered to prisoners and the rest was withheld. The Chinese then suggested to those who received no mail that their families and friends had abandoned them.
- Complete control of information was established. Only Communist press, radio, magazines, and movies were allowed to prisoners. This left them with no access to accurate information.
- Self-respect was undermined through public confessions, self-criticisms, and testimonials. After extreme harassment, usually in response to a minor violation of camp rules, a prisoner sometimes agreed to sign a confession that he later was forced to read before his fellow internees. Repeated use of this tactic tended to demoralize the prisoner and to generate contempt for him among other prisoners. The use of testimonials such as the germ warfare confessions signed by some United States Air Force officers had a decidedly negative effect on morale and provided an excuse for collaboration by other prisoners.
- Threats of death or nonrepatriation, occasionally supported by mock executions or severe physical punishment, curbed any violent resistance. Those who actively resisted Chinese indoctrination were referred to as "reactionaries" and were segregated in separate camps where conditions were worse and physical privation greater than in the regular internment camps.

In place of the prisoners' normal social ties, the Chinese substituted social relations that were possible only through common political activity. All prisoners were required to attend lectures that were followed by group discussions. The lectures elaborated upon the imperfections and injustices of the United States and other governments under which the prisoners lived before capture. Through fabrications and gross distortions of fact, the Chinese attempted to undermine prisoners' loyalties and beliefs in order to win sympathy or outright support for the Communist cause. Constant repetition of ideas and group participation in regulated discussion eventually influenced those with poorly formed political convictions. However, in general, this technique was ineffective because of the primitive nature of the propaganda and the insufficient training of the instructors, who failed to detect insincerity and mockery in the responses of prisoners.

The Chinese rewarded correct responses in group discussion or individual drilling sessions and punished incorrect statements. Food, clothing, and medical treatment were offered as rewards for cooperation and denied in response to resistance. Members of the "progressive" group—those prisoners who openly cooperated or collaborated with the Chinese—received special privileges and better food and medical attention when it was available. The "reactionary" group—those who openly refused to cooperate and actively resisted any attempt to be exploited—were segregated, sometimes sent to hard labor camps, and in general, received worse treatment than collaborators.

Propaganda activities were controlled by a propaganda branch within the training and education section of the camp. The propaganda staff coordinated its activities with those of the indoctrination group, determining what propaganda would be used in the indoctrination courses and adapting materials sent from China and the USSR to camp use.

The propaganda staff utilized the radio network, camp libraries, public address systems, recording equipment, and camp newspapers to constantly repeat its propaganda message. It was assisted in giving a Western slant to its material by Soviet experts and by a British and an Australian advisor. Like those in charge of the indoctrination program, the propaganda branch operated through various organizations in the camps, all staffed by prisoners of war. Among these were the Central Committee for World Peace, which maintained liaison with the North Korean government; the Propaganda Workshop, which produced propaganda; the Stalin Dramatic Society, which wrote and produced propaganda plays; and the Lenin Debating Society, which debated such topics as "the evils of capitalism," "who started the war in Korea?" and "the move toward communism."[4]

The Chinese attempts to convert prisoners to their views caused significant psychological distress among internees, and they were able to elicit a considerable amount of collaboration through unscrupulous manipulation of men in their care. Only a few prisoners were able to avoid collaboration fully and then only by ignoring completely the consequences to themselves and their fellow internees. The majority who collaborated did so in matters that seemed trivial to them but that the Chinese were able to turn to advantage. The techniques of breaking down spontaneous prisoner organization and activities did create strong feelings of social and emotional isolation and led to the psychological impairment of many prisoners.

United Nations Command Program

UNC (United Nations Command) intelligence procedures were patterned after those employed by the United States in World War II. After capture, prisoners were disarmed, searched, segregated, and quickly evacuated to the rear for more intensive interrogation prior to assignment to a PW camp. Most prisoners proved to be very cooperative, some even assisting patrols in rooting out guerrillas. A polygraph was employed in some of the early interrogations, and certain prisoners were temporarily detained for intelligence purposes prior to assignment to PW camps. However, the information acquired about prisoners of war during intelligence screening was not, as a general rule, reported to the camp administrators. Nor did the administrators attempt to develop an intelligence network among detainees through interrogation or any other means. Camp authorities were solely concerned with guarding the prisoners and preventing escapes.

In April 1951 the Civil Information and Education Section (CIE) was created and established as a special staff section of UNC Headquarters. Its mission was to initiate, organize, and operate a program of orientation and education for North Korean and Chinese prisoners and civilian detainees in UNC custody. The heart of the program consisted of orientation classes based on a series of instructional units.

Formal instruction began on June 1, 1951, and was carried on in United Nations PW Camp Number 1, at Koje-do. In each of the compounds where the program was given, CIE constructed and maintained an instructional center. Activities in the center were normally limited to the formal orientation program during daylight hours and locally produced drama in the evenings. Instructional materials consisted primarily of printed pamphlets prepared by the CIE Section. Several newspapers, magazines, and other materials were furnished to, or procured by, the CIE Section for use in the PW camps. In addition, CIE procured recordings of selected radio programs that were broadcast over the public address system. Moreover, United States documentary films illustrating certain instructional themes were obtained when available.

In addition to the formal orientation program, an educational program was implemented in physical education and athletics, vocational training and works projects, literacy training, instruction in health and sanitation, and a wide range of hobby and recreational activities. The objective of these programs was to instill attitudes favorable to the United States and the United Nations among prisoners and civilian internees.

On March 26, 1952 the chief of staff directed the elimination from the instructional materials of all overt anti-Communist propaganda. From that point on, prisoners were informed of the values of living in a democratic society, but treatment of the fallacies and weaknesses of communism in theory and practice was avoided. Instructional materials that were prepared prior to the change in policy were screened, and items inconsistent with it were withdrawn from the program. Camp disturbances in April 1952 resulted in reduction of the program; and reassignments of prisoners to new camps eventually resulted in its complete suspension at Koje-do. However, a complete program of orientation and education was extended to each of the new camps.

Operation Homecoming began on June 16, 1952 in anticipation of release or repatriation of internees, and included an orientation phase that consisted of five days of concentrated, intensive educational activities for civilian internees just prior to their departure for the distribution centers in the provinces. A continuous and intensive evaluation program was carried on by CIE at all PW camp locations. Achievement tests, attitude tests, public opinion polls, interviews, written expressions, performance tests, reports of recorders, observation, and tests of reading speed and comprehension were utilized. Evaluation showed that, generally, the program of orientation and education was received favorably by anti-Communists and unfavorably by Communists. However, delegates from ICRC objected strongly to the formal orientation program, which they referred to as an orientation in democracy. The delegates' objections were based upon their opinion that the principles taught in the program intensified the ideological struggles that went on in many of the compounds at Koje-do.

Control of Order

United Nations Internment Camps

The United Nations Command experienced significant difficulty in 1952 in maintaining order in its internment camps. Its main camps were infiltrated by Communist militants who organized pro-Communist prisoners and fomented violence to support the Communist position at the peace table. The United Nations Command described these incidents in its bimonthly reports to the United Nations Security Council.

At Koje-do on March 13, 1952 a work party of cooperative prisoners accompanied by a detachment of South Korean troops was stoned while passing an area containing a large number of Communist prisoners. The guards opened fire; in the ensuing fight twelve Communist prisoners were killed and twenty-six wounded, and a United States officer and a South Korean civilian were injured. ICRC was informed of the incident and was permitted to make an independent investigation.

On May 7, 1952 prisoners at Koje-do culminated a long series of incidents by seizing the United Nations camp commander, William Dodd, and issuing demands that specified the conditions under which he would be released. The seizure was intended to offset the United Nations Command announcement that almost half the 132,000 United Nations detainees would forcibly resist return to Communist control. To avoid bloodshed, the acting commander of Koje-do signed a ransom note that met the terms of the demands. With release of the hostage, the United Nations Command refuted the note on the ground that it was obtained under duress and instituted a full investigation of the incident.

Following the May 7 incident, steps were taken to insure control of prisoners by moving them into smaller, more separate compounds. The move started on June 10 with the 6,000 detainees in Koje-do Compound 76, one of the most violently pro-Communist installations. The plan was broadcast in advance to the prisoners, and at the time of the move they were ordered to form into groups of 150. When they refused to obey and openly armed themselves with improvised weapons, troops moved in to begin segregation. Using only tear gas, they were able to evacuate most of the prisoners without difficulty. However, a group of 1,500 resisted fanatically in one corner of the compound and were finally brought under control through use of tear gas and concussion grenades. Several of the ringleaders were segregated from the group. Once Compound 76 had fallen, the other compounds were moved without resistance.

A survey of Compound 76 after the riot uncovered 3,000 spears, 1,000 gasoline grenades, 4,500 knives, and an undetermined number of clubs, hatchets, hammers, and barbed-wire flails. The weapons had been fashioned from scrap materials and metal-tipped tent poles. As a result of this incident and as a further measure to insure control, the United Nations Command planned to construct additional camps away from Koje-do to house Communist prisoners who had already been segregated for return to Communist control upon repatriation. By July 12, 26,900 prisoners and internees had been transferred from Koje-do.

Two incidents at PW Camp Number 16 at Nonsan on July 27 and July 30 produced the first evidence of possible pro-Communist infiltrators into the nonrepatriate camps. Anti-Communist prisoners at Camp Number 16 alleged that a group of North Koreans who had been shipped from Koje-do were posing as anti-Communists in order to penetrate mainland camps and to cause unrest and violence. They planned to assassinate anti-Communist leaders and to take over control of entire compounds. In the July 27 incident they were seized by existing prisoner leaders, who interrogated them and attempted to beat confessions of resistance out of them. One prisoner died as a result of injuries and seven were evacuated for treatment. The United Nations report does not state what action, if any, was taken against the attackers. In the July 30 incident twenty-four North Korean prisoners were injured. Interrogation of the injured revealed that the violence was related to an internal struggle for power between pro-Communist and anti-Communist elements. Again, the United Nations Command report makes no mention of measures taken to avoid future incidents.

A series of acts of defiance by pro-Communist Chinese prisoners in the latter part of September at PW Camp Number 3, in the city of Cheju, culminated on October 1 in a planned attempt at open rebellion. Two platoons of United Nations troops forced their way into the compound to restore order and were attacked by prisoners armed with rocks, spears, barbed-wire flails, and hand-fashioned missiles. The prisoners were divided into three groups and had cover from a partially constructed rock wall. The United Nations troops opened fire; it took ten minutes to quell the riot. Fifty-six prisoners died in the incident, ninety-one were hospitalized, and nine received slight injuries. Nine United Nations troops were bruised by rocks or clubs. The United Nations Command report does not state what action was taken to prevent further incidents.

United Nations Command Report 57 for the period November 1 to 15, 1952 took the occasion of two incidents in November to discuss in general the problem of order in the camps. The incidents involved the capture of prisoners on two different dates that provided evidence of continuing intelligence activities within pro-Communist PW camps, with strong efforts being made to maintain contact with outside agencies. On November 5 two North Korean prisoners were caught while attempting to escape from PW Camp Number 1 at Koje-do. Sewn into the clothing of one of them were six petitions addressed to North Korean and Chinese officials and intelligence data concerning the PW camps at Koje-do. The petitions included accusations and threats against the United Nations Command and concluded with appeals for help and promises of continued harassment. Admissions of a prisoner who had escaped October 17 and was recaptured November 19 presented a similar story of documents passed to contacts outside the camp.

The United Nations Command concluded that these efforts were part of an overall network built up by Communist agencies in North Korea to utilize prisoners in the custody of the UNC to achieve their objectives. Communist negotiators at Panmunjon controlled riots and violence in PW camps for their propaganda value in turning free world opinion against the United States to weaken its leadership in the war, and in unifying opinion in Communist nations against the United Nations cause. The United Nations Command maintained that the Communist high command was willing to use every means, including murder, to maintain a hold on its captured personnel and to expend them in whatever actions would hurt or weaken the United Nations Command.

The United Nations Command took several steps to block such exploitation of prisoners. In addition to distributing confirmed Communists among smaller compounds as noted above, it instituted more frequent inspection of compounds by camp authorities, including careful searches for contraband. Security forces were strengthened, curfews from 1900 to 0500 hours were enforced, and intelligence systems within the camps were employed to gain data on identification of subversive leaders. A native village and isolated civilian homes were moved out of the camp area on Koje-do to make it more difficult for prisoners to pass messages to the North Korean high command. Steps were also taken to prevent the carrying of oral instructions by agents disguised as surrendering soldiers and to prevent the use of PW hospitals as centers for transmitting messages between compounds and enclosures.

Notwithstanding these steps, the United Nations Command did not believe it could guarantee the measures would stop all further violence. While the loss of communications would prevent the timing of outbreaks to coincide with developments at the armistice negotiations, the United Nations Command felt that the prisoner leaders knew without further instructions that incidents at any time could be exploited. Thus, during two attacks on United States personnel at Koje-do, reported in United Nations Command Report 58, prisoners were injured when United Nations Command troops attempted to segregate the assailants. The camp authorities indicated that incidents of that type would probably continue for several days as part of a plan to create incidents while ICRC delegates were inspecting Koje-do. The pattern of incidents and application of force to control them is a recurring theme in United Nations Command reports throughout this period.

North Korean and Chinese Internment Camps

No reports were found of North Korean and Chinese problems in maintaining order in internment camps. As described in earlier sections, the physical condition of United Nations prisoners in Communist hands was generally poor due to inadequate food, clothing, shelter, and medical care. These men were hardly in condition to cause significant disciplinary problems. In at least one camp, the Chinese felt confident enough of their control over prisoners to use only guard posts and walking guards. Even barbed-wire fences were not used at all enclosures there.

Discipline and Punishment

Actions by the United Nations Command

During the Korean conflict, neither the United Nations Command nor its national contingents took formal judicial action against prisoners in their custody. As noted earlier, conditions in the PW camps were generally orderly during the early part of the conflict. However, by August 1951 there had been incidents of violence among prisoners as well as between prisoners and their guards. The ICRC took note of these in its camp visits at that time, and questioned how the United Nations Command intended to comply with article 82 of GPW-1949 (which requires that PWs be subject to the laws, regulations, and order in force in the armed forces of the detaining power). In its report on these visits, the ICRC suggested that the United Nations Command make clear what law or code applied to disciplinary and criminal offenses and so inform the prisoners in its care.

In response, the United Nations Command issued an interim directive on the subject on September 5, 1951, which provided that:

- Trials of prisoners for postcapture offenses would be conducted by United Nations military commissions.
- Trials would be governed by the applicable provisions of the *Manual for Courts-Martial of the United States* (1951) concerning trials by military commissions.
- Prisoners would be subject to trial for all postcapture offenses, including, but not limited to, violations of the laws and customs of war; violations of the laws of the Republic of Korea; violations of rules, regulations, or orders of prisoner of war camp commanders or their authorized representatives; and other acts prejudicial to good order and discipline among prisoners of war.

In an explanatory letter to ICRC, the United Nations Command stated that prisoners held by the United Nations Command were held by the United Nations as the detaining power. In that capacity, it said, the United Nations could adopt, as its own laws, the procedures governing the armed forces of any of its member states. It indicated, however, that the United Nations Command was planning to adopt a system of law other than that of any one member nation.

On November 1, 1951 the UNC issued a penal and disciplinary code covering postcapture offenses. The code was divided into four major sections: (1) Articles Governing United Nations Prisoners of War—containing preliminary provisions and lists of penal offenses. (2) Procedure Governing Non-Judicial Punishment of Prisoners of War—containing the rules governing disciplinary punishment. (3) Supplemental Rules of Criminal Procedure of the United Nations Command—describing the special and general military commissions to be employed, membership and their jurisdiction, and the procedures for trials. (4) Regulations Governing the Penal Confinement of Prisoners of War—describing conditions and places of confinement of prisoners undergoing judicial or disciplinary punishment.

The special and general military commissions were unique in that any properly qualified commissioned officer of the United Nations forces in Korea, including the forces of the Republic of Korea, was eligible to be a member. Further, the convening authority was authorized to appoint as a member "any civilian who is a citizen of any nation of the United Nations, including any citizen of the Republic of Korea." If an offense involved victims of the national contingents, each such nation could, in the discretion of the convening authority, be represented on a commission. The persons subject to the jurisdiction of the commissions were those eligible for treatment as prisoners of war under article 4 of GPW-1949 and "all other prisoners interned by the United Nations Command in a prisoner of war or internment facility" (that is, civilians).

The listing and description of specific offenses followed familiar criminal code patterns, and covered such offenses as disrespect, mutiny, murder, manslaughter, assault, riot or breach of the peace, and riot or destruction of property. The supplemental rules of the code provided that the general and special military commissions were to have jurisdiction over all prisoner of war postcapture offenses, including all violations set forth in item 3 of the interim directive mentioned above. The code contained procedures drawn from GPW-1949, including notification of the ICRC of trials and death sentences, requirements for deferring execution of the death sentence, and requirements for appointing counsel. The *Manual for Courts-Martial of the United States* (1951) was incorporated by reference, and it governed rules of evidence and matters of interpretation.

Although the code was issued, prisoners of war were not tried. In January 1952 the UNC reported to Washington that trials for serious offenses would not be conducted while the armistice negotiations were in process, and this prohibition was adopted as a policy by the United States Joint Chiefs of Staff. The UNC believed that the steps already taken in segregating suspected criminals and investigating their acts had acted as a strong deterrent to further incidents. But violence in the camps became more severe, and General Clark, in July 1952, requested authority to try prisoners. He noted that in addition to the Dodd incident, preliminary investigations disclosed an estimated fifty-two cases (about equally divided between Communists and anti-Communists), which should be tried and that investigation had been completed on fourteen cases, involving 100 offenders, which were ready for trial.

From July through February 1953, General Clark pressed his requests repeatedly, and in February the Joint Chiefs of Staff authorized trials of postcapture offenses against United Nations security forces. General Clark was advised "to assure that the tenor of the trials maintained the aspect of routine legal proceedings." Concerning trials for offenses between prisoners the Joint Chiefs of Staff stated that there were serious political and legal implications that would require an overall review of the prisoner of war problem before a decision could be reached.

General Clark objected to the limited authority granted by the Joint Chiefs of Staff. He pointed out that most of the investigated cases involved offenses among prisoners, that the Geneva Convention was designed primarily to protect such persons, and that this protection could not be afforded without trials for infractions. His pleas this time were quickly heeded, and he was granted authority, effective March 3, 1953 to try prisoners for postcapture offenses involving acts of violence to all persons, whether prisoners or UNC security forces. However, trial was limited to offenses committed after segregation of pro-Communist and anti-Communist prisoners—a time measured from an administratively determined date of June 27, 1952. Approval was also given to try prisoners for participation in riots or breach of discipline after March 3, 1953, whether or not it involved violence to persons.

These grants of authority were conditioned on the adoption of certain procedures. First, the panels of the military commissions were to consist of approximately fifteen officers appointed from nominees of each of the nations contributing military forces. Second, certain amendments of the penal code were required: All records of trials were to be reviewed by boards of review convened by the commander, UNC. The boards were to have powers such as those conferred by articles 66c and 66d of the United States Uniform Code of Military Justice as well as power to commute and mitigate sentences. Actions of the boards of review were to be final except as to death sentences, which required confirmation by the commander, UNC. The boards of review were to be composed of at least three members, preferably from the various countries contributing UNC forces.

Still, the trials were deferred. The requirements for participation by the member states delayed action. By the end of March 1953 only four nations had agreed to serve on military commissions. With developments in April toward settlement of the armistice, the possibility of trials became remote. Eventually, it appears, the prisoners were repatriated or released without any trials by the UNC or its component forces.

The UNC applied administrative pressure in one incident in the Korean conflict to force recalcitrant prisoners to move into new PW camps. Three hospital compounds of Enclosure Number 10 at Pusan were controlled by hard-core Communist leaders who had resisted every UNC effort to restore law and order. The camp authorities had sufficient control outside the compound to prevent escape, but the prisoners had complete control inside, which prevented the authorities and medical personnel from entering to perform essential medical and sanitation tasks. After trying all methods of persuasion, the UNC attempted to secure control by moving the prisoners to a new compound in the immediate vicinity. Food and water were made available in the new compound, and the rebellious prisoners were informed that rations would no longer be delivered to the compounds they were then occupying. The prisoners were free to avail themselves of the facilities in the new compound and could do so by moving into them.

The ICRC, in a letter to the commander of UNC dated May 14, 1952, criticized this step, stating in part:

The withholding of food and water from PW's in three hospital compounds of UN PW Enclosure Number 10 constituted an infringement of Article 26, paragraph 6, of the Geneva Convention of August 12, 1949, relative to the Treatment of Prisoners of War which reads as follows: "Collective disciplinary measures affecting food are prohibited." The infringement is all the more serious as this measure was applied to hospital patients (postoperative, tuberculosis, mental, and amputee cases). . . .

The Chief of the delegation of the ICRC cannot agree with the point of view of the Detaining Power that in this case the transferring of prisoners' feeding-point to outside the compound is an administrative measure. In his opinion this measure could only be considered as such if its motive would be of an administrative nature. In the present case, however, the said measure can only be considered as a coercive means of enforcing obedience.

In a letter dated June 12, 1952 General Mark Clark reiterated the position of the UNC regarding its action, and stressed its scrupulous observance of GPW-1949. He reiterated the background of the situation, and asked that the ICRC report include a resume of the facts of the case.

In fact, the UNC actions were not successful; the prisoners still refused to move. It was not until United States troops, using tear gas and concussion grenades, entered the compound against strong and concerted resistance that control was secured. The ICRC protested the use of the concussion grenades. At least one prisoner was killed and several wounded in the incident, although the troops were efficient and well disciplined and held force to a minimum.

Actions by North Korea and China

Reports on the system of discipline used by the Chinese and North Koreans against prisoners come through individual reports by UNC repatriates. They indicate that the methods employed bore no relation to those contemplated by GPW-1949. The Chinese discipline was part of its program of total control of the prisoners' environment for military and political purposes. Discipline took such forms as providing a borderline starvation diet mitigated at times according to a prisoner's degree of acceptance of the Communist ideology and practices, self-criticism meetings, solitary confinement, and the selective use of physical torture.

Disciplinary measures varied widely. The following incident involving a prisoner who criticized Communist indoctrination illustrates what they could be at an extreme: Within his quarters, a prisoner who had been exposed to a political indoctrination speech stated that it wasn't worth the paper it was written on. A Chinese interpreter who had come into the room overheard the statement and took the prisoner to headquarters. The prisoner was tied up in front of headquarters, in view of all, and required to stand until he collapsed from exhaustion. The Chinese guard then dragged him away, kicking him and hitting him with the butt of a rifle in view of the prisoners in the compound. He was taken to an air raid shelter where he was confined and tied up with little food or water for three or four days. The prisoner was then returned to camp, where he died some three weeks later.

Other incidents elaborate the point. A United States junior officer who was a leader of an escape plan was punished by being trussed up with his hands wired behind him and then lifted by a rope thrown over a beam. A captain of the British Royal Artillery—who had distracted a guard, permitting three Americans to escape—was punished by having bamboo splinters inserted under his fingernails, having his fingers wired together, and having his genitals brutally twisted. A United States lieutenant who succeeded in escaping from an interrogation center was beaten (and later died). A United States major who criticized a statement of Chou En Lai in an indoctrination class was accused of a "hostile attitude toward the Chinese Government," a punishable offense under the law of China, and was beaten and hung by the hands.

Judicial proceedings were also highly irregular. One United States enlisted man was charged with having a hostile attitude, organizing a group to disrupt the work study program, removing pictures of Communist leaders and Picasso's "Peace Dove" in the camp library, falsifying a written autobiography, being a warmonger, falsifying answers to a questionnaire about his treatment, and, finally, stealing the prison-camp assembly bell. He was tried without defense attorney by a people's court of five Chinese officers presided over by the camp commander. He confessed to all charges except stealing the camp bell, for which a United States Army lieutenant was brought in to accuse him. While the lieutenant faltered in his accusation the first time, the next day he made the accusation firmly. Both the enlisted man and lieutenant received ten-month sentences.

An air force captain was brought before a Chinese military court in Mukden, China, on charges of bacterial warfare, psychological warfare, and violation of Soviet territory. The captain did not confess to the charges, although his interrogation resulted in solitary confinement, inedible food, quarters without heat, threats of nonrepatriation, incessant questioning at all hours, and a mock execution. During the trial he was imprisoned in a penitentiary in solitary confinement, allowed no lawyer or opportunity to present his case, and was required to stand at attention before the court for weeks. Eventually the trial was disbanded, but in September 1953, he was told that he would be repatriated if he would sign a statement saying he had been well treated. In compliance, he wrote that in his fourteen months of confinement he had received more of an education than in the previous twenty-nine years of his life.

At Kaesong, while awaiting repatriation, the captain was rejoined by the crew of his airplane. There they were put on a stage, had their pictures taken, and were told that they were at a joint Chinese-North Korean military and civil court. A document was read that referred to the prior trial of the captain and his innocence, but that in its last paragraph stated that the captain and the crew voluntarily admitted that *other* air force units had engaged in bacterial warfare. This was written into the record without signature of the captain or the crew. The captain attempted unsuccessfully to refuse repatriation until the statement was denied.

Harsh measures were used against seventy-eight American pilots accused of bacterial warfare by the Communists, and confessions were extracted from thirty-eight. The treatment of these pilots included the techniques mentioned above and others: threats of nonrepatriation and death, digging of their own graves and mock execution; isolation; conviction of war crimes, third degree questioning and physical abuse, substandard living conditions, denial of food, and other deprivations.

Release and Repatriation

The release and repatriation of prisoners of war in Korea was the result of long and difficult negotiation. Although the armistice negotiations had begun on July 10, 1951 (about a year after the start of the war), hard bargaining on repatriation began that December. By the end of April 1952 it was the only major unresolved question; an apparently irreconcilable impasse had developed. The United Nations Command insisted on the principle of nonforcible repatriation, while the Communists demanded an "all for all" exchange. In October 1952 the issue was brought before the United Nations General Assembly, which passed General Assembly Resolution 610 (VII) endorsing the principle of nonforcible repatriation. Renewed United Nations Command overtures in February 1953 regarding the sick and the wounded led to a breakthrough in negotiations. In March 1953 the Communists agreed to an exchange, which took place in late April and early May. Settlement of the entire repatriation issue followed; the Communists accepted the principle of nonforcible repatriation, and on June 8, 1953 agreement was reached on prisoners of war. The importance of the principle of nonforcible repatriation to the United Nations is shown by the battlefield toll: While negotiations were taking place concerning the approximately 11,000 prisoners held in North Korea and some 132,000 detainees held by the United Nations Command, there were 125,000 United Nations Command battle casualties and, according to United States Army estimates, over a quarter million Communist troops were killed, wounded, or captured.

A few prisoners were released during the war. Some were liberated by United Nations forces when they recaptured territory; these included eighty-six United States prisoners at Namwon, South Korea in September 1950 and twenty United States prisoners who escaped or were rescued from the North Koreans in the capture of Pyongyang. In their flight, however, the North Korean Armies massacred many United States and South Korean prisoners, most notoriously at Taejon in September 1950 and in the later retreat from Pyongyang. The Chinese Communist forces released fifty-seven United States prisoners for propaganda purposes in November 1950 at the start of their military drive into Korea. The pockets of these prisoners were filled with Communist leaflets in an apparent attempt to demoralize the United Nations troops. The next day the Communists started a massive offensive.

The United Nations Command insisted on exchange of PW lists prior to negotiating the terms of an agreement. In August and September 1950 it received word through ICRC of 110 United States prisoners, but this was the only official Communist report issued. In their broadcasts and news releases, the Communists had reported the capture of over 65,000 prisoners.

The Communists initially responded negatively to the demand for lists. They wanted to exchange prisoners without them, but submitted to the point at United Nations insistence. The lists were exchanged in December 1951 and disclosed that the Communists held only 7,142 South Koreans and 4,417 other United Nations personnel, of whom 3,198 were from the United States. In contrast, South Korean records showed more than 88,000 men missing in action, and the United States reported 11,500 personnel in the same category. The United Nations Command lists included 132,474 Communist prisoners, plus 37,000 men recently reclassified as civilian internees, which did not compare unfavorably with the 188,000 men listed as missing by the Communists.

When pressed on the small number of prisoners reported, the Communists stated that they had not detained all the persons they captured and that if they had done so their lists would have contained an additional 50,000 names. In explanation, they stated that they directly released those prioners of war who did not want to join a war against people who fight for their "real independence." While they admitted to "reeducating" prisoners, the Communists claimed that the many South Koreans who had been impressed into the North Korean Army had acted voluntarily.[5] At the same time, they did not let pass unnoticed the United Nations Command's reclassification of 37,500 persons from PW to civilian status, arguing that the United Nations Command should have included these persons on its lists.

In planning for repatriation negotiations, Washington suggested a flexible approach. The primary objective was to obtain release of the prisoners held by the Communists without giving a military advantage. However, the United Nations Command's first proposal quickly developed into firm insistence upon the principle of voluntary repatriation. The first detailed United Nations Command exchange proposal offered a one-for-one exchange of prisoners, with application of the principle of voluntary repatriation to the rest, who would be bound by a parole agreement not to bear arms later against their captors. In presenting this proposal, the United Nations Command adopted the Communists' own argument about the permissibility of voluntary action by the prisoners. The United Nations Command also proposed that South Korean Army personnel still impressed in North Korean service be reclassified as prisoners of war.

The Communists responded by insisting on an "all for all" exchange and did not change this position until the end of negotiations. However, following the initial United Nations Command proposal each side made concessions. It became apparent as early as January 1952 that both sides were willing to permit displaced civilians to go to the side of their choice, and this early understanding was eventually included in the armistice. The United Nations Command claimed that South Koreans captured by the United Nations Command while in the North Korean Army should be classified according to place of residence and, accordingly, need not be repatriated to North Korea. The Communists initially took the view that classification should be based solely on the army in which the prisoner was serving when captured. However, by the end of April 1952, they agreed that natives of South Korea held by the United Nations Command could choose to stay there. For its part, the United Nations Command dropped the idea of a one-for-one exchange and adopted the principle of "nonforcible repatriation" in place of "voluntary repatriation." The difference between the two concepts lay in the degree of resistance a prisoner would offer against efforts to return him to his home.

At this stage in the negotiations there was a hopeful shift from principles of repatriation to the practical question of the number of prisoners the United Nations Command would repatriate. It appeared that if the United Nations Command came up with a figure on repatriates that was not too low, agreement on repatriation could be reached. The United Nations Command negotiators estimated, without benefit of screening prisoners, that 116,000 might be approximately the number of prisoners it could repatriate.

When the United Nations Command stated its willingness to poll the prisoners to ascertain the actual number who would be repatriated, negotiations were recessed for this purpose. In the course of screening, the United Nations Command made every effort to include as many prisoners as possible on the list. At the request of the United Nations Command, who feared that the prisoners would be prosecuted upon their return to North Korean territory, the Communists provided a declaration of amnesty to encourage voluntary repatriation. (It will be recalled that Russian prisoners released by the Nazis in World War II were, in fact, imprisoned by Stalin upon their return to Russian territory.) PW and civilian internees were reminded of their family obligations, and no promises were made as to their disposition if not repatriated. If a prisoner said that he would like to return to North Korea or China, he was listed as a repatriate. If he said "no," however, he was questioned to determine the depth of his resistance. Unless he mentioned fighting to death, suicide, attempted escape at risk of death, or similar actions, he was listed for repatriation. It was in these respects that the United Nations Command shift from "voluntary" to "nonforcible" repatriation had significance, although the Communists initially failed to distinguish between the two approaches.

In spite of efforts to maximize repatriates, the results of the screening fell far short of the number the United Nations Command felt the Communists would accept. Of the approximately 170,000 military and civilian prisoners in United Nations hands, 70,000 was the number presented to the Communists as prisoners willing to be repatriated. This took the Communists by surprise and was completely unacceptable to them. Another attempt was made later in April to persuade the Communists to accept this figure through a package proposal, which combined the prisoner of war issue with the questions of whether airfields in North Korea could be rehabilitated after the Armistice and whether the USSR could be a member of the Neutral Nations Supervisory Commission. The United Nations Command planned to concede the airfield issue but to stand firm on the PW and USSR questions. This proposal was also futile, and the prisoner of war issue remained as the sole major question between the belligerents.

When United Nations Command screening to determine prisoner preferences started, the Communists mounted an offensive within the prisoner of war camps. Complete Communist organizations, which had loyalty enforcement squads and regular communications with the North Korean and Chinese military command, existed in some compounds. PW riots occurred that the Communists claimed were reactions to indoctrination by the United Nations Command aimed at forcing prisoners to abandon communism. As a result, the United Nations Command was unable to maintain order within these compounds, and screening was not possible. Prisoners at such locations were automatically listed as repatriates.

Discussions during the summer of 1952 brought no progress. However, on September 28 the United Nations Command presented three alternatives:

1. All prisoners who objected to repatriation would, after identification in the demilitarized zone, have a right to return to their captors.
2. All prisoners who objected to repatriation would be interviewed by neutral representatives in the demilitarized zone and be free to go to the side of their choice. The neutral representatives would be one or more of the following:
   a) ICRC
   b) Teams from impartial nations
   c) Joint teams of military observers
   d) Red Cross representatives from each side
3. All prisoners objecting to repatriation would be free to go to the side of their choice, without questioning or interviewing. This would be accomplished by each side under the observation of one or a combination of the following:
   a) ICRC
   b) Joint Red Cross teams
   c) Joint military teams

The Communists responded on October 8, 1952: All captured personnel of the Chinese army "must" be repatriated and Koreans "may" return to North Korea. The proposal of visits and classifications under the observance of inspection teams of neutral nations was acceptable. Thus, the Communists agreed to nonforcible repatriation of Koreans but not of Chinese.

With this latest rejection, the United Nations Command had no further proposals to make, and it called a recess of the plenary armistice sessions although liaison officers continued to meet. It was hoped that further progress would be made at the United Nations General Assembly, which convened on October 14. On December 3, 1952 the General Assembly voted against a USSR proposal calling for forcible repatriation and adopted instead a resolution presented by the Indian delegation. It provided that:

- The release and repatriation of prisoners should be in accordance with the principles of the Geneva Conventions.
- Force should not be used to prevent or effect "the return of prisoners to their homelands."
- Prisoners should be treated humanely at all times in accordance with the letter and spirit of the Geneva Conventions: No violence to their persons or affront to their dignity or self-respect should be permitted.

The Indian plan provided for establishment of a repatriation commission of four United Nations nations (two Communist and two others who were nonparticipants in the fighting) to receive all the prisoners in a demilitarized zone. Each side would have the opportunity to explain to prisoners their rights, and PWs would be free to return to their homelands. Prisoners who did not choose repatriation after ninety days would be referred for disposition to the political conference recommended in the armistice agreement. If, after another thirty days, there were any who had not been repatriated, the responsibility for their care and maintenance would be transferred to the United Nations.

The United Nations Command had proposed exchanging the sick and the wounded at the beginning of negotiations in 1951 and regularly thereafter. The Communists replied that this would occur with the first group of repatriates under the armistice. While there was no special reason to expect a change of heart, in February 1953 the commander-in-chief of the United Nations Command took advantage of a new resolution of the Executive Committee of the League of Red Cross Societies that called for the immediate exchange of the sick and wounded. He wrote the supreme commander of the Korean People's Army and the commander of the Chinese People's Volunteers, calling attention to the League's appeal and stating that the United Nations Command remained ready to repatriate such prisoners immediately in accordance with article 109 of GPW-1949. He asked whether the Communists were prepared to do the same and stated that the United Nations Command liaison officers were ready to make the necessary arrangements with their Communist counterparts.

The Communist reply on March 28, 1953 agreed to the proposal and added, "The reasonable settlement of the question of exchanging sick and injured prisoners of war of both sides during hostilities should be made to lead to the smooth settlement of the entire question of prisoners of war, thereby achieving an Armistice in Korea, for which peoples throughout the world are longing." The reply suggested that the suspended armistice negotiations be resumed.

Chou-En-Lai, the foreign minister of Communist China, went even further in a statement issued two days later. After reviewing the lengthy negotiations, he stated that the Communists "were prepared to take steps to eliminate the differences on the entire prisoner question" and proposed that the parties "undertake to repatriate immediately after the cessation of hostilities all those prisoners of war in their custody who insist upon repatriation and to hand over the remaining prisoners to a neutral state so as to ensure a just settlement of the question of their repatriation."

When the liaison officers met to implement the exchange, the atmosphere was cooperative. Operation Little Switch, the exchange of sick and wounded, began April 20 and was completed on May 3. The United Nations Command returned 6,670 North Koreans and Chinese in exchange for 684 members of the United Nations forces. The exchanges took place at Panmunjon, the site of the truce negotiations, without a general cessation of hostilities, and it was effected by military personnel on both sides. While Red Cross personnel did not participate in the actual exchange, ICRC delegates accompanied Communist sick and wounded to the exchange points and were permitted to observe the exchange. Mixed medical commissions were not used, nor did neutral or Red Cross representatives enter into the territory of either side to examine the prisoners being exchanged.

Upon the resumption of negotiations, the Communists first set forth a proposal that could have resulted in keeping prisoners in a neutral nation indefinitely. However, on May 7 they presented an eight-point proposal that had many similarities to the Indian plan and was accepted by the United Nations Command as a starting point for discussion of the final armistice terms. In this proposal the Communists gave up their earlier demand that prisoners be sent to a neutral country and proposed a five-nation neutral repatriation commission to take custody of prisoners not repatriated upon signing of the armistice. But substantial obstacles still remained. For one, the proposal would have allowed Communist explanation teams, unlimited as to number and accompanied by members of the Communist press, to travel over much of South Korea to persuade the nonrepatriates to return home. Secondly, the proposal lacked an acceptable method of assuring asylum without unreasonable delay to prisoners demanding it.

Moreover, the United Nations Command faced opposition from President Rhee concerning the proposed political division of Korea, the Chinese presence in North Korea, the lack of formal assurance of the future security of South Korea, and the procedures for determining the disposition of prisoners. He considered it an unwarranted encroachment in South Korean affairs to allow any troops of a neutral power to enter South Korean soil to take temporary custody of nonrepatriated prisoners or to offer explanations to them. He threatened to release the nonrepatriates unilaterally, without involving the United Nations Command. As a result, the United Nations Command on May 13 proposed to the Communists that the Korean nonrepatriates be released as civilians on the day of the armistice, with freedom to settle where they desired in North or South Korea, and that the Neutral Nations Repatriation Commission take custody of only the Chinese. However, in the interest of obtaining an agreement, this approach was abandoned, and the United Nations Command proposed that Korean and Chinese prisoners who were not initially repatriated be placed in the custody of the Neutral Nations Repatriation Commission under armistice provisions, described earlier in this chapter under "Systems of Control." The Communists accepted this proposal on June 4, and by the middle of June all that remained was to determine the date and arrangements for the armistice ceremony.

However, President Rhee continued to resist the repatriation agreement. His obstruction reached a climax on June 18 when some 25,000 anti-Communist Korean prisoners, guarded by South Korean security units, broke out of United Nations Command PW compounds in Pusan, Masan, Nonsan, and San Mu Dai. United States personnel at these camps, who were limited to the camp commander and a few administrative personnel, tried unsuccessfully to prevent the breakouts. Nine prisoners were killed and sixteen injured during the escapes. About 1,000 escapees were recovered, but the remainder disappeared into the local population.

The security guards were promptly replaced by United States troops. However, since they were reluctant to use force and generally confined their response to nontoxic gases and other nonlethal methods of control, many escapes were attempted and hundreds broke out. Sixty-one prisoners died and 116 were injured. The tally at the end of June showed 8,000 Korean prisoners in the camps where there had been about 35,400 on June 17.

World reactions to President Rhee's actions were critical. The president of the United Nations General Assembly wrote Rhee that the release of prisoners was a violation of the June 9 agreement on exchange of prisoners and the agreement between the Republic of Korea and the commander-in-chief, United Nations Command, which assigned to the latter the command authority over all military forces of South Korea during hostilities. A message from President Eisenhower similarly admonished President Rhee and suggested that other arrangements would have to be made unless he accepted the United Nations Command's authority to conclude the armistice. The Communists did not break off negotiations over the affair, but they expressed the opinion that the United Nations Command had conspired in the matter and questioned the United Nations Command's ability to induce President Rhee to comply with the prisoner of war agreement. To meet that problem, the United States assistant secretary of the army and the army chief of staff, sent as personal emissaries from Washington, entered into direct negotiations with President Rhee. An agreement was reached in which President Rhee promised to adhere to the armistice in return for promises that the United States would enter into a mutual security pact with the Republic of Korea and would provide it with economic and military aid. To meet Rhee's objections about the compromise of South Korean soil, the United Nations Command moved all the nonrepatriates to the demilitarized zone, notwithstanding the administrative and logistical problems of constructing entirely new PW camps and of transporting prisoners and the Indian custodial forces there.

Between August 5 and September 6, 1953 the United Nations Command transferred 75,823 prisoners to the Communists, of whom 70,183 were North Koreans and 5,640 Chinese. A total of 12,733 United Nations Command personnel were returned to the United Nations Command from North Korea. The Communist members of the Red Cross teams in South Korea and at the exchange point engaged in disruptive propaganda, alleging violation of their rights and complaining of mistreatment of prisoners. The North Korean authorities severely curtailed the activities of the United States and other non-Communist members of the team in North Korea.

On September 23 the United Nations Command turned over 22,604 non-repatriates to the NNRC in the demilitarized zone, and the next day the Communists delivered 359 United Nations Command personnel in the same category, of whom 23 were from the United States, one was from the United Kingdom, and 335 from Korea. PW interviews and explanations were delayed by the necessity of providing suitable accommodations for them and by disputes over rules of procedure caused by prisoner refusal to cooperate. The recalcitrant prisoners of war were politically organized and internally controlled by leaders who obstructed the interviews. When arrangements were made for explanations, groups of prisoners refused to emerge from their compounds, and others turned on the persons sent to interview them. The Polish and Czechoslovakian representatives of the NNRC wanted to segregate the leaders, but the other members found this undesirable or impracticable. The former proposed that prisoners be forced out for explanations, but the Swedish and Swiss members felt this would be inconsistent with paragraph 3 of the Terms of Reference under which NNRC functioned, which forbade the use of "force or threat of force" against PWs, and the Indian delegation would not require force without a unanimous vote. As a result, only 10 days were actually spent in providing PW explanations, and by December 23, when the explanation period expired, only a small proportion of prisoners had been through the process. While in the custody of the NNRC, 628 prisoners formerly held by the United Nations Command chose repatriation; two of the 23 Americans did likewise and were returned to United Nations Command control.

At the end of the 120-day period, the NNRC did not declare the release of the remaining nonrepatriates to civilian status as provided for by the armistice. It interpreted the armistice to require completion of the explanation process and referral of remaining PWs to the political conference before it could release them to civilian status. Since the NNRC regarded itself unauthorized to release the nonrepatriates to civilian status, it restored them to the custody of the original detaining powers with a caveat that these powers would have to agree on alternative procedures concerning them. The United Nations Command did not accept this interpretation and, on January 23, 1954 declared that the prisoners returned to its custody "now have civilian status."

A further question arose upon return of the prisoners to the detaining powers; it concerned the final disposition of PWs who had committed offenses while in the custody of NNRC. Seventeen anti-Communist Chinese and Koreans were held by India on charges of murder. Proceedings against at least three had been initiated by an Indian court-martial. These prisoners were returned to the former detaining power along with the others and, it appears, were released to civilian status without continuation of the charges. The legal necessity of this decision may be questionable. It does not appear to have been necessary for the United States to treat such persons as civilians in municipal as well as international law, since the requirement for release to civilian status can reasonably be considered to pertain to the treatment to be granted by the former detaining power but not to the status to be accorded by the prisoner's own country.

Shortly after the end of the 120-day period, the United States Army discharged its soldiers who refused repatriation. The announcement of the action indicated that the United States interpreted the armistice requirement on release to civilian status as preventing treatment of those persons as deserters.

Administration of Occupied Territory

Occupation by North Korean Forces

The government of North Korea claimed jurisdiction over all the country. In view of this and of the actions of the North Korean forces during the war, it appears that it considered the laws of belligerent occupation inapplicable.

North Korean forces quickly overran the South after crossing the 38th parallel in June 1950. By August the United Nations and South Korean forces had been pushed into a perimeter in the southeast corner of the country, but by the end of September they were back at the 38th parallel. During this period the North Koreans conscripted tens of thousands of South Korean civilians into the North Korean Army and forced civilian labor to carry military supplies. When the North Korean Army captured Taejon in lower South Korea, a North Korean "Home Affairs" Department was established to apprehend persons unsympathetic to the Communist cause. This office directed the arrest of business and professional men and other persons who had been employees of the Republic of Korea. All were interrogated and jailed under very crowded conditions in the Taejon city jail and within a Catholic mission. Military and civilian prisoners were interned together.

When the recapture of Taejon became imminent in September 1950, the Communists began killing groups of internees. Starting on September 23, several groups of from 100 to 200 each were removed from their cells, tied and bound to other prisoners, dumped into trenches dug for the purpose, and summarily shot. By September 26 the tempo of the killings had increased with the assistance of a North Korean Army unit. Thousands of bodies were ultimately exhumed. At Taegu, too, civilians thought to be against the Communists were murdered and left in rows in trenches by the retreating Communist forces.

Occupation by U.N. and South Korean Forces

United Nations General Assembly Resolution 376 (V) of October 7, 1950 was adopted at the time United Nations forces had reached the 38th parallel and two days before they advanced into North Korea. It supported the move north for the purpose of unifying Korea under an independent and democratic government and laid the basis for administration of North Korean territory. The government of the Republic of Korea, it will be recalled, had been established in August 1948 under the auspices of the United Nations, whose Temporary Commission for Korea supervised the free elections. The government of the Republic of Korea had subsequently been accepted by the United Nations in a General Assembly resolution adopted December 12, 1948, as the lawful government of Korea having effective control and jurisdiction over that part of Korea where the United Nations Temporary Commission for Korea had been able to observe and consult.

Reciting this background, the October resolution provided the framework within which Korea would become unified. Paragraph one recommended that:

1. All appropriate steps be taken to insure conditions of stability throughout Korea.
2. All constituent acts be taken, including the holding of elections, under the auspices of the United Nations, for the establishment of a unified, independent, and democratic government in the sovereign State of Korea.
3. All sections and representative bodies of the population of Korea, South and North, be invited to cooperate with the organs of the United Nations in the restoration of peace, in the holdings of elections and the establishment of a unified government.
4. United Nations forces should not remain in any part of Korea unless necessary for achieving the objectives specified in sub-paragraph (1) and (2) above.
5. All necessary measures be taken to accomplish the economic rehabilitation of Korea.

Paragraph two of the resolution established a seven-nation United Nations

Commission for the Unification and Rehabilitation of Korea (UNCURK), whose functions included representation of the United Nations in bringing about a unified government in Korea and other responsibilities for relief and rehabilitation. Until the commission took over in Korea, an Interim Committee of individuals from same member nations operated at United Nations headquarters to consult with and advise the United Nations Unified Command, which was initially composed exclusively of United States officers who were subsequently joined by a British deputy chief of staff.

Pending consideration of the problem by UNCURK, the Interim Committee's first action was to adopt a resolution on October 12, which, *inter alia*, advised the Unified Command to assume provisionally all responsibilities for government and civil administration of those parts of Korea that came under occupation by United Nations forces and that had not been recognized by the United Nations as being under the effective control of the Republic of Korea at the outbreak of hostilities. President Rhee objected to making the Unified Command the administrator of North Korean territories. He claimed that the Republic of South Korea had jurisdiction over all the country, as its constitution provided. However, the chairman of the Committee responded that the October 12 resolution was not unfriendly to the Republic of Korea and that it was merely a logical deduction from the resolution of the General Assembly of December 12, 1948, which stated that there was no government recognized by the United Nations as having legal and effective control over North Korea.

At other meetings during October the Interim Committee obtained the views of the Unified Command on its occupation responsibilities and gave advice and direction to guide the command. The occupational aims of the Unified Command were to establish peace and security, so that the Korean people themselves might solve their own problems. The command felt that the occupying forces should not impose a complete governmental administration in North Korea, although it might be necessary to establish a temporary substitute for the North Korean regime and to exercise some supervision and control over de facto provincial and local authorities there. It considered that the occupation would fall into three phases: The first would establish internal security, provide emergency relief and assistance, and establish law and order and de facto local and provincial governments. The second would be the transition to a unified government. The last phase would involve assumption of authority by the government of a unified Korea with only a minimum of United Nations forces remaining there.

The command's policy contemplated that, pending consideration by UNCURK, there would be as little change as possible in the fundamental structure found in North Korea, and that land reform measures and the ownership of industries would be maintained in their existing status. The tactical headquarters of the Unified Command would be separated as soon as possible from the headquarters directing the occupation, and the government of the

Republic of Korea would be consulted on occupational matters. The Unified Command issued these views as a directive to the commander-in-chief of the United Nations Command later in November, even though they were not formally approved by the Interim Committee.

When South Korean and United Nations forces had reached the Yalu river in October, the Unified Command reported that North Korean officials, even at the local level, had fled or been taken away as the United Nations forces advanced. It stated that provincial, city, and village administrations were being established and that United Nations military commanders had themselves selected local officials in some cases and in others the officials were elected by the people. In the absence of available persons from the North it appeared necessary to use persons from South Korea to be responsible for essential services, such as running trains. The Interim Committee agreed with the employment of South Koreans, subject to three conditions: that local persons be used to the maximum; that any South Koreans used or appointed by the Unified Command be under its full control; and that no one be used in a manner enabling him to bring political pressure on the inhabitants or to restrict their opinions. The Interim Committee also decided, as recommended by the Unified Command, to use South Korean currency in North Korea, since the United Nations forces had found no plates or adequate supply of North Korean currency and had decided against issuing occupation currency.

UNCURK was established in Seoul at the end of November 1950. As an initial act it consulted with President Rhee, who wished to extend the jurisdiction of the government of the Republic of Korea over the whole country as soon as possible. He proposed elections to fill the 100 vacant seats in the National Assembly (which had been left for representatives from the North), as well as the establishment by the government of the Republic of Korea of a civil administration in North Korea. The first North Koreans UNCURK interviewed— officials of two provinces in North Korea serving under the United Nations administration—also expressed the view that North Korea should be brought under the jurisdiction of the Republic of Korea. However, the commission disagreed with these steps, feeling that while the people in the North probably did favor joining the Republic of Korea, this was not a matter to be effected by an arbitrary act from without, but one in which those people themselves should take part. It felt, too, that certain legislative and administrative safeguards might have to be secured first and that military considerations of securing and maintaining order and lines of supply also supported administration by the United Nations Command. However, these questions soon became academic. In November the Chinese Communists invaded Korea in force and the war entered a new phase that sent the United Nations and South Korean forces into rapid retreat.

The armistice left the United Nations with a wedge of territory above the 38th parallel of approximately 2,300 square miles. The North Koreans were left with a small amount of territory below the 38th parallel in the extreme west around Kaesong. During the armistice negotiations the wedge occupied by the United Nations forces was in the zone of military operations, and UNCURK did not give it any fresh consideration. The area then was largely cleared of population. After the armistice, when the military situation stabilized, the area was resettled mainly by its original inhabitants, growing to a population of about 130,000. Administration of the territory both before and for some time after the armistice was in the hands of the commander-in-chief of the United Nations Command, as the military governor in the area. Few difficulties of administration occurred before resettlement, and after resettlement local affairs officers attached to the different commands maintained overall supervision and assisted the inhabitants to reestablish themselves. In August 1954, with resettlement completed and the population reasonably able to support itself, UNCURK recommended the transfer of administrative control of the area to the government of the Republic of Korea without prejudice to the final disposition of the territory. The transfer to the Republic of Korea was promptly effected.

Collection and Protection of the Wounded
and the Sick

Communist care of the wounded and the sick was similar to their general treatment of PWs. Doctors, medical facilities, and medical supplies were scarce. Even more fundamental, the wounded and the sick were often treated as expendable, particularly from the time of capture until they reached a permanent camp. The investigators of the United States Army Korea War Crimes Division revealed a Communist policy of summarily executing any prisoners whose physical condition would burden their operations. The bodies were always left unburied along the roadside.

Acts were reported in which the Red Cross emblem was ignored, and the wounded in a hospital were murdered. The incident involving the Red Cross emblem occurred in July 1950 when North Korean troops overran eighteen to twenty wounded United States troops being treated by the regimental surgeon wearing a Red Cross brassard. They immediately opened fire even though none of the men was armed. The doctor, although wounded, managed to escape. The hospital incident took place in Seoul on June 28, 1950. The invading North Korean troops immediately occupied the university hospital, in which 150 wounded South Korean soldiers were confined. Upon orders of the commanding officer, these patients were executed in their beds and buried behind the hospital.

A more coherent picture of what conditions were like is provided by the following account of a United Nations medical officer's experiences from capture through the early period in permanent camps.[6]

Captain X was surgeon of the 2nd Battalion, . . . and was taken prisoner in early December 1950. The Battalion Aid Station and Collecting Company, along with other units, were caught by a deep road block near Kunmori. The patients included four truck loads of litter patients . . . five ambulance loads of litter patients . . . and approximately 150 walking wounded. . . . Those captured were marched by the Chinese to "Death Valley," approximately 65 miles south of Pyoktong, which is on the Yahu River. The march took 25 days and they arrived at the Camp on 26 December 1950.

Within two or three days after capture there were about 100 prisoners in Captain X's group, of which ten to twenty were slightly wounded. No medical treatment was available. The prisoners had been stripped of all medical supplies and equipment and many of them had their overcoats and shoes taken away. This group was joined by other groups during the march and by the time they arrived at Death Valley, there were approximately 500 prisoners in the group. The officers and enlisted men were separated on the third or fourth day of the march. The marching was done at night. They would march two or three days [sic, actually hours] and then take half an hour break. This had an adverse effect on the men. The long marching period made them perspire and they became very cold during the long break. During the day they stayed in Korean mud huts. . . . Food consisted of about four ounces of cracked corn. . . . Water came from wells, rice paddies and melted snow. Two-thirds of the group developed bloody dysentery during the march. The men became weak and the weaker were helped by the stronger as long as possible then the weaker ones would be left with a guard. Frequently shots were heard and the guard who had been left with the prisoner would return to the column. Approximately 50 persons were lost on the march. . . .

Captain X separated the patients into three groups: the wounded, pneumonia and seriously ill, dysentery and miscellaneous. . . . There was not sufficient room to accommodate all of the sick in the hospital. Captain X visited the sick who were not hospitalized, twice a day. . . . He had repeatedly asked the Chinese for medicines, even to suggesting the Red Cross as a possible source, without avail. The only medicine provided until 3 January 1951 was Tannalbin, a Japanese product used for dysentery. Only enough of this medicine was available to treat two to three percent of the dysentery cases. . . . Prisoners were dying at the rate of two to seven daily between 26 December 1950 and 24 January 1951. . . . The United Nations doctors were not allowed to see patients except in the sick call area. Occasionally the Chinese doctor would visit the sick in the company areas when prisoners were seriously ill. About 75% of the prisoners the Chinese doctor visited would be given "pop-out" shots. Following the shots, the patient would appear more alert but usually died within 24 hours. . . . A patient had to be almost dead or have an obscure medical problem before the Chinese would allow him to go to the hospital. In spite of this, the UN doctors were severely reprimanded if they allowed deaths to occur in the companies rather than in the hospital.

While the experiences of Captain X concern the wounded and the sick in one set of circumstances it can be concluded from the other accounts of PW treatment that these conditions were probably typical.

Treatment of the Dead

United Nations Command policy in disposing of the dead was the subject of discussion between ICRC and UNC. The North Korean Army did not use identification cards, so it was impossible to identify most Korean bodies. The United Nations forces disposed of enemy battlefield dead by internment in recorded burial plots within established United Nations cemeteries. "However, health measures to prevent widespread disease and the exigencies of armed conflict" dictated on-the-spot group burials in many instances. Lists of graves were reported to ICRC. When possible, the UNC kept reports of internment of individuals that contained clues for future identification of unidentified remains, but this was infrequent because of the lack of identity cards or tags.

The Chinese and North Koreans did not account for prisoners live or dead, except for a list of 110 PWs reported early in the war. Prisoners in the Communist camps attempted to have the authorities allow identity tags to be used to identify the dead. In one instance reported, the attempt was not successful. Atrocities later investigated by the United States Army Korea War Crimes Division include accounts of mutilation of bodies, failure to bury the dead, burial in mass graves, and removal of identification from the dead.

Notes

1. Seyersted, United Nations Forces in the Law of Peace and War 35-36 (1966). (An exception was the British Commonwealth units that, after July 27, 1951, were combined into one division of their own under the United States Eighth Army.)

2. White, The Captives of Korea 25 (1957).

3. Department of the Army, Communist Interrogation, Indoctrination, and Exploitation of Prisoners of War 18 (Pamphlet No. 30-101) (1956), at 31.

4. Department of the Army, sup. note 3, at 54-59.

5. Hermes, U.S. Army in the Korean War, Truce Tent and Fighting Front 142-43 (1966) (prepared by the U.S. Department of the Army, Office of Military History); Vatcher, Jr., Panmunjon: The Story of the Korean Armistice Negotiations 129-30 (1958).

6. Biderman, March to Calumny, Appendix E, 289-97 (1963). (The account appearing in March to Calumny is taken from Grant, Operation Big Switch: Medical Intelligence Processing at 3-10, unpublished document.) Reprinted with permission of Macmillan Publishing Company Inc.: from March to Calumny by Alfred D. Biderman. © Alfred D. Biderman, 1963.

5 Vietnam

Introduction

The Geneva Accords, signed on July 21, 1954, divided the former French
Indo-Chinese colony of Vietnam at the 17th parallel, creating two approximately equal territorial areas. In North Vietnam the Vietminh administered the
Democratic Republic of Vietnam (DRV) created by Ho Chi Minh in 1945 (in the
wake of the Japanese defeat in World War II). In South Vietnam an amalgam of
non-Communist and anti-Communist elements administered the Republic of
Vietnam (RVN). For the leadership of both the North and the South, the
partition of Vietnam along territorial lines was essentially a military truce and
not a resolution of political differences within the country. The accords
provided that the political question was to be resolved by elections to be held in
July 1956. In the interim neither party was to make a military alliance or permit
the construction of a military base under foreign control. The estimated 600
United States advisors and technicians who had assisted the French were to be
allowed to be known in the southern zone.

Because of the greater severity of the colonial war in the North, the DRV
experienced substantial economic difficulties. It embarked upon an intense
collectivization program that resulted in an authoritarian state, differing from
those in Eastern Europe only in specific organizational features. The state was
under the control of the Communist Lao Dong, or Vietnamese Workers Party.
As a North Vietnamese prisoner was later to state, "Life ranged from hard to
grim." Even under conditions of relative peace, the DRV had to depend to a
considerable extent on assistance from other countries in the Communist bloc.

In the South, Ngo Dinh Diem succeeded Emperor Bao Dai. Diem, a
staunch-Nationalist and anti-Communist, emulated the Mandarin bureaucracy of
the pre-French dynasty. The economy of the South was strong enough to feed
its people and still produce a surplus rice crop. Its social fabric, however, was
fragmented, with two million Catholic and middle-class refugees from the
Communist North, an equal number of militant Buddhists, several other
powerful politico-religious faiths (Cao Dai, Hoa Hao, and Benh Xuyen), a trade
union movement, and strong student groups, each with its own values and
political ideals. In the course of consolidating his power, Diem primed the army
to repel any invasion across the 17th parallel. On October 24, 1954 President
Dwight D. Eisenhower wrote Diem offering United States aid "to assist the
Government of Vietnam (GVN) in developing and maintaining a strong, viable

state, capable of resisting attempted subversion or aggression through military means."[1]

The Communist leaders in North Vietnam based their hopes of national reunification principally upon the collapse of the Diem regime. However, a residue of the Vietminh resistance movement in South Vietnam, led by Le Duan, a senior member of the Lao Dong, was less sanguine. The party members serving under his command were to hide their arms in secret caches, reintegrate themselves in the society of South Vietnam, and remain inactive until called up to fight again should it become necessary. Thanks to United States aid, the government of Diem, far from collapsing, strengthened its position, resettled its northern refugees, and seemed well on the way to restoring peace in the cities, if not in the countryside. In March 1956 South Vietnam held elections for its National Assembly amid accusations of fraud and violence. At the same time it took the position that a nationwide election would be a travesty because the population north of the 17th parallel would be obliged to vote as directed. Two months later the United Kingdom and the USSR, co-chairmen of the 1954 General Conference and charged with conducting nationwide elections, postponed any effort to hold the elections anticipated in the accord.

When it became apparent that North Vietnam could not force Diem into elections, Le Duan proposed to the North Vietnamese Politburo that a people's war of liberation be launched in the South. From 1956 to 1958 the Vietminh were reorganized as the Veterans of the Resistance [subsequently to be known as the National Liberation Front (NLF)], appealing to villagers who had been alienated by the Diem regime. Guerrilla warfare began in earnest in 1958. The Diem government, referring to all military opposition as "Vietcong," meaning Viet Communists, moved to crush the guerrillas with conventional military force.

The Government of (South) Vietnam (GVN) gradually lost ground to the guerrillas. (From another quarter, Diem put down a military revolt in November 1960.) By the time John F. Kennedy became president of the United States in January 1961, the Vietcong had the upper hand in the rural provinces. Acting on the advice of missions led by Vice President Johnson and General Maxwell Taylor, President Kennedy gradually increased the number of United States advisors and irregular special forces from the 685 who were present in the country when he took office to 4,000 by the end of the year.

South Vietnamese defense forces were organized into a regular army of 150,000 men, a security force ("Bao An") of 60,000, 45,000 police, and a people's self-defense force ("Dan Ve") of 100,000. In October 1961 Premier Diem promulgated a decree declaring the whole of South Vietnam to be in a state of emergency. On December 14 President Kennedy recalled the United States declaration made at the end of the Geneva Conference in 1954 and reaffirmed that the United States was "prepared to help the Republic of Vietnam to protect its people and to preserve its independence." Arguing that the training, supply, and infiltration of guerrillas by the North was a continuing violation of the accords, the United States increased its assistance to South Vietnam under the principle that a material breach of an agreement by one party entitled the other to withhold compliance with an equivalent or related provision until the defaulting party is prepared to honor its obligations.

In January 1962 Radio Hanoi announced the formation of the Marxist-Leninist Vietnamese People's Revolutionary Party to serve as the vanguard for the NLF of South Vietnam. The 4,000 United States personnel in South Vietnam were increased to 11,000 by November 1962, a number roughly equivalent to the estimated infiltration rate from North Vietnam. Military operations, confined to the territory of South Vietnam, consisted principally of pacification measures involving local engagements and herding the rural population into 1,900 strategic hamlets to protect the civilians and to disrupt the Vietcong logistical and political basis for support. Both the Vietcong and the GVN strove to inculcate the traditionally inert and locally oriented peasantry with a sense of political identification; both persuaded, coerced, and intimidated civilians into participating in or supporting military operations.

In November 1963 the Diem government was toppled by a military coup d'état. Coincidentally, Presidents Diem and Kennedy were assassinated later the same month. When President Lyndon Johnson took office, there were 16,000 United States personnel in Vietnam. But by August 1964, with United States combat forces at 25,000, the tenor of the conflict changed. North Vietnamese torpedo boats attacked the United States destroyer *Maddox* in the Gulf of Tonkin, and the United States carried out retaliatory strikes against naval installations in North Vietnam. United States troop strength gradually increased to over one half million during President Johnson's term in office. The military character of the war from the Gulf of Tonkin incident until the onset of the Paris truce negotiations in November of 1968 was one of continued escalation by the principal parties to the conflict, accompanied by increased participation by the international community.

In February 1965 the United States began conducting air raids north of the 17th parallel. In August United States ground troops engaged in their first major direct confrontation with the Vietcong. Australia, Korea, Thailand, and the Philippines committed troops and supplies to the cause of the GVN. The USSR, Communist China, North Korea, and Mongolia supported North Vietnam with economic and military assistance. It was not until peace talks commenced in Paris in 1968 that North Vietnam even conceded the presence of any of its forces in the South; as late as 1969 North Vietnamese negotiators in Paris insisted that they were not holding any United States prisoners of war—just war criminals who were captured during acts of unprovoked aggression on the DRV.

From 1970 through 1972 the peace negotiations were characterized by offers, withdrawals, and rejections of alternate plans by all parties involving political settlement and repatriation of prisoners. Negotiations were punctuated by unilateral releases of the wounded and sick by the GVN and sporadic releases of United States airmen by the DRV. President Richard M. Nixon made the return of PWs a principal political issue in domestic politics as well as in the Paris negotiations. In 1973 the balance of United States prisoners were repatriated in a series of releases in consideration of the total withdrawal of foreign forces from Vietnamese soil. A fragile truce restrained the Vietnamese advisors as the conflict gradually reverted from a mixed international-civil basis to a civil conflict. United States combat troops were fully withdrawn by the end of 1973 and logistical personnel were largely withdrawn by the end of 1974. With the cessation of American assistance the forces of South Vietnam crumbled before North Vietnamese and Viet Cong onslaughts.

Type of Conflict

Although the Vietnam conflict directly involved the military forces of eight nations (Australia, Korea, New Zealand, the Philippines, Thailand, United States, North Vietnam, South Vietnam) and the logistical involvement of at least thirty others, there is still debate over the nature of the conflict. Thus, according to United States Under Secretary of State George W. Ball, "the central point of the debate in the discussions that have surrounded the South Vietnam problem is [whether] the war in South Vietnam is an external aggression from the North, or is it an indigenous revolt?"[2]

Prior to the direct involvement of United States ground forces in 1964, Hanoi made a compelling case for the hostilities to be regarded as a civil conflict. The Geneva Accords of 1954 consisted of twelve documents, eight of which were unilateral. Among these were statements of national policy; three military agreements signed by the Vietminh, Laos, Cambodia, and France; and a covering declaration that was not signed by any nation. The United States, which by 1954 was paying eighty percent of the cost of the war and exerting an increasing influence on the politics of the struggle, was not a signatory to any of the documents. It did take note of the three military agreements and declared that it would not use force or the threat of force to disturb the truce. As noted earlier, the accords did not create two new states *de juro*, but merely partitioned the divided country pending the proposed resolution of the political controversy in 1956 through free elections. Thus, the brief published by the United States in 1966 defining the legality of participation in the defense of Vietnam argued that "there is no greater license for one zone of a temporarily divided state to attack the other zone than there is for one state to attack another state."[3] Accordingly, even if the DRV were to concede its participation in the hostilities in South Vietnam, it could still have argued that hostilities vis-à-vis the GVN were civil in character rather than international.

The DRV, however, chose to base its principal argument for civil war on a flat denial of its participation in what it termed an indigenous conflict within the southern half of the country. The only conflict in the South by this theory was the continuation of the forty-year struggle of the Lao Dong party to seize political control of the country, initially through the Vietminh and currently through the NLF. Denied self-determination at the ballot box, North Vietnam asserts, the people were obliged to continue their struggle through arms. In sum, stated Ho Chi Minh:

> ... it is a dishonest argument to say that the southern part of our country is a neighboring country separate from the northern part. One might as well say that the southern states of the United States are a country apart from the northern states. ... As sons and daughters of the same fatherland, our people in the north are bound to extend wholehearted support to the patriotic struggle waged by the people of the south.[4]

The DRV's characterization of the war as a civil conflict was not changed even by the direct participation of the United States combat units and the bombing of the North. The aggression of the United States, from the point of view of the DRV, certainly did not entitle its servicemen to any superior standard of treatment under the Geneva Conventions. Thus the secretary general of the DRV Red Cross wrote to the president of ICRC (International Committee of the Red Cross) in September 1965 that "... pilots who have carried out pirate raids destroying the property and slaughtering the people ... are liable for trial in compliance with the laws of the DRV." She also reaffirmed her pledge that North Vietnam would comply with general humanitarian principles.

Prior to 1965 the Diem government was ambivalent about the characterization of its conflict with the North for the purposes of the application of GPW. On the one hand, it stoutly affirmed its sovereign independence and charged aggression from Hanoi—a position that would militate in favor of the international character of the conflict. On the other hand, the Communist guerrillas of the NLF, like the militias of the Binh Xuyen, Cao Dai, and Hoa Hao, were residents of the South—which argued in favor of local insurgency.

French support of the Binh Xuyen and the residual loyalty of senior Vietnamese officers to Bao Dai, who was still recognized by France as titular head of state, occupied the initial attention of the Diem regime. Although the NLF gave sporadic support to the sects, it was relatively quiet through 1958. The resumption of Communist guerrilla activity was taken by GVN as further rebel action against the government. Although it never credited the NLF with indigenous leadership, it was unwilling to extend the logic of its position to the conclusion that a rebel from a local village is entitled to be treated as a prisoner of war under international law because he is the agent of Hanoi. Moreover, the GVN had never signed the military armistice agreements at Geneva; on the contrary, their delegation protested its imposition. It was not until considerable pressure was applied to GVN by the United States in July 1966 that Saigon reluctantly acceded to the United States characterization of the war as an international conflict that entitled the Vietcong to PW status. Since the DRV stoutly denied the charge that its forces were fighting in the South, and prisoners suspected of northern origins refused identification, that characterization as to type of conflict was relevant only to the treatment of Vietcong prisoners.

The United States regarded the conflict as international at all times. It never presumed that any provision or inference of the Geneva Accords could deny the sovereign independence of the GVN. It argued that the GVN had been recognized by sixty governments, had been admitted as a member of some of the specialized agencies of the United Nations, and would be a member of the United Nations itself but for a veto by the USSR in 1957. The United States entered its intention to treat South Vietnam not as a "provisional zone" but as an entity entitled to "full independence and sovereignty" on the official record of the 1954 conference. It asserted that the NLF was sponsored by the Lao Dong from 1954 to 1958 and argued that in the next three years the DRV infiltrated 10,000 northerners of southern origins into the South. By 1964, after the North had "moved over 40,000 armed and unarmed guerrillas into South Vietnam [they] . . . apparently exhausted their reservoir of Southerners who had gone North and . . . began to infiltrate elements of the North Vietnamese Army in increasingly larger numbers."[5]

The United States held that its characterization of the conflict, in theory, invoked the application of GPW (Geneva Convention Relative to the Treatment of Prisoners of War). However, it was sensitive to the reluctance of the GVN, which it regarded as the detaining power, to apply the conventions to the Vietcong. This sensitivity had diminished by the summer of 1965 when United States forces directly participated in the conflict in substantial numbers. To assure the application of GPW-1949 to its own forces, the United States quietly began changing administrative policy to insure that captives turned over to the GVN would, in fact, be treated as prisoners of war. Subsequent to the withdrawal of United States forces in 1973 the parties to the conflict honored the Paris peace agreements by their breach rather than their observance, with all sides tacitly regarding the conflict as civil rather than international in nature.

Type of Forces

Among the conflicts considered in this book, Vietnam undoubtedly raises the most profound questions about the characterization of forces engaged in the capture and detention of PWs. The series of conflicts in Vietnam since the end of World War II have involved regular uniformed armies, irregular partially uniformed forces, nonuniformed guerrillas, and civilians who were often laborers by day and terrorists by night.

Before 1954 the principal conflict in French Indochina involved the guerrilla warfare of the Vietminh against the government of France. Although the Communist bloc provided logistic support to the rebels and the United States supported France, foreign forces were not participants in the hostilities. Typically, the guerrillas were a nonuniformed force that operated clandestinely, and France employed a uniformed army that carried arms openly. Hostilities from Dien Bien Phu through 1958 were confined to the territory of South Vietnam. Like the Vietminh, the large majority of Cao Dai and Hoa Hao forces wore civilian clothing. The balance, as well as a substantial number of Binh Xuyen, who were supplied by the French, wore military remnants of the French Army.

The armed forces of the Republic of Vietnam (ARVN) were attired in variations of United States Army uniforms with insignia identifying local corps. Similarly, the armed forces of the United States, including its Special Forces, and the armies of other nations participating in the hostilities, were principally regular uniformed forces. The Dan Ve, however, was basically a civilian militia under the jurisdiction of the province military commander. These nonuniformed civilians were a favorite target for VC (Vietcong) terrorists. The unconventional warfare in Vietnam also included several thousand civilian irregular mercenaries under the command of United States and ARVN Special Forces, which conducted counterterrorist activities against the VC.

Vietcong units, from the onset of serious military operations in 1958 through the Paris peace negotiations, took pains to create and preserve their image of an indigenous local force. However, they did not ordinarily wear military uniforms, and they carried arms openly while on offensive forays. Nevertheless, they were under tight command and control and conducted operations in accordance with the customs of civil conflict.

Systems of Control

In August 1965 ICRC addressed an appeal to the principal parties to the conflict to abide by "the humanitarian provisions of the Geneva Conventions." It is not clear, however, whether this meant to apply to all the conventions or only the common articles. It reminded the DRV, the GVN, and the United States that all were parties to the 1949 conventions. It also sent a copy of the appeal to the NLF insisting that it too was bound by "the undertakings signed by Viet Nam." The appeal specified five points: (1) ICRC should be permitted to serve as a neutral intermediary; (2) prisoners of war, identifiable as such by their apparel or an emblem, should be treated humanely; (3) PW lists should be exchanged; (4) ICRC delegates should be authorized to visit PW camps; and (5) civilians should be spared.

All four parties responded to the appeal. The United States, through Secretary of State Dean Rusk, and the GVN immediately acknowledged the communication and pledged their compliance with its requests. The DRV, replying through Mme. Tran Thi Tich, president of the Red Cross of the Democratic Republic of Vietnam, alleged that the United States had already violated the Geneva Conventions (through the bombing of the North) and merely used the conventions as a propaganda smokescreen to continue criminal aggression. She cited the DRV reservations to the conventions, inviting particular attention to the applicability to captured United States pilots of its reservation denying the protection of the conventions to PWs ". . . convicted of war crimes or crimes against humanity." She reiterated an intention previously announced by the DRV to treat prisoners humanely in accordance with domestic law (rather than international law).[6] The NLF, replying through Mme. Nguyen Van Dong, representative of the NLF to the USSR, denied the applicability of the conventions to an insurgent force that did not participate in the conventions and stated that it was not in a position to apply literally all the provisions therein.

Subsequently, the United States attempted, through diplomatic channels, to locate a protecting power that might accept the obligations of the conventions and be acceptable to all parties. It approached the USSR, Poland, East Germany, and other Communist-bloc nations, and the United Arab Republic. In May 1966 Ambassador Averell Harriman wrote to ICRC that United States efforts were in vain because ". . . the Government of North Vietnam has refused to accept a Protecting Power." It called upon ICRC to offer, pursuant to GPW article 10, its own good offices to the DRV. ICRC transmitted the United States request to Hanoi, but it was rejected by the DRV on the ground that the prisoners were not entitled to the benefits of the conventions.

The attitude of the DRV limited direct ICRC activities to the RVN. On several occasions ICRC offered its services to the Red Cross and the authorities of the DRV; these offers were also refused. On the other hand, the DRV readily communicated to ICRC complaints about United States bombing of villages, hospitals, and civilian targets. But when the United States denied the charges and proposed an investigation by ICRC, the matter was not followed up by the DRV. No evidence of other systems of control to facilitate communications between the parties to the conflict was found before the Paris negotiations of 1968.

All prisoners of war taken by the United States and other allied forces in South Vietnam were transferred to the custody of GVN in accordance with GPW article 12, which provides that prisoners of war may be transferred to a power that is a party to the convention and willing and able to apply its terms. Although the United States did not, and under the conventions could not, disclaim its role as a detaining power of those prisoners captured by its own forces, its ability to insure that they were treated in accordance with GPW was a problem. United States personnel scrupulously accounted for their captives identified as prisoners of war and similarly processed other detainees who were turned over to it prior to determination of PW status. But once they were transferred to the custody of the GVN, the United States lost control over their actual treatment, and was consequently cast in the role of a conspirator in the torture and murder of captured guerrillas.

Sanctions and Reprisals

The Vietnam war was characterized at all times by the lack of working guidelines and of precise distinctions between military and civilian personnel, between classical and guerrilla warfare, and between friendly and hostile territory. Accordingly, terror and counterterror in the "civilian" sector of the conflict rapidly escalated into reprisals and counterreprisals against "military" prisoners of war. NLF atrocities against civilians incited retaliatory measures by ARVN against VC terrorists. When the terrorists were tried and executed by the GVN, the NLF retaliated against United States prisoners of war. Personnel reprisals reached their zenith in the execution by the VC of a United States officer and two noncommissioned officers. The outrage expressed by the United States through diplomatic channels and to the ICRC resulted in a marked reduction of reprisals involving United States personnel. Continued reprisals of this nature clearly damaged Communist propaganda efforts, and subsequent reprisals against United States servicemen and civilian representatives (e.g., U.S. State Department) were more often threatened or feigned than carried out.

Another principal sanction invoked in the Vietnam conflict was the threat of the DRV to try United States airmen for "war crimes" in Hanoi. The initial position of North Vietnam (that the Communist reservation to GPW-1949, article 85, gave them the right to conduct local Nuremberg trials) yielded to international diplomatic pressure set in motion by the United States. As noted above, ICRC was considerably handicapped in its efforts as an intermediary because of the failure of the NLF or the DRV either to concede the applicability of the Geneva Conventions or to accept ICRC as a protecting power. However, it was quite clear from the pattern and tone of correspondence between ICRC and the Communists and from the occasional acceptance of ICRC medical assistance, that the international organization was an important moral influence even on combatants who denied its legal jurisdiction.

Heavy United States bombing of North Vietnam from 1971 through 1973, although protested domestically and internationally, were not acts of reprisal; nevertheless, offers by Presidents Johnson and Nixon to include the North as well as the South in any United States assistance plan to a Vietnam united and at peace had at least the ring of reparation. Short of that offer, spurned by the DRV, reparations in Vietnam had consisted principally of ransom and tributes paid by RVN civilian communities to the NLF.

Persons Entitled to PW Status

The United States and its non-Vietnamese allies took and retained prisoners only until custody could be transferred to the government of Vietnam. The official policy of these nations to comply with the Geneva Conventions was set forth in the declarations of the "Manila Conference" in 1966. All persons taken into custody by the United States Armed Forces were referred to as "detained" until classification. Pending classification, all were entitled to the full protection of GPW. Four classes of detainees were recognized in 1966:

1. Prisoners of war—all persons captured while actually engaging in belligerent acts other than terrorism, sabotage, or spying; all forces of the DRV or the NLF, whether captured in combat or not, except terrorists, spies, and saboteurs.
2. Regroupees—Vietnamese who lived in the RVN, moved North in 1954, and were captured when they subsequently returned to the RVN.
3. Returnees ("Chieu Hoi")—persons who returned to GVN control after having actively supported the VC.
4. Civil defendants—persons suspected of being spies, guerrillas, or saboteurs.

Subsequent refinements in classification extended prisoner of war status to irregulars, guerrillas, self-defense forces, and secret self-defense forces. Each of these additional classifications involved types of forces having some degree of military organization. The "secret self-defense force" category even included clandestine VC organizations involved in sabotage and propaganda. However, detainees suspected of being spies, terrorists, or saboteurs were at all times excluded from PW status under United States regulations.

The only persons who were held in permanent custody by United States forces were nineteen North Vietnamese seamen, who were held on board a United States vessel for almost two years until September 1968, when fifteen were repatriated. The circumstances of the hostilities, however, raised some peculiar problems in addition to the normal vicissitudes of conflict in the application of humanitarian standards. The Chieu Hoi, or returnee, program, which encouraged release and rehabilitation of qualified detainees, was not technically applicable to prisoners of war. Accordingly, there was a tendency on the part of the GVN to avoid the PW classification for detainees. In addition, since defectors or voluntary returnees are not PWs, a problem was posed by VC who fired their weapons at the adversary until out of ammunition, and then (if the captor were United States) threw up their hands and claimed to be civilian or "hoi chanh" ("rallier to the true national cause" and eligible for the Chieu Hoi program).

Yet another factor that encouraged a status short of prisoner of war is that VC who had voluntarily or involuntarily been removed from the conflict often preferred to surrender to civil authorities and to subject themselves to municipal criminal sanctions. This frustrated the efforts of the United States to have them treated as PWs. The apparent reason for the strategy was that a PW was likely to be interned for the duration of the conflict, whereas the average sentence served in local jails in South Vietnam was six months. It was reported that many chose to risk losing the protection of the convention rather than to undergo what appeared to be interminable detention.

The *Republic of Vietnam Armed Forces Guide Book for Handling Combat Captives* stated that:

VC troops have been warned by their commanders that once we capture them, we will kill them after collecting information from them. Therefore, captured VC's are "wise" to seek a quiet death rather than to be tortured . . . we must make them realize that they have been subject to false VC propaganda by handling them in a good manner.

The *Guide Book* continued:

The proper handling of Communist POW's is in response to humanity and reflects the good feelings of every ARVN soldier. Additionally, it is due to technical reasons that we must handle them properly to gain advantages for the defense of a righteous cause.

The policy was reiterated in a wallet-size card that was sealed in plastic and distributed by ARVN to its combat troops. The card, printed only in Vietnamese, said in part, ". . . when a CRP ('Communist Rebel Prisoner') is captured he will be treated humanely by you although he is not recognized as a POW in accordance with the meaning normally used internationally . . . Do not seek revenge under any reason."[7] The policy was more often honored in the breach than the observance.

For the purposes of the Geneva Conventions, the GVN initially took the Vietcong at face value and treated them as rebels and traitors who were not entitled to the amenities of prisoners of war. As the GVN, up to the end of 1965, had practically no facilities for detaining captured guerrillas besides the civilian jails and one or two indoctrination centers, the choice was either to release the captives or to kill them. Only with the greatest effort was the United States able to prevail upon the GVN to accept the Geneva Conventions at all. Even then, the official GVN policy was not universally respected by ARVN corps commanders who exercised broad local discretion under Vietnamese military custom and tradition. United States staff advisors and command personnel were able to persuade their Vietnamese counterparts to take PWs only by arguing strenuously for their value as military intelligence, the possibility of reprisals against United States prisoners, and the favorable international propaganda that would attend compliance with the conventions.

United States categories of classification suggest that civilians could be "regroupees," "civil defendants," or, in the case of civilians, not subject to further detention, "innocent civilians." However, ARVN, in practice, recognized only two civilian classifications: persons loyal to the GVN and persons who assisted the enemy. Civilians who were suspected of assisting the enemy were, more often than not, either released after interrogation or killed outright. In 1966, of 10,000 detainees captured and interrogated, only 2,500 were interned in all categories. The number of persons who could be interned was also limited by available facilities: In a reported instance in 1966, 3,000 persons from VC-controlled areas were transferred from United States custody to a GVN collection point; they were all released within three days of capture because the South Vietnamese simply lacked the facilities to accommodate them.

The NLF argued that it was not bound by the Geneva Conventions because "it did not participate in them." Moreover, it insisted that "these conventions contain provisions that correspond neither with its actions, nor the organization of its armed forces. Nevertheless, it was observing a humane and charitable policy toward prisoners."[8] (It sometimes appeared that the NLF spokesmen confused the Geneva Conventions with the Geneva Accords.) What kind of treatment the PW was entitled to at the hands of the VC appeared to depend upon his nationality and whether he was taken in a terrorist action or a military action. Although by 1968 the VC had assassinated over 17,000 Vietnamese and kidnapped almost 50,000, these terrorist actions did not involve "prisoners" as such. The frequent discovery of trussed civilians who had been shot in the back of the head was evidence of a discriminating attitude toward the taking of prisoners. The slaughter of such captives increased along the line of retreat as United States participation caused VC reverses in 1967. ARVN troops and Vietnamese civilians were more apt to be victimized than were United States troops. Intelligence sources agreed that United States soldiers were taken prisoners by the VC rather than killed. The wounded and the sick were often unilaterally released to avoid burdening the detaining power. Although there were some incidents in which United States soldiers were apparently killed after they had been removed from the battle, many reported murders and atrocities appear to have resulted in death during combat, or at the point of capture and prior to detention. There was virtually no reported information available concerning VC respect for the convention rights of ARVN captives.

No party to the conflict reported the taking of prisoners by DRV forces in South Vietnam. The DRV itself continued to deny the presence of any forces in South Vietnam almost to the day when its victorious army raised its flag in Saigon. As detailed in the discussions below, the 300 to 500 United States airmen held in Hanoi by the DRV were regarded by the detaining power as pirates "destroying the property and massacring the population of the Democratic Republic of Vietnam, as major criminals caught *in flagrante delicto* and liable for judgment in accordance with the laws of the Democratic Republic of Vietnam, although captured pilots are well treated."[9]

Standards of Internment[a]

GVN Internment Camps

The GVN operated six permanent internment camps, five of which had a population of 2,000 each by April 1968, with a capacity of 4,500 prisoners each. The sixth, the island camp of Phu Quoc, had a population of 12,500, with full capacity planned for 40,000 prisoners by October 1969. Phu Quoc was designed to serve as the final place of confinement before repatriation and release upon cessation of hostilities (ironically, it turned out to be the final refuge of thousands of civilians fleeing the victorious communist forces). The camps were isolated from civilian communities and other military and logistical activities, but in most instances appear not to have been marked with the letters "PW" or "PG." Even though United States forces had control of the air at all times, the camps, like the capital city of Saigon itself, were within range of enemy howitzers and rocket fire. With the possible exception of Phu Quoc, none of the camps were regarded by United States observers as being located in safe areas behind the battle lines, simply because the conflict engaged virtually the whole of South Vietnam. Even the northern portion of the island of Phu Quoc, beyond the perimeter of the internment camp, was presumed by United States camp advisors to be under VC control.

The camps themselves were constructed by United States military personnel to standard specifications: Each camp originally consisted of two fenced compounds separated by a recreation area. A compound contained four or five metal buildings with dirt floors to serve the housing, feeding, and support requirements of the prisoner population. The specifications calling for 1,000 persons in each of two compounds were later revised, for security reasons, to 500 persons in four compounds. From July 1966 through March 1967, while the camps were being constructed, the prisoner population increased from a total of 269 to over 12,000. Quarters constructed to house 200 prisoners frequently held as many as 600. A typical distribution at the time (Pleiku camp) was 250 VC, 250 civilian defendants, and the balance detained on suspicion. Female VC prisoners were usually sent to one of the forty-one civilian jails.

The camps were under the command of the GVN. The South Vietnamese camp commander was assisted by a United States advisory team typically composed of one officer and four enlisted men—a senior noncommissioned officer, a photographer, a security specialist, and an interpreter. The advisors had access to the camp commander at all times. Their influence on the command was often questionable, as indicated by the discovery of "tiger cages" of some GVN facilities, whose existence was allegedly unknown to the camp advisors. Similar cages were used by the Viet Cong, as noted below.

[a]The conditions and programs described in this section obtained principally in the period from 1966 to 1969, as indicated by the references.

Initial interrogation at prisoner collecting stations classified detainees into five categories: (1) "returnees"—South Vietnamese who had voluntarily returned from the Vietcong—who were sent to Chieu Hoi centers; (2) innocent civilians, who were returned to the place of capture or relocated if the village had been destroyed; (3) civil defendants, who were turned over to GVN civil authorities; (4) prisoners of war, who were confined to internment camps; and (5) doubtful cases, referred to a tribunal for further classification. Within some internment camps, PWs were further classified and segregated into Vietcong and North Vietnamese units. United States advisors to the ARVN camp commanders expressed discomfort about the justification under GPW article 22 for political segregation. It had been reported in interviews that at one time the GVN had further segregated Vietcong PWs into two categories: "hardcore" Communists and those considered susceptible to "rehabilitation." Copies of the Geneva Conventions were not normally available to the PWs, although in some camps extracts from GPW were posted in Vietnamese. "Instruction on Prescription of the Policies Concerning the Treatment of Rebel Communist Prisoners," A GVN guide to all aspects of PW treatment, published on December 10, 1965, was available at all camps.

Food in the camps invariably consisted of the local diet of rice and fish supplemented from time to time by meat and other perishables available from local vendors. The rice, shipped from Saigon to the camps, was often processed in the United States. The fact that American polished rice lacks the nutritional value of rough rice was found by a medical team to be the cause of at least one mysterious epidemic of beriberi in the first few months of camp operations. Once discovered, the condition was easily corrected by adding vitamins when polished rice was used. Food was prepared by the prisoners in areas set aside for the purpose. The daily monetary allowance for food was 24 piastres (20¢) per PW. The nutritional value of the diet was estimated at 2,800 to 3,000 calories per day.

Clothing PWs did not present a problem in the warm Vietnam climate. PWs in Vietnam were dressed in the customary garb of the Vietnamese peasant: a black pajama-like garment and sandals that are ordinarily made from automobile tire strips. For a period of time it appeared to have been GVN policy to mark PW uniforms with the Vietnamese symbols for "Communist Rebel Combat Captive" TPC. The detaining power insisted that the purpose of the marking was to assert domestic jurisdiction over PWs. After repeated complaints by ICRC and expressions of concern by the United States, the marking was obliterated to comply with GPW.

Standards of sanitation within the internment camp were maintained at a higher level than customary for the RVN depot troops. (This, plus United States pressure to observe the conventions' humane disciplinary rules and the existence of a recreational program for PWs was deeply resented by the RVN guards). Items required for personal hygiene, such as toothbrushes and soap, were always in short supply. Although the ICRC delegation in Saigon reported that hospitals and similar establishments were inadequately provided with essential medical supplies, there were no complaints recorded of lack of medicine or medical care in the internment camps themselves. Medical care within the internment camps was provided principally by North Vietnamese physicians. ARVN did not permit either the United States camp advisors or ICRC to check on compliance with convention requirements as to medical inspections or other matters.

The GVN Ministry of Defense Instruction assigns the "Political War Section" the mission of "providing necessary help to the VC PW's in religious ceremonies, as well as burial ceremonies when there is a death." Facilities were available, but few, if any, religious activities were reported at any of the South Vietnamese prison camps. The prisoners did not perform any labor besides camp maintenance, because provincial leaders would not tolerate PW competition for the few jobs that existed. Organized recreation was the principal element of camp life, consisting principally of several scheduled hours of group sports, such as volleyball, in the area between compounds set aside for the purpose. Beginning in 1968 some vocational training was provided. Each camp had a library or "collective activities room" stacked with censored newspapers and literature supplied by the Joint United States Public Affairs Office. Classes organized by the individual GVN camp commander through his political warfare officer consisted chiefly of political indoctrination for those NLF prisoners deemed susceptible to rehabilitation. Most of the time in camp was spent in idleness.

The principal contact with the outside world was through a family visitation program for VC PWs. United States advisors reported that this large-scale activity was administered even-handedly without particular problems. Of course, the program did not serve DRV PWs whose families were in North Vietnam. Neither incoming nor outgoing mail was permitted until 1967. To some degree this was a retaliatory response to the refusal of Hanoi to deliver PW mail. However, another factor was the refusal of DRV captives to communicate with the outside for political reasons. Since their government denied their presence in South Vietnam until well into the Paris truce negotiations, any communication could well have betrayed their national interest and imperiled their families.

Regular visits by ICRC began at the end of 1967, some six years after the escalation of United States participation in the conflict. Until then, the GVN stoutly resisted all efforts by ICRC to visit the camps, on the grounds that the conflict was civil and not international and because the DRV refused to permit ICRC observers. The South Vietnamese could not understand why United States advisors urged them to admit ICRC in the absence of reciprocity by the enemy. Ironically, it is reported that the PWs themselves were no more enthusiastic about seeing the ICRC representative than the detaining power was to permit the visits. To many of the rural PWs, a Caucasian visitor who spoke French evoked unpleasant colonial memories. Impressed by photographs frequently appearing in the United States press of atrocities, ICRC requested cessation of alleged mistreatment of PWs. GVN replied with a file on atrocities attributed to NLF forces and invited the committee to investigate the plight of Vietnamese prisoners held by the Vietcong. Small relief shipments to PWs were facilitated by the ICRC delegates in cooperation with the Red Cross of the Republic of Vietnam.

NLF Camps. Prison camps maintained by the Vietcong, the military arm of the National Liberation Front, were generally small and transient. United States intelligence information reports cited units ranging in size from three thatched huts near Ba Hy for fifty to sixty PWs to two large houses at Hoe Cuh containing 200 PWs. The Vietcong never publicized the location of prison camps or marked them in any way. Camps were generally located in jungles, which obscured aerial observation. Even neighboring villages were often unaware of—or perhaps reluctant to disclose—the existence of the camps.

Camps invariably held imprisoned civilians and United States and ARVN servicemen. Most of the civilians had been sentenced by NLF tribunals for failing to pay "taxes" or otherwise failing to support the military effort of the guerilla army. Within the camp, they were normally segregated by sex and nationality, but officers and enlisted men were not separated. Facilities were usually primitive. Several reports on transient camps stated that PWs were kept for periods of at least a week in "cages" approximately four feet high by three feet in length. Each cell was a barbed wire box framed by tree trunks with a bark roof. Cells containing one PW each were arranged in wards of five, and PWs were shackled with leg irons at night to prevent escape. The use of shackles was common even in the larger facilities: eighty of the 200 PWs at Hoe Cuh were observed to be shackled; twenty were soldiers and sixty civilians. This camp was believed to have had sixteen guards.

Intelligence reports uniformly stated that food was sufficient to sustain life. The daily diet of rice with the bits of meat or fish varied in quantity. It was, however, the same as or more than that received by the captors. The number of meals per day varied with the installation; two appeared to be the norm. However, weight losses of up to forty percent were experienced by PWs in captivity for an extended period of time. The normal attire of PWs was similar to the garments issued by the GVN; that is, a black pajama-like garment and tire strip sandals. In some instances PWs were permitted to retain their own fatigue clothing and boots.

Sanitation supplies and facilities were nonexistent or primitive at best. In the "cage" facility noted above, Vietnamese PWs were not permitted to cough or to sit erect without permission. They were obliged to urinate and defecate in large crockery jars and could empty them only once every four days. The intelligence report noted that United States servicemen were spared this indignity to which ARVN PWs were regularly subjected. Medical facilities were in short supply. In a transit camp at Phu Cam, 30 of 100 PWs were said to have died of wounds and sickness. Other than mercurochrome and occasional use of penicillin, there is no evidence of the availability or use of modern drugs or antibiotics. Another camp, however, principally for United States PWs, was visited monthly by a civilian nurse. But even this camp lacked medicine or special facilities for the wounded and sick. The medical care for PWs selected for release was the best that available personnel and facilities allowed.

Work was mandatory and regarded as therapeutic by the NLF, although labor was restricted to housekeeping, gathering firewood, and maintenance of facilities. PWs were paid fifteen piastres a month for their labor, less deductions for any amenities such as tobacco and soap. Work assignments were left to a representative selected from among the PWs by the detaining power without respect to rank. In practice, among United States PWs, the senior or noncommissioned United States officer assumed authority.

The principal form of organized "recreation" in the camps was[2] political indoctrination. PWs were frequently advised that a "good attitude" toward the indoctrination sessions would enable them to stay alive until the end of the war or might permit them to be transferred to a more "progressive" camp where there were said to be good living conditions, good food, and relative freedom of movement. One intelligence source observed a class of PWs, including twenty-six United States servicemen, apparently receiving political education in English. The Geneva Conventions were not posted in the camps or otherwise included in the "curriculum." At another camp, one hour per day was devoted to group criticism. A half-hour was also spent listening to music and news over Radio Hanoi. Programs stressed NLF victories and political goals, and urban unrest in the United States. This particular camp was the only one where PWs were, in theory, permitted to receive visitors or mail; they were not permitted to send mail. On the other hand, informants told of at least one camp where correspondence was not only permitted but encouraged. However, it was not established that any of the correspondence was ever posted; a general belief persisted among United States servicemen that the captors encouraged correspondence to secure their signatures for propaganda purposes. The Central Tracing Agency of ICRC forwarded letters to PWs from their families; but in spite of the existence of a "Red Cross of Liberation of South Vietnam," it was never able to find out whether such letters reached their addressees.

Camp administration was uneven, notwithstanding published policy regarding "humane treatment" for "war criminals" (United States servicemen). For example, the camp with the visiting nurse administered such additional amenities as tobacco, pure drinking water, extra rice, and haircuts, and was marked by the absence of harsh disciplinary measures. This camp was in stark contrast to the neglect and viciousness reported in other installations. Extensive indoctrination and propaganda efforts, particularly directed to United States Negro PWs and those about to be released, were common to all NLF camps. The ICRC repeatedly offered assistance to the NLF through its representatives in Prague,

Moscow, and Algiers. Such offers were rebuffed, and in 1966 the NLF ceased all contact with the ICRC.

DRV Camps. Prior to repatriation of American prisoners in 1973, it was generally believed that the North Vietnamese adhered to their announced humanitarian policies in spite of many technical violations. However, released airmen reported many instances of torture and brutality, although this did not appear to be the dominant theme of internment.

Perhaps the best publicized internment camp of the Vietnam conflict was the facility known as the "Hanoi Hilton," a converted city prison in the capital of North Vietnam. It was used principally, or perhaps exclusively, for United States airmen who had been captured by North Vietnamese personnel. By the end of 1968, 300 to 400 airmen had been captured by the North Vietnamese. The majority of them were believed to be in this camp or in transit camps en route to the "Hilton." Some are also known to have been confined in private homes in the suburbs of Hanoi for extended periods. The "humane" treatment of the United States PWs in the camp was the subject of a lengthy propaganda film by an East German company produced with the cooperation of the DRV. Most of the film details concerning camp administration were confirmed by repatriated PWs during the late 1960s and United States citizens acting as repatriation teams. However, the jurisdiction of ICRC was not recognized, and its inspection teams were not permitted in the camp. Subsequent to the general release of United States prisoners in 1973, one American officer reported having spent forty-two months in solitary confinement in this camp for a "bad attitude" that included failure to confess to war crimes.

Although the jurisdiction of ICRC was denied because the DRV did not consider itself to be involved in an international conflict, the full text of the Geneva Convention, in English, was distributed to all captured United States airmen. In fact, it was sometimes the only available reading material in English.

The city prison that served as a PW camp was a permanent stone structure consisting of several connecting buildings with an interior courtyard. PWs appear to have had individual cells. Cells contained a bed; a chair, in some reported instances; desks; and a wash basin. PWs were dressed either in standard Vietnamese black pajama-like garments and sandals, or in prisoners' uniforms with broad purple stripes. The United States PWs were fed three meals a day consisting of Western rations, comparable in nourishment, although somewhat less in quantity, than their accustomed standards. Food was prepared by the DRV, and there were no reports of canteen privileges.

PWs were paid a basic salary of sixteen piastres a day although labor was restricted principally to camp maintenance. A recreation program of sorts existed and included a minimum of one hour of physical activity per day and political classes conducted by the DRV. Attendance was voluntary, but it was often difficult to determine where interrogation (which was not voluntary) left off and indoctrination, offered through the recreation program, began. A few American prisoners reported having been beaten, tied, shackled, and starved during interrogation. In general, all of the PWs suffered from isolation and inactivity. They were known to be taken through the streets of Hanoi to view the effects of United States bombing missions and were shown photographs of children allegedly killed by United States aerial attacks. They were urged, cajoled, tricked, and frequently persuaded to make statements that were employed by their captors for propaganda purposes. The East German film, which was shown in much of Western Europe but whose publication was protested by the United States State Department, was a case in point.

The DRV returned all mail addressed to PWs through ICRC. PWs stated in propaganda broadcasts in 1968 that they were permitted to send one letter per month and to receive one envelope per month weighing up to twenty grams that could contain family correspondence and photographs. The letters were to be sent directly to the detention camp. Relatives of PWs received neither mail nor any other communication indicating that letters which had been posted as directed were received. In April 1969 the United States complained that mail had not been received from PWs in over a year. Yet, the United States government refused to accept prisoner lists offered to the "Committee of Liaison" and Senators Kennedy and Fulbright by the Communist negotiators, as the offerees were not parties to the negotiations. Information about PWs often came through indirect diplomatic channels, such as Communist correspondents in Moscow. Propaganda films showed PWs celebrating Thanksgiving and Christmas, including religious services for Christian captives. Additional religious activities were not reported. Neither North Vietnamese official sources, Vietcong, nor United States intelligence ever mentioned the existence of internment camps for South Vietnamese in North Vietnam, nor was there any evidence that PWs of the NLF were being held in North Vietnam.

Interrogation, Indoctrination, and Propaganda

Although available information suggests that the military requirement for immediate, useful intelligence makes the point of capture the most likely place for violations of international law, it is a difficult fact to prove: capture-point violations are less likely to be reported than violations removed from the battlefield. Relevant statistical data cannot be retrieved from official records; debriefings of combatants tend to shy away from statements that might incriminate the narrator or his associates. Journalists are prone to sensationalize and to suggest the aberration as the norm.

To these difficulties the Vietnam war added yet another: The four principal parties to the conflict conducted military operations through many semiautonomous units, such as the United States Special Forces, the Montagnard mercenaries, and the Pathet Lao. The local unit commanders, exercising extraordinary discretionary power, were the persons in the chain of command most likely to overlook mistreatment of prisoners for the purpose of intelligence.

Prior to 1965 relatively few prisoners were taken by either side. The GVN, for its part, simply "did not recognize the value of captured enemy personnel as source of intelligence information." Such exploitation of prisoner intelligence as was carried out by GVN personnel appears to have been principally an exercise in brutality. As a result of widespread publicity given to the torture of VC by the ARVN captors, the United States State Department attempted to prevail upon the GVN to curb the use of torture to extract information. As measured by subsequent reports of similar atrocities, the success of the appeal was negligible. On the contrary, it appeared that, at least during the advisory stage, United States Special Forces cooperated with Vietnamese interrogators rather than serving as a restraining influence. The brutality of the NLF toward ARVN personnel and civilian captives was at least equal to that of the GVN during this period.

As the role of the United States changed from advisors to combatants, a combined military intelligence exploitation system was established. It was agreed that the military interrogation command at the national level would be vested in the senior ARVN intelligence officer. Command of the interrogation centers at other levels would be vested in the senior representative of the nation whose tactical units were being supported by the center. Prisoners taken by the United States and other non-Vietnamese allies were searched, blindfolded, and evacuated from the capture point to one of eighteen brigade and division collecting points for interrogation. The collecting point transit camps were designed to accommodate about fifty persons for brief periods.

The responsibilities of the center included the screening of detainees, status determination by United States interrogating personnel, accountability, protection, and humane treatment of all detained personnel during interrogation. Directives emphasized prompt evacuation by the capturing unit and the limiting of interrogation at each echelon to information required to meet its own needs. The provost marshal reported that as the system began to produce more and better intelligence, ARVN "became more enthusiastic about according humanitarian treatment to captured enemy personnel."

The "enthusiasm" was slow to catch on in the field. Atrocity stories and photographs of brutal capture-point interrogation continued to flood the free-world press from 1967 through 1972. During this period the stories and photos involved United States captors as well as the ARVN. For example, in 1971 a House of Representatives subcommittee heard testimony from United States soldiers on "Operation Phoenix," which allegedly included the deliberate torture and murder of VC prisoners upon capture. The object of the brutality was to terrorize the enemy as well as to secure intelligence. In the transit camps, however, routines were tightened up. Subsequent to 1967, intelligence personnel were prohibited from taking prisoners outside the detention area unless a representative of the provost marshal was present. The PW "pipeline" was shortened to a five-day maximum. The use of capture cards became uniform. Still, the system for interrogation during detention was never designed to assure humanitarian treatment for all captives: the GVN intelligence personnel were not accountable for detainees classified as civil defendants. In addition, selected captives were regularly evacuated from the ARVN S-2 intelligence section or the United States Central Intelligence Command to the National Interrogation Center in Saigon. The operation of this facility, completely under the jurisdiction of GVN, was conducted in strictest secrecy.

Obtaining intelligence in the internment camps was a continuing process, involving PW informers, examination of incident reports, and observations of instructors in the camp recreational programs. One member of each United States camp advisory team was usually an intelligence expert. The camp indoctrination programs themselves were organized along guidelines published by the ARVN Ministry of Defense on December 10, 1965:

Article 33 . . . at each detention camp there will be a few daily papers in which the policies are truly in agreement with those of the ARVN government. . . .

Article 37 . . . The organization of entertainment performance by rebel communist prisoners must be approved by the Commanding Section of camps. . . .

The United States military command itself issued no guidance concerning indoctrination, training, education, or recreation. The principal efforts of the GVN to indoctrinate detainees considered "rehabilitable" appear to have been focused not on the PWs, but rather on the "returnees" under the Chieu Hoi program, who were not protected by the Geneva Conventions. The potential Communist defector was offered tangible rewards to "rally to the true national cause." These included fresh food, medical care, clothing, and, during the six to eight weeks spent in one of the fifty-two Chieu Hoi centers, an allowance of $1.60 per month. The program included seventy-two hours of political and ideological reorientation taught by GVN instructors. After reindoctrination, forty percent of the "hoi chanh" were drafted and the balance rehabilitated to a secure territory in South Vietnam. From 1964 to 1968, 83,000 VC allegedly defected from Communist ranks. As noted below, defections tapered off in more recent years. The Chieu Hoi program was regarded as a particularly important adjunct to allied intelligence.

The VC policy was to glean every possible advantage from publicity resulting from reports of leniency and humane attitudes toward prisoners. Accordingly, United States captives were less pressed for intelligence than they were for propaganda materials such as apologies for burning villages, repentance at the slaughter of innocent women and children, confessions of the use of chemical and biological warfare, and appreciation of the NLF for kind treatment. Prisoners were permitted to listen to Radio Hanoi, given written propaganda, and exposed to periodic interrogation sessions for reeducation lasting two to three hours. In general, punitive measures were not prescribed for unreceptive prisoners. However, reported instances of physical mistreatment of PWs when the captive refused to divulge more than name, rank, and serial number were confirmed when United States prisoners were repatriated in April 1973.

United States Ambassador Averell Harriman stated at the Paris negotiations that North Vietnam's professions of "humane treatment" could not be accepted in the absence of independent verification.[10] There was, in fact, substantial unofficial contact with the United States pilots, principally by persons friendly or sympathetic to the DRV cause. Interviews published by these sources were more convincing. Invariably, the prisoners publicly regretted United States participation in the conflict, credited their captors with humane treatment, expressed military admiration for the antiaircraft defenses of the DRV, and conceded that the purpose of the bombing of the North was to break the morale of North Vietnamese civilians rather than to destroy military targets.

Order and Discipline

Normally, prisoners were in United States hands for no more than five days before transfer of custody to ARVN. During that time, which was principally devoted to the extraction of intelligence, they were under close control and, having been repeatedly told by their own propaganda that they were likely to be killed if captured, were usually docile and obedient. There were several escape attempts by detainees in transit, some of which were successful. United States authorities did not normally discipline prisoners in the "pipeline" for escape attempts. Although the United States took military measures to prevent escape, neither the discipline nor the trial of prisoners was a significant United States problem. The only war crimes tried by United States authorities involved the court-martial of United States servicemen for violations of the laws of war.

GVN regulations, standard operating procedures, guides, and official training materials for handling captive prisoners of war since 1965 repeat or summarize many of the principles of GPW-1949. For example, the application of the basic rule that prisoners are subject to the laws, regulations, and orders in force in the army of the detaining power is explicit, as well as the rule that any offenses of PWs that would not be offenses in the army of the detaining power may be the subject of disciplinary punishment only. Disciplinary punishment alone is permitted for escape, except with regard to serious escape-connected offenses. The operating procedures authorized the following types of disciplinary punishment:

- Discontinuance of privileges provided by the prisoner of war regulations.
- Confinement to the disciplinary room.

- Fatigue duties, not exceeding two hours daily (not applicable to officers).
- Reduced rations.

Reduction of rations and discontinuance of other privileges, as mentioned in the procedures, are permitted by the disciplinary provisions of GPW-1949, article 119, which authorize "Discontinuance of privileges granted over and above the treatment provided for by the present Convention." The following limitations were also set forth; discipline may be imposed only by the camp commander or his representative; the action must be recorded in the PWs record and punishment book; no physical torture or ill-treatment is permitted; disciplinary punishments are limited to thirty days; the prisoner must be given notice of a disciplinary action; he may present a defense, have witnesses, and notify the prisoners' representative; pretrial confinement is to be deducted from the punishment; and confinement may not be inhumane.

Judicial sanctions contained in the regulations were less detailed than those pertaining to discipline. The general rule set forth was that PWs should be treated the same as GVN personnel of the same rank committing the same offense. Written training guidance provided by the GVN also stated that "each combat captive shall be given opportunity of their [sic] choice to lodge an appeal, and shall be assisted by a lawyer. . . . In case legal sentences are applied against combat captives, the GVN shall notify the defending nation within an appropriate time."

Reports from correspondents and veterans suggested that prior to November 1967 GVN rules were often honored more in the breach than in the observance. In 1966 ICRC, attempting to investigate stories of harsh discipline and other charges of mistreatment of prisoners in PW camps, took up the matter with the ARVN. The ARVN, by way of reply, conveyed to ICRC a file on atrocities attributed to the NLF. It also urged the committee to investigate the plight of ARVN prisoners in the DRV. The trial and discipline of PWs within the internment camps was not subject to outside scrutiny before 1967. However, court-martial trials of VC held outside the camps were well reported—resulting in threatened, and sometimes actual, reprisals by the NLF.

A VC terrorist was executed by the GVN on June 22, 1965, after his trial, conviction, and sentence to death by a South Vietnamese military court. The terrorist had been caught while attaching a fuse to a bomb that would have exploded five minutes after having been set. Thereafter, Radio Hanoi and the NLF radio announced that a United States noncommissioned officer whom the Vietcong held as a prisoner of war had been executed in reprisal. Three more VC terrorists were executed on September 22, 1965, in Da Nang, after trial, conviction, and a death sentence by a South Vietnamese court. On September 26 the "Liberation Radio" announced that the Vietcong had retaliated by executing two Americans held prisoners. Protests by the United States of these murders were ignored by the NLF. The VC policy of retaliation apparently succeeded in preventing further executions (or at least the publication of further executions) of convicted terrorists. Thus, three Vietcong terrorists who were convicted and sentenced to be executed in November 1967 were given a last-minute reprieve by the South Vietnamese premier.

A notorious murder in the streets of Cholon of a captured Vietcong guerrilla by General Nguyen Ngoc Loan, the head of the South Vietnamese National Police, in February 1968, was photographed and widely publicized. The general summarily killed the prisoner in a public street at point blank range after the prisoner had been brought to him during a bitter fight at a pagoda. Loan said the Communists "had killed many Americans and many of my people," and it was reported that the Communists themselves had staged similar executions during the fighting. Summary justice for and at the hands of terrorists was regarded by many observers to be standard procedure.

By June 1968 ARVN PW camps held almost 16,000 prisoners, 10,430 of whom were interned on the island of Phu Quoc. The decision to establish a PW camp on the island raised the spectre of another Koje-do. There were some VC on the island; logistical support and transportation facilities were inadequate, and facilities were overcrowded from the outset. Only a barbed wire barrier separated officers' quarters from those of enlisted men. In August 1967, eight PWs were involved in beating other prisoners, refusing to work, and rioting. In October 1967 there were similar incidents involving ten more PWs; this time a prisoner was murdered. Charges were brought against the accused, and they were tried by an ARVN military tribunal, receiving from ten months' close confinement to eight years' imprisonment.

Order in the NLF camps was, in general, imposed through intimidation and close restraint. There was a common use of leg irons and other shackles. In one "large" camp, shackles were employed at all times. Prisoners were often prodded by guards and in some instances actually beaten by camp authorities. Beatings were administered in private and, as noted below, were the exception rather than the rule. On the other hand, food and sleep were regularly withheld from uncooperative prisoners. It was universally rumored that prisoners would be shot in the event of attempted escape or of attack by the enemy. At least so far as United States prisoners were concerned; however, the escape rumors were not supported by the experience of captives. Statements by escaped or released prisoners indicated that United States personnel recaptured after escape attempts were often returned to their cells without further disciplinary action.

At the VC camps at Phu Cam, prisoners were bound each night with wire and bamboo strips to prevent escape. At another camp, PWs were protected from enemy air attacks on their unmarked camps by evacuation to open top trenches. Each trench held six prisoners. The total evacuation time was five minutes. Prisoners were shackled and heavily guarded during drills. There were no reports of actual raids on the camp. Incidents were reported of Vietcong beatings of prisoners who tried repeatedly to escape. A defector who had been an interrogator in a Vietcong PW camp related that Americans who unsuccessfully attempted to escape three or four times were beaten and had their feet manacled after each attempt. Their rice ration was also cut. The usual practice of the VC was one of reeducation rather than physical punishment; beatings were usually unauthorized acts motivated by anger of the moment. The first United States PW who escaped the VC in 1966 said that he had been struck with a rifle butt, though when he complained, his assailant was himself punished by the VC command.

The NLF reprisal policy was detailed in a broadcast by the NLF radio in June 1967. Referring to the death sentence handed down by a GVN court-martial of "Saigon patriots," the NLF stated:

With its humanitarian policy toward the captured American and puppet prisoners, a policy which has become known to everyone, the NLFSV, no matter how lenient it is, cannot stay its anger in the face of these cruel and fascist actions. . . . If the Americans and puppets execute the three above mentioned patriots, the Command will bring to trial many Americans who have committed many crimes against the Vietnamese people. . . . Blood debts must be paid in blood.

Like the NLF, the DRV replied principally on propaganda and reeducation to maintain order among prisoners. They also denied prisoners convention privileges as a form of discipline. A case in point was mail: Replying to an ICRC appeal for "respect for the rules of humanity" in 1965, the DRV stated, "Authorization had been granted them [captured pilots] to correspond with their families. However, the regulations concerning mail with the exterior having been recently infringed, the competent authorities of the DRV have decided to suspend this correspondence." Reconsideration of the issue was pledged "if those concerned demonstrate their willingness to observe the regulations."[11]

The communication cited above also informed ICRC of the intention of the DRV to try the captured pilots as war criminals. This position, reiterated repeatedly thereafter, created one of the gravest legal crises of the conflict. In July 1966 the pilots were paraded through the streets of Hanoi, among shouting and angry people demanding justice. Village petitions urged bringing the fliers to trial. Hanoi stated that trials would definitely be held. The legal basis for the threatened trials was the Nuremberg reservation taken by all the Communist signatories to the Geneva Conventions: "The Democratic Republic of Vietnam declares that prisoners of war prosecuted and convicted for war crimes or for crimes against humanity, in accordance with the principles laid down by the Nuremberg Court of Justice, shall not benefit from the present Convention, as specified in Article 85."[12]

The United States responded by bringing every possible diplomatic and legal pressure against the DRV. Secretary of State Dean Rusk warned that it would be a "very, very grave" development if Hanoi tried the fliers. United Nations

Ambassador Arthur Goldberg referred to "disastrous consequences" resulting from Hanoi's plans. Secretary General of the United Nations U Thant issued a statement in which he said that the trial and execution of United States pilots would lead to "new levels of suffering and sorrow and fixing more firmly still, the seal of an implacable war."[13] Eighteen United States senators who had been highly critical of United States actions in Vietnam called upon the Communist leaders not to abandon "the last remnants of reason" and thus invite "the gravest reprisals." A resolution was submitted to the United States Senate declaring that "the trial, punishment or execution of such U.S. personnel . . . would seriously diminish the opportunity for the achievement of a just and secure peace." United States leaders concertedly warned Hanoi not to miscalculate the United States reaction to trials of the pilots. Pope Paul VI also made a special appeal to Hanoi. United States government contingency plans if the trials were held included consideration of insistence on United States lawyers representing the fliers in Hanoi and specific military retaliation. However, the pressure yielded results: By the end of July 1966, Hanoi announced the appointment of a panel to study United States "war crimes." On the same day Ho Chi Minh, then the North Vietnamese president, cabled CBS news, in response to a prior cable of inquiry from CBS, that there was "no trial in view" for United States prisoners held in North Vietnam. The White House announced that this confirmed information it had. A few days later Ho Chi Minh was quoted as saying that the "main criminals" were not captured pilots "but the persons who sent them there—Johnson, Rusk, McNamara—these are the ones who should be brought to trial."[14]

Release and Repatriation

There were no bilateral exchanges of PWs in the Vietnam conflict through April 1969, although the United States and the government of South Vietnam repeatedly endeavored through many channels, both public and private, to bring about such exchanges. The DRV refused to consider exchange of PWs since it consistently maintained it had no troops in the South. Moreover, its public position that captured United States fliers were criminals and pirates was consistent with clemency but not with bilateral exchange. The National Liberation Front also refused to discuss the problems of United States PWs prior to the Paris peace negotiations on the grounds that the NLF was not recognized by the United States. Exchange of PWs was at first discussed at Paris in private talks with the United States delegation when Lyndon Johnson was President of the United States. After the administration of Richard Nixon assumed office in 1968 prisoner exchange was transferred from the private agenda to the public agenda. The return of the American prisoners became the single dominant theme of American negotiations and for almost five years appeared to be the political raison d'etre of continued United States participation in the conflict.

In a joint communiqué after a conference in Manila in October 1966, the United States and the Republic of Vietnam stressed the duty under GPW-1949 to repatriate sick and wounded PWs, and urged negotiations concerning prisoners of war. The communiqué also reaffirmed the determination of both governments to comply with the Geneva Conventions and to give full support to immediate action to repatriate the seriously sick and wounded. It also cited a resolution of the Executive Committee of the League of Red Cross Societies at Geneva in its 86th Session on October 8, 1966, which recommended that these actions be taken. In a White House statement issued in July 1967, the president noted that the GVN had undertaken and would continue the unilateral repatriation of seriously sick and wounded and urged the NLF to do likewise, while reiterating the desire and willingness of the United States and South Vietnam to discuss exchanges of PWs.

As a "humanitarian gesture" (which incidentally demonstrated the presence of DRV troops), the GVN unilaterally repatriated approximately 100 North Vietnamese regulars to North Vietnam in four actions starting in January 1966 at the Tet Lunar New Year's holiday. Twenty-one PWs were included in the first repatriation of January 1966; 13 in July 1966; 28 in February 1967; and 39 in June 1967. A substantial number of wounded PWs, including amputees, were in each of these repatriations. The repatriation of June 1967 included only seriously sick and wounded. These repatriations were effected directly from South Vietnam to North Vietnam, across the Ben Hai river bridge in the demilitarized zone. While North Vietnam refused to concede the presence of its forces in South Vietnam, DRV personnel met and accepted the PWs halfway across the bridge.

As of December 1967, ICRC doctors had screened for release an additional 141 seriously sick and wounded prisoners of war held by the South Vietnamese government, of whom forty expressed a desire to be repatriated. In June 1971 all but 13 of 570 disabled North Vietnamese refused to return to Hanoi. Notwithstanding requests from the ICRC, the International Control Commission established under the 1954 Geneva Agreements, and the GVN, the DRV refused to respond to appeals regarding exchange of the sick and wounded. However, in June 1971 DRV negotiators announced in Paris that they were willing to release all prisoners in exchange for unconditional withdrawal of United States forces from the conflict. The terms of the so-called "seven-point peace plan" were rejected by the United States and the GVN.

Irregular reciprocal PW exchanges were announced sporadically by all parties to the hostilities: In January 1967 the United States and the DRV announced the release of three Vietcong prisoners initially captured by the United States forces. This release was made at the suggestion of the United States. It followed and was announced to be in "direct response" to a release by the VC on January 4 of two United States civilian construction worker PWs and a Philippine woman. A total of thirty-four Vietcong PWs were released by the GVN from

January 1966 to August 1967. Additionally, in January 1968 it released thirty-five Vietcong woman PWs in a Tet celebration amnesty; on April 27 it freed three Vietcong in return for the release of three United States Army sergeants by the Vietcong in November 1967; and on October 24, 1968 it announced the release of 140 Vietcong in downtown Saigon as a "tolerant move and humanitarian gesture." In July 1971 the GVN announced the release of 3,000 VC prisoners in the largest unilateral gesture of the conflict. The release of VC prisoners was often confused with announcements of the thousands of persons released as defectors by the GVN under the Chieu Hoi program.

The only PWs captured by the United States who were retained in United States custody were nineteen crewmen of three Communist gunboats sunk by United States planes during a June 1966 attack on ships of the United States Seventh Fleet in the Gulf of Tonkin. These North Vietnamese sailors were held by the United States in a marine stockade in Da Nang. The United States returned two sick PWs in June 1967, three in March 1968, and the remaining fourteen in October 1968. The return of the three in March 1968 followed a release of three United States pilots by Hanoi in February 1968 and was announced as a goodwill gesture for the release of the pilots, and to stimulate further releases. The pilots were flown to Vientianne, Laos, in a private chartered plane accompanied by a United States Embassy official and an ICRC representative. The release of the remaining fourteen was effected on October 21, 1968, as an additional "goodwill" gesture. It was conducted under a thirty-six-hour limited truce negotiated in Vientianne between United States and DRV authorities, after the United States mentioned at the peace negotiations in Paris the willingness of the United States to release the rest of the captured sailors. The repatriations were voluntary, consistent with United States policy since Korea. Whether release had been effected by the United States or by GVN, a statement was invariably solicited from any PW initially detained by the United States that he understood his rights under GPW article 7 and that he was willingly and voluntarily repatriated.

Efforts to have the DRV return captive United States fliers were unsuccessful prior to the agreement to withdraw all United States forces in January 1973. In February 1968, however, the North Vietnamese released three fliers to a friendly delegation from the United States, and in July 1968 it released three more. The PWs did not know why they had been selected for release. The United States responded in kind in March by releasing three of the Gulf of Tonkin sailors. Subsequent to the Paris agreement of January 1973, the DRV released United States prisoners in small groups, beginning the following month. There were constant threats to stop repatriations completely if the United States failed to curb alleged cease-fire violations by their own and GVN forces.

Incidents were reported in which Vietcong prison camps had been overrun by United States or ARVN forces and PWs massacred. In an incident in November 1966 South Vietnamese troops overran a Vietcong prisoner of war camp in the

Mekong Delta; they liberated eight PWs and found five others shot or hacked to death. In January 1967 VC forces killed forty-four PWs before fleeing from advancing South Vietnamese forces. In March 1967 only two of twelve ARVN captives, who had been chained together, survived VC knife attacks perpetrated before the camp was overrun by South Vietnamese troops.

Economic Life

The economic consequences of United States military action were devastating. Measures taken to defoliate the countryside and to destroy crops are particularly relevant in considering the provisions of GC, article 53, concerning the destruction of real or personal property. In 1962 the United States began using defoliants to destroy the enemy's cover. The routes along which the guerrillas traveled were usually densely wooded strips lining the canals of the Mekong Delta. Fifty feet on either side of the canals the land is covered with heavy foliage under which the farmers build their villages. Movement under the trees is very difficult to spot from the air unless the men are concentrated in large groups. The South Vietnamese carried chemical warfare further and engaged in crop damage in places where VC control had been established. The United States did not participate in crop damage operations until the spring of 1965. The herbicides used were claimed at the time to be nontoxic to human or animal life. Such claims were subsequently challenged by critics of the war and it was not until 1975, two years after the cessation of United States participation in hostilities that the United States became a party to the 1925 Geneva Protocol on Poison Gas and Bacteriological Warfare.

The decision to defoliate and to damage crops in a given location was initiated by GVN district or province chiefs. The defoliated swath was ordinarily 0.6 mile (1,000 meters) on each side of a road or canal, and the effects were permanent. Each province chief was budgeted an indemnification fund from which innocent victims could claim damages. The occasional French plantation owner whose rubber trees succumbed to the airborne defoliant had no difficulty securing indemnification. Three thousand petitions were filed in the Kiem Tam District by peasant farmers. Petitions alleged:

We are people who live by farming alone and have fallen into a deficient, indigent situation because of the influence of defoliation. . . . American military performed this by planes spreading chemicals, and the effect . . . has made various types of fruit trees lose their leaves, ruined fruit, and crops such as green beans, white beans, peanuts, soybeans, and black beans lose their leaves, then die. . . . We sincerely request you to suggest that the higher authorities send personnel to inspect the crops affected in order to compensate for our losses.[15]

In practice, indemnification was often denied the peasant unless he was championed by an influential village official.

Destruction of growing crops was only one part of a program of "food denial" to the VC. Supplies of harvested rice were often destroyed in VC-controlled areas. In addition, "harvest protection" programs that required farmers to sell surpluses to the government while troops held off the VC "tax collector" were instituted. In some cases rice was confiscated in return for certificates that were redeemable later. United States economic assistance was funneled principally to cities and pacified territory in the countryside; rice, salt, sugar, medicine, and other commodities bound for VC territory were confiscated by police. The Vietcong smuggled penicillin from Saigon by the truckload. In 1966 the police seized from suspected smugglers 64,540 units of various medicines, including antimalaria drugs and vitamins as well as penicillin. The object of this kind of economic warfare was to deny food and supplies to the VC and to force the peasants to take sides or suffer the consequences.

It was GVN and United States policy to protect the property rights of individuals insofar as military operations permitted. Detainees were allowed to keep all personal effects except items of military significance. When United States personnel confiscated money or valuables from a detainee, a receipt signed by an officer was issued that accompanied the detainee to an internment camp. The same policy was printed on the GVN capture card issued to all its personnel, which provided instructions in the treatment of "Communist rebel captives." More detailed training material and directives outlined the personal property that could be seized and set forth procedures for the accountability of property taken. The GVN regulations also prohibited taking protective devices such as helmets and gas masks from a captive. Reports suggest that by and large the rules on detainees were observed. The rules did not, however, apply to the property of civilians who were not detained or to the militia and irregulars who were not under ARVN jurisdiction.

ARVN soldiers were not issued food rations on operations. They were expected to pay for the food they confiscated. In territory considered as VC, however, they took chickens, ducks, eggs, and rice without pretense of payment. Pillage of townspeople's property by ARVN troops was reported: Looting of bars, stores, and restaurants and the breaking and entering of private homes have been cited. The South Vietnamese particularly feared the Civilian Irregular Defense groups, which often beat and robbed the villagers they were supposed to protect. In one instance, a band of irregulars set up positions along a canal in Mochoa, RVN, and levied "taxes" on every boat that navigated the waterway.

In levying their private excise, the irregulars merely borrowed a page from the VC book: Throughout their entire campaign the NLF labored either to paralyze the economy or to divert it to their own purposes. Unlike some of the RVN forces, however, they showed no inclination to indulge in pillage. The VC had been known to cooperate with private contractors working on defense projects by allowing trucks to get through with building materials. They even supplied men to help finish the job, gaining both road taxes and wages to supplement their funds. Once the project was completed they were free to sabotage it without violating their agreement with the contractor. Many businesses paid "taxes" to the VC for the privilege of operating unscathed, including hauling fuel from Saigon to northern military installations.

Detainees of the VC were normally deprived of personal jewelry, wallets, notebooks, military clothing, and boots. Like the ARVN, NLF forces were subject to detailed written instructions regarding receipt and accountability of such property. A United States civilian, Donald Dawson, reporting his experiences during four months in a VC camp, stated that upon his release his captors gave back the 6,000 piastres he had brought with him plus an additional sum for work performed, which the VC claimed was paid to all detainees at a rate of fifteen piastres a month.

North Vietnam felt the direct economic consequences of armed hostilities in the bombing raids of Hanoi, Haiphong, and other North Vietnamese communities. When asked to comment on a series of reports from Hanoi by *New York Times* correspondent Harrison E. Salisbury regarding destruction of civilian property and civilian casualties, the White House replied, "No civilian targets have ever been authorized."[16] The distinction between military targets and civilian targets was not stated, and the distinction between authorized targets and those actually hit was left by the White House spokesman to the Department of Defense.

Authorized targets were principally limited to transportation routes, rail yards, fuel depots, heavy industry, and large structures that passed for heavy industry. Food prices in Hanoi fluctuated only slightly, although some shortages occurred in 1966, according to Salisbury. The rice crop was somewhat affected, and prices were held down principally by rationing and price controls. As North Vietnamese industry was never extensive, the deterioration in the standard of living caused by the bombing was "not really tangible." Imports through the port of Haiphong—which was not closed by air attacks—from Eastern Europe and the USSR actually permitted the government to reduce prices on a few consumer essentials such as bicycles, pharmaceuticals, and radios. The principal effect of the bombing was on the national distribution system for goods and services, a problem that was met by radical decentralization of economic activities.

Standards of Treatment of Civilians

The Battle for the Countryside

Four principal problems faced civilians in the Vietnam conflict:

1. ARVN treatment of Vietnamese civilians suspected of being, or harboring, Vietcong.

2. Civilian presence in the vicinity of armed conflict complicated by the fact that the allegiance of civilians, rather than territorial conquest, was to a large extent the measure of military victory.
3. The systematic campaign of propaganda, taxation, and terror by all parties, but principally the VC, to win control over the villages.
4. United States bombing of Vietnam that injured or killed civilians and destroyed civilian property.

The position of the Vietnamese farmer, who literally tilled a battlefield for forty years, was frequently expressed by the sentiment, "The VC only take our rice. The ARVN take our pigs, chickens and buffalo."[17] If the farmer was suspected of terrorist activity, the ARVN might also take his liberty or his life. The GVN, until its declaration of adherence to the Geneva Conventions in 1965, considered VC to be rebels and traitors, and as such they were subject to execution. Many of the captures were not made in actual combat where a VC soldier is identifiable as such. Instead, people were taken into custody simply because they were found in areas controlled or heavily influenced by the VC. A patrol, for example, would pick up a group of woodcutters working in a forest which the GVN had declared out of bounds to civilians. The decision as to whether they were VC or mere trespassers was largely hunch. If the detainee could establish that he sold his wood in a government-controlled village, he normally would be released with a warning or a fine. If the interrogator felt that the suspect "looked VC" or knew that he had been in a prohibited area on previous occasions, he might be shot.

The GVN and its allies never released any statistics on civilian casualties in South Vietnam at the hands of its own forces. However, they readily provided data on actions of the VC. Thus, on June 23, 1965, Secretary of State Dean Rusk said, "In the last eighteen months more than 2,500 local officials and civilians have been murdered. When an official is not found at home, often his wife and children are slain in his place. It is as if in our country 35,000 civic leaders and their families were to be killed at night by stealth and terror." The secretary's simile did not do justice to the complexity of the Vietnam conflict: United States civic leaders were not apt to be serving simultaneously in the militia. In South Vietnam, civic leaders who wished to avoid harassment from ARVN were apt to be officers in the "Dan Ve," or provincial militia (with the power to call for air strikes). Of course, once they accepted the commission in the people's self-defense force, they became targets of the Vietcong.

The victimization of civilians by the VC led the GVN to engage from 1962 to 1964 in a policy of fortifying strategic hamlets. Essentially, this meant forcible resettlement of entire villages from militarily insecure areas to territory that had been pacified by ARVN forces. As the 1,900 hamlets they were able to fortify constituted less than ten percent of the villages of South Vietnam and the resources of the government were unequal to the task of rearranging the population without utterly destroying the economy, the strategy was eventually abandoned.

The moving of civilians from their villages to provide protective custody, or to interrogate them as VC suspects, however, became a standard operating procedure in the conflict. ARVN or United States forces would enter a village and often "detain" every person—including women, children, and the aged—for interrogation. At that point they were referred to as "CD's" (civilian defendants). Typically, they would be taken to the brigade detention cage and then to a division collecting point, such as the Chulai POWC (prisoner of war camp) for interrogation. If they were found to be ICs (innocent civilians), they would be returned to their villages. If the villages had been destroyed or were in VC-controlled territory, they would be turned over to Vietnamese refugee authorities. By the summer of 1967 the United States and ARVN were detaining an average of 15,000 civilians per month. A civilian might be designated a "refugee" rather than a "detainee" prior to interrogation, depending upon the military judgment of the field commander, but this was rare under combat conditions in which every person was presumed hostile until proven friendly.

In some instances the presumption of hostility was fatal. Thus in March 1968, 130 Vietnamese civilians were slaughtered by United States forces in the village of My Lai. The incident, long concealed from the American public by military authorities, received national attention after publication of the book *My Lai 4* by reporter Seymour Hersh (for which he was awarded the Pulitzer Prize for journalism).[18] After a long series of investigations, hearings, and trials, Lt. William Calley was convicted in 1971 of the premeditated murder of twenty-two infants, children, women, and old men. The conviction was affirmed by the Court of Military Appeals in December 1973. This was the only publicized conviction of a person accused of grave breaches under GPW 147 arising out of the Vietnam conflict.

The emphasis on getting quick information to save the lives of military personnel commonly led to charges of intimidation and torture of civilians. A "detainee" was treated like a PW until exonerated by ARVN interrogators. Sixty-five percent of all persons detained proved to be ICs. North Vietnamese regulars, VC, or any other person who had committed an act against a "friendly force" were initially designated PWs, but an average of only seven percent of all detainees proved to be so. The balance were classified "CD" (civilian defendants), officially a category reserved for "spies, saboteurs and terrorists," but actually used to denote civilians about whom the interrogators could not make up their minds. If, and only if, a civilian was classified as a CD, the opinion of a field judge advocate was solicited concerning his status. A hearing could be requested to review a detainee's status, but detainees, frequently, were not informed of their rights, and hearings were rare. With the exception of the quasi-judicial element in CD classification mentioned above, classification procedures were otherwise administrative.

The treatment of "ICs" approximated the standards of GC. The CDs, however, were treated as criminals or political prisoners and imprisoned in local jails. The jails were very crowded, the treatment was rough, and conditions were squalid. These prisons were prime targets for VC raiders. For example, in August 1967, the Vietcong sprang the local jail of the capital city of Quangngai Province, freeing 1,200 prisoners, most of whom were CDs. The relatively large number of persons classified CD were not solely a result of administrative uncertainty. When they weighed the desirability of possible internment as a refugee for an indeterminate period against the average sentence of six months in a local jail (and the possibility of an early release by the VC), many villagers sought a CD designation.

ICRC reported of the refugees:

A large section of the South Vietnam rural population were compelled by air raids and military operations against the NLF to evacuate their homes. According to government statistics, approximately 484,000 Vietnamese have had to be sheltered in temporary reception centers since the end of 1964. Some 60 to 70 percent of these people are living in camps. The remainder have been taken in by the inhabitants of the towns where they sought refuge. In addition, the number of civilians who have been able to return to their villages is estimated at 123,000, while those who have been resettled in new villages are estimated at 325,000. These figures, reflecting the situation at the end of April 1966, vary constantly as a result of military operations. They do not include a large number of persons evacuated but not registered as "refugees." Most of the displaced persons were in the coastal provinces of the north and centre of the country, particularly in Quangngai, Phwyen, and Binh Dinh. They belong to all sections of the population including Vietnam families known for their sympathy for the rebel forces.[19]

If a United States unit took sniper fire from the direction of a village, this was usually sufficient justification for calling in an air strike to wipe out the "suspected enemy position" (i.e., the village). The Vietnamese constructed bunkers under their huts for just such an eventuality. When the ground forces finally moved into the village, anyone caught hiding in a bunker was automatically detained. In one instance, a United States paratroop captain told of how his company had managed to capture a number of Vietcong dependents hiding in a bunker. One group of the civilians—older men, women, and children—was discovered hiding in one section of the tunnel system. "When they saw we were not going to hurt them, they showed us where the others were hiding out," the officer said, adding, "It pays to be kind." This program was euphemistically known as "Winning Hearts and Minds—WHAM." The civilians were turned over to ARVN. It was reported that within forty-eight hours, all but the children had been executed. Dead Vietnamese discovered after an air strike were ordinarily considered VC in the daily body count.

The civilian population of South Vietnam was also exposed to the systematic terror and cruelty of the Vietcong. In 1963, 1,500 civilians and more than 500 government officials were murdered by the VC, 8,000 persons injured in terrorists attacks, and 700 kidnapped. These figures were published prior to the full-scale participation of United States ground forces. Thereafter, the Vietcong met superior firepower with military action at batallion and divisional strength and with selective terrorist activity. Subsequent to the VC offensive against the city of Hue in January 1968, allied forces reported the discovery of nineteen mass graves containing over 1,000 dead civilians. Evidence indicated that many victims were beaten to death, shot, beheaded, or buried alive. Unlike the United States forces, who used defoliants, napalm, and other chemical weapons that destroyed land and crops, the efforts of the VC were directed at diverting the agricultural economy to their own war effort. Where civilians were concerned, they did not indulge in indiscriminate slaughter or plunder, but they did use terror, torture, and mass murder when persuasion and propaganda failed to serve their ends. Characteristically, in the village of Vinh Ah in 1967, VC prison guards slaughtered forty-four men, women, and children moments before the village was liberated by ARVN forces. The victims were trussed by wires and then shot, grenaded, or hacked to death with bayonets.

In general, the VC went out of their way to treat United States civilians decently as part of a general policy of soliciting international goodwill. Among the more celebrated cases of kidnapped United States civilians was that of Gustav C. Hertz, chief of the U.S. Agency for International Development in Saigon, who died in captivity. Although, as it was later learned, Hertz apparently died of natural causes, the VC hinted that he would be executed as a reprisal for death sentences imposed on VC terrorists by a South Vietnamese military court in June 1967. The United States condemned the threatened reprisal under GPW, article 13. Another celebrated case was the capture of the beautiful French journalist Michele Ray, who was detained, interrogated, and released by the VC with all the courtesy due a former fashion model. The VC did not treat their captives with such solicitude unless it served their political interest to do so.

Stepped-Up Bombing in the South

Before February 19, 1965 the use of air power in the Vietnamese conflict was confined to tactical support of ground action. On that date United States forces began bombing enemy positions in South Vietnam with high explosives and antipersonnel devices such as napalm and cluster bomb units. A United States officer said to a *New York Times* reporter, "The Vietcong have terrorized the peasants to get their cooperation, or at least to stop their opposition. We must terrorize the villagers even more, so they see that their real self-interest lies with us. We've got to start bombing and strafing the villages that aren't friendly to the Government."[20] An average strike by a jet fighter carrying two one-ton cannisters of napalm ignited an inferno three times the size of a football field.

Burning for more than twenty minutes, the napalm would consume a dozen or so huts, as well as the oxygen from underground bunkers, causing death by suffocation. So-called free-bomb zones were established in which the pilot was not restricted to military targets. Any target, any structure, any movement at all was subject to destruction.

The F-105 fighter-bomber travels far too fast to see what it hits and must be guided by a forward air controller (FAC) in a spotter plane. If the FAC called an air strike inaccurately or by mistake, innocent people were killed; he literally had life and death power over the inhabitants of the villages within his reconnaissance area. In at least one instance, an FAC was relieved of duty because he declared himself a party to killing civilians. There was substantial evidence that paid Vietnamese informers triggered air raids on villages other than their own, for a variety of reasons. For example, a Jesuit mission refused to fly the NLF flag from its steeple. As a penalty, the VC herded twenty women and children into the church sanctuary and then tipped the local informer to report the hamlet. Napalm arrived ten minutes later. Indeed, it became well known in the villages that if the guerrillas came and shot at aircraft, the village was sure to be badly bombed at once.

In sum, United States firepower, used on an extremely large scale to save United States lives, to increase Vietcong casualties, and to destroy the VC base of economic and popular support, also killed and maimed estimated tens of thousands of Vietnamese civilians and destroyed their homes, farms, and livelihoods. Whereas the VC might select one or two key leaders of a government-controlled village for assassination, ARVN troops would either reply in kind or call a United States strike to obliterate the village. Although President Johnson urged the commander of United States forces in Vietnam to take all possible action to reduce civilian casualties and although search and clear operations were preceded by a helicopter calling civilians to collection points for protection, the effect of the bombing was to destroy the social structure of the countryside.

ARVN counterterrorist programs against civilians were not confined to air strikes. In 1966 there were 2,500 South Vietnamese commandos deployed in twelve-man forces under the command of province chiefs. Their mission included kidnapping and assassination. Paramilitary activities against civilians in VC-controlled areas included intimidation of women and destruction of farmland and livestock. Literally operating under a "skull and crossbones" emblem, the tactic of the commandos was to meet VC terror with counterterror—to intimidate, kill, and maim civilians believed sympathetic to the enemy in reprisal for similar attacks by VC against civilians loyal to the ARVN. The operations were supported by United States helicopters.

The Bombing of the North

In June 1966 United States planes bombed oil depots at Hanoi and Haiphong, North Vietnam. Although United States pilots had penetrated North Vietnamese air space as early as August 1964 to bomb military targets, the bombing of the capital city and the port of Haiphong fifty miles away marked a new escalation of the conflict. Bombing of the North continued until October 1968, when President Johnson ordered a curtailment of United States aerial attacks in stages to territory south of the 17th parallel. The bombing was resumed by President Nixon during the Paris negotiations of 1972. Information from the DRV concerning bomb damage was relatively sparse. ICRC was not permitted to observe the effects of bombing. The reports came principally from foreign correspondents, individuals, and delegations that were invited to enter North Vietnam by the DRV government, releases by the government itself, statements of United States pilots captured by the DRV, and intelligence reports.

The DRV frequently alleged that United States pilots were briefed to strike populated areas with cluster bomb units, napalm, and fragmentation bombs. "Confessions" of United States airmen typically stated that:

Our tactics would be to strike with fragmentation bombs encircling the villages first. This will cause many casualties, and the rest will seek shelter in the village. As they reach shelter, drop napalm which will drive them back into the open. Drop CBU's on the people as they run from their shelters. . . . In Nam Dinh it was the residential areas. . . . All the others were the same with the civilian population, centers of learning, medical facilities and market places being the only targets.[21]

Although the DRV called upon the United States on several occasions to stop the bombing of dikes and irrigation works and to otherwise cease the slaughter of innocent civilians, the actual number of civilian casualties and the effect of bombing on industry and agriculture were regarded as military secrets. In July 1972 the secretary general of the U.N., Kurt Waldhein, urged the United States to investigate charges of the bombing of dikes and was criticized by President Nixon for well-intentioned naivety. Nevertheless, *New York Times* correspondent Harrison Salisbury, the first United States correspondent to visit wartime Hanoi, stated five years prior in 1966 that:

- The heavily populated area of Phatchim, with no visible military objectives, suffered 150 attacks since 1965. In the worst raid, 72 persons were killed and 46 injured. The hospital was dispersed into half a dozen thatched huts because officials stated that it was too dangerous to occupy a substantial building. (No mention of marking of hospital.)
- The rhythm of city life in Hanoi was geared to bombing schedules, with shops open from 5 A.M. to 8 A.M., then closed until early evening. Frequent attacks occurred from 1 P.M. to 5 P.M.
- North Vietnamese military observers said that targets were often small and difficult to hit. For example, 14 trucks under repair in the suburb of Vandien scarcely seemed to be a significant military target; destruction of the Vietnam Polish Friendship High School, three-quarters of a mile from the repair yard was the consequence of the effort.

- Among the buildings hit was a Canadian mission to the International Control Commission. Near misses included the Rumanian, Chinese, Polish, and Russian Embassies.
- Bombs apparently directed at the Paul Doumer Bridge in Hanoi fell short in several strikes, destroying residences in the Hoan Kiem, Gialem, and Yenbien quarters of the city. Civilians were evacuated from the destroyed homes.
- The manhole concrete shelter, impervious to everything but a near hit, kept civilian casualties lower than might have been expected in comparison with the vast damage and destruction of living quarters.
- The works of the Hanoi museum of Fine Arts were sent to out-of-town caves. Polytechnic University departments were dispersed to the province. School children were evacuated to suburbs and schools themselves were dispersed, so that no more than one class was held in any building and all buildings were at least 150 yards apart. The children wore woven straw hats about an inch thick to safeguard them against fragmentation bombs.[22]

The resumption of the bombing of the North by President Nixon to spur cease-fire negotiations in 1972 was especially resented by the American public. Telford Taylor, the former United States chief prosecutor at Nuremberg, declared that if the war crimes standards applicable to Germany after World War II were applied to this conflict, the United States commander would be subject to conviction as a war criminal.

Collection and Protection of the Wounded, the Sick, and the Dead

Notwithstanding reports of atrocities against the wounded by ARVN and United States forces and reports of Vietcong atrocities against the wounded discussed elsewhere in this chapter, it appears that concern for collection and protection of the wounded and sick was among the few principles of the Geneva Conventions honored in the spirit, if not the letter, of the law. In view of the length and bitterness of hostilities and the high number of casualties, mistreatment of wounded combatants was not a major characteristic of the Vietnam war; the same cannot be said for neglect of civilian sick and wounded or the treatment of the dead.

Both Vietnamese and United States cultural values and published policies dictate compassion for the wounded and the sick of any nationality. All parties to the conflict collected the wounded and the sick after engagements and ministered to them according to available resources. ARVN and United States forces did not attempt to make any determination of detainee status of indigenous wounded on the battlefield. It was simply impractical as the wounded person was often too badly injured to permit identification. In addition, the Vietcong did not carry any identification—let alone the double identity disk prescribed by the convention. Subsequent to the participation of United States ground forces, most of the wounded were evacuated by helicopter. The availability of aerial evacuation ordinarily precluded evacuation of enemy dead from any conflict located at substantial distances from camps. The Vietcong and North Vietnamese, however, took great pains to collect and conceal not only the wounded but the dead as well, after each engagement. Vietcong removal of the dead served military and cultural purposes: In the first instance, it denied the allies evidence of the success of a mission as measured by a body count; in the second, the Vietnamese are traditionally solicitous about the burial of the dead.

Typical field operations in this regard were described by an American general:

A two battalion size artillery fire support base located some 60 kilometers from the nearest base camp is subjected to three separate ground attacks during the hours of darkness. The guerrillas suffer in excess of 300 killed. The majority of the bodies are located on or within the barbed wire surrounding the perimeter. The battalion surgeon insists on immediate removal (and) internment of the bodies to safeguard the health of the fire support base personnel. No air transportation is available for the evacuation of the dead. Cremation by napalm or utilization of a bulldozed mass grave are the only feasible courses of action available.[23]

Even in the meanest Vietcong prisoner camp lacking a medical facility on site, a Vietcong medic would be called from another camp to minister to the sick and wounded. Seriously ill patients would often be transferred to a larger camp for treatment. A typical first aid station, in a prisoner camp in Kien Phong province, was located in a low hut. Its two medics cared for six patients—two South Vietnamese PWs and four wounded Vietcong. However, wounded or not, it was not uncommon for prisoners to be killed by the Vietcong in the event of enemy attack. Captured documents indicated that the NLF also followed a practice of collecting identification from United States dead on the battlefield and then concealing the bodies for the purpose of simulating reprisals by releasing identification previously obtained. Thus, in June 1965, and again in September 1965, the NLF announced the execution of United States soldiers in reprisal for the deaths of terrorists executed by GVN. Bodies and personal effects of prisoners who were taken from the battlefield by the Vietcong or who died in Vietcong captivity were not returned to United States or ARVN authorities.

There were a substantial number of incidents of mutilation of the dead by United States and ARVN soldiers. A score of United States disciplinary and court-martial actions involved such matters as removal of the ears of the dead and decapitation. Other incidents by ARVN personnel involved public hanging and display of Vietcong corpses as a warning to villagers. Investigators attributed the crimes to the use of knives, hatchets, and bayonets in many hand-to-hand engagements, unrestrained reprisal for enemy terrorism, and a simple lack of knowledge that mutilation of the dead is a violation of the law of war.

It is estimated that there were ten civilian casualties for each military disability. In February 1968 the GVN, with the logistical support of the United States, initiated "Operation Recovery" for the collection and protection of South Vietnamese civilian casualties. The program was designed to assist victims of attacks on the cities and to convince villagers that the GVN was more concerned for their welfare than the enemy—but it reaped a propaganda harvest from Vietnamese suffering arising out of United States-conducted air attacks. This program received some international aid: Great Britain contributed $600,000, the Vatican $20,000, and international welfare organizations delivered medical supplies. Nevertheless, resources for the program were not commensurate with the need. Three military hospitals to have been constructed for the treatment of civilians were indefinitely delayed because of lack of funds. The failure of all parties to the hostilities to collect, protect, and offer adequate medical treatment to civilian casualties was a major tragedy of the conflict.

Protection of Hospitals

The wounded in South Vietnam captured by the allies were treated in United States Army field hospitals. Because it ordinarily took several days to establish the patient's detainee classification, problems of military security existed. The principal threat to United States hospitals was internal security. The hospital usually secured guards from the nearest military police unit as required. Patients classified as PWs who no longer required hospitalization were transferred to an army medical facility and subsequently to the GVN for internment. PWs requiring extensive hospitalization continued to receive care in the army hospitals.

Detainees who were classified as civilian defendants, refugees, or innocent civilians were turned over to ARVN or civilian hospitals as quickly as possible. A similar disposition was made of PWs who could not benefit from further hospitalization but did require outpatient treatment. The civilian hospitals, inadequate in the best of times, were strained beyond their resources. Nevertheless, the responsibility fell on the GVN for providing medical care to persons interned in PW camps as well as to Vietnamese civilians. The United States, acknowledging an uncertain obligation under GPW, article 12, continued to render outpatient care to PWs originally transferred to the ARVN by United States forces. Both the United States and Vietnamese hospitals were clearly marked. They were more often than not spared from VC mortar fire and terrorist attacks, with outstanding exceptions, including the civilian hospital at Hue, which was repeatedly struck during 1968 and 1969.

The DRV often accused the United States of bombing hospitals as well as other civil institutions. Thus a Reuters dispatch from Hong Kong in November 1965 alleged the deliberate bombing and strafing of a hospital in the town of Phu Tho. On several occasions in 1965 the DRV Red Cross accused United States aircraft of the destruction of "santoria and hospitals visibly bearing the Red Cross sign. ICRC took the "opportunity of drawing the attention of the American authorities to the respect which is due to hospitals and other medical establishments duly marked" and diplomatically advised the North Vietnamese that it had done so. The United States vigorously replied to ICRC that it had never bombed any target identifiable as a medical facility. It invariably disputed the validity of the accusations and proposed that an inquiry be made concerning them. Such proposals were not accepted by the DRV. Furthermore, the United States urged the authorities in Hanoi to clearly mark hospitals so that they could be easily identified from the air and to assure that they were not located near military installations.

Notes

1. U.S. Department of State, The Legality of United States Participation in the Defense of Viet Nam 26 (1966).

2. From the text of an address made by Under Secretary Ball before the Northwestern University Alumni Association at Evanston, Illinois, January 30, 1966.

3. U.S. Department of State, Office of the Legal Advisor, The Legal Advisor, The Legality of the United States Participation in the Defense of Viet Nam 13 (1965).

4. Dispatch from TASS, December 9, 1965.

5. U.S. Department of State, Office of the Legal Advisor, The Legal Advisor, The Legality of the United States Participation in the Defense of Viet Nam (1965).

6. Letter from Tran Thi Tich, DRV, to Samuel Gonard, ICRC, September 30, 1965.

7. Translations from the Vietnamese supplied by Col. George Westerman. The absence of a publication date or filing reference means that such references were not published on the original document.

8. American Red Cross News ss release 33021 December 1966 (The article quoted NLF communications to ICRC).

9. International Rev. Red Cross (1965) (statement of the DRV Minister of Foreign Affairs to ICRC).

10. Look Magazine, July 25, 1967, at 13.

11. 5 International Rev. Red Cross 528 (1965).

12. New York Times, July 8, 1966, at 3, col. 1. © 1966 by The New York Times Company. Reprinted by permission.

13. New York Times, July 17, 1966, at 1, col. 7. © 1966 by The New York Times Company. Reprinted by permission.

14. New York Times, July 26, 1966, at 1, col. 2. © 1966 by The New York Times Company. Reprinted by permission.

15. The Christian Science Monitor, November 25, 1967, at 4, col. 3. Quotation is from a petition filed by six farmers. © 1967 The Christian Science Publishing Society. All rights reserved.

16. New York Times, December 29, 1966, at 1, col. 7. © 1966 by The New York Times Company. Reprinted by permission.

17. Stone, War Without Honor 121 (1967).

18. See bibliography of alleged United States war crimes in Vietnam to come below.

19. International Rev. Red Cross 407 (1966).

20. Langguth, *The War in Vietnam*, New York Times, September 19, 1965, Magazine Section at 31. © 1965 by The New York Times Company. Reprinted by permission.

21. Foreign Broadcast Information Service, Daily Report No. 36 (representative sample of confessions of United States Navy pilots on bombing of civilians broadcast by Radio Hanoi, February 21, 1967).

22. New York Times, 1966. © 1966, 1969 by The New York Times Company. Reprinted by permission.

23. Schull, *Counterinsurgency and the Geneva Conventions: Some Practical Considerations*, 3 International Lawyer 49, 50 (1950). Reprinted by permission.

Bibliography of Books on U.S. War Crimes in Indochina

Barnett, Richard J. and Raskin, Marcus G. *An American Manifesto* (New Amer. Library).

Brown, Maj. Frederic J. *Chemical Warfare: A Study in Restraints* (Princeton).

Brown, Sam and Ackland, Len. *Why Are We Still in Vietnam?* (Vintage). Essays by J.B. Neilands and Jerry Tinker.

Browning, Frank and Foreman, Dorothy (eds.). *International Commission of Enquiry into United States Crimes in Indochina* (Harper & Row).

Calley, William L. *His Own Story* (Viking Press).

Chomsky, Noam. *At War with Asia* (Pantheon). Chapters 2 and 6.

Clarke, Robin. *The Silent Weapons* (McKay).

Concerned Asian Scholars. *The Indochina Story* (Bantam). Chapters 5-12.

Dellinger, David. *Revolutionary Non-Violence* (Bobbs-Merrill).

Donovan, James. *Militarism, U.S.A.* (Scribners).

Duffet, John (ed.). *Against the Crime of Silence* (Simon and Schuster). Prefaced by Noam Chomsky.

Everett, Arthur. *Calley* (Dell).

Falk, Richard; Kofton, Robert; and Kolko, Gabriel. *Crimes of War: After Songmy* (Random House, 1971).

Gershen, Martin. *Destroy or Die. The True Story of My Lai* (Arlington House).

Greenshaw, Wayne. *The Making of a Hero* (Touchstone).

Hammer, Richard. *One Morning in the War* (Hart-Davis).

Harvey, Frank. *Air-War–Vietnam* (Bantam).

Herman, Edward S. *Atrocities in Vietnam* (Pilgrim Press).

Hersh, Seymour. *Chemical and Biological Warfare: America's Hidden Arsenal* (Bobbs-Merrill).

———. *Coverup* (Vintage Books).

———. *My Lai 4* (Random House).

Lane, Mark. *Conversations with Americans* (Simon and Schuster).

Lang, Daniel. *Casualties of War* (McGraw-Hill).

McCarthy, Richard D. *The Ultimate Folly: War by Pestilence, Asphyxiation and Defoliation* (Knopf).

McFadden, Judith and Kroll, Erwin. *War Crimes and the American Conscience* (Holt, Rinehart, and Winston).

Melman, Seymour and Falk, Richard. *In the Name of America* (Turnpike Press).

Neilands, J.B. *Chemical Warfare in Vietnam* (Macmillan, 1971). Foreword by Gunnar Myrdal.

———. *The Social Responsibility of Scientists* (Macmillan).

Riddell, Thomas. *Efficiency in Death* (Harper & Row).

Rose, Steven (ed.). *Chemical and Biological Warfare* (Beacon).

Schell, Jonathan. *The Military Half* (Knopf).

———. *The Village of Ben Suc* (Knopf).

Schwartz, Laurent et al. *Massacres and Chemical Warfare in Southeast Asia* (Francois Masperau).

Stanford Biology Study Group. "The Destruction of Indochina" (pamphlet, 1970). Available from Stanford Biology Study Group, Box 3724, Stanford, Calif. 94305).

Taylor, Telford. *Nuremberg and Vietnam* (Quadrangle).

35 Organisations des Assis Nationales. *Livre Noire des Crimes Americains au Vietnam* (Fayard).

Tiede, Tom. *Calley, Soldier or Killer?* (Pinnacle Books).

Tinker, Jerry. *Refugee and Civilian War Casualty Problems in Indochina* (Staff report for U.S. Senate Subcommittee on Refugees, September 1970).

Uhl, Michael. *A Soldier's View* (University Press).

U.S. House Committee on Armed Services. Committee briefing on Project Egress (Superintendent of Documents, 1972).

U.S. Senate Committee on Foreign Relations. Hearings, "Chemical and Biological Warfare." Free copies available from Committee Office.

———. Hearings on U.S. POW's and MIA's in Southeast Asia (U.S. Government Printing Office, 1974).

Prior bibliographies were compiled in the first edition of *Against the Crime of Silence* (Duffet) with legal framework provided by Richard Falk, and in the *New Republic Review* (January 1971) of *An American Manifesto* by Mark Sacharoff.

6   Dominican Republic

Introduction

The relevance of the Geneva Conventions to a regional peacekeeping force—such as those of the Organization of American States (OAS), the North Atlantic Treaty Organization (NATO), the Southeast Asia Treaty Organization (SEATO), or the Warsaw Pact nations—raises even more perplexing problems than its application to United Nations operations. If the United Nations, a legal entity composed of, but separate from, its member states, may be compared with a corporation for illustrative purposes, then the regional compacts are in the nature of partnerships. Some, such as NATO and OAS, are tightly structured with permanent administrative organizations, including a military command. SEATO, on the other hand, is a much looser arrangement. The application of the law of war to hostilities involving these organizations invokes considerations similar to those observed in the United Nations studies. How do the peacekeeping forces differ, if at all, from traditional treaty alliances for the conduct of hostilities? Who is the detaining power when regional forces capture and detain hostile forces? Who is responsible for the administration of occupied territory? The purpose of this section is to examine a single regional peacekeeping operation, the OAS in the Dominican Republic, as a basis for subsequent analysis.

Armed conflict in the Dominican Republic began on April 24, 1965, when a group of young officers, calling themselves Constitutionalists, rebelled against the provisional administration of President Donald Reid Cabral. It was substantially terminated on May 27, 1965, by a cease-fire imposed by military intervention in the name of the Organization of American States. In the seven weeks following the cease-fire, however, there were 900 cease-fire violations, resulting in over 200 casualties.

Rafael Trujillo had been the dictator of the country from 1930 until his assassination in May 1961. His successor to the presidency, Joaquin Balaguer, was forced out by a military junta in mid-January 1962. The junta, in turn, was deposed by a countercoup that, through a Council of State, called general elections in December 1962. Professor Juan Bosch, identified with the democratic left as candidate of the Democratic Revolutionary Party, won a clear majority. He was inaugurated in February 1963, and was removed from office by a military coup d'etat in September of the same year. Opposition had developed from the right, which accused him of surrendering to communism, and from the left, which accused him of capitulating to "Yankee imperialism." The military vested power in a three-man civilian committee that, after a turbulent 90-day administration, yielded the presidency in early 1964 to Foreign Minister Donald Reid Cabral. President Cabral promised new elections to be held in September 1965. But in April the crisis erupted.

The Constitutionalists, composed principally of junior officers and elements of Bosch's Democratic Revolutionary party, who felt that economic and military reforms were inadequate, were eventually led by Col. Francisco Caomaño Deño. The other side, calling itself the Government of National Reconstruction ("Loyalists"), was composed principally of the senior officers who had supported the administration of President Cabral and his immediate predecessors. They felt that reforms were moving too fast. The government faction was identified with the leadership of Generals Elias Wessin y Wessin and Antonio Imbert Barreras.

The police force of the capital city of Santo Domingo was a principal military target of the Constitutionalists. Public order disintegrated as the force collapsed, and armed mobs terrorized the city with indiscriminate shooting, pillage, and arson. On April 28 the Loyalist Command notified the United States Embassy that United States lives were in danger and that conditions of public disorder made it impossible to provide adequate protection for the safety of the citizens of the United States. It requested temporary intervention and assistance for the purpose of restoring order. President Lyndon B. Johnson ordered the landing of 400 marines to assist in the evacuation of 2,400 United States citizens and other foreign nationals.

The following day, the Council of the OAS expressed its concern over the fighting and announced its confidence that the matter would be resolved within the "framework of the institutions of the inter-American system." The United States rapidly built up its forces to over 20,000 within the next few days. Explaining the augmented presence to the American people, President Johnson stated:

The revolutionary movement took a tragic turn. Communist leaders, many of them trained in Cuba, seeing a chance to increase disorder, to gain a foothold, joined the revolution. They took increasing control. And what had begun as a popular democratic revolution, committed to democracy and social justice, very shortly moved and was taken over and really seized and placed into the hands of Communist conspirators.[1]

However, the official United States view was that its prompt unilateral action was merely a prelude to a multilateral peacekeeping operation by the regional organization and not an intervention into the domestic affairs of the Dominican Republic. The OAS wrestled with the legal exceptions to the prohibitions on intervention spelled out in the Charter of Bogota; on May 6, 1965 it declared the existence of an Inter-American Peace Force (IPF). Thereafter, and until they were relieved by military contingents of other Latin countries, United States forces acted under the IPF command.

The military action of the IPF was largely confined to Santo Domingo. United States Airborne and Marine units were encamped on the spacious polo grounds of the Hotel Embajador in the southwest corner of the city. On Friday, April 30 the United States forces secured the western residential sector of the city as an international safety zone. Paratroopers, landing during the night, mustered at the San Isidro Air Force Base, which was the military command of the Loyalists. They rapidly secured the Duarte Bridge across the Ozama River, which was the only entrance to the city from its eastern suburbs. Although the United States troops had instructions not to shoot at rebels unless fired upon, the position was taken only after heavy fighting. Eventually, the intervening forces split the city in two, dividing the rebel forces and establishing military positions that remained relatively unchanged during the subsequent weeks of talking and fighting.

Type of Conflict

The United States landed armed forces in the Dominican Republic as a humanitarian intervention in a civil conflict. It was the first large-scale joint military operation in the Western Hemisphere involving the United States since the French and Indian wars. It also marked the first major involvement of United States forces in a peacekeeping role on foreign soil during a civil war. Finally, it was the first intervention by the OAS in a conflict situation. Prior to the arrival of foreign forces, only those articles of the Geneva Conventions that relate to a conflict not of an international character were applicable to the Dominican combatants. To Loyalists and Constitutionalists, foreign intervention did not change the character of the conflict.

The principal issue was the legality of the intervention itself. Viewing it as a violation of Dominican sovereignty, several member states of the United Nations alleged that the United States had breached article 2 (7) of the United Nations Charter, which prohibits intervention by a United Nations member state into the domestic jurisdiction of another state, and had violated the Rio Treaty, which obligates signatories not to resort to the threat or use of force in any manner inconsistent with the United Nations Charter. Finally, it was contended that article 17 of the OAS Charter declares the inviolability of the territory of all member states under all circumstances. The only possible legal intervention would have been the collective action of the OAS or the United Nations. Under this argument, the United States would have been, as predictably argued by Cuba and the USSR, an aggressor in an undeclared war.

The legality of the United States position was defended under the rules of customary international law that permit any state to protect the lives and liberties of its citizens abroad in conformity with civilized standards. In the sixteen meetings of the United Nations Security Council between May 3 and May 25, the United States consistently disclaimed involvement in Dominican internal affairs and argued for OAS responsibility in attaining a cease-fire and promoting a political solution to the disorder. Finally, in order to underscore its impartiality and to spur military commitment by other Latin nations, the United States formally turned over its forces to the paper IPF command under the political leadership of José A. Mora, secretary general of the OAS.

The IPF, like the UNF in the Congo, was a peacekeeping force that was not intended to initiate military operations. Unlike the UNF, however, they lacked regulations relevant to the application of international conventions to the particular dispute. In practice, however, the OAS, like the ONUC, appeared to apply the customary laws of war rather than the Geneva Conventions per se.

The Loyalists were composed chiefly of uniformed, well-directed, disciplined, regular military units including ground troops and a tactical air force. They were, for the most part, under the military command of General Wessin y Wessin and of Colonel Pedro Bartolomé Benoit, elected "president" of the San Isidro junta. The uniformed police of Santo Domingo were also a party to the conflict on behalf of the Loyalists; they constituted the principal political base of General Antonio Imbert Barreras, who became head of the Government of National Reconstruction during cease-fire negotiations.

The Constitutionalist leadership consisted of regular, uniformed officers such as its commander, Colonel Caomaño Deño and key naval officers. It also included André Rivière, a French mercenary who served as a top rebel commander until his death during battle with the IPF. The rebel rank and file was made up principally of nonuniformed civilians who carried their rifles and submachine guns quite openly, but did not wear armbands or other identifying insignia. Colonel Caomaño Deño claimed to have 10,000 armed men in the center of the city and 37,000 elsewhere. This was probably a gross exaggeration; but the situation was complicated enormously when the Constitutionalists, on the second day of conflict, passed out arms to an estimated 5,000 inhabitants. In addition, thousands of Santo Domingans were reported to possess Molotov cocktails.

At first, armament ranging from rifles to .50-caliber machine guns were issued only to armed forces veterans, and each recipient had to sign a receipt. Later, the depositories were thrown open by the Constitutionalists to anyone who wanted to grab a weapon. This tactic was largely responsible for the creation of a group of thrill-seeking youngsters called "Tigres," whose incessant sniping caused much of the injury, most of the recriminating charges of truce violation, and the frequent identification of the rebels with irresponsibility, brigandry, and Communist opportunism.

By the second week of operations, the IPF, commanded by General Bruce Palmer, involved over 30,200 men, 21,500 of whom were on Dominican soil.

The total contingent included 14,000 paratroopers, 7,000 marines, and 8,000 sailors manning the 30 ships and 274 aircraft involved full time in logistic operations. By the fifth week of the conflict, General Palmer passed command of the IPF to General Hugo Panasco Alvim of Brazil, whose nation committed 5,000 troops to the operation. Uniformed contingents were also contributed by Nicaragua, Honduras, and Costa Rica.

Systems of Control

No fewer than five international agencies attempted to mediate a truce between the parties to the Dominican civil war and to interject humanitarian standards into the conflict. The political activities of the OAS were directed by its secretary general, Dr. José A. Mora; the secretary general of the United Nations was represented by Dr. A. Mayobre of Venezuela; the Papal Nuncio in Santo Domingo, Msgr. Emanuele Clarizio, was a tireless mediator in the name of the Roman Catholic church; M. Pierre Jequirier, the Latin American ICRC delegate general, promoted truce and civilized warfare in the name of the Geneva Conventions; and President Johnson sent a virtual delegation of personal representatives and observers to report the facts and to negotiate a truce. At one time or another, key figures included Attorney Abe Fortas (later appointed associate justice of the United States Supreme Court); McGeorge Bundy, special assistant to the president for national security affairs; and John Barlow Martin, former United States ambassador to the Dominican Republic. The peacemakers sometimes marched together and sometimes worked at cross purposes. More often, they ignored each other and communicated through their own chains of command. With each of three groups of armed forces and five mediation teams going its own way in a city of little more than half a million population, the confusion was monumental.

On April 28, 1965, the day of its intervention into the Dominican civil war, the United States informed the OAS of United States actions and requested OAS intercession. The United States position was spelled out by Ambassador Ellsworth Bunker seventy-two hours later at the Tenth Meeting of American Ministers of Foreign Affairs. The creation of a regional military force was opposed by virtually all of the major powers of Latin America except Brazil. Nevertheless, the United States mustered the required two-thirds vote, and by the time the matter reached the United Nations Security Council on May 3, the regional organization was on record as accepting the primary responsibility for attaining a permanent cease-fire and promoting a political solution to the disorder.

Even though article 52 of the United Nations Charter permits regional agency settlement and even calls upon the Security Council to encourage such settlement, the right of the United Nations to investigate a threat to the peace under article 34 is not preempted. The OAS had kept the Security Council fully informed of its activities as required by the charter. However, dissapproval of the United States action by member states resulted in adoption of a resolution to have the secretary general send his own representative to the Dominican Republic. The concurrent jurisdiction of the United Nations and the OAS was criticized in the United States Senate and by the Pan American Union.

The Loyalists and the Constitutionalists lost no time in choosing champions. Both requested the OAS to send the Inter-American Commission on Human Rights to investigate alleged violations of rights. The Constitutionalists also demanded the dispatch of the United Nations Commission on Human Rights. The United Nations Commission could not comply because, lacking an invitation from the "government," its action would have constituted an illegal intervention in the domestic affairs of the state. Actually, neither the Loyalists nor the Constitutionalists were the established government, but the OAS concluded that a request from both had the implied consent of the state. The secretary general dispatched Dr. Mayobre and General Indar Rikhye to report on the military scene. There was a twenty-four-hour courtesy truce during General Rikhye's tour, which was broken the moment he left Dominican soil. Dr. Mora's and Dr. Mayobre's activities were supplementary much of the time, with the former tending to build bridgeheads from the Loyalist side of the dispute and the latter from the Constitutionalist side.

The Papal Nuncio was actually able to negotiate a fragile cease-fire on April 30. President Johnson announced the accomplishment in a televised speech, only to be advised within a matter of hours that the truce had been shattered. President Johnson's own emissaries attempted to secure the peace through kingmaking. United States influence resulted in elevation of General Imbert to the junta leadership in an attempt to secure the peace (and was later used to try to have him succeeded by backing Silvestre Guzman for president). General Imbert proved hard to control, however, and Dr. Mayobre recommended Security Council action because of Imbert's refusal to adhere to a truce. The OAS, in the meantime, criticized Caomaño Deño for violating the cease-fire and claimed that President Johnson's emissary (Bundy) was obstructing its efforts as well. It also leveled the same charge at the United Nations team.

The extensive peacemaking effort appeared largely to defer considerations of detainment, civilian relief, and other humanitarian purposes to the greater issue of a permanent truce. Even the ICRC delegate was swept up in the effort to mediate a cease-fire. Working with the Dominican Red Cross and the World Health Organization representative, he did at least successfully negotiate a twenty-four-hour truce for removal of the wounded and dead, as discussed below. ICRC also visited the detention centers on both sides, broadcasted warnings to the population about the misuse of the Red Cross emblem, and observed respect for the Geneva Conventions during the truce period.

Persons Entitled to PW Status

The Inter-American Commission on Human Rights, an organ of the OAS, was invited by both factions to investigate alleged deprivations of life, liberty, and personal security. It reported the arrest and imprisonment of thousands of persons, the bulk of them political prisoners held without cause, without charges, and without hearings. Of 4,000 persons still in prison in June 1965, only several hundred were military prisoners and none was a member of IPF.

The United States mission, which arrived on April 28, seemed totally unaware of the scale of political imprisonment, and appeared quite uncertain about whether to take, let alone how to handle, the prisoners that fell into its hands. United States correspondents accompanying the armed forces reported that prisoners were taken, but the reporters were frustrated in their efforts to determine the number of prisoners or their disposition. Although newsmen had pictures of Dominicans in stockades under guard of United States troops, military spokesmen insisted they knew nothing about this. Some reports said that United States troops were releasing rebel prisoners to the junta forces. The reports appeared correct, for within forty-eight hours of the United States landing, General Palmer issued a memorandum changing "the command policy on turning detainees over to the Loyalist forces." The number and fate of prisoners turned over to the Loyalists during the first two days after the United States forces landed were unknown—apparently the principal reason for the change of policy. The military mission of the peace keeping force was to create and police the demilitarized International Safety Zone through the center of the city of Santo Domingo between the hostile factions. As noted above, there was no mass confrontation of forces. Most of the conflict was characterized by sniper fire from buildings and rooftops.

During the first week, IPF took about 100 Constitutionalist prisoners. In addition, IPF detained suspicious persons who were carrying arms in the international corridor in the central city. United States diplomatic officials on the scene did not regard the IPF as a party to the conflict, did not consider the detainees to be prisoners, and did not believe that the Geneva Conventions were applicable. The Constitutionalists, in turn, captured several United States marines who blundered into their sector of the city or pursued snipers too far beyond the international zone. American soldiers were detained only by the Constitutionalists since the Loyalists operations were conducted principally behind the United States power shield (in spite of the best efforts of the United States to maintain neutrality). These prisoners were invariably released in a day or two. The most serious of several of such incidents occurred on May 6, when seven marines mistakenly drove a jeep from the international corridor into the rebel zone. Two were killed and one fatally wounded; the balance were taken prisoner and repatriated within forty-eight hours. The bodies of the dead marines were delivered to a marine checkpoint by Dominican civilians. The two uninjured prisoners were interrogated by Colonel Caomaño (for the benefit of United States TV camera crews) before being turned over to the United States Peace Corps director.

Standards of Internment

The vast majority of captives were held in prisons scattered about the City of Santo Domingo. The Inter-American Human Rights Commission, assisted by an investigating and review board set up by the Government of National Reconstruction, began in early May to determine conditions of internment, to assess complaints, and to arrange the release of prisoners. The commission maintained continuous contact with the top officials of each faction and the prison commandants. It kept up a steady pressure for proper hearings and trials, improved sanitary and medical facilities, and treatment of the sick and wounded in detention. Conditions in all the prisons were reported as substandard, although they gradually improved with a decrease in crowding after the first two weeks of bloodshed.

The principal Loyalist prison, La Victoria Penitentiary, held 350 civilians and 132 military prisoners in mid-August, a full two months after the cease-fire had been negotiated. At the same time, San Isidro Air Force Base, headquarters of the junta (and, ironically, of the United States 82nd Airborne Division which had taken over one of the hangars) held eighty political and military prisoners. Fifty more were held by the junta in the National Police Palace and ninety in the interior of the country. The Constitutionalists held their prisoners in the Ozama Fortress, site of the heaviest fighting during the early weeks. They also held prisoners at a detention center near Sans Souci, a small peninsula separated from the city by the Ozama River.

As noted above, for the first two days IPF prisoners were turned over to the Loyalists. Subsequently, the commanders of the (United States) 82nd Fourth Medical Battalion and Fifth Logistic Command were ordered to establish detainee centers to provide for "expeditious handling of captured personnel, documents and material to preserve their intelligence value. . . . The Detainee Collecting Point became a Detainee Center. This meant that the temporary holding facility became semi-permanent and entailed feeding, housing, and safeguarding detainees for an extended period."[2] United States Army records suggest that the logistics of existing internment facilities were merged with those of civilian relief and assistance. Apart from detaining individuals causing disturbances and providing sanctuary to persons who would be in danger if released, the IPF did not actively seek to detain forces of either side.

At the outset of military operations, ICRC (International Committees of the Red Cross) informed the Dominican Republic Red Cross of its willingness to assist the victims of the civil war. Although it was a principal contributor to the cease-fire negotiations and was able to arrange a truce for the removal of the wounded and dead, ICRC was not as concerned with conditions of internment in this conflict as it was in other conflicts. The OAS, on the other hand, flew in a group of criminologists in July to investigate charges of murder in the prisons, assassination, and kidnapping.

The specific incident that sparked the investigation was called the Hacienda Haras case and involved charges of Loyalist execution of seventeen prisoners. The charges were confirmed by a detailed committee report that concluded that not "only had the prisoners been killed after detention," with the knowledge of Loyalist authorities, but there was "cause for believing not only in their military origin, but in an established policy of prosecuting the elimination of adversaries, executing them precipitately without trial, and leaving the bodies abandoned so that the fate of the victims would serve as a lesson and an exemplary warning to the people."[3] The Loyalists, for their part, accused the Constitutionalists of killing a dozen captives in cold blood and of beheading an officer and parading his head through the rebel area on a pole. This particular charge was given by Colonel Benoit to John Barlow Martin, President Johnson's special envoy, as a reason for the unacceptability of a cease-fire proposal. The charge was not confirmed.

Within the limits of its manpower, the commission investigated all reported atrocities and grave breaches in places of internment and throughout the city. The standards of the Geneva Conventions were not overtly invoked (except in the matter of removal of wounded and dead, discussed below).

Standards of Treatment of Civilians

The citizens of Santo Domingo were participants, bystanders, and victims of the war that wracked their city. On a "typical" Sunday, May 16, 1965, Caomaño headquarters reported that junta tanks and infantrymen were firing point blank into residences in which they thought rebels were hiding. Women and children were indiscriminately slaughtered, and hospitals confirmed the arrival of hundreds of new casualties with bullets and shrapnel wounds. The cease-fire had been shattered again. The official death toll three months after the civil war began was 2,850 Dominicans and 28 United States troops. Most of the dead Dominicans were civilians. In addition to the loss of life, the property of individuals had been taken and destroyed and the economy of the country crippled.

The 82nd Airborne Division, spearheading the military operations of the IPF, participated in a broad civic action to provide food, clothing, water, and medical care to the civilian population. General Palmer's report observed that 36,000 civilians received medical care, and 1,400 tons of food were distributed to

23,000 families. A Dependents Assistance Center was established on April 30, 1965, to write to the next of kin of persons who were separated from their families by the hostilities. Some troops were even reported to have handed out their own combat rations to people in greater need of food.

United States civilian agencies were similarly active. Within a month after the outbreak of hostilities, and while military operations and political warfare went on everywhere, a United States Department of State staff of sixty officials acted, for all practical purposes, as the civilian government of the country. Their activities included restoring the important peanut oil factory in Santo Domingo, supplying a United States tanker so that the city would not lose its electrical power, and even lending money to the junta to pay the salaries of the Loyalist soldiers. Understandably, the rebel-controlled Radio Santo Domingo described the United States as an "occupying power," a status stoutly denied by Washington. In addition to regular State Department and AID personnel, the United States Department of Health, Education, and Welfare and the American Red Cross provided relief, transportation, and temporary housing for thousands of foreign nationals and Dominican refugees. The American Red Cross reported the evacuation of 3,982 persons to Puerto Rico. Refugees evacuated from the island at United States government expense could return at their own expense at any time.

The Hotel Embajador, as well as several large hospitals and the International Safety Zone itself, became refugees for the homeless and ill. Fleeing from indiscriminate firing by Loyalist forces in mid-May, thousands of refugees left the northern district of the city and set up improvised camps on either side of the highways outside Santo Domingo. Refugees were permitted in all areas patrolled by IPF troops after a careful search for weapons. The policy was that all unarmed persons, civilians, or rebel soldiers would be permitted to cross IPF lines. (The policy was less clear with respect to crossing by armed junta personnel.)

United States soldiers were actually quartered in some requisitioned private homes in the International Safety Zone. Sometimes the United States purchased food instead of issuing field rations. In one instance, a hotel was rented from its owners; more often, IPF forces bivouacked in vacant lots and parks. There did not appear to be any uniform command policy on the use and taking of civilian property.

A poignant vignette of civilian life in a low-intensity conflict was given by correspondent Tad Szulc.

Heavily armed [U.S.] soldiers chatted easily with Dominican girls, leaning on garden walls in front of the little houses. Flowers were growing in many of the tiny front gardens. Here and there a paratrooper would relax in a rocking chair on a porch, talking to the family with whom he and his buddies had moved in for the duration. It was an idyllic picture. But it could all change in a fraction of a second. Someone could start firing from somewhere—as usually happened several times a day—and the young paratroopers who had been sitting in the rocking chairs or flirting against garden walls would grab their rifles, machine guns or bazookas. Then the peaceful street would turn again into an inferno of flying bullets and exploding shells. There would be curses through clenched teeth and occasionally, cries of 'Medic' . . . In a few minutes, or in a few hours, the fighting would die down and all would be tranquil again.[4]

Collection and Protection of the Wounded and the Sick

The locations of all the city hospitals were well known to the local combatants. They were spared direct attack and served relief as well as medical purposes. The situation during the first week of hostilities in the Dominican Republic, as described by Harry Benson, the photographer of the *London Daily Express*, from one of the downtown hospitals in Santo Domingo, was that the building

. . . had no electric power and no running water. It was out of anesthetics and most medicines. The wounded, including women and children, sometimes underwent surgery on the dirty floors . . . about a thousand people were lying on the floor awaiting death. Doctors said there was nothing they could give these people or do for them anymore. Swarms of flies on the festering wounds of the injured . . . People were often buried where they died and frequently bodies were burned in big piles to prevent epidemics. Nobody had any idea what the toll of dead and injured was. But at this point, after five days of fighting, it obviously ran into hundreds and hundreds.[5]

Another correspondent, describing conditions in the Salvador B. Gauthier Hospital, later wrote, "that inside the hospital, where medicine was usually dispensed, women and children in torn clothes, and some without any, were milling around."

The United States Marines brought along medical supplies, particularly analgesics and anesthetics, for hospitals in Santo Domingo but these were depleted by the first week. Seven of the United States Peace Corps volunteers, who had been social workers and nurses in clinics in the city's poor districts prior to the hostilities, moved into the hospitals to assist the staffs. The director of the American Red Cross accompanied State Department and United States AID personnel on a special mission to determine relief needs, which resulted in shipments of blood, inoculation equipment, vaccines, and nutritional supplements to the Dominican Red Cross for distribution.

M. Jequirier, Latin American ICRC delegate general, did not arrive until May 15, 1965. Working with the Dominican Red Cross, he immediately set about negotiating a twenty-four-hour truce for removal of the wounded and dead, basing his appeal upon the Geneva Conventions of 1949. Although the ICRC proposal was well received by Colonel Caomaño Deño, the junta delegation led by General Imbert was reluctant to conclude the truce. It appeared to have been not the Geneva Conventions, but rather the additional pressure brought to bear by the United Nations special envoy, Dr. Mayobre, that secured compliance. General Imbert, who was quite unmoved by the reminder that his country was a signatory to the conventions, was pointedly advised by the ICRC of "the unfortunate effect which his hesitation would produce on the Security Council."

The collection and protection of the wounded during the street fighting was ultrahazardous because of the presence of roof-top snipers. United States paratroopers were under orders to avoid entry into rebel zones except in hot pursuit of snipers. In one instance during the third week, several paratroopers who had penetrated a few hundred yards into rebel territory were pinned down and wounded by heavy machine gun fire. To enable medics to reach the wounded men, the paratroopers fired at the machine gun emplacement with 106-mm. recoilless rifles. The shots from this powerful weapon virtually sliced the tops off of the houses from which the fire had come. The Constitutionalists later complained that a number of civilians were killed in the action. The rebel military action against the IPF was impersonal and inconsistent. A typical incident occurring during the same period as the one described above, involving an inadvertent penetration of rebel territory, had a different conclusion; one United States soldier was killed, whereas another, mortally wounded, was sped by the rebels themselves to a hospital several blocks away.

Notes

1. Department of State Pub. 7971, Inter-American Series, 92, Part 3, Released October, 1975.

2. Palmer, Stability Operations, Dominican Republic, U.S. Army Report No. USFDR-JO, in vol. II (no pagination and no date).

3. OEA, Tenth Meeting of Consultation, Doc. 231, July 11, 1965.

4. Tad Szulc, *Dominican Diary*. © 1965 by The New York Times. Reprinted with permission of Delacorte Press.

5. Id.

Part III:
Application of the Law:
Russia, China, and
Other Powers

7 Russia

Legal Tradition

Any attempt to predict how the USSR would treat prisoners of war in a future general or limited conflict is a highly speculative undertaking. Essentially what one must do is to extrapolate and project past attitudes and practices into a wholly hypothetical conflict situation. In the case of the USSR, those attitudes and practices date from World War II and earlier, for Soviet forces have not been directly involved in recent conflicts, such as Korea or Vietnam, where large-scale prisoner of war experience has accumulated. The occasional border incidents involving United States aircraft shot down off Soviet coasts are scarcely typical of a wartime situation, and there are no data on PWs taken in the Sino-Soviet border clashes along the Ussuri River. Moreover, it is not unreasonable to expect treatment of prisoners of war to vary, depending upon the scope and nature of the conflict. One may suppose that it would make a difference if the USSR were fighting on its own territory, or if nuclear weapons were used on a large scale, or if Soviet PWs and the civilian populace were being humanely treated by the enemy. During World War II, of course, Soviet experience was that of a victim state whose population, both civilian and military, was subjected to enormous atrocities, in violation of the laws of war, at the hands of the Nazi armies. It may be important also that, in the past, war has primarily meant land warfare to the Soviet Union. Naval operations have, until recently, played only a minor role in Soviet military operations. Although the struggle for air supremacy in the USSR during World War II was important, Soviet cities suffered far more from being surrounded and shelled than they did from being bombed.

In spite of these and other differences between past experience and possible future situations, the public record relating to Soviet treatment of prisoners of war during World War II and earlier conflicts is relevant to any attempt to identify fundamental Soviet attitudes. In addition, the Soviet government played an active and instrumental role in the drafting and adoption of the 1949 Geneva Conventions of prisoners of war and has enacted legislation pursuant to those conventions. The following survey, based on those materials, seeks to identify fundamental Soviet attitudes and practices likely, in one manifestation or another, to affect Soviet behavior to prisoners of war and civilians in the future.

The Russian Empire and its antecedent entity, Muscovy, evolved in very special circumstances that had a profound influence on the status and value of the individual in Russian society, the formation and character of the Russian

215

legal system, and the reception and development of international law and diplomatic practice in Russia. In spite of periods of self-imposed isolation, the greater part of the history of the Russian state and its predecessors bears the imprint of constant, often violent, contact and conflict with highly diverse foreign cultures and legal systems. To the south there had been centuries of trading, diplomacy, and war with the Byzantine Empire and later the Turks. To the east were the Tartars, whose conquest and domination of much of Russia for nearly 240 years (1240-1480) retarded the reception of European law and diplomacy but whose own practices in the conduct of war influenced Russia for centuries thereafter. To the west lay Europe, whose influence, somewhat belatedly, was the last to reach Russia. Often engaged in conflict simultaneously or successively on three fronts, Russia became the repository of diverse patterns and values in the art of war whose synthesis was to become peculiarly Russian.

The Muscovy period (1480-1689) was characterized by very slow and tentative expression of interest in Western ideas. Although for religious and political reasons Russia was isolated from the Western Renaissance, the origins of a science of international law began to emerge. By order of the Tsar, a German manual on military art published in 1565-73 was translated into Russian in 1606-7 and reworked in 1621. The manual dealt in part with the treatment of prisoners of war but was not published until 1777, when the manuscript was rediscovered in the Kremlin. The first translated treatise on international law published in Russia, in 1647, also was a German work dealing in part with war prisoners. But Russian practice remained heavily influenced by tradition and religion in this period; for example, a prisoner in Russian hands could terminate his captivity by being baptized, with the permission of the Tsar, in the Russian Orthodox Church. The prisoner thereupon became irrevocably a Russian national.

With the advent of the Imperial Period (1690-1917), the drive for the modernization of Russia was accomplished by the importation of Western notions of a legal order and of international law. The first original unofficial work on international law in the Russian language appeared in 1717. Written by a Russian diplomat, the volume discussed the legal grounds for the war then being fought against Sweden and criticized, *inter alia*, Swedish violations of the status of prisoners of war. In the nineteenth century Russia enacted a series of statutes notable for their humanitarian and rational spirit in treating prisoner of war questions. These had considerable impact on international legislation (notably, the Brussels Declaration of 1874, the Hague Conventions of 1899 and 1907, and the Geneva Conventions of 1929). A Statute on Prisoners of War adopted in 1914, shortly after Russia entered World War I, differed from the 1907 Hague Convention only in minor respects.

Thus, prerevolutionary Russian experience may be said to have comprised the following principal elements: War was a central concern of the state in order to secure and then expand its borders; diplomacy was conducted with a wide range of political entities, from sovereign states to the West (and China) to vassal-tribute relations in Central Asia; international law was part of Russian thought and practice from at least the Imperial Period on (and perhaps earlier); a continuing involvement in conflict and reliance on massive land armies as its principal weapon were influential in causing Russia to undertake a leading role in articulating principles for the treatment of war prisoners.

Bourgeois laws and legal systems had been singled out early in the Marxist movement as one of several major instruments through which the ruling classes perpetuated their domination over the proletariat. In October 1917 the Bolsheviks not only revolted against prerevolutionary law, but also dreamed of creating a new type of classless society in which all people would live in fellowship and would be governed by their social consciousness, without need for legal institutions. Initially, they restored to law, primarily as a means of maintaining the "proletarian dictatorship" over class opposition in the transition period. In time, however, the Soviet rulers found that without law they could not maintain political order even among friendly supporters, nor could they run a planned economy. Also, they came to recognize not only that law is an important instrument of politics and economics, but that it also helps to shape them. Thus, by the early 1920s Soviet jurists had begun to draft codes based on those of Western Europe, with due account being taken of Soviet conditions. Although the notion of "law" went through numerous transmutations during the interwar period, and the status of the legal profession often was in doubt, a distinctive Soviet legal system, devoted in its own way to concepts of order, rationality, and equity, did emerge. Even during the worst of the political purges—conducted for the most part outside the legal system—law continued to function in everyday relations among citizens, enterprises, and agencies.

Before 1917 Bolshevik ideology had very little to say about international law; a detailed ideological critique simply had not been made. In their international relations the Soviet rulers began with the most cynical view of international law as a means of exploitation of weak states, colonial peoples, and revolutionary movements by the powerful imperialist capitalist class. However, as the Soviet Union sought, in its own interests, to stabilize relations with other countries, international law was seen to be a necessary means of self-protection. It was recognized that international law constituted both a means through which accommodations with the enemies of the Soviet government must be made, and a set of principles that, if properly employed, could help to secure the integrity of the Soviet state over the long run. So, with some exceptions (e.g., unequal treaties, secret diplomacy, right to abrogate Tsarist loans) the Bolsheviks found themselves accepting traditional international law, developing a body of state practice, and reserving an ideological rationale or explanation for this phenomenon for the future. When ideological explanations were forthcoming (principally by E.A. Korovin in 1924 and E.B. Pashukanis in 1935), they were unsatisfactory and appeared to have little impact on Soviet practice. After World War II, when the USSR emerged not only as the second greatest military power in the world but also as the center of a system of Socialist states, its stake in the maintenance of a complex international order led it to a much more optimistic view of the role of law in helping to resolve conflicts between states and to create channels of international cooperation. Formulations of doctrine by G.I. Tunkin and other modern Soviet publicists accept contemporary international law, stressing the principles of state sovereignty, equality, reciprocity, and Soviet practice. In addition, since the 1930s, and especially since the end of World War II, the USSR has participated actively in international legal conferences, the United Nations International Law Commission, and the International Court of Justice. As party to many multilateral and bilateral agreements, the USSR appears to observe and to demand observance of their provisions in the same manner as other states.

Major Variables

In addition to ideology and historical experience, some very concrete factors, difficult to estimate in advance, will influence Soviet treatment of prisoners of war under the Geneva Conventions of 1949. One factor will be the attitude of the Soviet government toward the state whose nationals have been captured or otherwise detained. During World War II, for example, the Nazi German government waged a total war of annihilation and extermination in violation of the most elementary principles of international morality and law. The Soviet response, broadly speaking, was twofold: (1) The USSR vigorously and bitterly protested German activities in traditional international legal terms while declaring its intent to avoid resort to reprisals; (2) the USSR decided early in the war that the highest levels of the German command should bear personal responsibility for atrocities committed. This decision led to a very broad concept of war crimes for which German prisoners were held accountable under Soviet law. We shall return to the question of war crimes below, but it should be stressed here that that Soviet experience at the hands of the Germans in World War II left an indelible mark so far as the prosecution of German nationals for violations of the laws of war is concerned.

Postwar Soviet-West German relations offer another example. Before 1955 the USSR admitted to holding several thousand German nationals allegedly serving sentences, or under investigation, for war crimes. West German requests for names and other particulars repeatedly were denied. When Soviet-West German diplomatic relations were established in 1955, the German PWs were released, apparently as part of the deal; many reported improved rations and other instances of better treatment in the months before release.

There is also some evidence that domestic political conditions in the USSR affect the treatment of PWs. Those Soviet citizens and foreign nationals who survived Soviet concentration camps during the late Stalin years (1947-53) reported an improvement in general conditions and in camp administration the day after Stalin's death. Other accounts given by Soviet citizens imprisoned in labor camps very similar to prisoner of war camps show that the camp administration was sensitive to changes in purge policies; when for short periods it appeared the purges might come to an end, rations increased and more reading matter was allowed.

Another factor bound to affect Soviet treatment of prisoners of war is the notion of reciprocity. Since the very first days of the 1917 October Revolution, the USSR has been confronted in one form or another with restrictions or disabilities imposed by states that opposed either the Soviet government per se or certain policies pursued by that government. As a result, the Soviet Union has become highly sensitive to the notion of reciprocity. In Soviet treaty and legislative practice, one constantly finds examples of privileges being granted or withheld on the basis of reciprocity. Although the Soviet Union disavowed the taking of reprisals against German PWs in World War II, numerous reports attest to the fact that German nationals were subjected to harsher treatment than they would have received had their own government treated Soviet PWs with humanity.

When the Soviet government has had no faith in the intention or ability of enemy governments to observe international law, it has retaliated by refusing to honor international obligations that otherwise would be respected. In 1941, for example, the USSR refused to acknowledge the immunity of German hospital vessels in the Baltic Sea and Northern Arctic Ocean, concluding that "after . . . facts of systematic, perfidious violation by the German Government of international treaties and agents . . . " there was "every ground to suspect that the German Government will also not observe the decrees of the [1907] Hague Convention and that hospital vessels will be used by it for military purposes."[1] The influence of reciprocity and retaliation in Soviet practice is noted in our discussion below.

Treatment of PWs detained by the USSR may also vary according to their rank, their actual role in the hostilities, the circumstances of their capture, and their attitude toward Soviet authorities during detention. During World War II German officers were often singled out for preferential treatment and reeducation since, as the leadership elite, they might prove to be malleable for the purposes of postwar Soviet policy in Germany. On the other hand, German SS officers were always suspected of heinous acts, and this was frequently reflected in their treatment. Insofar as war crimes were concerned, higher officers were regarded as the original perpetrators of atrocities and were subject to punishment accordingly. We will return to the question of indoctrination and war crimes below.

Finally, we would list as a major variable the attitude of the PW himself. Recalcitrant individuals who resist interrogation or violate camp rules are likely to be dealt with harshly, as experience from Soviet concentration camps shows. Persons who cooperate with the authorities receive better treatment, and great pressure is applied to obtain cooperation. The Soviet legal system is strongly partial to the notions of confession, sincere repentance, and rehabilitation. If past experience is an accurate guide, PWs charged with war crimes are likely to be cajoled with promises of a lower sentence or charge, or of better treatment if a confession is signed or other persons are implicated by the accused in the alleged deeds. It was common for German PWs to implicate senior officers and civilians in crimes committed by them, and the testimony was carefully collected and used later against those individuals. It is also noteworthy that during the trial of U-2 pilot Gary Powers his expressions of sincere repentance and his implication of United States government officials were probably significant factors in his receiving a relatively light sentence and early release.

The Soviet Union and the Law of War

Our discussion thus far has indicated some of the factors that in one way or another may affect how and when the Soviet Union applies the law of war with respect to PWs in a given conflict. Before we reach the question of how Soviet treatment of prisoners of war may diverge from the principles accepted by major Western countries, it is worth stressing that the Soviet Union takes the law of war very seriously. The law of war is not looked upon as simply a bourgeois invention to which lip service is to be paid; on the contrary, it is regarded as a body of law common to bourgeois and Socialist countries alike, and deserving of respect from all states. The Soviet denunciations of Chinese mutilation of corpses of Soviet soldiers killed in the clashes at the Ussuri River may be taken as a genuine reflection of Soviet antipathy to such acts. Also it may be noted that United States fliers shot down and captured off Soviet coasts during the 1950s and 1960s seem to have been treated humanely. The examples do not by any means tell the whole story, but they do indicate that the Soviet Union takes seriously the existence of a body of international law governing such matters.

Shortly after its accession to power, the Russian government "recognized" and declared its intention to comply with all the international conventions relating to the Red Cross (the Geneva Convention of 1906 and the related Hague Convention No. IV of 1907) and on June 16, 1925, formally adhered without reservation to both conventions. Appropriate steps were taken to enact criminal legislation pursuant to the requirements of those conventions. The USSR also has ratified the 1925 Geneva Protocol prohibiting gas and bacteriological methods of warfare (with a reservation) and GWS-1929 (Geneva Convention for the Amelioration of the Condition of the Wounded and Sick in Armed Forces in the Field–1929).

The Soviet government played a major role in drafting the four Geneva

Conventions of 1949, which were ratified (with reservations) by the USSR on April 23, 1954—a year before their ratification by the United States. In 1955, in response to an inquiry from the Netherlands, the Soviet government for the first time formally declared its recognition of the Hague Conventions and Declarations of 1899 and 1907 "to the degree that these conventions and declarations do not contravene the United Nations Charter" or have not been suspended by later conventions to which the USSR is party. Some years before 1955, however, a prominent Soviet jurist, A. Trainin, had claimed:

... it is also natural that the USSR recognized all laws and customs of war since they were directed towards the humanization of war, and that it has insisted on their observance. The USSR has thought that from the point of view of international law belligerent states have no right to use any and every form and method of war, but only those which are not forbidden by international agreements (conventions). The USSR has adhered to all proposals which could mitigate the consequences of destructive wars, the main weight of which falls on the mass of the people.[2]

Although the Soviet Union is among the great majority of parties to the Geneva Conventions of 1949 that have failed to adopt criminal legislation punishing "grave breaches," it did enact a new Statute on Military Crimes in 1958 providing penalties for the mistreatment of prisoners of war. The 1958 statutes did not differ significantly in this regard from earlier Soviet and Tsarist legislation.

Thus, at this point in history the Soviet Union is formally committed to observe the network of international treaties and agreements regulating the treatment of PWs and civilians. It remains for us to consider whether these rules may be interpreted or applied by the USSR during a future conflict in a manner significantly different from the way in which they are interpreted and applied by the United States.

Since the USSR participated in the drafting of the Geneva Conventions of 1949, one should expect its understanding of the conventions to be basically that of the other parties. Fortunately, we have had no occasion since 1949 to determine whether that would hold true in an armed conflict. However, the USSR did enter reservations to the conventions, and Soviet jurists from time to time have published articles interpreting the conventions. Drawing on these materials and Soviet attitudes and practices in World War II, we have a body of data that may provide some clue to problems that could arise in the future detention of PWs by the Soviet Armed Forces.

Common article 3 of the Geneva Conventions, which prohibits murder, torture, and other violence to life and person, humiliating and degrading treatment, and the sentencing of persons without affording "all the judicial guarantees which are recognized as indispensable by civilized peoples," applies to conflicts not of an international character. Soviet jurists have regarded this provision as being applicable to insurgent and rebel groups engaged in wars of national liberation against a colonial or other non-Communist regime and have strongly criticized Western powers for committing "atrocities" in putting down domestic rebellion in colonies or dependent territories. In Soviet legal literature the war of national liberation is linked to what Soviet writers regard as a legal right of peoples to self-determination. Noting that article 3 does not require that both parties to the conflict recognize a state of belligerency, one Soviet publicist characterized the provision as involving "the obligation . . . of the participating nations to apply the basic humane principles of these conventions . . . to persons participating in civil and colonial wars."[3]

From the United States point of view, this interpretation of article 3 could become important if the United States and the USSR found themselves embroiled on opposite sides in a Vietnam-type situation. Even if the conflict were denominated a "police action" or some other similar term, the Soviet Union would be likely to insist that PWs captured by the other side be accorded article 3 treatment. If the other side failed to conform, the Soviet side might then treat its own prisoners accordingly.

Treatment of Civilians

Soviet legislation expressly makes punishable the use of force against the population in areas of military operations. The term "force" includes assault with intent to rob, illegal destruction of property, or the illegal removal of property under pretext of military necessity. The offense is punishable by deprivation of freedom for a term of three to ten years or by death. A similar penalty may be imposed for the offense of pillage against civilians, as well as against wounded military personnel.

Soviet jurists are satisfied that the Geneva Conventions of 1949 once and for all have outlawed the practice of taking hostages. According to E.A. Korovin, a prominent Soviet international lawyer, the USSR abandoned the practice of taking hostages as early as 1919:

Hostages are defined in Soviet legal literature as: Persons from amongst the local population of occupied territories illegally arrested by the occupants with the aim of preventing (by threatening the execution of the hostages) the local population of the occupied areas from committing acts directed against the occupant, and also with the aim of uncovering individuals who had committed such acts. The taking of hostages is generated by unjust, predatory, imperialistic wars and is an illegal act of the occupants aimed at terrorizing the population of the occupied territories.[4]

Such arrests or executions of civilians are regarded as an international crime and a form of "international banditism."

Guerrillas

Extensive Soviet use of partisan and guerrilla movements in World War II and their obvious relevance to contemporary wars of national liberation are primarily responsible for a distinctive postwar Soviet approach to the question of whether partisans or guerrillas are entitled to prisoner of war status. Several theories have been advanced by Soviet jurists to support this position.

With regard to Soviet partisan activity in World War II, Soviet jurists argued that resistance by Soviet civilians was not guerrilla warfare in the strict sense but a form of mass uprising against an ineffective military occupation, a levy en masse. Substantial numbers of Soviet citizens were conscripted into units of the "people in arms" (*narodnoe opolchenie*), and in 1941 such persons were declared to be subject to the USSR Statute on Military Crimes and under the jurisdiction of military tribunals. Wide areas behind German lines were in fact under Soviet administration. Under this argument, when German troops approached, the members of the levy were entitled to the normal protections of HR-1907 (Hague Regulations–1907) (so long as such persons satisfied the stipulations of article 2 of the convention that arms were carried openly and the laws and customs of war were respected). Consequently, these guerrilla forces need not otherwise meet the requirements HR imposed on militia and volunteer corps (that is, requirements that they be commanded by a responsible person and have distinguishing marks visible from a distance).

It was also argued in justification of the partisan movement that its members were a militia or volunteer corps constituting the army or part of it and therefore within the protection of article 1 of HR. The actual operation of the partisan movement lends much credence to this point. In government directives and Stalin's speeches, the partisans were named as equals of the other branches of the armed services. Many of their commanders were Red Army officers, their work was synchronized with operations of the Red Army, and their units were often absorbed into the army upon the liberation of an area. Furthermore, in many cases the units actually were Red Army detachments ordered to stay behind during retreat and fight the enemy with guerrilla tactics.

In current international legal literature, Soviet jurists are prone to overlook their earlier justifications for the guerrilla movement and to go well beyond the bounds of the 1949 Geneva Conventions by asserting that "in a war of national liberation every person who takes up arms to fight against the aggressor fulfills a high patriotic duty, and his actions may not be regarded as criminal."[5] This assertion is in conformity with the Soviet position at the Geneva Conference of 1949, where the USSR proposed the coverage of Common Article 3 be enlarged to provide that in armed conflicts not of an international character each party thereto should be bound to apply all rules relating to the regime of prisoners of war to all combatants.

Thus, on the basis of past experience, it would be reasonable to anticipate that in a future conflict the Soviet Union would claim PW status for guerrillas or partisans detained by the enemy and would interpret the status of "guerrilla" in the broadest possible fashion so that almost anyone taking up arms against the enemy would be entitled to PW protection. The status of partisans captured by Soviet forces is much in doubt, however, for in World War II Soviet authorities customarily dealt summarily with such persons, regarding them as bandits or worse. The principle of reciprocity may be influential in persuading the Soviet leaders to assume a more tolerant attitude toward the treatment of such PWs; however, this is at best conjectural.

Protecting Powers, ICRC, and Other Systems of Control

During the drafting of the Geneva Conventions of 1949, the Soviet delegation expressed great apprehension over the role of protecting powers and humanitarian organizations in any future conflict. Since the early 1920s when foreign relief societies were permitted to distribute aid in portions of Russia struck by severe famine, Soviet authorities have been reluctant to permit any foreign inspection or supervision of Soviet nationals abroad or of persons detained in the USSR. The Soviet Red Cross Society is willing to serve as a conduit for mail, supplies, and so forth, to prisoners, but without outside supervision. One would expect this to remain true in the future, unless perchance in a limited conflict the USSR considered it desirable to publicize the well-being of PWs. It is also noteworthy that the Soviet Union expressed a preference for the term "relief society" during the 1949 Geneva Conference; this suggests that the Soviet authorities would not look with favor on religious or similar humanitarian organizations' assuming any role on Soviet territory.

Soviet suspicion of the impartiality of ICRC or of potential protecting powers was reflected in reservations made to article 10 of GPW.

Article 10: The Union of Soviet Socialist Republics will not recognize the validity of requests by the Detaining Power to a neutral State or to a humanitarian organization, to undertake the functions performed by a Protecting Power, unless the consent of the Government of the country of which the prisoners of war are nationals has been obtained.

In the Soviet view, the government of the state of which the PWs are nationals should have sole discretion to select a neutral state or humanitarian organization to serve as protecting power. The Soviet delegate stated in the plenary meeting of the 1949 Diplomatic Conference of Geneva that the Soviet delegation:

... will never approve an Article which leaves to the enemy the choice of Protecting Power which he may wish to impose on a legitimate government.

Treatment of PWs

The most recent experience of Soviet treatment of PWs and camp conditions dates from World War II. Two general observations about that experience undoubtedly will have relevance for the future. First, the Russians simply were not equipped at the early stages of the war to handle large numbers of PWs. Conditions were exceedingly poor, especially for the transport of PWs to the camps, and many German soldiers perished in overcrowded boxcars en route to their place of confinement. Second, although the Russians reportedly honored, by and large, the obligation to give prisoners of war the same rations that were issued to members of their own armed forces, food was in short supply in the USSR and rations were meager. By United States standards, the quantity of food would be appallingly low.

Prisoner of war camps were administered by the People's Commissariat of Internal Affairs [(NKVD); later renamed by Ministry of Internal Affairs (MVD)], the agency that also managed correctional labor camps to which Soviet citizens convicted of crimes were sent. The NKVD had its own military formations, and the commanding officers of the main prisoner of war camps usually were military personnel. This meant that an experienced cadre of camp administrative personnel was available and that a basic routine for such camps had been worked out.

German officers usually were separated from enlisted men and were sent to special officers' camps. Unlike enlisted men, whose labor often was utilized in nonmilitary industries, officers were obliged only to maintain their camps, in conformity with GPW-1929 (Geneva Convention Relative to the Treatment of Prisoners of War—1929). They were granted larger and better food rations and more leisure time than enlisted men. In camps for enlisted men individual PWs were assigned to work in accordance with requests from local industry. Norms of productivity were established, but allowances were made for PWs who were physically unable to work the maximum length of time or to fulfill the requirements of production per hour.

Basic medical care was available in prisoner of war camps. There was a central hospital at each main camp, with various first-aid stations located in labor areas. Vaccinations were given as a matter of course against certain communicable diseases. Malaria, enteritis, and dysentery were diseases most common in the camps.

In any future conflict, the Soviet government can be expected to demand, as it did in World War II, maximum protection under the Geneva and other conventions for captured Soviet military personnel and civilians. So great were the violations of the law by Germany on the Eastern Front in World War II that Soviet protest notes referred to general policies of atrocities and the unsatisfactory condition of German camps instead of pointing to individual instances of violations. Protests were frequent and sharp, although to no apparent avail.

The Soviet legal system is inclined to treat more favorably those accused who confess and express sincere repentance for their wrongful acts. In criminal cases arising under Soviet law, Soviet investigators have always placed a great premium on obtaining confessions from the accused, especially confessions that would implicate others. The same practice was followed in the prosecution of German military personnel as war criminals. During interrogation a PW could expect to be offered various inducements or to be subjected to varying degrees of mental or physical abuse, depending upon his cooperativeness. This might range from promises of a lighter sentence or reduced charge to a restricted diet, curtailed exercise, solitary confinement, or physical beatings and torture. Post-Stalinist reforms in the Soviet legal and penal systems are believed to have curtailed most abuses of this type, although A. Solzhenitsyn in *The Gulag Archipelago*, and others, argue to the contrary. Soviet conduct in this regard during a future conflict would to a significant degree depend upon the viability of institutional checks against abuses in interrogations. At this point in time, we can merely note that the groundwork for such institutional checks has been laid.

Conditions of Internment

The Constitution of the USSR and those of the union republics guarantee "freedom of religious worship" and "freedom of antireligious propaganda" for all citizens, including aliens. In contrast to the first Soviet Constitution of 1918, the freedom of religious propaganda is no longer guaranteed; and article 227 of the 1960 RSFSR Criminal Code, similar in this respect to the criminal codes of the other fourteen union republics, makes punishable the "active participation" in a religious group that is "connected with . . . inducing citizens to refuse social activity or performance of civil duties, or with drawing minors into such groups." In Soviet law the exercise of religious "duties" as referred to by article 34 of GPW would very likely be construed narrowly to encompass only worship or liturgy.

Similarly, article 227 of the RSFSR Criminal Code would pose difficulties for members of those religious sects, such as Jehovah's Witnesses, which stress conversion and missionary activity. Article 35 of GPW, providing that chaplains or others are to be allowed to exercise "freely their ministry among PWs of the same religion," is not likely to be interpreted by Soviet authorities to permit proselytizing of any kind and would probably be punishable under the ban against religious propaganda. In prisoner of war camps one would expect Soviet authorities to permit religious workshop on formal occasions, perhaps with minor harassment, but to resist any activities with political overtones or activities that might reach Soviet citizens as well as PWs. With physical culture enjoying such wide respect in the USSR as a vital component to public health, one would expect normal recreational pursuits and physical exercise be allowed, and perhaps encouraged.

Even under normal peacetime conditions, the Soviet government places severe restrictions on the kinds of books and literature that may be imported into the Soviet Union. Although the Constitution expressly provides for secrecy of correspondence, mail is in fact often opened and read before delivery; packages with unacceptable or undesirable contents are lost or confiscated. Prisoners of war will suffer like treatment. Similarly, it is difficult to imagine that visitors to prisoner of war camps would be allowed, except Communists or fellow travelers for propaganda purposes. The fact that in the *Powers* case (as well as in some other cases of foreigners tried for crimes in the Soviet Union) members of the family were permitted to come to Moscow to see him and attend his trial does not appear to have relevance. The Soviet Union does have a sizable number of lawyers and other legally trained personnel available, so that it would be possible to provide lawyers to assist PWs in the preparation of legal documents, pursuant to GPW, article 77.

The Soviet government has always viewed the prisoner of war as an appropriate object of political indoctrination. Political agitation in the Russian army was a key ingredient in the Bolshevik accession to power in 1917, and Bolshevik political activity among German prisoners and soldiers remained a sore point in German-Soviet relations even after the Treaty of Brest Litovsk was signed. Soviet policy in World War II followed the same pattern. Great emphasis was placed on the political indoctrination of prisoners of war, not only to correct misimpressions about Soviet life but to create a cadre of reliable leaders who, when the war ended, would assist the Soviet Union in establishing Communist rule in their own countries.

In World War II each Soviet prisoner of war camp had a political director (*politicheskii rukovuditel* or *politruk*) who was subordinate to the NKVD but who was primarily responsible to the Communist party apparatus. Often it was possible to appoint a German Communist to the post of political director. After some initial mistakes, the Soviet authorities were successful in organizing for the East European countries the nuclei of governments-in-exile that were capable of appealing effectively to the patriotism of the PWs. Another technique was the organization of anti-Fascist schools, where PWs were taught dialectical and historical materialism, Marxist philosophy, history of the labor movement, and other related subjects. Participation was voluntary, but there were, of course, material inducements for joining the courses.

Undertakings of this character were clearly tailored to Soviet expectations of a primary role in Eastern Europe after the war. The formation of a Communist government-in-exile expressly prepared to follow the Red Army and of a cadre of followers sympathetic to its cause is widely credited with playing a decisive role in consolidating Soviet rule over territories liberated by Soviet forces. There is no reason to expect that this same policy would not be utilized by the USSR in a future conflict.

Penal and Disciplinary Sanctions

Whatever abuses may have occurred in the sphere of political offenses, the Soviet Union has had a functioning domestic legal system since the 1920s, with codes modeled on the continental European system, a judicial system, a legal profession, and procuration. In short, the USSR possesses the essential institutions necessary to implement the requirements of articles 82-108 of GPW-1949. Defense counsel, under the Fundamental Principles of Criminal Procedure, must be afforded to accused persons; "show" trials in the tradition of the Stalin era have been infrequent. Procurators pay regular visits to prison camps to listen to complaints of prisoners and, when justified, may require the prison administration to make changes or to correct illegal behavior. There is no guarantee, of course, that the formal requirements of due process will be transgressed by government or party fiat; however, the political climate in which such transgressions were widespread has not existed in the Soviet Union since shortly after Stalin's death in 1953.

One provision of the Geneva Conventions of 1949 deserves further comment in light of Soviet law. Articles 115 and 119 of the conventions refer respectively to "disciplinary punishment" and "indictable offenses," but the conventions nowhere define the distinction between the two. It is worth noting that such phrases as "indictable offense" have no exact counterparts in the Russian language; the word "indict" is rendered in Russian as "accuse," and under Soviet law one may be "accused" of a disciplinary or administrative offense that is not a crime.

War Crimes

So far as GPW-1949 is concerned, the major question of legal interpretation relating to war crimes will revolve around article 85 and the Soviet reservation thereto. The Soviet government flatly rejects the application of article 85 to prisoners of war "convicted under the law of the detaining power, in accordance with the principles of the Nuremberg Trial, for war crimes and crimes against humanity, it being understood that persons convicted of such crimes must be subject to the conditions obtaining in the country in question for those who undergo their punishment." The reservation does specify that *conviction* of the PW is necessary before the benefits of the 1949 conventions are stripped away, so that summary executions would not be allowed under this language. In response to an inquiry from the Swiss government, the USSR Ministry of Foreign Affairs, in a note of May 26, 1955, clarified the Soviet reservation to article 85. Prisoners of war convicted for war crimes or crimes against humanity pursuant to Soviet legislation must submit to the same penalties as any other persons similarly condemned and will not benefit from the protection of the

GPW-1949 once the judgment of a court has been entered into force. The protections of the conventions are again extended when the sentence has been served, and such persons may be repatriated upon the terms of the convention. However, even though the convention protections may not apply to convicted prisoners of war, Soviet law prohibits corporal punishment and requires that standards of humanity and hygiene be observed. Convicted persons also retain the rights to submit complaints and to request review of their sentences.

The definition of war crime in Soviet literature and practice is a very broad one. In a recent article devoted to United States policy in Vietnam, a Soviet jurist included the following amongst war crimes: "the bombardment of peaceful cities and population in North and South Vietnam, the use of such prohibited barbaric devices as napalm and the use of chemical agents for the destruction of crops (defoliants)."[6]

In prosecuting war crimes arising out of World War II, the Soviet concept of criminal negligence was of great importance. Thus, the Russians asserted that one who was in command of a unit was responsible for crimes against the laws and customs of war committed by any member of the unit of which he knew or should have known and which he did not take measures to prevent, and of crimes against prisoners of war under his supervision when he knew or should have known of the possibility of the commission of such crimes. (It may be noted that Soviet courts and writers define negligence as including both an objective and subjective standard; that is, in determining whether the person in command could have foreseen an action they take into account the personal qualities of the defendant, his capacities, education, and the like.) Also, Soviet criminal law (compare article 15 of the RSFSR Criminal Code) makes the preparation of a crime, short of attempt, itself equally punishable with the crime itself.

In addition, the USSR employed a broad definition of complicity, to some degree borrowed from the Anglo-American doctrine of conspiracy. Complicity could come about negligently as well as intentionally. Also, heavy penalties for participation in illegal organizations could be meted out to persons who were only loosely associated with such organizations. These doctrines were widely used during the purges of the 1930s to implicate persons who had even the slightest associations with political offenders. In the post-Stalin law reforms, however, the principle of complicity has been limited to intentional joint participation in the commission of the (specific) criminal act (article 17 of the RSFSR Criminal Code). Also, the rule of "individualization of punishment" is applied in Soviet judicial proceedings, whereby the Soviet court examines each defendant's personal degree of guilt in every individual case. Of course, the concept of "criminal organization" as defined in the Charter of the Nuremberg Tribunal may be expected to influence Soviet treatment of PWs in a future conflict as well.

Repatriation of Prisoners of War

Soviet repatriation after the end of hostilities in 1945 proceeded very slowly, partly because of the attitude toward war crimes described above. In 1950 the Soviet government announced the complete repatriation of German PWs but also stated that there remained 9,000 men who had been convicted of serious war crimes and 3,815 men whose crimes were still under investigation. The USSR refused to furnish lists of such persons or of civilian internees. It was equally uncooperative with respect to Japanese prisoners of war, of whom only 3,676 were repatriated from December 1, 1947 to April 30, 1948. Ultimately, the repatriation of German PWs was settled by a bilateral agreement between the Federal Republic of Germany and the USSR in 1955, when the Soviets agreed either to grant amnesty to the 9,626 Germans then held as war criminals or else to turn them over to the Federal Republic of Germany.

It is difficult to predict whether the dispute over "voluntary repatriation" in the Korean conflict will affect future Soviet interpretations of article 118 of GPW. The Soviet Union did support the Chinese and the North Korean view that the provisions of article 118 were mandatory for all detained PWs and not merely those who desired to return. Nevertheless, in a large number of treaties concluded by the Soviet government after World War I, the principle of asylum for PWs was specifically recognized. During World War II as well, the same principle was acknowledged. On January 8, 1943, the Soviet army at Stalingrad promised every German soldier who surrendered that after the war he would be returned to Germany or to "any country for which he expressed a preference."[7] The same promise was made to surrounded German troops near Budapest. The distinction between these two attitudes is that in the latter cases foreign nationals were involved, whereas in the Korean case nationals of a Communist state were threatening to remain in the detaining state. Soviet disposition of the question may well depend upon whether it will suffer a net disadvantage under a system of voluntary repatriation.

Conclusion

The provisions of GPW-1949 are basically compatible with Russian and Soviet tradition, with Soviet concepts of law and due process, and with the body of state practice that up to now has emerged. Nothing in the convention is fundamentally alien to Soviet notions about the laws and conduct of war. Russia (under Tsarist and Bolshevik regimes) has contributed significantly to attempts to make war more humane. At the same time the Soviet Union has proved itself to be enormously sophisticated in manipulating the laws of war to its own advantage where the rules admit of flexibility in application or construction.

If there is one principle upon which Soviet observance of the convention is conditioned in a future conflict, that would be the principle of reciprocity and its corollary, retaliation. Only in the most unusual circumstances has the Soviet Union been willing to grant treatment to foreign nationals superior to that granted by other states to Soviet nationals. The response of retaliation against discriminatory treatment is often expressly sanctioned by Soviet legislation. There can be little doubt that the treatment of Soviet PWs will strongly influence their own attitudes toward PWs detained by Soviet armed forces.

Also, the task of verifying Soviet compliance with the convention in any future conflict would be a difficult one. Soviet resistance to verification by neutral states or humanitarian organizations is reflective of a broader, more deeply rooted opposition to any outside intervention or involvement in Soviet affairs. The Soviet legal system as a whole, for example, would pose major obstacles to the effective functioning of an international inspection unit on Soviet territory. These are not obstacles created specifically against such an eventuality; they merely inhere in the legal system as presently constituted. At the same time, the legal system presents a generally suitable framework for overcoming some of these obstacles.

Soviet compliance with the Geneva Conventions of 1949 would appear to be marginal or doubtful in three major areas. The first is the status of guerrillas, partisans, or other civilians bearing arms against the Soviet Union. Unless the USSR were in a position where it would, by reason of reciprocity, have to grant prisoner of war status to such persons, there may be a tendency to regard them as ordinary criminals or rebels subject to summary justice. At the same time, the Soviet Union will insist, citing the "just" cause for which they fight, that partisans captured by the enemy are entitled to PW status. Soviet policy at any given moment will probably reflect its view of where the net advantage lies.

The second problem area is the political indoctrination of PWs. Although there is no basis in past experience for supposing that they would resort to the brainwashing techniques used in the Korea war, the Soviet authorities do tend to regard PWs as political objects. PWs may expect to be subjected at least to rudimentary propaganda, and willing subjects, recruited with material inducements, may be subjected to much more.

The third area is that of war crimes. The Soviet Union remains adamant in its view that war crimes and crimes against humanity are best prosecuted under the national legislation of the state where the crime was committed and therefore are within the exclusive domestic jurisdiction of that state. Soviet jurists resist notions of a general international criminal law, and Soviet concepts of criminal organization, although narrowed since World War II, are still sweeping in scope. Also, Soviet willingness to punish the preparation of a crime, short of attempt, as an independent offense equally punishable with the crime itself, affords the Soviet Union wide grounds to prosecute PWs in its domestic courts, especially given the availability of the complementary doctrines of criminal negligence, complicity, and criminal organizations. It should thus be apparent that developments in Soviet criminal law will be perhaps the most important source of predicting what treatment PWs may receive while in Soviet captivity. In addition, the precedent of the Nuremberg trials, as interpreted in the Soviet Union, probably will exert a strong residual influence on Soviet attitudes toward war criminals in any future conflict.

Finally, it should not be forgotten that the Soviet Union, like most states, uses law to achieve political ends. What those ends are in any future conflict involving the USSR will affect Soviet interpretations and applications of the 1949 conventions.

Notes

1. Izvestia, March 9, 1955. (The note is translated in 3 Soviet Statutes and Decisions, No. 4 (1967) at 72-73.)

2. Trainin, *Questions of Guerrilla Warfare in the Law of War*, 40 Am. J. Int'l L. 552 (1946). Reprinted by permission.

3. Latyshev, *Zhenevskie konventsii 1949 g. o zashchite zhertvy voiny* [The 1949 Geneva Conventions on the Protection of Victims of War], Sovetskoe gosudarstvo i pravo [Soviet State and Law], No. 7 at 122 (1954).

4. Bratus et al., Iuridicheskii slova' [Legal Dictionary] 206 (Moscow: Gosiurizdat, 1953).

5. Ginsburgs, *Wars of Liberation and the Modern Law of Nations—the Soviet Thesis*, in H. Baade, ed., The Soviet Impact on International Law 73 (New York: Oceana Publications, 1965).

6. Latyshev, sup. note 3.

7. Izvestia, January 17, 1954, at 1.

8 People's Republic of China

Legal Tradition and Outlook

It is obviously hazardous to attempt to predict how, in some future conflict, any state will treat prisoners of war and detained persons. To some extent the personnel of every state can be expected to depart from generally accepted international principles, and personnel of the People's Republic of China (PRC) constitute no exception to this observation. What we seek to do here is to ascertain the extent to which the government of the PRC is itself likely to authorize or to tolerate departures from accepted norms in spite of its 1956 accession, with certain reservations, to the four Geneva Conventions of 1949. To put the matter more positively, what are the distinctive policies, attitudes, and practices that the PRC is likely to adopt?

The following extrapolation of the PRC's future behavior rests upon the public documentary record. That record is necessarily fragmentary, even if we give due weight to the variety of official and semiofficial statements spawned by the Korean conflict. Moreover, the Korean conflict came to an end over twenty years ago, and the continuity of the PRC's position on any particular question cannot be assumed. Nevertheless, it is possible to piece together other bits of evidence deriving from more recent experiences, including the Sino-Indian border conflict, and from the writings of Chinese publicists. These materials, when combined with knowledge of the Chinese legal tradition of contemporary treatment of persons charged with antisocial conduct in China and of Chinese Communist political theory and practice, provide a solid basis for anticipating, if only tentatively, future Chinese treatment of prisoners of war.

It is important at the outset to mention a number of factors that, although of uncertain magnitude, are of manifest relevance. For over 3,000 years, traditional China evolved its own distinctive civilization in virtually absolute isolation from that of the West. Although many Chinese attitudes toward law were analogous to those held in Western countries, so long as both civilians remained in premodern agricultural stages, China did not undergo the political, economic, and social revolutions that transformed Western attitudes toward law in the seventeenth to nineteenth centuries.

Traditional China's ideological blend of Confucian and Legalist doctrines held formal law in low regard. Large areas of economic and social activity went

This chapter is contributed by Jerome Alan Cohen, Director of the East Asian Studies Program, Harvard University Law School.

233

unregulated by law; rather, they were governed by custom and by the unofficial rules and institutions of villages, clans, guilds, and other groups. By and large, law served as an instrument for enforcing the will of the state upon benighted segments of society, who, it was thought, deserved the harsh treatment that was usually associated with law. The Chinese did not perceive law as a guarantor of the rights of individuals against the coercive power of the state, and no such phenomenon as an independent profession of legal advocates and counselors was permitted to develop as a stimulus either to the growth of law generally, or to the enterprise of limiting the exercise of sovereign power.

Nor did traditional China's contacts with the other people of East Asia introduce notions of a rule of law. With only occasional exceptions, foreign relations in East Asia were not regarded as taking place among independent states that treated each other as sovereign equals and that developed reciprocally binding rules to govern their intercourse. Rather, China, "the Central Realm," stood at the apex of a regional hierarchy in which the place of other peoples was determined according to the degree of their assimilation of Chinese civilization. The governments of these other people periodically paid tribute to the imperial "Son of Heaven" in the Chinese capital; he in turn bestowed munificence and legitimacy upon them, but his freedom of action was not significantly curbed by these rituals.

Thus, when international law, as we know it, was brought to China by the Western powers, it constituted an exotic foreign import rather than the outgrowth of domestic or international legal principles and institutions that China shared with the Christian nations of the West.

Chinese Communist ideology views the political arena, both internal and external, in terms of struggle among economically defined classes. Although Marxism-Leninism-Maoism differs markedly in its content from traditional Chinese ideology, there is a high degree of continuity between the two with respect to fundamental attitudes toward law. The Chinese Communists, who see law both domestically and internationally as the tool of the dominant class, regard it as something to be manipulated by the state to advance its interests; they, too, hold law in low regard, exempt broad areas of economic and social activity from its ambit, fail to perceive it as a guardian of individual rights, and refuse to tolerate the growth of a legal profession.

One area of direct relevance to treatment of prisoners of war in which contemporary practice has broken with the past is the treatment of persons who have been adjudged criminals or who otherwise have been classified as antisocial. "Thought reform" of prisoners was not part of old China's penal system but is a Chinese Communist contribution that was in part perfected during the Chinese Civil War by its application to captured Nationalist troops. After the Communist victory in 1949, its techniques were applied to the population as a whole, but with special emphasis upon the population of prisons, labor camps, and other detention places.

The Chinese Communists view international law as it has developed in the West as the tool of the ruling force in the world community—bourgeois imperialism, which manipulates the rules of the game to suit its interests and to suppress those of subjugated states and peoples. As the heirs to China's semicolonial "century of humiliation," which was symbolized by the system of extraterritoriality imposed by imperialist states in the guise of the rule of law, the Chinese leaders appear to hold this view of international law more ardently than their former Soviet mentors, whose ancestors, after all, were imperialists and whose revolutionary fervor has mellowed over almost six decades.

Yet, following the Soviet lead, the Chinese do not reject "modern" international law, the term they use to describe the modified version of general international law that they are shaping to suit China's present needs. This modified version retains many principles of nineteenth century Western international law that emphasize state sovereignty and that provide the PRC with a valuable defensive weapon against attempts by the dominant powers in the world community to impose their standards upon all states. For example, the Chinese have resisted the trend to regard international organizations as subjects of international law and as instruments for enforcing minimum standards of "human rights" upon all states, although since their entry into the United Nations they have joined in General Assembly condemnations of the racist policies of the white-dominated regimes in South Africa. They have also vehemently refuted any suggestion that a multilateral treaty might bind a state that is not a party to it. Moreover, as the dispute over repatriation of prisoners of war in Korea illustrated, the PRC frequently adopts a fundamentalist, "old-fashioned" policy of interpreting treaties literally rather than in the light of their major purposes and changing circumstances. And, with considerable skill, both its official spokesmen and its scholars often invoke familiar customary and conventional norms to induce other states to conform to traditional standards in their relations with China. In certain respects, such as the law of diplomatic and consular privileges and immunities, the law of intervention, and the protection due aliens, there has always been a gap between the version of international law that Peking applies to others and the version that it applies to its own conduct. But with the exception of the Cultural Revolution of 1966-69, to the extent that its practice is known, the PRC's behavior appears to have reflected an awareness that reciprocity is the foundation of international law and that the problem of the "double standard" must be kept within manageable proportions if China is to guarantee respect for its own claims.

Thus, in spite of the fact that both Chinese tradition and the Communist world outlook make the PRC's leaders reluctant to accept legal restraints, the need for contacts with the world community, the utility of certain aspects of international law in carrying on those contacts, and other reasons of political expediency have led the PRC to handle its foreign affairs, including prisoners of war, within the general framework and rhetoric of international law. Hence,

Peking acceded to the 1949 Geneva Conventions. It is a safe assumption that in any future conflict the PRC will call for application of the provisions of those conventions by its enemies. The question remains, however, to what extent is the PRC likely to allow those treaties to govern its own conduct? The answer to that question may be determined by a number of variables.

Major Variables

One important factor is the "line" that the Chinese leadership is currently pursuing toward the state whose nationals are detained. For example, in 1950, the Communists sought to eliminate United States influence in Japan by resort to "resolute struggle" against the Japanese government. In order to foster resentment against the United States the PRC adamantly called for harsh punishment of Japanese prisoners of war who were then being detained by the United States occupation force in Japan and who were subject to trial for war crimes. In 1956, however, after the PRC had shifted its policy to one of courting Japan's recognition of the Chinese Communist regime, the PRC went to great lengths to publicize its new policy of leniency in its own treatment of Japanese prisoners of war who were accused of war crimes and to contrast it with the allegedly harsh treatment that the Philippines and Japan itself had meted out.

The Korean conflict offers another illustration. During the early stages, when the PRC did not seem interested in a negotiated settlement, it advocated a "lenient policy," which treated all prisoners of war as war criminals who could be shot but who would be treated generously in exchange for demonstrated "repentence"; this policy was touted as superior to that of the Geneva Convention Relative to the Treatment of Prisoners of War (GPW), to which the PRC had not yet acceded and for the invocation of which prisoners were sometimes punished. In mid-1951, however, when the PRC decided to enter armistice negotiations, it began to emphasize China's observance of the standards set forth in the convention, albeit with certain important reservations, and treatment generally began to improve. Moreover, it was subsequently reported by released prisoners of war that they received better treatment at times when their Chinese captors were pleased with the status of the armistice negotiations than when they were displeased.

Indeed, Peking's general foreign policy line at any given time is a critical factor in determining its attitude toward international norms governing prisoners of war. During periods such as 1949-51 and 1966-69, when great emphasis is being placed on inciting world revolution, the likelihood of respect for international norms is significantly reduced. During periods of "peaceful coexistence," such as 1954-57 and 1970-74, on the other hand, the Chinese are likely to lay considerable stress on adherence to accepted rules in order to gain favor with world opinion.

Similarly, although the PRC's foreign policy has not always paralleled its domestic political evolution, the treatment of prisoners of war is also likely to reflect domestic as well as international factors. It is probably more than coincidence, for example, that lenient treatment was first announced for Japanese war criminals in 1956, the first year in which there was a general "thaw" in law enforcement under the Communist regime. It should also be noted that in 1950-52, when the PRC was committing many brutal acts against prisoners of war, it pursued an equally harsh policy toward both Chinese and foreign prisoners in domestic Chinese jails. The worst abuses of domestic jails ceased in 1952-53, a time when the PRC was improving treatment of prisoners of war as well.

Whether opposing parties to the conflict appear to be protecting their prisoners of war is, of course, another relevant factor. Although measures of reprisal against prisoners of war are prohibited, although in Korea the PRC claimed that it continued to provide conforming treatment in spite of alleged violations by United Nations forces, and although in other contexts the PRC has not always taken "the corresponding measure" in response to a perceived infraction against China, on many occasions the PRC has retaliated for alleged violations on international law. It might well extend this practice to prisoners of war. Moreover, the seriousness with which the PRC takes the Geneva Convention may be adversely affected if it believes the other side is using subterfuge in interpreting the convention's provisions, as it believed on the "voluntary repatriation" issue in Korea.

Fortunately, there has been no occasion to test the hypothesis that, in a conflict perceived by the PRC to be an all-out struggle, it would be less likely to observe the Geneva Convention than it would be in a limited war. In the Korean and Sino-Indian conflicts the PRC was alert to the importance of appearing to behave humanely toward PWs, if only as a means of highlighting the position of opposing states by demonstrating China's reasonableness, its unhappiness over hostilities, and its willingness to bring fighting to an end. It is certainly at least conceivable that the PRC might be less concerned with such a posture if large-scale warfare were to occur in the interior of China, for example.

This suggests another possible variable—whether Maoist guerrilla strategy emphasizing the role of a vast, but relatively unprofessional, "people's militia" will be preferred in a future conflict to the more conventional strategy proffered by dismissed Chinese generals, such as P'eng-Teh-huai, who advocated relying principally upon professional military units. The latter, of course, being better trained, equipped, and disciplined, presumably would be more likely to have the capabilities to provide adequate treatment of prisoners of war.

Whether, as a matter of regime policy, individual captured persons will be given prescribed prisoner of war treatment will also depend on the nature of the role they were perceived to have played in the hostilities, the circumstances of their capture, and their behavior after capture. For example, the PRC made it clear in 1954 that in a conflict outside China, even though personnel are in uniform, prisoner of war treatment would not be given to United States military personnel who are apprehended in the course of flying into China at night in unmarked planes for what appear to be intelligence purposes. Chinese conduct during the Korean conflict strongly suggests that PWs who cooperate with their captors by showing "repentance," receptivity to "thought reform," or other favorable attitudes are more likely to receive prescribed treatment than ordinary PWs, and that those who are recalcitrant may often be handled in substandard ways: This was an application of the domestic penal concept of "leniency for those who repent, severity for those who resist," which continues to prevail in Chinese criminal law and is likely to prevail against prisoners of war in spite of articles 16 and 17 of the convention.

Finally, the regime is likely to grant prescribed, and even privileged, treatment to prisoners of war generally, if it believes that a policy of generosity will win the political sympathies of a substantial number of them who may prove to be valuable assets when they are released. The unexpected generosity of their Communist captors, when combined with "thought reform," converted many Chinese Nationalist troops to the Communist cause during the Chinese Civil War. And the Chinese Communists' experience in Korea appeared to teach them that better living conditions and greater emphasis on "voluntarism" enhance their chances of persuading Westerners who are prisoners of war.

Specific Problems

Exigencies of space and time require that this discussion focus on those major aspects of Chinese treatment of prisoners of war that can be expected to diverge from accepted principles. Here, unless otherwise indicated, "accepted principles" will be taken to mean GPW-1949. It can generally be assumed that our silence with respect to important provisions indicates that the Chinese are likely to observe them.

Applicability of the GPW Convention

Article 2 of GPW states that "the present Convention shall apply to all cases of declared war or of any other armed conflict which may arise between two or more of the High Contracting Parties, even if the state of war is not recognized by one of them." Article 3 of the Convention provides that in "the case of armed conflict not of an international character occurring in the territory of one of the High Contracting Parties," the parties to the conflict shall be held to far less exacting standards than those that are made applicable to conflicts that fall under article 2.

The Chinese Communists' position toward their Chinese Nationalist rivals suggests that, had the Korean and Vietnam conflicts been confined to the rival indigenous governments, in Peking's view these conflicts would not have attained "an international character" and only the limited provisions of article 3 would have applied. Even though the virtually exclusive territorial base of the Nationalists is the island of Formosa, the Communists regard the continuing struggle between themselves and the Nationalists as the continuation of the civil war that chased the Nationalists off the mainland in 1949. Because they do not regard that war as an international conflict, they refuse to renounce the use of force to settle it. Moreover, PRC statements directly regarding Vietnam and Korea described both of those conflicts as having originated as civil wars prior to the intervention of United States and other non-Communist foreign forces.

The fact that a conflict may be of an international character does not, of course, eliminate related questions concerning the applicability of the convention. After the 1962 outbreak of hostilities on the Sino-Indian border and India's harsh measures against aliens of Chinese nationality, India sought to justify its interference with China's efforts to protect Chinese nationals. India claimed that it had complied with GPW-1949 Relative to the Protection of Civilian Persons in Time of War (hereafter GC) by permitting ICRC (International Committees of the Red Cross) to visit the detention camps in which it had confined Chinese nationals. This led the late Chou Keng-Sheng, one of China's leading scholars of international law, to agree that the convention was generally applicable in the circumstances but to argue that its provisions relating to the role of humanitarian organizations were only designed to apply where a state of war existed and diplomatic relations were broken off. In the Indian case, he pointed out, though there was an armed conflict, diplomatic relations continued, and the Chinese Embassy must therefore be allowed to protect its nationals; need for the protection of a third party such as ICRC cannot arise in these circumstances, he said, wholly apart from the additional fact that the PRC had not consented to activities of ICRC.

In the 1954 dispute over the post-Korean-armistice conviction of eleven United States Air Force personnel for espionage, another leading Chinese scholar of the day, Ch'en T'i-ch'iang, used language that unnecessarily suggested a more restrictive view of the applicability of the GPW Convention. The United States had argued that prior to the armistice the fliers had been shot down either over the "recognized combat zone in Korea or over international waters." Instead of simply limiting his argument to the official Chinese position that the fliers had been shot down deep in Chinese territory after secretly entering for purposes of espionage rather than combat, Ch'en ambiguously stated:

Only captured members of the armed forces of a belligerent can be considered prisoners of war by the captor side. No state of war exists between China and the U.S. U.S. spies who have intruded into China for espionage purposes are not prisoners of war.[1]

Ch'en's remarks were only the murky dicta of a single publicist, to be sure, but they suggested the possibility that the PRC could some day choose to read the phrase "any other armed conflict" in article 2 restrictively, as North Vietnam appears to have done, in spite of the more conventional position voiced by Chou Keng-sheng vis-à-vis India.

Who is a Prisoner of War?

As all the parties announced by 1953 that they regarded the "spirit" of GPW as applicable to the Korean conflict, the principal question raised by the case of the captured airmen was whether the specific circumstances in which they were apprehended entitled them to the benefits of the convention and the armistice agreement. The official PRC position was that the conviction of "foreign spies" is China's internal affair and that the case had nothing to do with the question of prisoners of war. Many legal commentaries by Chinese scholars buttressed this conclusion. They argued (1) that the fliers had entered China clandestinely for espionage purposes; (2) that their uniforms merely constituted a disguise designed to conceal their mission and to endow them with colorable prisoner of war status if caught; (3) that international law and even the 1917 United States "Rules of Land Warfare" are analogous to these; and (4) that nothing in either the armistice agreement or the GPW Convention precludes this: Nonetheless, it should be noted that, without yielding on its legal position, the PRC did release the fliers as an act of "leniency" in response to United States efforts; it did not release two other Americans convicted of espionage at the same time for whom no colorable claim of prisoner of war status could be lodged.

Treatment of Detained Civilians

In no circumstances has the PRC sought artificially to extend the characterization as prisoners of war to civilians. It has pointed out that Japanese civilian nationals detained in China since the end of World War II were free to return to their homeland, but that this could not be called repatriation since these people were not prisoners of war and repatriation only applied to prisoners of war. By the same token, a carefully orchestrated newspaper campaign to press Japan to send back to China Chinese civilians who were forced to go to Japan during the war never claimed prisoner of war status for those people. We should point out that during the Korean truce talks on the question of voluntary repatriation, the PRC rejected the argument that prisoners who did not wish to be repatriated were actually "political refugees" rather than prisoners of war. Since the Korean conflict it is unclear whether the PRC regards United States military personnel who stray into Chinese territory as prisoners of war. Servicemen on leave who have occasionally wandered across the Hong Kong border have been released following a few days of detention and interrogation by local police with no reference made to their legal status. But two pilots who were shot down over Chinese territory during the Vietnam conflict were subjected to lengthy confinement, without clarification of their legal status.

This is not the place to discuss the PRC's treatment of ordinary foreign nationals who are not involved in armed conflict, except to note that its record was very poor during the 1950-53 period and again during the "Cultural Revolution" of 1966-69. Although Japan has been pressing to learn the fate of thousands of Japanese who were in China during World War II and whose whereabouts are unknown, it has not otherwise been suggested that the PRC may have detained large numbers of foreign nations. After two of the United States civilians held in criminal custody had committed suicide, the others who were either serving long criminal sentences for espionage convictions or awaiting the end of extensive investigation were released in the wake of Sino-American detente. Civilian materials of other Western countries and Japan were also released as their governments normalized relations with China.

Following the Sino-Indian border clashes of 1962, Chou Keng-Sheng asserted that the PRC had not detained a single Indian national (shortly afterward, an Indian residing in Shanghai was convicted on a rape charge, with no consular access granted until the sentence was approved on appeal). Chou charged that India's detention of many resident overseas Chinese violated various provisions of GC by taking the Chinese as hostages (article 34), not allowing them to leave India (article 35), interning them without reasons of national security (article 5, 42), failing to report the identity and location of interned Chinese (article 43), taking reprisals against their personal property (articles 33, 97) and failing to provide adequate medical and hygienic facilities (articles 81, 85). Other Chinese scholars took a similar position. As previously indicated, the Chinese press was also vigorous in calling for the return of Chinese who had been forcibly taken to Japan during the Sino-Japanese War.

Protecting Powers, ICRC, and Other
Systems of Control

Nothing has happened since the Korean conflict to suggest that the PRC is likely to enforce those provisions of the GPW Convention that provide a role for protecting powers, ICRC, or neutral nations (articles 3, 8, 13, and so forth). In Korea the Chinese showed no interest in having protecting powers appointed or having neutral nations inspect prisoner of war camps. They refused to cooperate with ICRC until after the armistice, and even then their gestures were a sham. Although the PRC did not hesitate to make use of ICRC reports on conditions in the United Nations prisoner of war camps to the extent the reports were favorable to the PRC position, the PRC frequently denounced ICRC as a tool of United States imperialism that pronounced the situation in United Nations camps "excellent" in spite of Chinese allegations that bacteriological experiments were being conducted there. Moreover, the PRC charged that ICRC resorted to spurious legal arguments in order to avoid investigating Chinese complaints but leaped into action when the United States requested it to investigate accusations that the United States had engaged in germ warfare. The depth of the PRC's suspicion of the disinterestedness of ICRC and of potential protecting powers was reflected in one of the reservations to the PRC's 1956 accession to the convention, which stated regarding article 10 that it

will not recognize as valid a request by the Detaining Power of prisoners of war to a neutral State or to a humanitarian organization, to undertake the functions which should be performed by a Protecting Power, unless the consent has been obtained of the government of the State of which the prisoners of war are nationals.

The PRC is likely to behave the way the North Vietnamese government did in the recent conflict by refusing to agree to the appointment of a protecting power or to requests that ICRC or any other impartial international organization be allowed to visit prisoner of war camps during hostilities. Moreover, when a joint team from ICRC and the Chinese and North Korean Red Cross organizations was finally allowed to visit Communist camps after the Korean armistice, "the visit was a farce," as the inspectors were not permitted to have access to whatever camps they wished or to question PWs freely. Yet, the Chinese charged that the United States was obstructing visits by a joint Red Cross team to United Nations prisoner of war camps and claimed that China facilitated such visits.

During the Sino-Indian conflict the PRC again rejected a role of ICRC, but, while not permitting any visits by the Indian Red Cross, it did at least allow the Chinese Red Cross to provide the Indian Red Cross with information concerning prisoners of war and to transfer released PWs to the Indian Red Cross. That national Red Cross organizations of parties to a conflict may play a larger role vis-à-vis China than international organizations was even more clearly suggested in 1956 when the PRC, as part of its effort to woo Japan, permitted representatives of the Japanese Red Cross to inspect the conditions in which China had detained convicted Japanese war criminals.

Treatment of Prisoners of War

The Chinese must be expected, of course, to claim maximum protection under GPW for captured Chinese military personnel. During the Korean conflict they often protested against alleged "slaughter," mutilations, and maltreatment inflicted upon prisoners of war by their United Nations captors. The PRC seemed especially concerned, as it has in other contexts, with use of "irritating spray" or "poison gas" to quiet PW riots.

Whether the PRC can be expected to improve upon its own poor record of treatment of prisoners of war is unclear. Although the parties to the Sino-Indian conflict made a number of self-serving statements about Chinese treatment of Indian PWs little in the way of reliable reporting on that episode exists. Similarly, we have as yet no reliable verification of Soviet charges that in the March 1969 Sino-Soviet frontier clashes Chinese soldiers brutally wounded and bayoneted Soviet frontier guards.

Individual atrocities may always be expected, but it is probable that the Chinese government will seek to curb the worst Korea-type abuses of physical mistreatment, just as it has made its domestic penological policy more humane since 1952. Yet, intimidation, insults, and exposure to public curiosity are very likely to continue, just as they have for domestic prisoners, for such acts of humiliation are deeply rooted in Chinese tradition. It is not irrelevant to note that the North Vietnamese, who share this tradition in important part, subjected (captured) United States personnel to harrowing propaganda parades and public obloquy. The North Koreans, who also share this tradition, subjected the crew of the U.S.S. *Pueblo* to a good deal of physical violence as well as psychological intimidation.

A basic principle of Chinese treatment of prisoner of war continues to be that those who are "progressive" and recognize their misdeeds deserve good treatment and those who are "reactionary" deserve harsh treatment. Again, this emphasis upon the necessity of confession as the first step to repentance is millennial in China and is a prominent aspect of contemporary Chinese law enforcement. Thus, the Chinese almost surely will not honor the requirement of article 16 of GPW that no discrimination be based on "religious belief or political opinion." For similar reasons one must be dubious about the PRC's future compliance with article 17's prohibition of sanctions against those who refuse to provide information to interrogators, for this notion is simply alien to Chinese tradition.

Conditions of Internment

The condition of conflict on Asian soil are, of course, something of a limitation upon the capacity of any power to implement the provisions of GPW. This was made clear in Korea. It is doubted whether the PRC, even if it had acted in good faith, could have lived up to these obligations during the period between capture of United Nations troops and their arrival at prisoner of war camps. Because of the logistics involved and because of the PRC's decision to give greater priority to its military effort than to its prisoner of war obligations, conditions at the camps themselves were far worse in 1950-51 than they were in 1952-53. PRC public relations media were never candid, but the idyllic picture that they painted during the latter period reflected a real change in situation. A similar evolution is likely to take place in the future, although in the Sino-Indian conflict, where much smaller numbers of PWs were captured, the PRC repeatedly claimed that it met all humanitarian standards from the outset.

The PRC is more likely to meet those standards of GPW that are defined in relative terms than those that are defined absolutely. It is probable that prisoners of war will be quartered in conditions as favorable as those for Chinese forces in the area, as required by article 25's first sentence, but those conditions will be Asian conditions unsuited to the habits and customs of United States prisoners and may well be prejudicial to their health; it is unrealistic to expect the PRC to adhere in all circumstances to the standard set forth in the second sentence of article 25, that is, that "said conditions shall make allowance for the habits and customs of the prisoners and shall in no case be prejudicial to their health."

Similarly, although the Chinese claimed that the food rations of their prisoners were both above those required by the convention and the same as those received by the Chinese People's Volunteers (CPV), the evidence suggests that rations were often far below convention standards, particularly during the early years, but were usually the same as those of the CPV. Much the same can be said of clothing, hygiene, and medical treatment. In all these aspects, however, it must be reemphasized that the granting of these conditions often depended on the extent to which an individual or unit demonstrated its "progressiveness."

In spite of frequent Chinese propaganda pronouncements during both the Korean and Indian conflicts about the full scope for religious observance offered to prisoners of war, the Korean evidence and the PRC's domestic policies toward religion make it appear very unlikely that prisoners of war will "enjoy complete latitude in the exercise of their religious duties" (article 34) or that chaplains (or others) will be allowed "to exercise freely their ministry among prisoners of war of the same religion" (article 35). This does not necessarily rule out limited opportunities for worship on formal occasions such as Sundays and holidays. But these "reactionary activities" so antithetical to Maoism will only be permitted as an exercise of discretion and will be subject to termination at any time if perceived to be politically inexpedient.

Certainly, if experience is a guide, the PRC may be expected to "encourage the practice of intellectual [and] educational pursuits," but not "while respecting the individual preference of every prisoner" (article 38). The PRC's "encouragement" will be limited to the pursuit of the Chinese Communist outlook through exposure to appropriate lectures, films, literature, broadcasts, small group discussions, private chats, and other techniques of "reeducation." Although in Korea, after a period of experimentation with compulsory methods, these programs became "voluntary," the "voluntarism" was synthetic, being based on the manipulation of privileges and even necessities such as food.

Moreover, PWs were offered no educational alternatives to the Communist programs. In view of the fact that similar "reeducation" continues to be foisted not only upon domestic prisoners but also upon the entire Chinese population, it appears to be an abiding characteristic of Communist policy.

A more optimistic assessment can be made of prospects for compliance with requirements for encouraging recreational pursuits and physical exercise (article 38). By the latter part of the Korean conflict the PRC had begun to take these obligations seriously by providing facilities for sports such as basketball, volleyball, and swimming. Since Chinese domestic policy has consistently emphasized sports or other exercise for everyone, albeit to a lesser extent for prison population, the PRC is likely to employ the same policy toward prisoners of war to the extent that conditions permit.

It is quite likely that the responsible officers of Chinese prisoner of war camps will have copies of GPW in their possession and will communicate its provisions, at least in appropriately qualified form, to staff and guards (articles 39, 127). As early as 1951 the Chinese press announced that before a Chinese "volunteer" was recommended for decoration, consideration was given to the extent to which he complied with China's prisoner of war policy of "leniency, based on humanitarianism." This is regarded as much a part of his war conduct as heroism on the field of battle.[2]

In spite of Chinese propaganda to the effect that camp authorities in Korea reprinted the full text of the convention in wall newspapers for the information of prisoners of war, reports from PWs and Chinese Communist attitudes toward law suggest that this could only have been done as a token, selective, or tardy basis. In contemporary China, published laws are few; most written proscriptions are limited to internal distribution for application by the bureaucracy and are not for dissemination to the public. By and large, the Chinese have taken a dim view of the invocation of published legal rules to protect one's "rights" ever since such rules were promulgated on bronze vessels as early as the sixth century B.C., and the PRC is no exception. Therefore, at least until PRC policy substantially conforms to the convention, it is unlikely that the convention will be posted in prominent places of the camps as required (article 41).

Although Chinese propaganda claimed that prisoners of war held by them in Korea were permitted more than the minimum correspondence prescribed (article 71), this was not generally true in the early period, and the sending and receiving of mail, like other facets of PW existence, were manipulated as political weapons, rewarding the cooperative and penalizing the uncooperative. Undoubtedly, there must have been a grave shortage of competent translators capable of carrying out censorship, but this could not entirely have accounted for the initial mail blackout and subsequent manipulation. Similarly conditions are likely to prevail in the future.

It is uncertain whether the PRC will permit prisoners of war to receive whatever books, papers, or study or religious materials are sent to them (article

72), for, as indicated above, this would hinder the Communists from controlling the PW's "reeducation." It should be pointed out, however, that the United States civilians detained in Chinese prisons on espionage convictions were permitted to receive books, periodicals, and correspondence.

Interestingly, after the cessation of hostilities, prisoners of war who have been convicted of war crimes may be allowed more contact with the exterior than ordinary prisoners of war enjoyed during hostilities. The Chinese press has stated that Japanese war criminals held in China were permitted to receive packages, communications, and even visits from their families, and the United States civilians serving prison sentences for espionage enjoyed these privileges, including family visits at several different times. The only visitors who are likely to be allowed to enter prisoner of war camps during hostilities are Communist sympathizers who can be counted upon for propaganda.

The PRC cannot be expected to furnish lawyers to advise prisoners of war on preparation of legal documents (article 77), for the simple reason that there are virtually no lawyers actually functioning in China.

Prisoners of war in the hands of the PRC are likely to be as cut off from channels of protest against illegal treatment as are civilians who are detained by China's domestic law enforcement agencies. Since in Korea the PRC refused to approve any protecting powers or to cooperate with ICRC or other international organizations, there was no impartial agency to which prisoners of war could complain (articles 78, 79, 81). Moreover, the election of prisoners' representatives authorized to file complaints in behalf of PWs was largely rigged by the PRC, which would generally approve only the candidacies of "progressives," who painted an idyllic picture of conditions in the camps. Genuinely elected representatives usually were ineffective. Complaints that prisoners of war managed to lodge with their Chinese captors usually failed to elicit favorable responses and often resulted in sanctions against those who complained.

One study of the experience in Korea has concluded that the convention failed to take account of "the Chinese concern for 'face' that made it almost impossible for them to accept any suggestion which did not emanate from themselves."[3] In any event, although the Chinese did improve conditions as they saw fit, little of the credit could be assigned to the complaint system. Nothing that has happened to Chinese attitudes toward law since that time, either domestically or internationally, offers any basis for supposing that the PRC will treat either complaints or the election of prisoner representatives in the spirit of the convention.

Penal and Disciplinary Sanctions

No other portion of GPW has more of an air of unreality about it in relation to the Chinese Communists than chapter 3 of section 6. When in 1956 the PRC acceded to the convention, one might have argued that its good faith was not in question concerning this chapter, because at that time it appeared to be developing a domestic legal system that would have familiarized the Chinese with the essential institutions and practices that the convention assumed to exist. Unfortunately, the "antirightist movement" of 1957 ended all this, so that, unless China undergoes very great changes in the direction of "revisionism," it is ludicrous to read articles 82 to 108 with the thought that the PRC might be expected to comply with these provisions.

Although the fundamental concept of GPW, chapter 3, in dividing disciplinary sanctions from judicially imposed sanctions, and in prescribing substantially more elaborate safeguards for PWs who are subjected to the latter, has not been entirely obliterated in form in China, in practice virtually none of the judicial safeguards set forth in the convention exist. For example, the principles of *nulla poena sine lege*, of no coerced confessions, and of opportunity to make a defense and to be represented by qualified counsel (article 99) are simply not practiced in China. The same must be said of trial by a court that offers "the essential guarantees of independence and impartiality as generally recognized" (article 84).[4] China has chosen to do without a legal profession, seldom permits law professors or others to serve as advocate in criminal cases except in "show" trials, and even then does not grant them a meaningful opportunity to freely consult with the accused, to summon and interview witnesses, or to argue for more than mitigation of punishment. Furthermore, Chinese judges serve in extremely insecure circumstances. Until the Cultural Revolution they were under the close scrutiny of police and prosecutor and ordinarily had to obtain the approval of the local Communist party secretary before handing down criminal judgments; during the Cultural Revolution the Chinese Army replaced policy, prosecutorial, and party officials in controlling the courts, and only in recent years has its role in the administration of justice been receding. In cases involving aliens, the Ministry of Foreign Affairs habitually issues secret instructions and is often consulted in concrete cases.

As both the Korean experience and domestic law demonstrate, the Chinese do not shrink from extending a prisoner's sentence beyond the prescribed term without resort to significant formality, in apparent violation of article 86; and occasionally after completing the first sentence, prisoners of war can be expected to receive a second, presumably for misconduct while serving the first. It is also unlikely that the limitations upon disciplinary punishments will be observed (article 90).

The PRC will probably want to mete out death sentences to prisoners of war when there are less formal ways of attaining the same result. If it should, however, it cannot be expected to implement the special procedures set forth (articles 100, 101, 107), if only because it will refuse to recognize a protecting power.

The Chinese probably regard the convention's provisions restricting punishment for escape as bizarre and based on a "sporting" view of escape. They should not find it easy to understand why article 91 prohibits them from punishing a prisoner of war for the escape if he is recaptured after making good his escape within the meaning of the article. Nor should they comprehend why a PW who unsuccessfully attempts to escape is liable only to a disciplinary punishment both for the escape (article 92) and for certain offenses designed to facilitate the escape, or why escape cannot be considered an aggravating circumstance at a trial for other escape-related offenses (article 93). The artificiality of such "legalistic thinking" and the circumscribed nature of disciplinary punishment make it unlikely that the PRC will be bound by these provisions in practice, as indeed it was not bound during the Korean conflict, when it meted out long sentences of solitary confinement for attempted escapes. The PRC's Korean record offers little basis for confidence that it will not on occasion impose collective punishment for individual acts, imprison prisoners of war in premises without daylight or engage in other cruel acts (article 87).

The only possible issue of legal interpretation that might arise in this chapter concerns the scope of the PRC's reservations to article 85's requirement that the convention's benefits continue to apply to prisoners of war even after their convictions under the laws of the detaining power for precapture acts. Like other Communist states, the PRC claimed that it would not be bound by this provision "in respect of the treatment of prisoners of war convicted under the laws of the Detaining Power in accordance with the principles laid down in the trials of war crimes or crimes against humanity by the Nuremberg and the Tokyo International Military Tribunals."

The reasonable meaning of these words would seem to be that, in the PRC's view, after conviction of such crimes prisoners no longer enjoy the convention's benefits. In 1966, however, North Vietnam appeared to argue that under the terms of its reservation, which applies to PWs *prosecuted for* and convicted of" war crimes, and so forth, the convention also did not apply to those PWs who have simply been accused of war crimes but not yet convicted. Although the wording of China's reservation lends itself less readily to such an argument, we cannot rule out the possibility that it may some day be made by the PRC, in view of its initial position in the Korean conflict that all United Nations prisoners were war criminals by virtue of having participated in aggressive war and therefore were subject to summary execution. It should be noted in this connection that North Korea failed to give prisoner of war treatment to the crew of the *Pueblo* and even threatened to try crew members for espionage.

When the PRC indicated after the Korean armistice that it might not repatriate prisoners of war who had been convicted of crimes and were still serving sentences, the United States insisted that this would be a violation of the armistice agreement and that it would not repatriate Chinese and North Korean prisoners who had been convicted of serious crimes until the convicted United Nations personnel were released. The Chinese reply pointed out that article 119 of the convention authorizes continuing detention, after general repatriation, of those prisoners who have been charged with or already convicted of indictable offenses until they complete their punishment.

Nevertheless, and this may be useful in future disputes over whether prisoners of war can properly be deemed war criminals, the PRC announced shortly thereafter the release of eleven United States airmen who had been suspected of invading Chinese airspace and dropping germ bombs and special agents in China and who had therefore been extradited by North Korea to China. Some of the eleven had admitted that the United States Air Force had engaged in such criminal activities, it was said, but investigation by the Northeast People's government had led to the conclusion that they personally had had no direct connection with aggressive activities against China. It was therefore decided to exempt them from prosecution and to return them to Korea for repatriation.

That war criminals would be prosecuted by the PRC in its domestic tribunals was confirmed by the experience of Japanese prisoners of war captured in World War II. In 1956 the PRC articulated the factors that it considered in deciding whether to prosecute the Japanese for war crimes or to release them. In addition to reasons of state, such as Japan's new prominence and China's desire to normalize relations with Japan, which motivated a general policy of leniency, in individual cases the PRC took into account factors such as the seriousness of the alleged crime, the degree of remorse shown by the accused, and the extent to which the accused seemed to have been coerced into committing, the crime by Japan's militaristic leadership.

Release, Repatriation, and Death

Although the PRC may be slow in, and may attempt to gain political advantage from, the return of seriously wounded and ill prisoners of war, it can be expected at least partially to comply with the convention (articles 109, 110). Very late in the Korean hostilities it carried out an exchange of sick and wounded. According to Chinese claims, the PRC behaved admirably in the Indian conflict. The pattern seemed to be that the Chinese Foreign Ministry would inform the Indian Embassy in Peking of the number of PWs captured, and the Chinese Red Cross would then follow up with particulars about each individual, including his name, location, and physical condition. On a number of occasions the Chinese Red Cross released Indian sick and wounded. Nothing in the record suggests, however, that the PRC might be prepared to accept the appointment of mixed medical commissions that could interfere with its unilateral determination of who among the prisoners was eligible for release (article 112, 113).

It is unclear whether the PRC will accept the outcome of the nonforcible repatriation dispute in Korea as precedent for the future application of article

118. The Chinese, together with the North Koreans and Russians, had argued for what they claimed to be a literal interpretation of article 118's provision that "prisoners of war shall be released and repatriated without delay after the cessation of active hostilities." This, they said, meant that all PWs had to be repatriated, even against their will. For support they pointed to the contrasting language of article 109, which provided for the obligatory return of seriously sick or injured prisoners prior to cessation of hostilities but which went on to state that no such person "may be repatriated against his will during hostilities." The implication of this, it was said, was that PWs could be repatriated against their will after cessation of hostilities. Moreover, the Chinese argued that article 7's provision that PWs "may in no circumstances renounce in part or in entirety the rights secured to them by the present Convention. . . ." meant that they could not refuse repatriation. The Chinese persisted in this position for more than a year before finally yielding to military necessity, including, it is commonly thought, a United States threat to resort to nuclear weapons against China.

The question of the proper interpretation of article 118 apparently did not arise in the Indian conflict, where the Chinese claim to have unilaterally released all Indian PWs after an unsuccessful effort to persuade India to negotiate the arrangements. The PRC refuted Indian claims that it had delayed repatriation of prisoners and violated the convention. Anticipated political realities suggest that the question will arise again in any conflict in which numbers of Chinese are captured. In these circumstances the PRC may not accept the Korean agreement but may brand it as an "unequal treaty" imposed under the threat of nuclear weapons.

Experience in both the Korean and Indian conflicts indicates that, despite China's claims to have provided complete data, the PRC's handling of information concerning persons who die as prisoners of war is likely to be unsatisfactory, especially because of tardiness. Japan has also been unhappy about the PRC's reporting on thousands of Japanese nationals who were purportedly in China during World War II and who have never been heard from since. Whether or not it establishes "an official information bureau" (article 122), the PRC will use the Chinese Red Cross to carry out the international duties contemplated by the convention. It seems unlikely, however, for reasons outlined above, that the PRC will cooperate with a central prisoner of war information agency or any other public or private international organization as contemplated (articles 123-25).

Conclusion

If taken seriously by the Chinese, GPW would constitute a vehicle for bringing to the PRC Western concepts of due process of law, much as exposure to general international law in the nineteenth century introduced China to Western concepts of law. Unfortunately, the evidence is that Chinese Communist theory and practice, as reinforced by traditional Chinese theory and practice, have in large measure resisted these standards. Nevertheless, the Chinese have shown that they are not wholly insensitive either to world opinion or to the intrinsic desirability of humane treatment at least of those prisoners of war who are not "reactionaries."

Can anything be done to enhance prospects for acceptable behavior by the PRC toward prisoners of war? Although there are no panaceas, a variety of recommendations ought to be considered. As the Vietnam conflict suggests, from the very outset of any hostilities the United States should be more alert than it has been to see that it and its allies fully implement the convention, that this is made known to our enemies, and that they are requested to make reciprocal efforts. Moreover, the United States should meet China's concern about aspects of the law of war the importance of which we tend to underestimate, such as the use of bacteriological and chemical weapons. The recent ratification of the 1925 Geneva Protocol might be a useful step in eliciting Chinese cooperation toward prisoners of war.

In the event of hostilities we should also contemplate proposing bilateral agreements between the Chinese and American Red Cross agencies in an attempt to overcome the difficulties created by China's demonstrated reluctance to accept any role for third states or for international organizations. Our problems negotiating and administering agreements in Korea and the 1955 Sino-American agreement for the repatriation of civilians will, of course, remind us that this will not be easy.

We should bear in mind, however, that the Chinese regard us with grave suspicion when it comes to making and keeping agreements and abiding by international law. Their perception of United States behavior concerning the Cairo Declaration's pledge to restore Taiwan to China, the Uniting for Peace Resolution, the legal maneuvering that long excluded China from the United Nations, the interpretation of GPW regarding nonforcible repatriation, the branding of China as an "aggressor" in Korea, the condemnation of Chinese justice for "trumped-up charges" against the CIA agents convicted of espionage, the continuing invasions of China's airspace, and other issues, hardly dispose the Chinese leaders to trust the United States to abide by the rules of the game. Any effort to improve the PRC's treatment of prisoners of war must thus be viewed in the broader context of the antecedent need to create a modicum of trust in our willingness to take international law seriously.

Now that the PRC is represented in the United Nations and many other international organizations, enjoys diplomatic relations with most countries, and is engaged in the process of normalizing relations with the United States, there are ample opportunities to demonstrate the credibility of our commitment to international law and to elicit China's cooperation in responding to the multiplicity of challenges confronting the world community. The visit to China in late 1971 of the ICRC president provided an initial occasion to discuss the development of international humanitarian law and the work program of ICRC's conference of experts. After declining two previous invitations to participate in the efforts of the committee of national experts convened by ICRC to consider revision of the Geneva Conventions of 1949, the PRC did send a delegation to the 1973 meeting of the committee, and it also took part in the first session of the Diplomatic Conference on the Reaffirmation and Development of International Humanitarian Law Applicable in Armed Conflicts convened by the Swiss government in 1974.

These early contacts indicate that enlisting Chinese collaboration in the enhancement of protection for prisoners of war will not be easy. Yet, prospects are currently brighter than they have been at any previous time since the founding of the PRC in 1949.

Notes

1. *Uniformed Spy Is a Spy, Says Legal Expert Ch'en T'i-ch'iang*, Survey of the China Mainland Press, No. 955, at 31-32 (1954).

2. Wang Yen-lin, *How We Treat the P.O.W.'s*, People's China, No. 12, at 22 (1951).

3. See Ministry of National Defence, United Kingdom, Treatment of British Prisoners of War in Korea 16 (1955).

4. Cohen, *The Chinese Communist Party and "Judicial Independence": 1949-1959*, 82 Harvard L. Rev. 967-1006 (1969).

9

Other Powers

Introduction

This chapter is concerned with the attitudes toward, and willingness and ability of selected nations in five areas of the world to comply with, the humanitarian principles of the Geneva Conventions. Predictions as to how nations may treat prisoners of war in a future limited conflict are highly speculative and become increasingly more so the further into the future the forecast extends.[a] However, useful behavioral consistencies in the nations examined provide useful insights into future conduct. To some extent, these conjectures also expose difficulties in the application of the Geneva Conventions arising out of their Western European ethnocentricity. Analyses of nations in this chapter were based upon in-depth interviews with eminent academic specialists who have spent a substantial portion of their professional careers studying (and, in most instances, residing in) the nations discussed. The purpose of the interviews was to determine the extent to which the histories and cultural values of these nations might condition their attitudes toward the application of the principles of the conventions. With a single exception the specialists interviewed are neither lawyers nor persons particularly familiar with the international law of the protection of victims of war. They are, rather, persons with deep knowledge and understanding of the traditions and values of the nations in question. Although their names are listed in the footnotes as principal reference sources for much of the information included in this chapter, they are neither the sole sources nor the authors of the words below and cannot be held responsible for the text.

Eastern Europe[1]

For the purposes of this section "Eastern Europe" includes Yugoslavia, Poland, Hungary, Bulgaria, Czechoslovakia, and Rumania. In most of these nations ethnic and regional identifications are exceedingly strong and often extend beyond national boundaries. The cultural differences between populations within such states are apt to be greater than the political differences between states and may strongly color the treatment of prisoners in armed conflicts. Moreover, in each of these nations the population would be disposed to treat

---

[a]The caveat is especially in order if the reader will recall that most of the predictions in this chapter were made in 1968.

prisoners of war better than they would treat their own common criminals. Most of the Balkan nations have developed a heightened sense of discrimination between the kinds of people held in detention. The result of centuries of political turmoil and subjugation is that political imprisonment carries no public opprobrium. Many of the national heroes, particularly those of Communist nations, have spent some time in jail. For example, it is regarded as natural that as esteemed a statesman and author as Milovan Djilas should be imprisoned in Yugoslavia, and just as natural that his personal stature remained high even in the administration that deprived him of his liberty. Slavs are mindful that from Lenin to Tito (to say nothing of Ghandi and Bolivar), political servitude in some cultures is virtually a certification of integrity. Since war is regarded as a political act, prisoners of war would enjoy ". . . in all circumstances . . . respect for their persons and their honor" in accordance with GPW (Geneva Convention Relative to the Treatment of Prisoners of War), article 14, barring other factors such as traditional enmity, war crimes, or the personal conduct of the prisoner.

There are apt to be social reservations and gaps in the application of GWS-1949 (Geneva Convention for the Amelioration of the Condition of Wounded, Sick, and Shipwrecked Members of Armed Forces at Sea—1949) with regard to the wounded and sick. In those parts of countries where an aristocratic heritage remains, the wounded and sick are likely to be given the same medical care as that which is given to the troops of the detaining power. However, in many communities industrialization has broken down the previous standards of a rural morality and no humanitarian ethic has taken its place. It is not nearly as likely that the wounded and the sick would be respected and protected. Above all, ethnic enmities are paramount. In case of any kind of a conflict between Yugoslavia and Germany, Montenegrans, for example, will shoot Germans whether they are East Germans or West Germans and even if they are wounded. The traditional fears, hatreds, and emotional responses exacerbated by the experiences of World War II would dictate public reaction toward the wounded and the sick.

To the extent that the concept of a protecting power depends upon the belief in true neutrality, it would be rejected by the Communist authorities. Communist leaders simply do not believe that neutral nations exist. The conventions suggest that a state is either a party to the conflict or it is a neutral. Communist doctrine teaches that the conflict between the bourgeois and the proletariat is as much an underlying reality in so called "neutral" countries as it may be in those involved in an armed conflict.

The broad base of the population in Eastern Europe does not necessarily comprehend or accept this Marxist sophistication. To them the notion of a protecting power is quite feasible. However, important distinctions would be drawn between neutrals. For example, Poles respect Swedes and would be inclined to accept them as protecting power. However, they do not like Austrians, and the neutrality of Austria could never be established merely by

Austria's political position with respect to a given conflict. The same generalizations hold true for the impartiality of ICRC (International Committees of the Red Cross); that is, the populations accept the humanitarian, impartial commitment of a Red Cross organization composed entirely of Swiss nationals. The Communist elite does not. In this instance, however, popular reaction is more likely to affect official policy than the party leadership.

Unfortunately the application of GPW, article 3, or for that matter any portion of the GC (Geneva Conventions Relative to the Protection of Civilian Persons in Time of War) to disputes of other than an international character is remote. For example, within Yugoslavia, in conflicts between the Serbs and the Croats, each party has always tended to think of the other as oppressors and traitors. In multinational countries, traditional rivalries and intense hatreds are likely to dominate humanitarian impulses in civil conflicts.

The restrictions of GPW, article 50, respecting permissible labor for prisoners are not likely to be observed. It is less a matter of public or official opposition to the policy, than of massive disillusionment and cynicism arising out of the experiences of World War II. People in the Balkans simply do not believe that a detaining power would show any restraint in the use of PW labor. Thus, the belief is that as no major power (notably Russians and Germans) is likely to observe the rules, why should a minor power act with greater circumspection?

As noted in Chapter 7, capture connotes some degree of disgrace to the Russians, which may result in reduction of the amount of relief and assistance that the prisoner may expect from the power on which he depends. However, this attitude is less true in the case of the other Slavic countries, whose troops often expect to be captured. Conditions of internment would also be affected by other national attitudes: Yugoslavs are likely to show more concern for their captured comrades than would Rumanians. Mountain people would tend to temper regard for their comrades by the nationality of the captured troops or whether they fought honorably on the battlefield. Poland is perhaps, the only nation that could be expected to honor commitments unilaterally.

Living conditions within internment camps are likely to follow regional traditions. Thus, it is probable that the requirement of GPW-1949 regarding food, clothing, shelter, mail, and so forth would be scrupulously observed in Montenegro even if the conditions of the prisoners were superior to that of the depot troops because of the traditional hospitality of the mountain people. On the other hand, it is extremely unlikely that any standard higher than the assimilation rules of GPW-1929 are likely to be observed in Bohemia and other industrialized areas. In East Germany the one Western European country in the Communist bloc, local custom will not be important. The camps will be run in accordance with official policy whatever it might be. In the other nations the attitude of the local population toward the country on which the prisoner depends is likely to determine his treatment in the internment camp.

Attitudes toward group punishment appear to vary with the extent of industrialization. Here, again, the preindustrial social structures are likely to administer collective punishment in the internment camp than the more industrialized sections of nations. Almost thirty years since the end of World War II it is probably still true that the East German will be principally motivated by whatever will most favorably impress the Russians. Thus, the use of coercion, humiliation, degradation, and even physical torture is likely to follow the prevailing Russian pattern. These prohibited practices are more likely in Germany than in the other countries with which this section is concerned.

No Communist nation regards a prisoner of war as a person removed from the conflict. Nevertheless, the Communist elite of Eastern Europe is likely to observe the spirit of the conventions to insure reciprocity. The overriding consideration with respect to the political treatment of prisoners would be their nationality. For example, any German prisoner of war in Poland may be expected to be treated as a political criminal. On the other hand, the Slavic attitude toward war crimes is not likely to delay repatriation at the conclusion of hostilities, as was the case in the Soviet Union following World War II, since the return of their own prisoners of war is apt to be an important consideration.

The Indian Subcontinent[2]

Sociologically, if not by operation of law, the highly developed class systems of India permeate the application of all legal concepts. Thus, there is no notion of a "criminal" or of a "prisoner" without reference to the captive's status. There are many gradations of treatment, depending upon this factor. There is little doubt that India and to a lesser extent Pakistan and Bangladesh, would tend to discriminate among prisoners of war at least on the basis of rank, although discrimination is not likely to be invidious to any class. The discrimination that might be expected with regard to healthy prisoners would not necessarily apply to the wounded and the sick. Given the personnel and material to do so—a condition that is problematical—the nations of the subcontinent could be expected to comply with all elements of GWS, including equal treatment of enemy wounded and sick.

India is one of the few nations of the world that might welcome a protecting power to fulfill its convention obligations in international conflict. A principal reason for this is that the role of the impartial intermediary, or arbitrator, is central in the adjudication of domestic legal disputes. The parties to the controversy always expect to call upon a disinterested mediator, arbitrator, or conciliator. Thus, India was willing to accept the good offices of the USSR (if not the full convention role) in mediating the 1965 Pakistan conflict. The Pakistanis are somewhat less enthusiastic about the role of the disinterested neutral, but no less so than, say, the United States. In a mixed civil-international conflict, such as Bangladesh's war for independence from Pakistan, India's role as a "neutral" supporter of the revolution all but precluded third party mediation. The impartiality of the ICRC is fully accepted by both India and Pakistan.

In the event of civil conflict (which is likely to arise over religious and language differences within regions hard pressed by poverty and famine) there is little doubt that the senior civil service and the police would make every effort to apply applicable convention articles and, in particular, common article 3. Consistent with what has been noted as a part of the Indian juridical tradition, an outside constabulary is regularly called in to control riots, on the theory that the law enforcement authorities in the affected communities may not be sufficiently impartial.

Application of the conventions would reflect the economic realities of the region. Given the problem of chronic unemployment, it is unlikely that prisoners of war would be used for prohibited labor. It is far more likely that prisoners of war would not be permitted to do any work in the labor-rich Indian subcontinent. In the event of a brief conflict with Pakistan or China, Indian PW internment camps, for logistical reasons, would be located near the borders of these countries. Except in the mountain provinces, the area is extremely hot. There is some evidence that when the Indians interned Pakistani soldiers during the Bangladesh revolution there was a sanitation problem, but no problem of housing or clothing. Minimal rations would be provided as the Indians attempted to comply with the conventions as best they could. Neither India or Pakistan has the resources to care for large numbers of prisoners of war in any kind of prolonged conflict. For example, if the 1965 Indian conflict with Pakistan had occurred one year later, food would have been insufficient to feed the prisoners held by India. The parties would do their best to meet their commitments, however, and would ungratefully welcome international assistance. Their attitude in this respect would be a strong contrast, for example, to that of the parties in the Nigeria-Biafra dispute.

Collective punishment within PW internment camps or in occupied territory is most unlikely. The subcontinent rigorously observed the notion of the individual guilt that is common to both English law and Hindu and Moslem traditions. By the same token, the Indians would readily comply with the legal prohibitions respecting torture, humiliation, and degradation of prisoners and interned civilians. Compliance is probable but less certain in the Moslem countries.

Aliens in the territory of a party to the conflict would be scrupulously protected to the letter of the conventions, and to their spirit if the conventions were technically inapplicable. Indeed, during the Sino-India conflict of 1968 some aliens were placed in assigned residences, some were interned in camps, and all were offered an opportunity to return to China under convention safeguards. This protection took place in spite of the fact that diplomatic relations continued and Chinese nationals were theoretically under the protection of the

Chinese embassy. On the other hand, it became equally clear during the Bangladesh revolution that the Indians will continue to hold interned aliens for political purposes (in this instance the recognition of Bangladesh by Pakistan) rather than repatriate them upon cessation of hostilities. In this respect their failure to observe GPW was consistent with the behavior of the Communist nations in the Korean and Vietnamese conflicts.

Indians, Pakistanis and Bengalis regard a soldier as an instrument of government who is simply performing his duty. The prisoner of war would not be regarded as a personal party to the conflict. Accordingly, in theory and in practice they would tend to respect the disarmed prisoner of war. There is no disgrace attached to surrender; the captured prisoner would receive the support of the power upon which he depends and would be accepted home upon release or repatriation. However, the philosophy and natural temperament of the subcontinent is tempered by the reactions of the mass population in time of conflict. Thus, although the military and civil leadership would be inclined to treat military prisoners with humanity and compassion even if the other side denied any obligation to do so, such forbearance should not be expected from civilian masses involved in the conflict. Indeed, the Moslems and Hindus slaughtered one another without restraint in the India-Pakistan war. The Pakistanis and Bengalis for their part, observed the Moslem maxim: "My brother and I against my cousin; my cousin and I against the world." In one instance in 1965 the Moslems killed every passenger on the train carrying Hindus except the engineer and fireman. When the twenty-car hearse arrived at the next Hindu village, the inhabitants slaughtered every Moslem in sight.

Indonesia and Malaysia[3]

Indonesian attitudes toward prisoners are influenced principally by Dutch traditions and Javanese culture. The Malaysian experience was shaped by English common law and, in particular, by the way in which Great Britain handled the Communist terrorists on the Malay Peninsula. An overlay of Chinese cultural heritage is common to both Indonesia and Malaysia.

In Malaysia, during the Malaysian conflict, the British judge advocate wanted the Communist guerrillas, terrorists, and spies to be treated as criminals. The military personnel and those responsible for administering policy urged that they be treated as PWs in accordance with the Geneva Conventions in order to encourage surrender. There was no clean resolution of the issue. In the best English tradition both points of view were reconciled by creating two categories: captured enemy personnel (CEP), who were to be treated as criminals, and surrendered enemy personnel (SEP), who were to be treated as prisoners of war. As the name implied, the prisoner who surrendered prior to capture would be entitled to the more favorable SEP treatment. In fact, classification was rarely based upon the difficult criteria of whether the prisoner surrendered after he ran out of ammunition or was captured with a few rounds left in his rifle. Rather, the actual standard of classification was the post-capture attitude of the prisoner. If he had an ideological orientation toward Communism, he was a CEP. If it appeared that he could be prevailed upon to support the lawful government, then he would be classified as a SEP. The treatment within the two classes was substantially different. Neither rigorously complied with GPW because SEPs who received favorable treatment were also subject to compulsory propaganda and were neither released nor repatriated at the end of hostilities. Rather, they were impressed into the service of Singapore and Luang Probang. Malaysian authorities would tend to classify prisoners according to these categories in any conflict in which they might reasonably be expected to become involved.

Indonesian tradition makes a sharp distinction between the common criminal and the treatment of the PW in favor of the latter because of the distinction between criminal and political crimes in its colonial heritage. The PW would be regarded as more akin to the political prisoner, to whom no personal culpability attaches. The depth of the distinction is illustrated by the late President Sukarno's autobiography in which he bitterly complained, many years after the fact, about having been compelled to mingle with common criminals when he was arrested for political activities. This complaint strikes a responsive Indonesian chord.

Literal application of the provisions of GWS would be at variance with the Indonesian heritage. Their reaction to the disabled is influenced by Javanese culture, in which the greatest courtesy that one can extend to a fallen enemy is not to inflict further pain and suffering. The Indonesian, for example, would never understand the American concern for the victims of the earthquake in Honduras. Ironically, nominally equitable application of GWS could come in Indonesia as a result of scarce resources. Sufficient medical personnel and equipment would probably be lacking to even begin to treat enemy wounded and sick. Thus, the degree of neglect for the disabled would thus be equal for all. To a lesser degree, based upon the economics of scarcity, Malaysians would have the same attitude toward caring for their own and letting enemy wounded fend for themselves.

Indonesia would find the notion of a protecting power intolerable. The society is permeated by a high degree of secretiveness. Secrecy and mystery are the very embodiments of Javanese culture. Moreover, the notion of a protecting power would be offensive in their own eyes to their dignity as a major world power. In their view, the word of an important person is not questioned. His baggage is not searched. His tax return is not audited. Therefore, by analogy, the stature of a "major" power will not permit surveillance by a neutral. This attitude is far less likely to prevail in Malaysia with its strong sense of British legality. Relative to other nations in Southeast Asia, Malaysia is an open society whose government considers itself publicly accountable. The impartiality of

ICRC and the humanitarian efforts of the Red Cross are accepted at face value by both Indonesia and Malaysia.

The application of convention principles, and article 3 in particular, to civil conflict by either country would be questionable. In the Indonesian civil conflict, all the Communist prisoners were held as political prisoners under conditions of internment that approximated PW care. However, rather than being released they were tried individually as criminals. The existence of tens of thousands of prisoners after the Indonesian coup against the Sukarno administration makes it likely that many are resigned to spending much of their lives in internment camps awaiting trial. Malaysia, as above noted, made the SEP-CEP distinction in its own Communist conflict. The SEP were proselytized and then exploited by the government. The CEP were detained, tried, and sentenced, to long prison terms that were not commuted at the end of hostilities.

Both Malaysia and Indonesia used prisoners of war for all kinds of labor. Neither country should be expected to hesitate to employ prisoners in war-related work if required. It should be recalled that during World War II President Sukarno actually provided conscript labor of the Japanese. No GPW-1929 assimilation standard for providing food, clothing, and shelter to prisoners of war would be likely to be honored by Indonesia and Malaysia. However, there is no chance that prisoners of war would ever receive better food, clothing, and shelter than the depot troops in either country.

GPW article 33 prohibiting collective punishment is foreign to the traditions of either country. In Malaysia's post-World War II civil conflict, the English high commissioner regularly imposed collective punishment on "bad villages." The propriety of group responsibility was never questioned. Similarly, the Sultans in Indonesia used to punish an entire town for offenses committed by individuals. Most significant is the Chinese tradition, as expressed through its overseas population, resident in Malaysia and Indonesia, that as long as a relative of an offender is available for punishment, it is not particularly important to find the individual who committed the crime. In short, the concept of collective guilt is firmly implanted in the culture. Moreover, the humanitarian prohibitions against torture humiliation and degradation of prisoners are completely at odds with the cultural traditions of Malaysia and, particularly, Indonesia. Southeast Asians have developed humiliation and degradation of the person to a fine art. Conventional restraint on these practices is more likely to be honored in the breach than the observance. These nations might show some restraint with respect to torture that would incur unfavorable publicity, but such restraint would be reluctant and would be at odds with tradition. The use of pain as an instrument of compliance is quite customary, and refraining from causing pain to others is regarded as an exemplary courtesy. Indeed, the prisoner who insisted upon his rights against torture could well be viewed as committing a provocative act.

GC provisions that would protect aliens from hostile activities short of internment or placement in assigned residence are foreign to the culture of both countries. The alien is a natural target of resentment. The only unusual factor in the slaughter of Chinese Communists in Indonesia in the mid-1960s was the grand scale of activities, not the nature of the activity itself. A captured Malaysian or Indonesian is not regarded by his captors as having been removed from the conflict in any sense. If he has surrendered, it is quite likely that he will be killed by his own people when he returns; accordingly, the soldier who surrenders ordinarily assists his former enemy. The reaction of his own people does not arise out of any notion of disgrace as, for example, in Japanese tradition. Rather, it springs from simple motives of retribution—which are not likely to have been legislated out of existence by the conventions in that part of the world.

Although the application of the conventions is unilateral in theory, there is little chance that either Indonesia or Malaysia would ever apply them without reciprocity. This may be seen from the fact that in the Indonesian-Malaysian conflict local military actions ranged all the way from a refusal to take PWs at all to decent treatment (by local standards), depending upon how the enemy was treating its captured personnel.

Turkey[4]

The Turks tend to view the world in terms of in-group and out-group relationships. The prisoner of war in an international conflict, unless he is ranking officer, is likely to be regarded as a member of the out-group and treated the same as a common criminal. The word "common" in this regard refers to the peasantry, for within Turkish society, the intellectual elite and the peasantry receive decidedly different standards of treatment. Although there is no ideological or cultural obstacle toward humanitarian treatment of the enemy wounded and sick, it should be assumed that Turkish wounded and sick would always receive preferential care and the enemy wounded and sick are likely to be ignored. This is a consequence of a system of ethics born of scarcity: The Turk will automatically assume that there is insufficient medical personnel and supplies to treat all the wounded and sick, for this has been his experience through most of his life. On the other hand, the wounded and the sick would be readily exchanged. In fact, these provisions were rigorously observed in the 1974 battle between Greek and Turkish Cypriotes.

The Turks would be ambivalent about a protecting power. Through practice, they are disinclined to accept the role of the impartial arbitrator. However, since Kemal Ataturk they desire at all costs to be regarded as a "modern" nation. Thus, they would probably accede to the appointment of a protecting power in an international conflict if the major powers accepted the concept and pressured them to do so. On the other hand, they have no difficulty in accepting the impartiality of the Red Crescent Society and, through it, the role of ICRC.

The application of GPW article 3 in an internal conflict is remote. In any kind of conflict in which Turk is pitted against Turk, as indicated by their own revolution, it would be a "no holds barred" contest, and each of the four prohibited activities in GPW article 3 (1) (a) through (d) would be expected to occur. In a mixed civil-international conflict, such as the Turkish invasion of Cyprus in 1974, the guidelines were predictably unclear.

If the conflict does not create labor shortages, the Turks might be expected to comply with GPW with respect to the use of prisoner labor. If they are pressed for workers, however, their participation in the conventions is not likely to outweigh their pragmatism. Conditions of internment within Turkey are likely to be grim. The Turks are well disciplined and used to hardship. War is regarded as a necessarily brutal activity. Food, clothing, and shelter should not be expected to meet even minimum standards unless there were substantial international pressure for compliance and inspection. Only national disgrace or ridicule would be likely to improve internment conditions. But they are particularly sensitive to criticism implying backwardness and failure to comply with standards of modern Western nations. Within the internment camp, the application of group punishment is probable. The Turkish view respecting the collective guild of a family or community to which a wrongdoer belongs is closer to that of the Orient than Western Europe. In any event, the "enemy," as an out-group member, is beyond the pale—he has no claim to rights.

The application of coercion, humiliation, or physical torture to prisoners or civilians in occupied territory would depend upon the whim of local commanders. It is certain that military discipline will not tolerate insubordination in the name of humanity. The trial of an enlisted man in Turkey for obeying an order to commit a criminal act against a civilian or a prisoner is inconceivable. The rank or status of the civilian or prisoner is as likely to affect the probability of torture as the ostensible reason for which the torture is administered.

Within its own society, humanitarian considerations play a substantial role in the vicissitudes of life. Moreover, the Turks have no problem with the concept that a prisoner of war is removed from the conflict. It is simply that he is removed to a low social status. Outside the Turkish legal community there is not likely to be any high regard for the commitments of international law. To the rural Turk it is still true that only power commands respect. In a nation in which the rule of *lex talionis* still prevails, unilateral application of the convention in a conflict against a foe who is suspected of dishonoring the conventions is improbable. The Turkish government and its people would be guided by reciprocity. The Turks have a proud military heritage and consider martyrdom during battle as a glorious form of death. By the same token, they respect their fighting men and would identify with and support their own captured personnel in the PW camps of the enemy. There is no opprobrium to capture if one has fought well. Repatriation would be welcome. Prompt repatriation of prisoners taken in the Cyprus conflict was effectuated by the ICRC and the United Nations peacekeeping force upon the cessation of the 1974 hostilities.

Zaire, Nigeria, and Central Africa[5]

In Zaire, and in much of Central Africa, territorial divisions are political distinctions created by the former colonial powers and are far less significant than tribal and racial divisions. The treatment of prisoners of war will depend upon whether the conflict is truly "African," that is, if it involves only black Africans, or whether European interests and forces are also engaged. Other variables include the background of the detaining personnel, the identity of the prisoner of war (including race, tribe, and class), the place of detention, and the circumstances of the capture. These variables result in a spectrum of attitudes toward prisoners of war ranging from complete arbitrariness to utmost respect for the laws of war.

The notion of a faceless antagonist who kills without animus or personal motivation in the service of an abstract principle is totally foreign to African thinking. Armed conflict in Central Africa is, thus, not depersonalized. The soldier is not merely an agent of his government, he is a man who may have just attempted to kill his captor and who must be dealt with accordingly. The prisoner of war is not even a "political" enemy in the Western sense, but a personal enemy entitled to retribution. An enemy captured in an intertribal or international conflict (the distinction is not always clear in Central Africa) thus occupies a lower status than a person detained under municipal criminal law or custom.

Most of the cultures of Central Africa would favor compassion to the wounded and sick of any tribe or nation. The degree of compassion would be a function of the relationship of the disabled person to one's own extended family. (In this respect, it must be understood that the African "extended family" may take in thousands of people.) The question, however, tends to be academic for the foreseeable future: There are scarcely sufficient medical resources to treat the wounded and the sick in time of peace. During times of war, medical care is all but nonexistent. Thus the Congolese armies during the Katanga revolution like most of those of Central Africa were composed of combat units only with little or no logistical support. This is changing, but it will be quite some time before a medical corps is established.

The concept of a neutral nation as a protecting power would be acceptable in a dispute involving African states only if the neutral were African itself, for example, the protection offered by Mali in the dispute between Somaliland and Kenya. If the conflict is not truly "African," as for example, aspects of the mid-1960s conflicts in Nigeria and Zaire, then because of colonial heritage, no African nation would be accepted as truly neutral. All non-African nations would, likewise, be regarded with a degree of suspicion. The ICRC is not likely to be acceptable as a protecting power, nor is it even likely to be regarded as impartial, simply because it is non-African. Moreover, the concept of detached impartiality, aside from personalities, is only imperfectly understood. It is felt that acceptance of ICRC assistance after the uprising of mercenaries in 1967 was a reluctant concession to considerable international pressure. Unfortunately, the United Nations Congo operation vitiated whatever remote possibility there might have been for the United Nations to be regarded as a neutral. Many Africans found themselves unable to distinguish between United Nations forces and white mercenaries who were retained by the Belgians and Katanga. There were even Congolese accusations of looting by United Nations forces. The enormous political power of the "Third World" in the United Nations General Assembly in the 1970s could neutralize the earlier impression.

In a civil conflict, the punishment of rebels, whether military or whether a means to retaliate against the enemy, should be expected. The Nigerian civil war was a case in point: The best that the Biafrans could hope for was indifference by the detaining power. To a degree, this is a part of the colonial heritage. Group punishment was common and merciless in any instance in which a European was killed in a colony. On the other hand, group punishment of prisoners of war in an internment camp is not likely without provocation by the group itself. Black African logic is personalized. There is no philosophy of impersonal retribution, expiation, or even deterrence as factors of punishment. Rebels have usually been regarded as traitors; however, depending upon the circumstances, they have also been treated as common criminals, international scoundrels, mere political activists, and supernatural forces. For example, Mr. Mulale, who was triumphantly accepted by his countrymen upon a return from Brazzaville, Republic of Congo (while Premier Mobuto was out of the country), was tried by a military court and publicly executed the moment Premier Mobuto returned—as were several ministers of the Congo who attempted to assassinate the prime minister.

As in the case of the Indian subcontinent discussed above, it is idle to consider abuse of PW labor. There is not enough work in the best of times. Conflict would increase the needs of the people, but at the same time it would impair the slim capital and management base required to convert human requirements to economic demand. Moreover, if prisoners are taken, they would not be permitted to do any kind of work, because they would be considered to be inherently untrustworthy.

A certain degree of torture, coercion, and degradation of prisoners of war is likely in Central African conflicts. It will not be officially encouraged or condoned, but nevertheless it is customary, less as a method of extracting information than as an appropriate response to evil. Simply stated, an enemy is an evil person. Thus, captured Italian pilots flying for the United Nations were tortured and killed in Zaire during the Katanga dispute. Torture would never be arbitrarily imposed, but to the Western mind the African reasons for torture or degradation are likely to appear arbitrary or even capricious.

It is most unlikely that PWs would be fed, sheltered, and clothed at a standard equivalent to the detaining power. The two principal reasons are: (1) the perennial shortage of facilities of all sorts in Central Africa and (2) the personal animus that is borne by captors against prisoners. Under ordinary circumstances, non-African PWs may expect to fare somewhat better than African PWs. An additional complication is the relative lack of central administrative control in most central African states. Standards concerning the internment of prisoners are likely to be made by local commandants applying local standards value.

The classification and logistics problems would also affect internment. In the first instance, it is often quite difficult to separate political prisoners from prisoners of war. The sophistication required to determine who is entitled to PW treatment should not be taken for granted in Central Africa. Moreover, in the absence of an adequate support function, detained persons often depend upon the outside for sustenance. There were cases in Zaire of persons arrested as "paratroopers" (a favorite charge since the United Nations Congo operation) and left in jail to starve until relief was sent by friends or agencies.

The protection that might be afforded to an enemy alien in time of conflict or the treatment given to civilians in occupied territory is questionable. The principal problem involved in considering such matters is that the legal issues are based upon territorial rights and African political sensibilities and are far more oriented to tribe and caste than to territory. The notion of political rights that arise out of a relationship or a person to a parcel of land on which he resides, or from which he is removed, lacks reality in African thinking. It might very well be a general feeling, for example, that an "enemy alien" should be protected from the resentment of local citizens in time of conflict; but no one in authority would be likely to extend such protection in the absence of specific instructions to do so. On the contrary, uniformed forces (police and soldiers) have been known to detain the foreigner rather than to control the population. Whether detention would be arrest or protective custody is a fine point that might not be resolved.

Capture of a prisoner of war or surrender of a soldier would not ordinarily be regarded with any kind of opprobrium or involve any degree of disgrace to the PW, since imprisonment per se is not considered disgraceful. Nor does surrender entail a loss of prestige for the person or the armed force of which he is a member. Rather, the African reaction is akin to that of the European when a member of the family gets into trouble. The power on which the prisoner depends is not likely to disown him. Prompt repatriation by the detaining power upon the cessation of hostilities and efforts to secure repatriation by the power on which the PW depends—his family or tribe, not necessarily the state—are probable.

Family and tribal relations are strong, and the sick and the wounded will be collected by their kin. Indeed, the only relief that he may receive may be from his own tribe or family. Even in time of peace, when a person is hospitalized it is expected that family members will support the sick or the disabled patient; the hospital will not ordinarily do so.

In practice, there is a total disregard of the Geneva Conventions throughout

Central Africa. In large part this is based upon the lack of knowledge of the conventions; but even where knowledge exists, the underlying legal presumptions of the conventions make no particular sense in African terms of reference. The central theory of the conventions is based upon territory and nationality. The African thinks in terms of tribe and religion. Personal humanity and compassion are unrelated to disinterested Western legal philosophy. On the other hand if an African power treated prisoners well, it would not be because of either compassion or the anticipation of reciprocity from the enemy. It is more likely to arise out of personal relationships between the particular prisoners and the particular camp commandant. Similarly, if a detaining power heard that the enemy treated its prisoners poorly, it would unquestionably engage in retaliation.

The conventions themselves are, in some manner, embodied in the military law of all of the former British colonies and in most of the French codes of conduct. This is significant only so long as the law is enforced by European-trained officers. When the cultural or colonial link is broken, the law of war is all but forgotten. Thus, in Nigeria, General Gowan issued a statement that he would apply the Geneva Conventions, "except in the case of white mercenaries." In Zaire, the principal problem was that all the British colonial laws were too complicated to be administered by the Congolese. In practice, for many years after independence there were few local administrators who could even comply with the legal procedures to secure a driver's license without difficulty. It should not be expected that as complex and as culturally foreign a body of law as the Geneva Conventions would carry appreciable weight in Central Africa.

Latin America[6]

In all Latin American countries two categories of persons are distinguished in the administration of criminal justice: upper sector and common people. The term "sector" is used because it is not a "class" distinction as that term is understood in the United States; nor is it truly a class difference as in India, and certainly not an ethnic or racial distinction as in other parts of the world mentioned in this study. Rather, it relates to a sociopolitical division between those with power and influence and those without connections. Because of the extended family system that prevails in Latin American states, and the nature of hierarchical political parties, even a remote connection to the upper class will secure favored treatment in any kind of criminal action.

Traditionally, persons in the upper sector are, for all practical purposes, exempt from detention. Civil authorities are reluctant to take any action against individuals with proper connections because of unpleasant consequences to the enforcement agency itself. For example, with the exception of Mexico, police are wary about controlling student riots because the injury or death of a student, whatever the circumstances, will cause universal revulsion. In Guatemala, Communist terrorists who were apprehended by law enforcement authorities in the 1960s were usually acquitted of all charges when the local magistrate discovered that they are students five days a week and revolutionaries only on weekends. Fidel Castro, once actually apprehended by the Batista regime, was released when it was discovered that his cousin was one of Batista's ministers. In any event, political crimes are viewed as honorable crimes, and the leaders of political movements are treated with respect. Thus, the murder of Che Guevara in Bolivia is readily attributed to the CIA influence, because the act was inconsistent with Latin American values. However, the rules appear to be changing: Thus in Chile, in 1932, sixty-three students initiated a miniature fascist uprising and were slaughtered by the police. The national reaction resulted in the downfall of the government at the polls. But when the government of President Salvador Allende Gossens was overthrown by a military junta in September 1973, the brutal repression and torture that followed did not spare any of the former president's supporters, regardless of class. There are no equal rights in Latin America. Treatment of a prisoner depends upon how far removed he is from power and influence.

The application of GWS in any international conflict involving Latin nations is likely to be limited only by a participant's medical resources. Prisoners of war could expect medical attention equal to that given to forces of the detaining power, without respect to rank or status. Latin American nations have a high respect for international law and the role of international and neutral intermediaries as well as the function of relief organizations. Governments have generally cooperated with investigations conducted by the Inter-American Commission on Human Rights and agencies of the Organization of American States. The impartiality of ICRC is, in general, accepted by South American governments. Nevertheless, though several systems of control might be acceptable in international disputes, it is not likely that a protecting power, or any intervening third parties, would be welcomed by the participants in a civil conflict. From the perspective of the Latin Americans, the Dominican Republic regional peacekeeping operation was not an exception to the rule.

The social status of a rebel is critical in determining his treatment as a prisoner. As noted above, upper sector persons were traditionally treated by both sides with dignity and respect. If the tradition is crumbling, it is still a long way from the aristocracy to the masses. Common people should be expected to be interned, tortured, or killed without reference to personal behavior or political position. Captives taken in internal conflicts are regarded as political prisoners whose legal rights are no better than those of spies, guerrillas, or saboteurs. Whether the prisoners are taken in open combat or apprehended during clandestine activity and whether arms are carried openly or concealed have little or no effect on their classification or treatment.

In international conflict, Latin American respect for the law of war may normally be presumed. Thus, without reference to specific cases (there have only been three or four international conflicts in Latin America since 1820), there is every likelihood that Latin American countries would comply with convention requirements concerning PW labor. An officer will always be accorded the protection and respect of GPW. With respect to discipline and punishment the Latin concept of "machismo" (manliness) has an element of chivalry that is extremely important in the treatment of officers. Enlisted personnel with poor connections, however, are likely to be subject to some degree of torture, coercion, and degradation. Widespread confirmed reports of torture by military governments in Uruguay, Brazil, and Chile from 1972 to 1974 suggest a wholesale disregard of article 3 in civil conflicts. In the administration of occupied territory, regional practices suggest the likelihood of a group punishment to maintain order and mass reprisal against common people in the event of serious breaches of discipline. Over a year after the overthrow of the Allende government over 5,500 political prisoners were still detained to preserve public order.

Conditions of internment would depend on the status of the prisoner. Officers would be fed, sheltered, and clothed in full compliance with GPW even when the standard was superior to that of the detaining power. Enlisted men would be fortunate indeed to enjoy even the assimilation standards of GPW-1929. Thus, in the Chaco War between Paraguay and Bolivia in 1932, Bolivian peasants enjoying the standard of the detaining power received better treatment as PWs than they received from the ruling classes in their country. The capture or surrender of Latin American military personnel, does not connote opprobrium. Speedy release and repatriation are likely to take place in rigorous compliance with GPW, Part IV, Section II. Repatriation is not apt to be delayed to insure reciprocity or to retaliate for enemy violation of the conventions. On the contrary, the Latin American sense of honor makes unilateral compliance with the conventions likely in spite of enemy violations. In this respect, they regard the United States preoccupation with reciprocity (for example, United States offers of troop withdrawal in the Vietnam conflict in return for prisoners return by the North Vietnamese) as a commercial ethic that is less than admirable.

Notes

1. William Griffith, Associate Professor of Political Science, Massachusetts Institute of Technology. He is the author of "Communism in Europe," Cambridge: M.I.T. Press.

2. Myron Weiner, Professor of Political Science, Massachusetts Institute of Technology. He is the author of "Party Building in a New Nation," Chicago: University of Chicago Press, 1967.

3. Lucien Pye, Professor of Political Science, Massachusetts Institute of Technology. Professor Pye was born in (The Peoples Republic of) China and lived in the Far East for many years. His publications include "Guerilla Communism in Malaya," Princeton: Princeton University Press, 1956.

4. Fred Frey, Professor of Political Science, Massachusetts Institute of Technology. He is the author of "Turkish Political Elite," Cambridge: M.I.T. Press, 1959. (The conspicuous omission of a discussion of Greece in this section was a function of the concerns of the United States government at the time that the project underlying this book was commissioned. Cyprus was relatively quiet in the late sixties and the behavior of Greeks was regarded as predictable within the context of Western European cultural values.)

5. Professor Zdenck Cervenka, Institute of Law, Academy of Science, Prague, Czechoslovakia, holds a Doctor of Civil Laws degree from Charles University, Prague. He was a resident of Accra, Ghana during the Katangan revolution.

6. Ernest Halperin, Professor of Political Science, Massachusetts Institute of Technology. A Swiss citizen, Professor Halperin lived in Brazil and Chile for extended periods.

**Part IV:
Deficiencies and
Recommendations**

10 Deficiencies and Recommendations

In 1968 the United Nations Conference on Human Rights, held in Teheran, recommended that the General Assembly invite the secretary general of the United Nations to study the steps that should be taken to secure better application of the conventions. Reports were submitted to the General Assembly by the secretary general and a decision was taken by the ICRC (International Committee of the Red Cross) to convene a conference of governmental experts on the subject. The experts convened in June 1971 and adjourned for one year because of complaints that there had not been a sufficiently representative group of states. In June 1972 the experts met and drafted two protocols that were to be submitted to a "Diplomatic Conference on the Reaffirmation and Development of International Humanitarian Law Applicable in Armed Conflicts." One hundred and twenty-five of the 135 states that are parties to the Geneva Conventions responded to the invitation. If the first session of the conference produced anything at all, it was the conviction that the political fragmentation of the world in the mid-1970s all but precludes the current possibility of significant change to a body of outdated international law.

Time and scholarly analysis have exposed substantial lacunae in the provisions of the conventions. For example, there are no provisions to allow United Nations or regional organizations to serve as protecting powers. There are no guidelines for determination of "belligerent status." There are no definitions of the individual forms of "grave breaches" listed in each convention. The distinction between civil and international conflict is vague and uncertain. The articles on PW labor are too restrictive, the definition of persons entitled to the protection of the law too narrow. These and many other valid criticisms of the conventions have been leveled and will be set forth in the following pages. There are also observations of the weakness that characterizes any complex body of statutory law; it can derive from oversights in the drafting, from political compromise during the drafting and negotiating process, or from awkwardness in application. The deficiencies attributable to these causes, albeit important, are second in priority. First priority must be given to deficiencies inherent in the application of the Geneva Conventions: (1) the difficulty of applying sanctions in the international law of war, (2) the changing nature of warfare since the 1949 conferences, and (3) the unconscious cultural reservations of many signatories to a complex body of law that presupposes a common humanitarian system of values.

273

General Recommendations

General

The first and foremost recommendation this book makes is that the General Assembly of the United Nations should adopt by resolution a declaration setting forth and affirming the basic principles of the Geneva Conventions of 1949.

Such a resolution would add little or nothing to the present legal force of the Geneva Conventions of 1949, except insofar as it might link the treaties more closely to the customary law as enunciated in the declaration. The effect of such a declaration would be primarily psychological and educational—psychological in the sense of emphasizing the concern of the community of nations with the main safeguards of the conventions, and educational in the sense of summing up the treaties in terms that would be comprehensible and meaningful to the ordinary reader, who cannot now be expected to follow all the intricacies of legal draftsmanship. It is particularly important that the declaration emphasize the apolitical humanitarian character of the conventions.

The principles affirmed should reflect the content of the conventions and not go beyond them. Inconsistencies between the declaration and the existing treaties could diminish respect for and observance of them. The principles should not be drafted in terms of abstractions but should be written in down-to-earth terms meaningful to military personnel. They should be brief and simple.

Because of implicit cultural reservations of many signatories to a complex body of law that presupposes a common humanitarian system of values, parties to the Geneva Conventions of 1949, should undertake to report annually, in time of war and in time of peace, on their record of compliance with the conventions and on the degree to which the conventions are working effectively.

Compliance reports should include at least a copy of operational regulations that implement the conventions, the status of national laws that support the conventions (including penal sanctions for their violations) and a report of criminal prosecutions for violation of the conventions. Such a reporting procedure would resemble that employed under the international labor conventions. Annual declaration should lead to stricter compliance with the conventions; if a state refused to report, its record could be justifiably suspect.

Types of Conflict

Although common article 2 of the Geneva Conventions of 1949 makes the law applicable "to all cases of declared war or of any other armed conflict which may arise between two or more of the High Contracting Parties," the provision does not resolve the question of what constitutes an "armed conflict" for the purpose of these treaties. There are various levels of violence in the relations of states, and the convention does not make clear how far down on the scale the conventional law of war is applicable. Such an ambiguity existed in the 1963-66 confrontation between Malaysia and Indonesia, when both parties were reluctant to regard the hostilities as sufficiently intense to warrant the application of the Geneva Conventions. The very application of treaties directed to the protection of war victims could, in the view of various states, further exacerbate relations between two belligerents by giving rise to the inference that a low level of violence was now to be regarded as war. An unwillingness to apply the conventions may thus contribute to a checking of violence.

The parties to a conflict may both deliberately refrain from recognizing an armed conflict between them as a state of war. (If one of the two contending parties to the conflict recognizes the "state of war," the Geneva Conventions apply pursuant to common article 2, even though the state of war may not be recognized by the other party.) With the obsolescence of the institution of the declaration of war, the abnormal situation has become the normal one: Neither party resorts to a formal declaration of war. This was true in the Korean and Vietnam conflicts, as well as in most of the conflicts discussed earlier, and has caused numerous difficulties not only in international law but also in municipal law. For other purposes, United States courts have sometimes had to strain to find the existence of a "declared war."

By the terms of common article 2, the conventions are applicable in an armed conflict not constituting a "declared war" only if the state of war is recognized "by one of them"; literally, arguing to the contrary, it could be said that the provision excludes situations in which both parties do not recognize the state of war. This last would appear to be an improper reading of the provision in light of its humanitarian purposes, but so long as there are strict constructionist and so long as the provision reads as it does, the state failing to recognize the state of war will always be in a position to deny that the conventions should be operative during a conflict—even a conflict of major proportions.

Even if there is no such reluctance, the best-intentioned states may have a problem in determining whether particular outbreaks of violence constitute an "armed conflict" between states. Is the incursion of a small body of armed men into the territory of another state, followed by their repulsion by a small defending group, a case of armed conflict? The ICRC (International Committee of the Red Cross) seems to take the position that for these purposes "armed conflict" should be defined as widely as possible, in order to give the safeguards of the law of war to as many individuals as possible. This is humanitarian, but hardly definitive. Since the conventions fail to specify precise and objective guidelines identifying belligerency, they might well be supplemented by an international determination of the criteria of belligerent status and the entitlement of the combatants to full prisoner of war status.

Common article 3 is a declaration of the minimum rights of all captives in any war. It outlaws murder, torture, taking of hostages, degrading treatment, trials without due process of law, and discrimination on account of race, religion, sex, class, or economic status. Although article 3 purports to bind all the parties to the conflict to the rules set forth therein, the legal effectiveness of this article in binding rebels has been questioned. Presumably, the authorities in power of a state are bound by reason of that state's being a party to the conventions. But, the line of argument runs, rebels, who are revolting against the authority of the supposed lawful government, cannot be expected to accede to any obligations initially assumed by that lawful government in the past. Nevertheless, rebels opposed to a particular government are still nationals of a state that is party to the conventions. The authorities in power might well be disposed to apply article 3 to the rebels if the latter also accept and apply article 3. Even if this question can be resolved, there remains the problem of whether rebels can, as a matter of fact, carry out the obligations imposed upon both parties to the conflict by common article 3. It is quite clear that the Bolivian rebels in the 1974 Santa Cruz rebellion would not have had the means of according to their prisoners the safeguards and protections stipulated under the Geneva Conventions. It is often physically difficult for rebels to comply with even the minimum rules framed to regulate the conduct of the preexisting government that initially controlled all the territory of the state.

There will inevitably be problems about the legitimacy of this application of internal law, especially when two contending factions within a state purport to apply municipal law to persons belonging to the opposing faction. As the conventions now stand, there is no effective integration of the requirements of article 3 with the power of political factions to try persons for violation of municipal law. Experience has indicated that the safeguards contained within article 3 are grossly inadequate. As an alternative, all the provisions of the four Geneva Conventions of 1949 could be brought into force. However, not all these provisions are suited to a civil conflict, and it is difficult to adapt conventions essentially directed to international conflict to the conduct of contending political and military forces within a single state. (Although the parties are free to select those provisions of the four conventions that they wish to apply in the course of a civil conflict, there is nevertheless a tendency to choose all or nothing—to apply either article 3 alone, or at the opposite extreme, to apply the conventions as a whole.)

For example, in international conflicts civilians can be identified as enemies by nationality and by related tests of "enemy character." In a civil war such distinctions cannot be made. In civil conflicts, article 4 of GC, which provides that "persons protected by the Convention are those who at a given moment and in any manner whatsoever, find themselves in case of a conflict or occupation, in the hands of a party to the conflict or Occupying Power of which they are not nationals, is impossible to apply. In civil wars it is also impossible to identify "occupied areas," since each side in the war will normally contend that it exercises governmental authority over the whole territory of the state. In the Spanish Civil War, for example, there were no areas "occupied" by the Nationalist forces; these were simply looked upon as being parts of Spanish territory that had been wrested from rebel control. The same problem existed in the Vietnam war, particularly insofar as it was conducted within the territory of South Vietnam. The whole of South Vietnam was theoretically subject to the jurisdiction of the government of South Vietnam. When the Vietcong were driven from several villages, the territory was "liberated," not occupied. Indeed, in a civil conflict the territory of the state is never occupied in the same sense it is in international wars.

However, modern conflict is rarely either purely international or purely civil. The more common form in these days is part civil and part international—often civil in its inception, quickly followed by participation by other states. If a foreign state intervenes in order to assist government A against rebels, this foreign participation may or may not convert an essentially civil conflict into an international one. Rarely does foreign participation change the position of the two contending political factions within the state. It can be maintained that the assisting foreign state itself is governed by international law in its relations with the rebels; however, if the foreign state is only stepping into the shoes of the lawful government, the civil nature of the war is reinforced. If another foreign state assists government B, the other faction in the state, it will look upon government A as rebels; again, the relationship of government B to the rebels is uncertain. The relationship of Greece and Turkey to the contending factions in Cyprus in 1974 is illustrative. Should the two assisting foreign governments engage in armed conflict with one another, they may be viewed as engaging in international conflict; yet, it would be peculiar if their relations were governed by international law of war, while those of the foreign state with the opposing local faction were governed by the law governing civil war. In actuality, the combatants often mingle; the conventions do not provide guidance about the law to be applied when the conflict assumes this mixed civil-international character. Although it is recognized that both at the 1972 Conference of Government Experts and at the 1974 Diplomatic Conference the suggestion of international characterization of conflicts that are basically civil was not favorably received, the conventions should always be given the broadest possible interpretation. Proposals that would extend or restrict the application of the conventions depending upon the purpose of a war or other political considerations will tend to narrow the coverage and, in the end, weaken the fabric of the law.

A word should be said about operations by United Nations forces (see also the discussion under "Types of Forces"). The first question is whether United Nations forces should operate on an equal footing with the troops they are combating, supervising, or inspecting. Greatly simplified, this is like asking whether the policeman should be in the same position as the criminal. The basic question is whether a body of law resting on the assumption of juridical equality between belligerents is appropriate to operations conducted under the authority of the General Assembly or in pursuance of a direction of the Security Council. If, for example, United Nations forces occupy an area after combat with opposing forces, should the United Nations forces be subject to all the restraints on a belligerent occupant under HR (Hague Regulations) and GC (Geneva Conventions Relative to the Protection of Civilian Persons in Time of War)?

In the past, United Nations forces have been markedly reluctant to hold prisoners or to "occupy" territory in the hostile sense contemplated by the law of war. United Nations forces have normally been closer in position to visiting forces than to occupying forces; the presence of UNEF (United Nations Emergency Forces), ONUC (Organisation Nation Unis de Congo), UNFYCP (United Nations Forces in Cyprus) and on the Arab-Israeli truce line was in each case arranged with the state exercising sovereignty over the area. United Nations forces entered combat reluctantly in the latter two operations and resorted only to measures necessary to maintain peace and otherwise to carry out the General Assembly's mandates.

In respect for the humanitarian intent of the law on civilians, prisoners of war, and the wounded and the sick, United Nations forces should comply fully with the treaties and customary law. However, portions of the law—notably, the provisions of HR on the administration of occupied territory—look not to the preservation of human rights but to the limitation of a political régime. Thus, for United Nations forces in the field, it may be of benefit to distinguish between provisions pertaining to human rights and provisions regulating other aspects of the conflict situation.

The 1975 session of the Diplomatic Conference should be convened to define elements of belligerency, and the level of conflict that would entitle combatants to invoke the Geneva Conventions of 1949 should be identified. Few, if any, nations are prepared to apply the conventions to civil commotion and riot or to the incursion of a small body of armed men across a lightly defended border. Thus, the conventions were not involved during the persistent disturbances in Northern Ireland or the independence movements of Portuguese East Africa. The task would try to define the threshold of the maxim *de minimis non curat lex*. We hope that the conference would recommend the deletion of the words "even if the state of war is not recognized by one of them," in common article 2 and substitute therefor the words "even if the state of war is not recognized by the belligerents." Such a change would give the conventions effect at the level of belligerency defined by the subcommittee even if neither party to the conflict recognized a state of war.

Types of Forces

Contemporary warfare frequently involves international forces made up of contingents from a number of states, including the forces operating under the authority of the United Nations, original organizations constituted under article 52 of the United Nations Charter, and military alliances, such as NATO and the Warsaw Pact. UNEF, ONUC, and UNFICYP were all military operations mounted by the United Nations, acting through its Secretariat, as authorized by the General Assembly or the Security Council or both. The United Nations Command in Korea fell somewhere between forces instituted by military alliances and those on behalf of the United Nations, as it involved the conduct of warfare with authority delegated to a single member state, the United States, without any continuing responsibility for the political or military control of the operation being retained by the United Nations. International forces may also be established, as in the case of the Inter-American Peacekeeping Force in the Dominican Republic, which was a regional organization under the authority of the Organization of American States.

The Geneva Conventions of 1949 are simply not geared to operations of this character. The conventions, under common article 2, look to "cases of declared war or of any other armed conflict which may arise between two or more of the High Contracting Parties"; and these High Contracting Parties can only be states. It follows from the provisions of the conventions that an international organization or the military forces of an alliance cannot be a detaining power, since a detaining power, as defined, must be an individual state. Immediate difficulties arise when one attempts to integrate the law laid down in the conventions with the existence of multinational forces. Since a coalition, such as forces of the United Nations, the Warsaw Pact, or NATO, has no general municipal law of its own, it has no law that could be applied to prisoners. It is highly probable that it will be difficult to determine the national custody of prisoners at any particular time due to the characteristic of passing prisoners from one unit to another unit of a different nationality.

Policy toward prisoners may also be set by the upper echelon of the multinational force or by an officer of a different nationality and service from these forces that actually have custody of the prisoner at the moment. Who has responsibility if the military authorities of the detaining state are directed by an officer of another state to act toward prisoners of war in a way that is in contravention of international law? Correspondingly, if national units who have prisoners in their hands choose to disregard the law, a higher commander of another nationality has no penal or disciplinary jurisdiction over these forces. The requirements of the convention with respect to transfer of prisoners of war, as expressed in paragraph 2 of article 12 of GPW, already complicates the ready movement of prisoners of war from one military unit to another within a multinational command. Though one unsuccessful attempt has been made within NATO to deal with these problems, there should be further efforts to work out a common policy.

The United States and its treaty allies in NATO, OAS, SEATO, and other bilateral or multilateral military alliances should determine, in advance of coalition warfare, the law of the detaining power to be applied in the event of war. It is acknowledged that such a determination is a complex matter involving parties, venue on procedural matters as well as substantive law. Nevertheless, the very exercise in attempting to pattern common doctrine in advance of conflict would be a healthy exercise of more than academic value.

Consideration might be given to imposing joint responsibility on all members of a coalition for the treatment of prisoners held by any single member. It would certainly seem desirable to provide for easy transfer between national contingents making up a multinational force without the necessity of complying with all the existing requirements of article 12 of GPW (Geneva Convention Relative to the Treatment of Prisoners of War). Care would have to be taken that such transfer not be employed in order to avoid the requirements of the convention with respect to prisoners of war. In the event that joint responsibility were imposed, it might provide that the common standard to be applied to prisoners should be the standard of that state in whose custody the prisoners are at the time of the action. The adoption of a national standard would enable the draftsmen to avoid some of the difficulties posed by the concept of a detaining power. In any event, the form that such new provisions might take and the degree to which they might depart from existing language of the Geneva Conventions of 1949 is not foreseeable.

United Nations forces operate for the good of the international community. Suggestions have been made from time to time that a different body of the humanitarian law of war should be applied to United Nations forces and that they should occupy a position superior in law to an aggressor. Similarly the 1974 Diplomatic Conference toyed with different standards for "wars of national liberation." According to these views, the aggressor opposing the United Nations or the liberation movements should not be in a position to exercise any of the "rights" conferred by the law of war; should not be allowed to acquire title to property through seizure under the provisions of HR; and should not be permitted to carry out the functions that are conceded to a belligerent occupant of enemy territory.

However, there is every reason to reject tampering with the law to create dual standards—one for the forces acting on behalf of the world community or the just cause, and a separate one for that state that is acting unlawfully. In the overwhelming majority of instances the United Nations forces are enjoined only to restore peace by separating two or more belligerents. The Security Council and the General Assembly normally do not attempt to determine whether individual states are acting in conformity with international law or in violation of it. Thus it is extremely difficult, if not impossible, to determine which state is the aggressor and which state is acting lawfully. Certainly, the United Nations forces themselves are not necessarily operating for the vindication of international law and justice, but are charged solely with the responsibility of restoring peace. Even if it were possible to determine which state were the aggressor and acting unlawfully, lack of reciprocity and mutuality in the operation of the law could only lead to disrespect for that law by the state whose conduct had been characterized as unlawful. With this double standard, therefore, states would be strongly tempted to throw off the restraints of the law completely. This question should be studied further by the international community.

Systems of Control

The system of control envisaged by the conventions and described in Part I is not working effectively, for the principal element of that machinery—the institution of a protecting power—has broken down completely. In no major conflict since World War II has there been any designation of a protecting power by any of the belligerents. Even the Arab States and Israel, which have fought three conflicts considered civilized by today's standards, have not been able to agree upon a protecting power.

There are a number of explanations for the past failure and probable future ineffectiveness of the institution of a protecting power. Experience in Korea and Vietnam illustrates that a simple mistrust of foreigners and of third-party intervention has contravened its application. Chinese xenophobia suggests, for example, that a protecting power could never be agreed upon in a conflict with the People's Republic of China (PRC). (In the Sino-Indian dispute the PRC argued that there was no proper role for the ICRC since the parties maintained diplomatic relations throughout the conflict.) Even in cases where aversion to foreigners is absent or exists in a lesser degree, states will have difficulty identifying states that are truly neutral and acceptable to both belligerents. Thus, India's integrity as a neutral was totally compromised by its active involvement in the Bangladesh secession from Pakistan.

The problem grows more complicated when one of the belligerents has not recognized the other or when one or both of the belligerents maintain diplomatic relations with comparatively few neutral or reportedly neutral third states. For example, the nonrecognition of Israel by the Arab States has undoubtedly obstructed a protecting power agreement between the two contending parties; and in the case of North Vietnam, the range of states that might have been in a position to act as protecting powers was limited by the number of nations maintaining diplomatic relations with Hanoi. Even if all of these political factors could be overcome, neutral nations would find the responsibilities of a protecting power to be a thankless task that might involve them unwillingly in the dispute.

The 1972 Conference of Government Experts has proposed the substitution of the ICRC for the protecting power. Some scholars have suggested the use of the United Nations. Proposals that utilize the ever-available services of ICRC or occasionally available services of the United Nations if no state can be found to serve as a protecting power could be implemented through multilateral treaties.

Although ICRC would be the preferred substitute, some of the lesser developed countries might prefer a United Nations commission without European representation. From the humanitarian perspective of the law, this would be quite acceptable. One procedure could be like that of accepting the "optional clause" governing the jurisdiction of the International Court of Justice. Thus, in a conflict between States A and B, both parties to the protocol, ICRC serves as protecting power for personnel of State A in the hands of State B and for personnel of State B in the hands of State A. A simpler procedure would be for states to become parties to a protocol to that effect.

In order to reduce noncompliance arising out of ignorance of the law, parties to the Geneva conventions of 1949 should allow ICRC to audit, encourage and evaluate the training of armed forces in the Geneva Conventions of 1949. This proposal could not prevent willful noncompliance or spur humanitarian interests that do not otherwise exist. It would, however, reduce noncompliance, as well as open communications between states' armed forces and ICRC in peacetime that would be useful during times of war.

While there is no necessary connection between the activity of the protecting power and the exchange of prisoners and establishment of a prisoner of war information bureau, the failure of belligerents to agree on protecting powers or to accept the services of ICRC has severely complicate the securing of prisoner information lists. This material is the single most important element of the system of accounting for prisoners of war established by the conventions as a means of compelling responsible treatment of prisoners by belligerents. Although it was not easy during the Korean conflict to secure an exchange of lists of prisoners, during the conflict in Vietnam lists were received from the North Vietnamese and the Vietcong only immediately prior to repatriation of American prisoners.

Somewhat greater success has been achieved by ICRC in visiting places where prisoners of war and civilians are detained and in securing and exchanging information about prisoners. Even though ICRC has not served as a substitute protecting power in either the Arab-Israel conflicts or the Malaysia-Indonesia confrontation, it was nevertheless granted access to places where prisoners were held in those countries, in the Republic of Vietnam, and in those Korean camps under the jurisdiction of the United Nations Command. ICRC clearly owes some of its success to its functioning as a relief organization and as an organization providing medical aid to the belligerents. Where ICRC has been unsuccessful, its unacceptability is probably linked to its identification in the minds of certain Asian and African countries as an essentially white, European, and Christian institution to be regarded with varying degrees of mistrust. When passions run high in civil conflict and the provision of relief tends to have political or even military implications, ICRC may appear to belligerents to lose the neutrality that always marked its work.

In spite of the decline of the institutions envisaged in the conventions, United

Nations involvement in the protection of civilian and military war victims and concern with the operation of the law in individual instances have grown. The General Assembly has adopted several resolutions over the years urging compliance by Israel with the law of war in the areas that it occupies and observance of the conventions in relation to the protection of human rights. ICRC appears to be reconciled to the growing involvement of the United Nations in these questions, but the ineffectiveness of existing machinery clearly requires the formulation of other alternatives.

Parties to the Geneva Conventions of 1949 should through appropriate instruments, form an organization of states for the purposes of monitoring the application of the conventions, fact-finding, inviting the attention of states to their responsibilities under the conventions, and initiating revisions of the conventions from time to time; the International Committee of the Red Cross should serve as its permanent bureau.

The form of organization proposed closely resembles that of the United Nations Conference on Trade and Development. The existence of the organization could secure the support of the General Assembly in bringing about compliance with the conventions. There is an argument for subordinating such an organization to the General Assembly, but the offsetting disadvantages are compelling:

- The United Nations is not universal; a number of countries that could be the scene of hostilities (for example, North Vietnam, and North Korea) are not members.
- Not all states that belong to the United Nations are parties to the Geneva Conventions of 1949, and vice versa.
- The United Nations has been a participant in conflicts.
- The involvement of the General Assembly would inevitably lead to politicization of the application of the conventions.
- Political partiality could be a factor in determining whether or not states should be called to account for failing to comply with the conventions.

Parties to the Geneva Conventions of 1949 should agree upon diplomatic, economic, and military sanctions to be applied against nations whose breaches of the conventions are serious, substantiated, and persistent. This follows from the suggestion above that an organization be created for the purposes of fact finding and inviting the attention of states to their responsibilities under the conventions. The obligations of the conventions are unilateral in principle. Retaliation is expressly forbidden as a tool of enforcement. The belligerents are already at war. Therefore, they have no enforceable tool, only the expectation of reciprocity. It is incumbent upon the other parties to the conventions to secure respect for the law by exerting pressures. Without the above agreement among the parties, attempts to exert pressure might be deemed hostile acts inconsistent with neutrality. Agreement on sanctions provides a few teeth for mouths otherwise predisposed to bite. It is doubtful that the United States has adequately discharged its responsibility to enact effective legislation to deal with violations of the law of war committed by its own personnel, military and civilian. Enemy personnel may, of course, be tried by general courts—martial or military commissions for any violation of the customary law of war. Equal justice under law for United States personnel seems to be another matter. The revelations of the report of inquiry by Lt. Gen. William R. Peers of the cover-up of the My Lai massacre in Vietnam are all too instructive. Although the killing of 130 civilians did eventually lead to the conviction and brief imprisonment of one junior officer, the deliberate withholding of details of My Lai, and of a similar incident in My Khe hamlet in Vietnam, prove the double standard applied in the domestic implementation of the law.

Some of the provisions of the conventions have their counterparts in the municipal military law of the United States. The unjustifiable killing of an enemy soldier or civilian can be prosecuted as manslaughter or murder under the Uniform Code of Military Justice. Corresponding acts committed by civilians within the United States may likewise be punished under municipal law applicable to civilians. But, where the provisions of the conventions have no counterpart in military or civilian law, severe legal obstacles lie in the way of any prosecution of the offenders. This is because of the absence of any legislation defining violations of the law of war as also violations of the law of the United States. The provisions are simply not self-executing. Over and above this difficulty, civilians serving outside the United States and not subject to the jurisdiction of any civilian court (because of the general territorial limitation on the application of United States law and on the jurisdiction of United States courts) or military court (because of limitations on the trial of civilians by such tribunals) may escape punishment for their "grave breaches" or other war crimes. The same is true for servicemen who were separated from the military after commission of a violation of the law of war in a foreign country. The United States might well follow the example that other nations have adopted by enacting legislation covering punishment of war crimes committed by their own personnel.

Persons Entitled to Treatment as Prisoners
of War

So long as a distinction is maintained between combatants and noncombatants in the international law of war, it will be necessary to define with some precision those to be regarded as combatants. In general, noncombatants are persons who are left at liberty and pursue their normal activities, to the extent compatible with the conduct of military operations. Persons who are trained to fight, or who have taken an active part in hostilities, present such a danger to the enemy that it must have the power to detain them. The problem lies in determining whether an individual is a peaceful citizen who may be allowed to remain at liberty, or a member of the armed forces who may be held as a prisoner. Inevitably there are cases in which the nature of modern warfare totally blurs the distinction between peaceful civilians and members of the armed enemy forces. The situation is particularly severe in civil and civil-international conflicts such as the ones in Cyprus and Vietnam.

The device that the law of war employs to determine which category a person falls into is to require him to declare himself a "member of the armed forces of a party to the conflict" (article 4 of GPW-1949). It has been assumed that members of the regularly constituted armed forces of a state will meet the requirements laid down for members of other militias and volunteer corps; namely, that they will be "commanded by a person responsible for his subordinates," that they will have "a fixed distinctive sign recognizable at a distance," that they will carry arms openly, and that they will conduct "their operations in accordance with the laws and customs of war." In addition, a member of the regularly constituted armed forces would normally be expected to wear a uniform.

A question that has come up constantly during the past century is what categories of persons other than members of the regularly constituted armed forces should be held as prisoners of war. It has been asserted that anyone captured with arms or after engaging in hostile activities should be treated as a prisoner of war. There are situations in which combatants will assume the coloring of noncombatants in order to protect themselves, but when captured, they will claim the same regime applied to captured, nondisguised members of the regular forces. It was thought that a reasonable compromise had been worked out at Geneva in 1949 by granting prisoner of war status to members of "other militias" and of "other volunteer corps," including members of "organized resistance movements" even in occupied territory, provided they met the four requirements of openness and regularity set forth in GPW, article 4, subparagraphs A (2) (a) to (d).

In a number of the conflicts to which attention has been directed in this study, but most notably in the conflict in Vietnam, there has been extremely wide use of forces that do not meet the four classical requirements. Should such persons be treated as spies and saboteurs under what would amount to a policy of "no quarter"? All the reasons for taking prisoners (for example, weakening the resistance of the enemy, intelligence gathering, propaganda, humanitarian aspects of interning rather than killing) weigh in favor of treating these "irregulars" as prisoners of war upon capture. Members of the Vietcong main force were, in fact, held as prisoners of war even though they did not qualify under the strict language of article 4 of GPW. What was done as a matter of grace emphasizes one of the shortcomings of the convention—its strict definition of prisoners of war.

Upon the revision of the Geneva Prisoners of War Convention of 1949, the definition of persons entitled to treatment as prisoners of war under article 4 should be broadened to embrace, in addition to "members of the armed forces of a Party to the conflict," as currently understood, members of other military forces who (1) are organized as military units, (2) are commanded by a person responsible for his subordinates, and (3) conduct open warfare against legitimate military objectives. This position seems to have been the consensus of the Conference of Government Experts. Therefore, pending revision of the convention, it is recommended that the armed forces of the United States unilaterally adopt the policy of treating the persons defined above as prisoners of war, without regard to the more stringent requirements of the Geneva Prisoners of War Convention.

The position of guerrilla forces and resistance groups that spring up after an armistice or a capitulation is far from clear. Persons such as members of the resistance in France had often been asserted to be acting in violation of the law of war, to be war criminals, and therefore not entitled to treatment as prisoners of war (quite aside from their failure to meet the standards prescribed for other militias and volunteer corps). If this position had been taken in any of the Arab-Irael conflicts, where both sides freely engaged in hostilities in violation of the General Armistice Agreements and the cease-fires, there would be no prisoners and thousands of war criminals. Fortunately, the uncertainties of GPW have resolved in favor of treating such persons as prisoners of war. In a revision of GPW, it would be well to remove any possible ambiguity in the definition of prisoners.

The following persons should *not* be treated as prisoners of war:

- Members of regularly constituted armed forces who engage in hostilities while out of uniform.
- Members of regularly constituted armed forces who evade capture or recapture after escape by donning civilian clothes as disguise and, so disguised, engage in hostilities.
- Members of the regularly constituted armed forces who assume the uniform of the enemy or civilian dress as a ruse of war prior to or during combat.
- Members of the regularly constituted armed forces who are nationals of the detaining power as well as of the state whose armed force they serve.

This recommendation would exclude from PW entitlement such combatants as Palestine Liberation Organization guerrillas and United States soldiers out of uniform airlifted to Laos in unmarked aircraft. However, if otherwise qualified as prisoners of war, members of the armed forces who resume hostilities in violation of an armistice and deserters from the armed forces should not be denied their PW status.

Standards of Internment

The internment provisions of the Geneva Conventions of 1949 were born in the Nazi prison camps in 1941-42. Sixty thousand Soviet prisoners of war died of hunger, neglect, torture, and murder in Sachseahausen alone. German violations on the eastern front in World War II were of such magnitude that Soviet protest votes referred simply to the generally unsatisfactory condition of German camps instead of pointing to individual instances of violations. Determined to erect legal safeguards against the recurrence of such atrocities, the Geneva conferees drafted extraordinarily detailed and rigid internment regulations, leaving relatively little latitude for the detaining power to apply its own interpretation of humanitarian standards. As a result, the detaining power can be in a position of technical violation even when there is substantial compliance with GPW. This was the case in North Vietnam, where the DRV, although charged with a multitude of violations including failure to permit inspection, failure to transmit mail, refusal to supply names of prisoners, and improper detention in solitary confinement, was not accused of grave breaches of the convention prior to the repatriation of American PWs. On the other hand, the United States, although in technical compliance with GPW when it transferred prisoners to the South Vietnamese government, had an extraordinarily difficult time policing the application of the convention, responsibility for which, under GPW, article 12, "rests on the Power accepting them while they are in its custody." In sum, in most of the conflicts since World War II the internment provisions have appeared both overly precise in parochial matters, such as the operation of the canteen, and unduly narrow in the larger issues.

The location and marking of prison camps presented problems in the Korean and Vietnam conflicts. None of the parties to either conflict scrupulously observed marking requirements. The Communists not only failed to properly mark their camps in both conflicts, but also disciplined prisoners who attempted to identify the camps so that they could be seen from the air. For its part, the United States found it difficult to observe GPW, article 19, which requires that camps be located far enough from the battle zone to be removed from danger. This was one reason why the repatriation camps, Koje-do in Korea and Phu Quoc in Vietnam, were located on islands in spite of logistical difficulties. The United States was also in technical violation of GPW, article 22, when it confined nineteen North Vietnamese seamen in a prison ship for several months. In many of the low-intensity conflicts studied, prisoners were frequently confined in local jails. However, because their locations were known to the population, common knowledge and military intelligence appear to have been adequate substitutes for standard marking; even in those instances where the camps were close to the combat scene, they do not appear to have been often deliberately attacked.

Overcrowding has proved to be the most common internment violation. In virtually every conflict for which statistics were available, the captor has failed to provide as much space for the prisoners as "for the forces of the detaining power who are billeted in the same area" (GPW, article 25). Adequate housing is a problem in the wealthiest nations in the best of times. In warfare the captor has usually failed to anticipate the sudden billeting requirement; resources are scarce; and the incentive to provide decent, sanitary quarters for prisoners is negligible. As ICRC said of one of the French camps for Algerian rebels, "We cannot prevent ourselves from thinking that the miserable conditions in this camp are desired and form part of a system. . . . " The "system" often implied substantially more than scarcity of resources. In the Korean and Vietnam conflicts, the consistent inadequacy of shelter and food provided by the Chinese and Vietcong was a deliberate effort to weaken the prisoners' wills, to demean them in the eyes of the population, and sometimes to aid interrogation and to induce propaganda statements. Invariably, the worst conditions have been found in transit camps, as in the Korean conflict, and in municipal prisons, as in the Dominican Republic civil war. GPW acknowledges the necessity of transit camps in which prisoners shall be held only for brief periods (article 20) and requires that transit camps of a permanent nature comply with rules applicable to other camps (article 24). However, it lacks explicit provisions applicable to the permanent mobile camps characteristic of guerrilla warfare. A singular characteristic of such camps, particularly in South Vietnam, was the isolation of prisoners, in cages and otherwise, for long periods. (The excessive use of solitary confinement is discussed below under "Interrogation, Indoctrination, and Propaganda.")

There has been little in the history of modern warfare to test the effectiveness of the substantial changes in nutritional requirements from the 1929 conventions to the 1949 conventions. It will be recalled that whereas GPW-1929 applied an assimilation standard to PW diet (that is, prisoners would be given the same quality and quantity of food as that fed to forces of the detaining power), GPW-1949 required that account be taken of the habitual diet of prisoners. The Vietcong and other irregulars employed the 1929 standard because of limitations of resources, if for no other reasons. The Chinese and North Koreans simply ignored the convention standard altogether and violated international law by feeding PWs as they would class enemies in their own country. The systematic withholding and dispensation of food as a tool of coercion violated GPW, article 26. The United States, the North Vietnamese (for the most part) and the Israelis took pains to supply a quantity, quality and variety of food consistent with the prisoner's customs and with maintenance of health. Although GPW might theoretically be strengthened by substituting a minimum nutritional standard for its present unscientific qualitative terminology, there is no indication that such a change would increase either comprehension or compliance.

Sanitary facilities and medical attention in prison camps were more often inadequate than not. The fault is not in the law, except to the extent that systems of control are inadequate to prevent the destruction and confiscation of scarce drugs and supplies and to secure the passage of relief packages. The government of South Vietnam persistently violated GWS article 33, by diverting medical supplies required by the NLF in the Vietnam conflict. The Nigerians persistently blocked Biafran medical relief as a matter of military policy. The niceties of the law respecting diagnostic tests, disability certificates, unlimited correspondence privileges for retained medical personnel, and the like, are sheer frosting in most internment situations, standards to be emulated if incapable of observation. Technical violations of internment laws, that is, violations of rules other than those affecting the health and physical well-being of prisoners, were common in all the conflicts.

Compliance with the Geneva Conventions should be discreetly linked with the provision of relief and medical assistance, especially through any United Nations emergency relief force. The acceptance of proferred relief from international organizations or neutrals by the detaining power should be deemed to be in compliance with the conventions. The failure of the detaining power to either provide relief or accept assistance from others should be regarded as a violation. This recommendation, which has been advanced by several persons, arises from a resolution adopted as part of the Final Act of the Geneva Conference of 1949. In the past, the provision of relief supplies or medical aid has been the opening wedge for obtaining outside security of the position of war victims. With the establishment of a relief service, arrangements to verify correct treatment of prisoners of war become practicable. There is little that can improve the conventions in the matter of internment except enforcement and supplementary relief. Bilateral arrangements should be concluded between United Nations emergency relief forces and individual states before actual conflicts. Relief should be depoliticized by making it more international and less closely identified with the Western states.

Labor

The experience with prisoner of war labor since World War II has not provided empirical data to judge the effectiveness of the labor provisions of GPW-1949. However, the language of the convention itself reveals areas of difficulty. The wording of article 50 is vague with regard to three categories of work that prisoners of war may be compelled to perform provided the work has "no military character or purpose" (that is, public works and building operations, transport and handling of stores, and public utility services). The phrase "no military character or purpose" continues the deficiency of GPW-1929, which requires that most compulsory work have "no direct connection with the operations of the war." Moreover, the preparatory work for the 1949 conference in Geneva and the discussions at that conference provide no significant indication of the intended meaning. The term "military character or purpose," declares one authority, "defies definition in the ordinary sense."[1]

Many questions arise. How much emphasis should lie in the word "no"? Should the whole phrase be interpreted qualitatively in such a way as to confine work of a "military character" to items that are exclusively or primarily of a military character? How much connection with the military is required before work not having a "military character" assumes a "military purpose"? And what manner of connection with the military is required—a connection with military operations, a connection with military personnel, a connection with civilian personnel employed by the military? If the work is performed at a military installation, does that automatically give it a military purpose? What if the end item is for recreation or for the basic needs common to the general civilian population as well as the military?

The answers to such questions given in current regulations of the United States Army adopt a practical approach. The regulations provide, in part, that the term "military character" applies to those items or to those types of construction that are used exclusively by members of the armed forces for operational purposes (for example, arms, helmets, gun emplacements, and confidence courses) as contrasted to items or structures that may be used by either civilian or military personnel (for example, food, soap, buildings, public roads, and railroads). The term "military purpose" applies to activities that are intended primarily or exclusively for military operations as contrasted with activities intended primarily or exclusively for other purposes. The term "military operations" refers to actual combat activities and their immediate logistical support. On the other hand, for example, the ICRC Commentary on the Convention, in attempting to give substance to the words "military character," states very broadly, "Everything which is commanded and regulated by the military authority is of a military character, in contrast to what is commanded and regulated by the civil authorities." But the commentary says that the term "military purpose" may be interpreted flexibly, and that an incidental military purpose is not the only consideration.

The prohibition on work of a military character should be relaxed. The present key distinction, between work having some military character and work having none, is totally inadequate. Work that has no military character or purpose is rare. Any job filled by a PW frees a national for the war effort, and most wartime occupations contribute in some way to aiding the national economy or morale. Prohibitions on direct military work could be substituted for the present listing of permissible labor in article 50.

Another matter of concern is voluntary work. The prohibition discussed above, and the general prohibition on compulsory work by officers and on nonsupervisory work by noncommissioned officers, do not prohibit voluntary work, and voluntary work may be unhealthy or dangerous. The 1949 conferees took a calculated risk in excluding voluntary labor from the article 7 prohibition upon waiver by a prisoner of war of his rights.

Upon the revision of the Geneva Prisoners of War Convention of 1949, article 49 should be amended or supplemented to permit persons whose work is voluntary to withdraw their consent to employment on terms consistent with the domestic labor laws of the detaining power and, in any event, to withdraw their consent after three months of employment. The conventions were particularly concerned about forced labor, and they carefully defined the conditions under which a prisoner may be compelled to work. The psychological pressure of idleness, however, may prompt a prisoner to volunteer for work. His right to quit a job for which he has volunteered is not clear. In Socialist countries, and in capitalist countries in times of war, a voluntary commitment could become involuntary servitude. If labor is bound by domestic law, this suggestion will at least give the prisoner quarterly options to continue or withdraw from voluntary employment.

Interrogation, Indoctrination, and Propaganda

The interrogation and indoctrination of prisoners of war extracts useful military and political intelligence from prisoners and exerts psychological influence upon prisoners to get them to accept their captors' philosophy of the conflict and its role in world events. As the French put it in the Algerian conflict, the components of a successful program are *lavage de crâne* ("brainwashing") and *bourrage de crâne* ("brain filling"). The policy of the detaining power is the primary determinant in the treatment of the prisoner; moral and legal sanctions rarely intrude and, if they appear, are more likely to serve the purpose of rhetoric than to spring from any attachment to humanitarian principles. Either the conferees at Geneva did not fully appreciate the ideological content of modern warfare, or (more likely) they chose to keep the restraints on intelligence minimal in order to assure some measure of compliance with the conventions.

GPW, article 17, obligates a prisoner to divulge identifying information to the detaining power. Beyond that the captor may not inflict physical or mental torture to secure any kind of information whatsoever, nor may prisoners who refuse to answer questions be threatened, insulted, or exposed to unpleasant treatment of any kind. The prisoner's participation in recreational pursuits, including educational activities, are voluntary under GPW article 38. All these articles were violated in the Korean conflict by the Communists and in the Vietnam conflict by both the North and the South. Far more meaningful than the gross tortures employed by the North Koreans and the South Vietnamese were the sophisticated interrogation and indoctrination methods of the Chinese and the North Vietnamese captors, many of which are not prohibited by a strict reading of the Geneva Conventions. Systematic physical torture was not employed with this method. For the most part, physical punishment resulted from offenses such as attempts to escape, stealing, and infraction of camp regulations.

As noted in Part II, techniques of interrogation in Korea and North Vietnam varied, but frequently included requiring prisoners to write detailed essays and autobiographies, questioning prisoners to exhaustion, "walking" conferences, alternating threats of punishment with promises of reward, and careful control of the interrogation atmosphere. Prisoners were indoctrinated by separating them into minority groups receptive to particular strains of propaganda; utilizing controlled socialization such as lectures, group discussions, group self-criticisms, and educational courses; publicly undermining a prisoner's self-esteem or authority; and maintaining tight control of communications within the camp. In North Vietnam isolation was often imposed. In Korea the Chinese organized theater groups to perform ideological skits and plays for the press as well as for other prisoners; sports and musical activities were interspersed with instructive lectures; discussion groups were encouraged to study Communist ideology; self-criticism and national criticism were obligatory during group therapy sessions; and current affairs classes discussed heavily censored news. In all cases the activities were led by "progressive" prisoners, the large majority of whom cooperated. "Progressive" PWs received privileges not granted to the rest. It is clearly evident that the conventions established a minimum standard of care and treatment but no restrictions as to how these should be administered. What cannot legally be extracted by the stick can be psychologically induced with the carrot.

Upon the revision of the Geneva Prisoners of War Convention of 1949, GPW, article 17, should be amended to deny the detaining power permission to induce the cooperation of prisoners of war by promises of preferential treatment in captivity. Under this recommendation the detaining power may still solicit the cooperation of the prisoner, subject him to propaganda (within the restrictions of the convention), and offer parole and early release, but he may not promise extra food or less work to induce cooperation. The theory is not that interrogation, indoctrination, and propaganda are improper activities but that all prisoners are entitled to equal care and protection.

The broad language of GPW, article 17, gives little help in forestalling psychological coercion during interrogation. It would be unduly fastidious to ignore the fact that the domestic criminal procedure of most of the nations that are parties to the Geneva Conventions sanctions or overlooks police threats, deceit, promises, and insidious persuasion to obtain information from prisoners. As Solzhenitsyn detailed in *The Gulag Archipelago*, the Soviet Union, for example, exhibits an almost compulsive concern with the legal trappings of trial and confession. From the purge period of the thirties to the trials of intellectuals in the sixties, the outward appearance of legality was maintained even when all the participants are aware of the fictitious nature of the confessions. In Chinese culture (not merely the People's Republic of China) the criminal is expected to find salvation in confession and ultimate recrudescence through selfless submission to group service for the state.

United States criminal procedure has undergone such changes in the past two decades that United States jurists can readily interpret the broad language of article 17 to restrain the extraction, or at least the utility, of confessions by prisoners in ideological conflicts since Korea. The analogy to domestic criminal law is obvious. From the perspective of domestic notions of justice both the analogy and logic of the American experience could be forcefully applied to the convention. However, it is idle to pressure that such standards would be acceptable to the world community.

The effect of a "Fifth Amendment" interpretation to article 17 would be to place a burden upon a detaining power to prove that a confession was really given voluntarily. This must be done before the confession will be given probity by world opinion. Parties to GPW might agree that no statement by a prisoner of war be accepted as true without an assertion by the protecting power of its surrogate that the statement was voluntary. The protecting power shall consider the actual circumstances under which the statement was made, its own freedom to investigate the statement, and other pertinent factors affecting voluntary statements against interest. Acceptance of this recommendation would not reduce the number of confessions coerced for propaganda purposes. It should, however, increase both the use and importance of independent verification by protecting powers. Increased access to PW camps by protecting powers is an essential goal in the administration of the conventions.

Control of Prisoner of War Order

The Spanish and Algerian civil wars, the mixed civil and international conflicts of Korea and Vietnam, and the international wars between Israel and the Arab States all involved the relocation and internment of large numbers of civilians and prisoners of war. Discipline within prison camps and civilian internment camps was not always maintained in compliance with the international law of war. Indeed, the studies in Part II reveal numerous violations in each conflict, including shackling of prisoners, degradation, group punishment, withholding of rights, denial of legal process, and failure to provide the necessities of life. However, in only one conflict since World War II has the matter of control of order raised fundamental questions about the workability of the law itself. The serious riots in the United Nations prisoner of war camps on the island of Koje-do and in the city of Cheju in the summer of 1952 focused the world's attention on the behavior of prisoners of war and on the resources that the detaining power was prepared to allocate to restore order in the compounds.

The principal tenet of the law of war concerning order and discipline in prison camps has been that prisoners of war are subject to the laws, regulations, and orders applicable to the armed forces of the detaining power (HR, article 8; GPW-1929, article 12; GPW-1949, article 82). The authority to deal with offenses against discipline is vested in the camp commander, who must be a commissioned officer of the regular armed forces of the detaining power (GPW, article 96). Prisoners of war in United States custody during World War II were subject to disciplinary sanctions in the form of company punishment and trial by summary courts-martial, provided the punishment did not exceed thirty days. Informal disciplinary proceedings by the camp commander to control order in PW camps frequently included a "no work, no eat" policy to induce compliance with work orders. Bread and water was sanctioned by a ruling of the Provost Marshal General in October 1943, which interpreted GPW-1929, article 27, as permitting the detaining power to use reasonable means to force prisoners of war to comply with orders. "Administrative pressure" by Allied commanders was also regarded as compatible with GPW-1929.

In their control of order in prisoner of war camps, Germany and Japan simply ignored conventional law in whole or in part. Soviet prisoners, specifically, were considered to be outside the protection of GPW-1929 and all standards of honorable treatment. German orders explicitly enjoined "ruthless and energetic action" against them. Insubordination and resistance were to be broken immediately by force of arms. Guards were instructed to fire upon prisoners without previous challenge or warning shots. Prisoners of all nationalities who attempted to escape were killed whether or not they could have been recaptured alive. In Japanese prison camps corporal punishment and torture were administered, under published regulations, for the slightest breach of discipline, insubordination, insult, or offense—or for no reason at all. The mildest form of disciplinary action was beating and kicking. Other disciplinary action included exposure to the tropical sun without protection, physical suspension, confinement in cramped cages for days or even weeks, forcing prisoners to run over broken glass, and other forms of brutal collective punishment. Japanese prisoner of war regulations were amended to apply the same punishment to a prisoner attempting escape as to a deserter from the Japanese army, that is, death. Accessories to escape were also punished by death. The motion picture "Bridge on the River Kwai" was an accurate documentary of the period. This was the background against which the conferees at Geneva in 1949 drafted the comparatively benign disciplinary articles of GPW. The articles were tested, under fire, for the first time in Korea.

ICRC, whose humanitarian role was recognized by the United Nations Command but not by North Korea or the Chinese Communists, repeatedly inquired how the UNC intended to comply with GPW, article 82, which requires that prisoners of war be subject to the laws, regulations, and orders in force in the armed forces of the detaining power. The UNC (United Nations Command) stated that prisoners held by it were detained by the United Nations itself, which had the option of adopting the procedures governing the forces of any of its member states or of adopting its own system of law. The United Nations Command issued a penal and disciplinary code covering postcapture offenses. The subsequent first breaches in discipline eventually culminated in the kidnapping of the United Nations camp commander by the prisoners and a series of well-planned and coordinated Communist riots.

After several detailed investigations, the UNC concluded that the disorders in the prison camps were part of an overall plan by Communist China and North Korea to utilize prisoners in UNC custody to achieve their objectives. The Communist negotiators at Panmunjon orchestrated the riots and violence in the camps for their propaganda value during the interminable truce negotiations. The UNC made several basic errors: It failed to prevent the organization and growth of Communist cadres within the camps. It failed to counteract Communist indoctrination of prisoners during the first few months of capture when they would have been susceptible to indoctrination by the United Nations forces. It did not locate and support anti-Communist leadership within the camps. It failed to investigate the causes of disturbances and was content with a facade of order that was frequently achieved at the expense of the anti-Communists among the prisoners. Finally, it left discipline, as well as many unofficial camp programs, to the prisoner representatives who were, invariably, dominated by the Communist leadership. These shortcomings were ascribed to deficiencies in the law—to an asserted fallacious presumption implicit in the conventions that a prisoner is removed from the conflict and to the alleged naiveté of the detaining power in adopting a philosophy of democratic administration of prison camps (a philosophy also alleged to derive from GPW-1949).

The breakdown of order and discipline in the UNC camps in Korea was the result of poor management rather than of deficiencies in the law. The law does not create prisoners of war; it regulates the relationship between captor and captive once that factual relationship has been established. The law did not require the UNC to place 150,000 prisoners in a single camp in compounds averaging 6,000 prisoners each. GPW did not bar careful screening and segregation of potential troublemakers on a basis consistent with article 16, which forbids *adverse* distinctions based upon nationality, political opinions, and like criteria. GPW does not require ignorance of, or indifference to, political realities in the camp. The legal presumption is that the prisoner is removed from combat, not from the ideological struggle that underlies it. As the Commentary to the United States Code of Conduct states ". . . the fight is everywhere. Even in the prison camp! When the use of physical weapons is denied, the mental and moral will to resist must be kept alive in every prisoner." Subsequent conflicts, particularly in Vietnam, which posed the same potential for instability in prison camps did not witness a recurrence of the events in Koje-do. More to the point, the disciplinary restraints of GPW do not appear to have handicapped the United

Nations in subsequent Egyptian, Congo, and Cyprus actions or the Israelis in their several conflicts with the Arabs. Nevertheless, the tendency of those charged with the custody of prisoners to blame their failures on the limitations of the law should not serve as an excuse for ignoring the deficiencies that do, in fact, exist.

At least three systems of law converge upon the prisoner: (1) the municipal law of the power on which he depends, (2) the law of the detaining power, and (3) international law. The situation is even more complicated when a party to the conflict is a multinational force such as the United Nations, OAS, NATO, or the Warsaw Pact nations. ICRC pressure upon the UNC to state the method by which it would comply with GPW, article 82, pointed to the need for an annex to the convention or a set of regulations that would recite in precise terms the law applicable to multinational and international peacekeeping forces. This annex should authorize the multinational force itself, rather than any member state, to serve as the detaining power; vest in such a force the authority to convene military tribunals to try and to punish its own personnel irrespective of nationality; promulgate disciplinary rules for prisoners of war similar to those pertaining to the forces of the detaining power; and devise a method of determining the applicable substantive criminal law. The annex would assist in clarifying an ambiguity in the convention that suggests but does not explicitly declare that the camp commander's responsibility for the proper application of the convention is owed both to his own government and to all of the countries that are parties to the convention. If his own government gave the commander orders contrary to international law, he would remain personally responsible for upholding the convention.

Discipline, Punishment, and War Crimes

The trial of individuals as war criminals deserves serious consideration as the sole convention sanction for the violations of the law of war by individuals. Yet, there has been little occasion since the ratification of the conventions to employ the comprehensive and detailed provisions concerning penal and disciplinary sanctions against prisoners of war (articles 82 to 108 of GPW) and the corresponding provisions concerning civilians (articles 64 to 77 of GC).

In the two recent Asian wars in which the United States has been involved, "trials," whether conducted or only threatened, have been intended to intimidate prisoners and to serve propaganda and psychological warfare purposes. During the Korean conflict, charges by the USSR and North Korea that United States and United Nations forces had engaged in bacteriological warfare and the threatened trials of United States aviators for alleged war crimes (such as killing civilians and the destruction of hospitals) raised the spectre of legal circuses. It is evident that the Communist proclivity for "show" trials is foreign to the concept of individual responsibility embodied in the conventions. The UNC investigated and was prepared to prosecute war criminals but feared that such war crime trials would be likely to trigger retaliatory Communist trials. The potential peril to innocent victims in such trials offset the advantage of trying prisoners for crimes committed against civilians and fellow prisoners. The ultimate result has tended to be tacit agreement that neither side will conduct war trials during hostilities.

One can have no confidence in the impartiality or fairness of such proceedings if conducted by an enemy force during hostilities. If, as in Korea, no war crime trials are conducted before the end of hostilities, war criminals will be repatriated routinely. If trials are held toward the end of a conflict and immediately prior to repatriation, repatriation negotiations will be imperiled, as was the case in the Bangladesh conflict. Moreover, such trials cannot have any deterrent effect upon potential war criminals in that particular conflict. In summary, trials during hostilities are likely to be unfair; trials toward the end of hostilities will not effect any higher standard of compliance with the conventions, and prisoners cannot be denied repatriation to be held for trial after the conflict is concluded. Understandably, then, penal sanctions have not played any substantial role as a system of control in enforcement of the conventions.

Parties to the Geneva Conventions of 1949 should enact domestic legislation that makes all types of war crimes, including "other than grave breaches," punishable under local law. No less is required by GPW, article 129. The Uniform Code of Military Justice (UCMJ) does not cover all the criminal acts under GPW. The United States has come close to embarrassment on such matters as the court-martial of its military personnel for mutilation of the dead. Lacking a specific statutory implementation authorities have had to rely upon vague sanctions. General criminal statutes, such as UCMJ, article 134, can be stretched just so far before their constitutionality is challenged. As noted above in connection with My Lai, additional problems arise in connection with the prosecution of members of the armed forces for crimes committed abroad prior to operation. Other nations have adopted legislation covering war crimes committed by their own personnel as well as by enemy and allied personnel. The United States should as well.

Parties to the Geneva Conventions of 1949 should enact extradition treaties to implement the requirement of GPW, article 129, that persons "alleged to have committed . . . grave breaches" shall be handed "over for trial to another High Contracting Party concerned, providing such High Contracting Party has made out a prima facie case." The Eichmann trial by Israel might not have been preceded by a kidnapping if Argentina had concluded extradition laws. Because of the Communist-bloc reservations to GPW, article 85, regarding the prosecution of prisoners of war for crimes committed before capture, enactment of such legislation might receive support that would not otherwise be expected from the Afro-Asian "Third World."

When the Geneva Conventions are revised, GPW article 101, should be amended to provide for administrative delay, in carrying out death sentences given to PWs until the end of the conflict. Article 101 currently requires the death penalty to be delayed for six months after the protecting power receives the detailed communication required by article 107. However, article 101 is defeated if no protecting power is appointed. Theoretically, then, the sentence could never be executed. A standard is recommended that does not require third-party participation.

Release and Repatriation

During Hostilities. The general exchange of able-bodied prisoners during hostilities appears to be a thing of the past. None took place during World War II, and in more recent conflicts exchanges of the able-bodied during hostilities are not common, although isolated instances of release and repatriation have occurred, for example, in Vietnam, and the Near East.

The only provisions of the Prisoners of War Convention requiring repatriation during hostilities are those dealing with the seriously sick and wounded. During World War II a total of about 20,000 axis seriously sick and wounded were exchanged for about 13,000 allied personnel. Germany, Great Britain, and the United States came to the conclusion that direct repatriation of the less seriously sick and wounded was preferable. This is understandable in view of the costs of accommodation in neutral countries and the somewhat ambivalent status of prisoners of war in a neutral country. The United States attempted, without success, to obtain agreement of the opposing belligerents in Korea to the repatriation of the sick and wounded during hostilities; in Vietnam it effectively suggested to the GVN (Government of [South] Vietnam) that the sick and the wounded be repatriated. Repatriations of wounded and sick by the GVN in fact took place at periodic intervals until 1968, and sporadically thereafter.

The old institution of ransom is still viable but has grave dangers. United States policy makers considered the possibility of offering ransom in Vietnam for our fliers but backed away because of the political consequences. Offering ransom suggests that prisoners can be held as pawns or hostages and might also be considered a sign of weakness by the offeror. It provides the opportunities for unlimited "raising of the ante," as in the first Cuban go-around with Castro. In Vietnam it would have given propaganda opportunities to the DRV (Democratic Republic of Vietnam [North Vietnam]) such as identifying the offer of ransom with war crime charges being made against United States fliers.

At the End of Hostilities. One might think that with the termination of active hostilities, belligerents would find no difficulty in securing the prompt repatriation of prisoners of war, as required by article 118, GPW. There was full compliance with the law on this subject at the end of the 1956, 1967, and 1973 hostilities between Israel and Egypt, and at the conclusions of the conflicts between India and Pakistan. However, the record ranged from spotty to miserable in the exchange of Israeli and Syrian prisoners after the 1973 "Yom Kippur" conflict, between Greeks and Turks in the Cyprus conflict and between Pakistanis and Bengalis in Bangladesh. The issue of nonrepatriated prisoners was of active international concern as late as eight years after the termination of hostilities in World War II. The United Nations ad hoc commission established to determine the fate of prisoners of that war and to promote repatriations and accountings was still unsuccessfully seeking cooperation by the USSR and other nations in tracing the missing.

It would be optimistic to expect much success in a future conflict in obtaining compliance with the requirement of GPW-1949 for unilateral repatriation without delay after the end of active hostilities if the parties should fail to come to an understanding. To give up the bargaining position obtained by holding prisoners before knowing what the other side is going to do requires idealism, faith, and a respect for law that by contemporary standards would be regarded as naive. Since there is always a chance that negotiations may develop favorably in due course, delay within the framework of the law is easily rationalized. If there is a dispute over accounting for, or asylum to, prisoners of war, it is unlikely that one side will release and repatriate prisoners until it knows what prisoners it will get back. The problem was evident in the Korean war and Vietnam conflicts. Not only were there delays in repatriating prisoners, but active hostilities dragged on for years while the parties attempted to negotiate arrangements for the exchange of prisoners of war. While extension of the hostilities because of bargaining over prisoner exchange, as the United States did in Vietnam, may do violence to the spirit of the convention, it does not run counter to the law.

The armistice negotiations and arguments before the United Nations General Assembly in the Korean conflict reviewed virtually every argument and counterargument about the right of a state to grant asylum to prisoners of war. An ambiguity in the convention was highlighted when plausible legal arguments were presented against the position of the United Nations Command that the North Koreans would not repatriate prisoners of war at bayonet point and were not required to do so by the language of GPW. The results in Korea clarified and developed the law, by the resolution of the United Nations General Assembly that, in accordance with GPW-1949, force need not be used to compel prisoners to return to their homelands. Moreover, ICRC endorsed the principle, first during the conflict when it communicated with the United States Department of State and later in its Commentary of GPW-1949. The United States became fully committed to the principle in Korea.[2] In the words of President Eisenhower, "The Armistice in Korea inaugurated a new principle of freedom—that prisoners of war are entitled to choose the side to which they may be released. In its impact on history, that one principle may weigh more than any battle of our time."[3] In fact, the great question of voluntary asylum by prisoners of war on the territory of the detaining power was not fully settled either by the General Assembly in the Korean conflict or by United States commitment to the principle. The entire matter is so unresolved that the interminable repatriation negotiations, as Korea and Vietnam, may be regarded as a model rather than as an exception.

Recommendations Regarding Civilians

Standards of Treatment

From a practical point of view, the administration of occupied territory and the treatment of civilians are inseparable: In classical cases of belligerent occupation such as the Arab-Israel Six Day War in 1967, enemy nations in occupied territory were the only civilians who enjoyed any protection, as *protected persons*, under customary international law. The Geneva Conventions of 1949 broadened the protection of entire populations to include the whole area of conflict, detailed the rights of protected persons, and for the first time declared basic human rights in all armed conflicts. Nevertheless, when the Geneva Conventions extended the definition of "protected persons," it trod softly on virgin territory. For the purposes of this analysis it is important to recall that a "protected person" is one who enjoys all the benefits of the conventions and that some of the benefits are applicable to persons and populations that do not qualify technically as "protected persons."

The main object of the convention relative to the protection of civilian persons in time of war was to protect a strictly defined category of civilians from arbitrary action on the part of the enemy. It was not intended to protect all civilians or, indeed, any civilians from the dangers inherent in military operations, much less from the politico-military activities of their own governments. To view every atrocity and outrage against innocent civilians as a violation of international law is wishful thinking.

To the extent that GC, Section III, amplifies and extends the customary law of belligerent occupation, analysis of legal deficiencies may be productive. But merely detailing the inadequacies of protection of civilians from a humanitarian point of view loses sight of the traditional political attachment to sovereign prerogatives. Lesser developed nations, perhaps even more than wealthy, powerful states, resent and resist any encroachment on domestic jurisdiction. For example, Nigeria received substantial moral support from other African nations in its determined opposition to any kind of interference with its domestic affairs in the Biafra conflict. Is the reluctance of nations to enforce a body of law whose moral presumptions are considerably higher than those of the combatants to be counted as a deficiency in the law? The inclusion of common article 3 in the Geneva Conventions, which extends the humanitarian principles of the conventions to civilians in civil conflicts, already promises substantially more legal protection to victims of war than states seem willing to enforce.

To understand the limitations of the law, it must be recalled that in 1937 the Council of the League of Nations was able to condemn "the employment, in the Spanish struggle, of methods contrary to international law and the bombing of open towns."[4] But after a world war and four conventions later, the North Koreans and South Vietnamese denied the applicability of the law of belligerent occupation to their own inhuman treatment of civilians by simply claiming jurisdiction over the entire country. To appreciate the progress of the law, it should be noted that in the Spanish Civil War the wanton killing of hostages, the imprisonment and execution of tens of thousands by the Spanish Nationalists and Republicans, and the frequency of rape, torture, and murder were barred only by the conscience of mankind and the limited prohibitions of HR article 23. However, in the Korean and Vietnam conflict even if the law of belligerent occupation was inapplicable to the Communists, the deliberate slaughter of thousands of civilians prior to the recapture of Taejon in the former, and the Tet offensive in the latter, was a violation of the "principles" of the conventions.

The problem of applying the Hague Regulations and the Civilians Convention to conflict in a divided country was never more aggravated than in Vietnam. South Vietnamese civilians in South Vietnam were not "protected persons" vis-à-vis their treatment at the hands of the Army of the Republic of Vietnam because they were nationals of the government harassing them. Neither the GVN nor the Vietcong could properly be called an occupying power in its own country. Nor were the civilians "protected persons" with respect to United States actions, since the United States was a cobelligerent of the Republic of Vietnam with which it maintained normal diplomatic relations (GC, article 4). The civilians of South Vietnam were, however, entitled to protection from their own forces, from the Vietcong and from the United States air strikes under GC, article 3, and GC, Part II, pertaining not to individual rights, but to the population as a whole. (Part II, which comprises GC articles 13 to 26, deals with safety zones, noncombatants on the battlefield, and civilian hospitals. It is applicable when the convention as a whole is applied by the combatants. The United States and the government of South Vietnam both accepted the conventions in this conflict. The Vietcong did not.) In addition, although the Hague Regulations have been supplemented by provisions of the Geneva Conventions, relating to sieges and bombardments civilians would be protected if the conflict were regarded as international. The United States argued this position during the period of its own troop involvement.

Granting the limitations of coverage, South Vietnamese civilians were still denied the minimum protection of the law by all parties to the conflict: Terror and counterterror against civilians culminating in the blasphemy of My Lai[5] violated the prohibition against murder in GC, article 3 (1)(a); kidnapping by the Vietcong violated GC, article 34, and 3 (1)(b) against the taking of hostages. The indiscriminate use of antipersonnel weapons by United States forces destroyed "persons taking no active part in the hostilities" (GC, article 3(1)). Excessive use of napalm and the extraordinary intensity of aerial bombardment against villages in the south may have constituted the prohibited employment of "arms, projectiles or material calculated to cause unnecessary suffering" (HR, article 23e). (The use of nonlethal poison gases by the United States might well have been prohibited by the 1925 Geneva Protocol on Poison Gas and Bacteriological Warfare that, however, was not signed by President Gerald Ford until 1975.) The separation of families and forcible evacuation and destruction of villages violated "family honor and rights, the lives of persons and private property" (HR, article 46). The parties to the conflict did not make any effort to conclude local agreements regarding the removal of sick, aged, minors, and maternity cases from besieged areas (GC, article 17).

The limitations of coverage create distinctions far too subtle to be observed in combat. For example, United States civilians were detained by the Vietcong under conditions that violated virtually every standard of internment under GC, articles 79-135. Surely such persons, who were not nationals in the hands of the party to the conflict that is holding them, ought to have been entitled to the full protection of the convention. Yet, as long as the United States was a cobelligerent of South Vietnam, with which it maintained normal diplomatic relations, they could not be regarded as protected persons even if the National Liberation Front were a party to the convention—which it was not. GC, article 24, enjoins the parties to take special care of children under age fifteen, an extraordinarily difficult provision to honor when children of that age were actually involved in combat. GC article 49, prohibiting mass forcible transfers as well as deportations of protected persons from occupied territory to the territory of the occupying power, was a vital new provision of the law, but technically inapplicable to the GVN strategic-hamlet program simply because its jurisdiction did not extend to the belligerents' own territory.

To a lesser extent, similar problems and limitations would have been faced had there been greater efforts to apply the Civilians Convention to the Algerian, Dominican Republic, and Congo conflicts. The issue is academic because the French refused to apply even common Article 3, and the intervening forces in the other two conflicts chose to rely upon customary international law. In the Arab-Israel conflicts, however, the law was fully applicable and generally honored (notwithstanding The Report of The Special Committee to Investigate Israeli Practices Affecting the Human Rights of the Population (26 October 1970) to the contrary, by a committee of neutral nations, which secured the data for its criticism of Israel from the Arab governments). The civilian suffering caused by Israel after the Six Day War in 1967 was generally in the nature of forced deportation, destruction of dwelling, and offenses against property rather than persons.

Arabs in occupied territory were encouraged by Israel to migrate to Arab states, but there was no forcible migration by the occupying power. Though there were early complaints about the quality of food and the failure to receive mail, ICRC inspections of the civilian internment camps at El Arish confirmed compliance with the internment provisions of GC. Of course, the scrupulously careful treatment of Egyptian civilians in Gaza occurred in an unusual environment, in that seventy percent of the total population was already being supported by the United Nations Relief and Works Agency. The United Arab Republic insisted that the burden of feeding the indigent, unemployed population of East Kahtara be shifted to Israel as an occupying power. Whatever its violations, Israel's observance of the outdated law of belligerent occupation still compares most favorably with its neglect by the parties to other contemporary conflicts.

The Civilians Conventions are poorly organized, wanting in precision, and badly in need of clarification. Unfortunately, there is a little encouragement in the conference records, in the willingness of nations to apply the law, or in the political temper of the times to suggest that they could be improved. Common article 3, after all, is clear, basic, and simple; yet, at least in civil conflict it is honored more in the breach than the observance. An attempt to revise the Civilians Conventions might even prove to be counterproductive.

Those portions of the Hague Regulations of 1907 dealing with the protection of prisoners of war and of the wounded and the sick have for all practical purposes been superseded by GPW and GWS (Geneva Convention for the Amelioration of the Condition of Wounded and Sick in Armed Forces in the Field). To a lesser extent, Section III, "Military Authority Over the Territory of the Hostile States," is supplemented by GC. The remainder of HR consists of the provisions on means of injuring the enemy, sieges, and bombardments; spies; capitulations; and armistices. These provisions do not in a major way affect the position of the persons protected by the Geneva Conventions of 1949. The only portion of HR falling directly within the scope of this study deals with belligerent occupation. HR is badly out of date on that subject; hopefully, it may be updated by the Diplomatic Conference in 1975. The Vietnam and Arab-Israel conflicts suggest as a modest goal of the conference the specification of the conditions under which an occupant may resettle civilians in order to deprive insurgents of their support. From the United States point of view, such a conference could raise issues about the use of certain types of weapons and modes of warfare that this country was reluctant to discuss during the Vietnam conflict. It could also be a form to raise issues that have been left open since the Arab-Israeli peace negotiation in Geneva.

The fate of civilians and the fate of their property go hand in hand in warfare. The bombs that kill people destroy their property. The same forces that tear them from their families deprive them of their homes and belongings. Human life and health cannot be sustained unless economic life is maintained or food and other relief supplies are provided. It is significant that "plunder of public or private property, wanton destruction of cities, towns, or villages, or devastation not justified by military necessity" were coupled with such crimes as "murder, ill-treatment or deportation to slave labor or for any other purpose of civilian population or in occupied territory, murder or ill-treatment of prisoners of war or persons on the seas, killing of hostages" in the list of the most serious war crimes in the Charter of the International Military Tribunal at Nuremberg. Similarly, article 147 of GC lists amongst grave breaches of that convention "extensive destruction and appropriation of property, not justified by military necessity and carried out unlawfully and wantonly." Control of the economy, relief, and civil claims against belligerents must be considered as factors of economic life. A civilian starved to death through the destruction or taking of his means of sustenance is as dead as the civilian murdered by an enemy shot.

Civil Conflicts. After World War I ICRC tried unsuccessfully to persuade the international community to accept the principle that mercy shipments should be permitted to pass through blockades. During the Spanish Civil War the Republican government requested assistance from the League of Nations and other organizations. Relief from ICRC and from religious and government organizations was permitted to pass through Nationalist lines to feed the vast number of starving refugees. The Republicans also attempted to augment the food supply through the seizure and collectivization of farmlands. Expropriation of real and personal property was widely practiced by both parties to the conflict. Neither of the parties to the conflict respected the principles of the Hague Regulations pertaining to the seizure of property and pillage, which are technically inapplicable to civil conflicts. If the belligerents can agree to bring into force during a civil conflict the law applicable to international wars, then the provisions of HR relating to property and economic life (both *qua* treaty and *qua* customary international law) and the corresponding provisions of the four Geneva Conventions of 1949 will be operative. These provisions, for the most part, concern occupied areas. Articles 13 to 26 of GC, setting forth general protections for the whole populations of parties to the conflict, affect property only insofar as they call for the free passage of medical supplies and equipment and of essential foodstuffs for women and children.

The relief provisions have been applied only with the greatest difficulty in civil conflicts such as the Nigeria, Bangladesh and Cyprus disputes. They were all but ignored in the French-Algerian war. United States officials have expressed the view that, for a variety of reasons, ICRC has been far less effective in the former conflict than the domestic welfare experts of some of the states providing relief. Discreet attempts might be made to link compliance with the Geneva Conventions with relief and medical assistance, especially through any United Nations emergency relief force.

Peacekeeping Operations. In the Cyprus and the Arab-Israeli operations, the United Nations concluded agreements with the countries concerned for the handling of official-duty and nonofficial-duty against intervening peacekeeping forces. In practice, the distinction between duty and nonduty claims was never observed, and the frequency of claims was low. In two other peacekeeping operations (the Congo and the Dominican Republic), the application of the law to relief shipments, property management, and economic affairs assumed greater importance.

The Inter-American Peace Force in the Dominican Republic, operating without the benefit of a formal treaty, not only dispensed massive relief to the civilian population, but also directed the civilian economy through a team of United States officials in Santo Domingo. The United States supplied electric power and equipment to hospitals and fuel to the capital city's electrical generating equipment and restored a vital peanut-oil factory to operation. On the other hand, United States forces confiscated Dominican military equipment and looted a Dominican arms museum. The rebel-controlled radio described the United States as an "occupying power," a status stoutly denied by Washington. Assuming, for the sake of argument, that the United States did confiscate military equipment as an occupying power it could have retained such of them as were public property and would have been obliged to return private property and to pay compensation therefor when peace was made (article 53 of HR). But if, as claimed by the United States, a party to a peacekeeping mission is not an "occupying power," the obligations are not clear under the law of war. The Organization of American States, which initially refused to compensate Dominican civilians for damage or loss due to combat on the theory that most of the damage was caused by Dominican belligerents, later reversed its position. Until then, individual tortfeasors were personally liable to the injured party.

The administration of claims arising from actions of multinational "peacekeeping forces" is ordinarily based upon regulations published after the fact. The United Nations has no standing published regulation on the matter; neither did the OAS. The IPF (Inter-American Peace Force) regulation merely followed United States practice and procedures. While the settlement of claims arising from peacekeeping operations by the United Nations or by a regional organization can prove troublesome, individual arrangements have normally been worked out. These arrangements are closely related to the claim provisions of "civil affairs" agreements on liberated territory and of visiting forces agreements. For this reason, no recommendation is made to codify these arrangements as part of conventional international law.

A useful supplement to the conventional law would specify the conditions under which a foreign military force engaged in peacekeeping operations could destroy, or deprive civilians of the use of, property (for instance, in order to deny support to insurgents). The Hague Regulations could be improved by eliminating the archaic distinction between the inviolability of private property and the vulnerability of public property. In any international conflict between capitalist and Socialist states, the former could take large quantities of enemy property as "public," while the latter would be theoretically restricted by proprietary considerations peculiar to capitalism.

Mixed Civil-International Conflicts. The position of the United States in Vietnam vis-à-vis South Vietnamese civilians was troublesome. If the United States were regarded as an occupying power throughout South Vietnam, then its extensive defoliation and crop destruction programs would be governed by GC, article 53, prohibiting destruction of real or personal private property by an occupant except when rendered absolutely necessary by military operations. Excessive destruction not justified by military necessity would, in fact, be a grave breach of article 147 of the GC. The law of belligerent occupation defines occupied territory only as that under the authority of a hostile army (HR, article 42). Hostile to whom? To South Vietnamese civilians who harbored Vietcong? As nationals of a cobelligerent, they were not protected by the Civilians Convention, nor was their property (GC, article 4). To the Vietcong? Municipal law, rather than the international law of war, governs property relationships in civil combat, and the GVN bore the responsibility for indemnification of South Vietnamese civilians for combat-related as well as noncombat-related damage. (In point of fact, the United States supported the GVN military civic action program on claims of crop damage, bodily injury, and loss of personal property. Civilian claims resulting from noncombat-related activity of the United States forces were payable under the United States Foreign Claims Act, 10 U.S.C., Sections 2734 et seq.)

The issue does not rest as easily as that: Seymour Melman and Richard Falk (authors of *In the Name of America*) link United States bombardment of South Vietnam with those prohibitions of the Hague Regulations that remind combatants that in international conflicts the means of injuring an enemy are not unlimited (HR, article 22). In particular, article 23 of HR prohibits the destruction of enemy property unless it is imperatively demanded by necessities of war, and article 25 is a flat prohibition on the attack of undefended villages, dwellings, and buildings. These provisions of HR are technically only reflections of customary international law; however, as both customary and conventional law, HR applies only to international conflicts. Thus, even though the United States treated the conflict as international for the purpose of dealing with prisoners of war under GPW, the applicability of HR was not affected. The crop destruction and defoliation programs (as well as the use of napalm and gas) also were condemned by critics of United States participation in Vietnam.

International Conflicts. In the Arab Israel War of 1967, a pure international conflict that involved the administration of occupied territory, the conventions had been largely observed in occupied territory. Following an initial disruption of trade, goods were freely exchanged among the occupied territories, Israel, and the Arab countries. Although GC does not require the occupant to initiate and develop the economic life of the territory, Israel assumed just such a role. It purchased agricultural surpluses of the Jordanian West Bank, raised the rate of exchange of the Jordanian dinar and the UAR pound in relation to the Israel pound (to equalize price levels between Israel and its occupied territory), and created branches of the Bank of Israel where local currency was scarce. In these respects Israel's performance surpassed the inadequate standards of GC, which fails to mention, in any specific ways, occupation currency or other modes of maintaining or undermining economy of the occupied area. On the other hand, economic support of occupied territories subsequent to the Six Day War of 1967 was followed by Israeli settlement of the Golan Heights in Syria and the Jordanian West Bank and expropriation of the Abu Rudeis oil fields of the Egyptian Sinai in blatant violation of GC. The economic situation remained basically unchanged following the United States negotiated truce that ended hostilities after the 1973 Yom Kippur War. The United Nations General Assembly repeatedly censured Israel for forcible eviction of Jordanian citizens in Jerusalem, demolition of homes, and the establishment of Israeli settlements within the city. Annexation of occupied territory is prohibited by GC, article 47. In effect, this article outlaws territorial acquisition by war unless the conquered nation yields the occupied territory. It simply does not seem workable in modern conflict when interminable hostilities are merely suspended by truces rather than resolved by treaties of peace.

Recommendations Regarding the Wounded
and the Sick

Collection and protection of the wounded and the sick are two of the more culturally sensitive requirements of the international law of war. That is, compliance or noncompliance with the requirements of the conventions tends to be a function of (1) cultural concern for, or indifference to, pain and suffering and (2) the availability of medical resources, rather than a reaction to legal imperatives. The Geneva Convention for the Amelioration of the Condition of the Wounded and Sick in Armed Forces in the Field (GWS) and the relevant articles of the other three Geneva Conventions of 1949 define affirmative requirements and prohibited acts—but only the latter, such as willful killing, torture, or biological experiments, constitute grave breaches under GWS, article 51. A compassionate people, with the means to tend the disabled, will do so as a matter of religion, morals, or ethics; people who are inured to pain or suffering or who lack the means of alleviation cannot be converted to good Samaritans by the requirements of international law.

In the Indonesian-Malaysian 1963-66 conflict, the Indonesians ignored GWS, article 15, requiring the combatants to search for the fallen after engagements. The neglect of the wounded by the Katangans in the Congo conflict (1960-64) was at least partly due to the lack of medical facilities and supplies. The brief and bloody Dominican civil war, which had many of the earmarks of an urban riot rather than an organized military operation, was a senseless collage of observance and breach. In one instance, the Constitutionalist would assist IPF medical personnel to collect and transport the wounded to hospitals; in the next, snipers would fire upon the medics. Although common article 3, merely requiring collection and care of the wounded, would apply to Dominican parties to the conflict, presumably the entire text of GWS (which under article 24 requires respect for medical personnel) would be invoked in operations involving the IPF.

The high-intensity conflicts in Korea and Vietnam showed clear patterns of violation and also disclosed problems in the application of the law. North Korea and the United Nations Command (UNC) offered to be guided by the "principles" of the Geneva Conventions. However vague and ambiguous the commitment may have been with respect to the other three conventions, GWS does in fact have a single central principle and several corollaries thereto. Since the first Red Cross Convention of 1864, the treaties have established that "members of the Armed Forces who are wounded or sick, and thus harmless and defenseless, must be respected and cared for without distinction of nationality. . . . In the exclusive interest of the wounded, ambulances and military hospitals, and also medical personnel, are to be protected against hostile acts." The single "great principle" itself (as it was called by M. Pictet in his Commentary on the Geneva Conventions of 1949) was assiduously ignored by the North Koreans.

The wounded and the sick were often treated by the North Koreans as expendable, particularly from the time of capture until they reached a permanent camp. The investigators of the United States Army Korea War Crimes Division revealed a Communist policy of summarily executing any prisoner whose physical condition would be burdensome. This was a grave breach of GWS, articles 12 and 14, and GPW, article 13. The bodies were left unburied along the roadside in violation of GPW, article 17. In the summer of 1950 North Korean troops reportedly slaughtered unarmed military patients being treated in the field and in hospitals by physicians wearing the Red Cross emblem (GWS, articles 19 and 24). The rules for the identification of wounded and dead, elaborated in GWS, article 16, were totally ignored.

The record of the UNC in disposing of the dead was not without blemish either: Enemy battlefield dead were interred in mass burial plots without records of the individuals dead. To the consternation of ICRC, which requested compliance with GWS, article 17, requiring individual burial and identification, the UNC pleaded lack of identification on the enemy dead and the requirements of public health that justified prompt interment. The same problem arose in World War II, particularly in the Pacific theater of operations, where corpses deteriorated rapidly in the tropical heat. The burial problem after major engagements was foreseen by the Geneva draftsmen who, in article 17, required individual burial "as far as circumstances permit." The obligation is not absolute, but burial in a common grave must always remain an exceptional measure.

The recital of violations in the Korean conflict says little about deficiencies of substantive law. It is certainly clear that in the first major conflict to which the conventions were at least partially applicable, the Communists gave only lip service to the most fundamental principles, let alone observed the niceties of law.

It was otherwise in Vietnam. United States and South Vietnamese (ARVN) military personnel were evacuated from the battle zone principally by helicopter. Rarely, if ever, was GWS article 36 observed. (Article 36 requires that the aircraft be clearly marked with a Red Cross emblem, be used exclusively for the removal of wounded and sick and the transport of medical personnel, and fly at heights, times, and routes agreed upon between the belligerents.) There was little regular communication between the combatants, and the conflict lacked a protecting power. Because of the shortage of aircraft, a "chopper" used for a rescue operation in the morning would be required for a military mission in the afternoon of the same day. The United States pilots did not trust the Communists. Given a choice between armaments and the distinctive emblem, they chose the former every time. It is not certain that article 36 is applicable under combat conditions. Without a protecting power to assist the parties in the necessary arrangements, the chances of its application are remote. Some progress was made on the marking and radio identification of aircraft at the first Session of the Diplomatic Conference on Humanitarian Law in 1974.

The North Vietnamese (DRV) and the Vietcong (VC) collected and protected enemy wounded, sick, and dead in addition to their own. They also tended to conceal the identity of enemy wounded and dead, in contravention of GWS, article 16, which requires prompt transmission of vital data to an information bureau set up under GPW. The purpose of concealment was to use the names for propaganda purposes. Thus the VC would announce the reprisal "execution" of a prisoner who had died earlier in captivity. The United States practice of measuring the success of a mission by a "body count" of the dead stimulated Communist collection of their own dead to deny the proofs of victory to the enemy. The body count appeared to be one of the causes of an undue amount of mutilation of the dead. On several occasions ARVN troops "proved their kill" to United States advisors by presenting dismembered portions of the enemy. United States servicemen also mutilated the dead and were, in several instances, disciplined and court-martialed. The conventions do not explicitly mention mutilation; however, the practice is precluded by the requirements of respect for the dead and honorable burial specified under GWS, article 17.

The principal victims of the Vietnam conflict were the South Vietnamese civilians, who suffered at the hands of all the parties to the conflict but most notably through aerial bombardment by United States aircraft. The civilians were not protected persons. The ratio of their casualties to military casualties was estimated at ten to one. The nominal effort made by the United States in "Operation Recovery" to collect and protect civilian casualties was totally disproportionate to the need or to the attention given to military casualties. However, as a matter of law, the civilians were not entitled to affirmative assistance, because they were caught up in the civil aspect of mixed civil-international conflict. When the belligerents are obliged to care for military casualties in combat, it is difficult to see why civilians should not receive equal protection under the law. Further, even when a conflict is only partially international in character, there is little reason why GWS and GC Part II (protection of populations against certain consequences regarding hospitals, safety zones, and humanitarian transport) should not be extended to the whole of the populations in conflict without any adverse distinction based upon the nationality of the forces injuring civilians.

These problems were, in fact, the core of the agenda considered by one of the three committees that composed the first session of the 1974 Diplomatic Conference. Unfortunately, the technical annex on the identification of medical and civil defense personnel, transports, and installation was not adopted—nor was much of anything else. When a decision was made in 1974 to edit and publish a manuscript that had been researched in 1968 it was presumed that many of the deficiencies and recommendations would have been largely outdated by diplomatic activity during the intervening six years. Unfortunately for the progress of humanitarian law this has not been the case. The painstaking work of the experts of the ICRC was all but brushed aside by gross political and partisan considerations in Geneva in 1974. The task is yet ahead. As stated by George H. Aldrich, United States representative to the Diplomatic Conference, "The law making task is to develop and improve standards intended to reduce suffering and protect those who cannot protect themselves. But this task also has a broader purpose—that of ensuring that feelings of compassion and brotherhood are not destroyed in the vortex of violence that is modern war. . . . Future generations may not thank us if we succeed, but they will surely pay the price if we fail."[6]

Notes

1. Eisenhower, Public Papers of the Presidents at 128 (1954). For a contrary view see Stone, Legal Control of International Conflict 680-683 (1954).

2. See Melman and Falk, In the Name of America (a publication which was reprinting news articles of the sufferings of South Vietnamese civilians at the hands of their own government beneath citations from GC (Geneva Conventions Relative to the Protection of Civilian Persons in Time of War) pertaining to "protected persons," grossly exaggerated the scope of legal protection).

3. Eisenhower, Public Papers of the Presidents at 128 (1954).

4. 18 League of Nations Official Journal 333 (1937).

5. See Rabin, *Legal Aspects of the My Lai Incident*, 49 Oregon L.R. 260 (1970).

6. Report of the U.S. Delegation to the Diplomatic Conference on the Reaffirmation and Development of International Humanitarian Law Applicable in Armed Conflicts p. 41.

Index

Index

About the Author

Richard I. Miller was the project director of the U.S. Army JAG prisoner of war study. He is a Vice President of Harbridge House, Inc., a multinational management consulting firm. Among his other publications are, "An Introduction to the Law of War," Boston Bar Journal (November 1970) and "Far Beyond Nuremberg," 61 Kentucky Law Journal 925 (1973). He is Chairman of the Public International Law Committee of the Boston Bar Association and a member of the International Law Section of the American Bar Association. He received the B.A. from the University of California in 1950, where he studied international law with Hans Kelsen, and the J.D. from Yale University Law School in 1953. Subsequently, Miller pursued post-professional studies at the Fletcher School of Law and Diplomacy. He is a member of the New York and Massachusetts bars.